THE YALE LIBRARY OF MILITARY HISTORY

Donald Kagan and Dennis Showalter, Series Editors

SURGE

*My Journey with
General David Petraeus and
the Remaking of the Iraq War*

Peter R. Mansoor

Foreword by General David Petraeus

Yale UNIVERSITY PRESS
New Haven & London

Copyright © 2013 by Peter R. Mansoor.
Foreword copyright © 2013 by General David Petraeus.
Maps drafted by Joe LeMonnier.
All rights reserved.
This book may not be reproduced, in whole or in part, including illustrations, in any form (beyond that copying permitted by Sections 107 and 108 of the U.S. Copyright Law and except by reviewers for the public press), without written permission from the publishers.

Yale University Press books may be purchased in quantity for educational, business, or promotional use. For information, please e-mail sales.press@yale.edu (U.S. office) or sales@yaleup.co.uk (U.K. office).

Set in Minion type by Integrated Publishing Solutions.
Printed in the United States of America.

Library of Congress Cataloging-in-Publication Data

Mansoor, Peter R., 1960–. Surge : my journey with General David Petraeus and the remaking of the Iraq War / Peter R. Mansoor ; foreword by General David Petraeus.
pages   cm—(Yale library of military history)
Includes bibliographical references and index.
ISBN 978-0-300-17235-5 (cloth : alk. paper)   1. Petraeus, David Howell—Military leadership.   2. Iraq War, 2003–2011—Campaigns.   3. Counterinsurgency—Iraq—History.   4. United States—Military policy—History—21st century.   5. Iraq—Politics and government—2003–.   I. Title.
DS79.76.M359 2013
956.7044'340973—dc23
2013015740

A catalogue record for this book is available from the British Library.

This paper meets the requirements of ANSI/NISO Z39.48-1992 (Permanence of Paper).

10 9 8 7 6 5 4 3 2 1

To the soldiers and civilians who answered their nation's call of duty in Iraq,
and especially for those who never returned

Contents

Illustrations follow page 152

Foreword

L eading the coalition military effort during the surge in Iraq in 2007 and 2008 was the most important endeavor—and greatest challenge—of my thirty-seven years in uniform. And Colonel, now Professor, Pete Mansoor, who was at my right hand for the first fifteen months of that endeavor, is uniquely qualified to write a history of what took place.

The situation in Iraq was exceedingly grim at the end of 2006, when President Bush decided to implement the surge and selected me to command it. Indeed, when I returned to Baghdad in early February 2007, I found the conditions there to be even worse than I had expected. The deterioration since I had left Iraq in September 2005 after my second tour was sobering. The violence—which had escalated dramatically in 2006 in the wake of the bombing of the Shi'a al-Askari shrine in the Sunni city of Samarra—was totally out of control. With well over fifty attacks and three car bombs per day on average in Baghdad alone, the plan to hand off security tasks to Iraqi forces clearly was not working. Meanwhile, the sectarian battles on the streets were mirrored by infighting in the Iraqi government and Council of Representatives, and those disputes produced a dysfunctional Iraqi political environment as well. And with many of the oil pipelines damaged or destroyed, electrical towers toppled, roads in disrepair, local markets shuttered, and government workers and citizens fearing for their lives, generation of government revenue was down and the provision of basic services was wholly inadequate. Life in many areas of the capital and the country was about little more than survival.

In addition to those challenges, I knew that if there was not clear progress by September 2007, when I anticipated having to return to the United States to testify before Congress in open hearings, the limited remaining support on Capitol Hill and in the United States for the effort in Iraq would evaporate.[1]

In short, President Bush had staked the final years of his presidency—and his legacy—on the surge, and it was up to those on the ground to achieve progress. In the end, that is what we did—together, military and civilian, coalition and Iraqi. But as my great diplomatic partner Ryan Crocker, the U.S. ambassador to Iraq, and I used to note, Iraq was "all hard, all the time." Pete Mansoor captures this reality superbly.

The Surge of Forces and the Surge of Ideas

The surge had many components. The most prominent, of course, was the deployment of the additional U.S. forces committed by President Bush—nearly thirty thousand of them in the end. Without those forces, we never could have achieved progress as quickly as we did. And, given the necessity of progress by the hearings anticipated in September, improvements before then were critical.

As important as the surge of forces was, however, the most important surge was what I termed "the surge of ideas"—the changes in our overall strategy and operational plans. The most significant of these was the shift from trying to hand off security tasks to Iraqi forces to focusing on the security of the Iraqi people. The biggest of the "big ideas" that guided the strategy during the surge was explicit recognition that the most important terrain in the campaign in Iraq was the human terrain—the people—and our most important mission was to improve their security. Security improvements would, in turn, provide Iraq's political leaders the opportunity to forge agreements on issues that would reduce ethnosectarian disputes and establish the foundation on which other efforts could be built to improve the lives of the Iraqi people and give them a stake in the success of the new Iraq.

But improved security could be achieved only by moving our forces into urban neighborhoods and rural population centers. In the first two weeks, therefore, I changed the mission statement in the existing campaign plan to reflect this imperative. As I explained in that statement and the guidance I issued shortly after taking command, we had to "live with the people" in order to secure them. This meant reversing the consolidation of our forces on large bases that had been taking place since the spring of 2004. Ultimately, this change in approach necessitated the establishment of more than one hundred small outposts and joint security stations, three-quarters of them in Baghdad alone.

The establishment of each of the new bases entailed a fight, and some of those fights were substantial. We knew that the Sunni insurgent elements and Shi'a militia groups would do everything they could to keep our troopers from establishing a presence in areas where the warring factions were trying to take control—and those areas were precisely where our forces were needed most. Needless to say, the insurgents and militia would do all that they could to keep us from establishing our new operating bases, sometimes even employing two suicide car bombers in succession in attempts to breach outpost perimeters. But if we were to achieve our goal of significantly reducing the violence, there was no alternative to living with the people—specifically, where the violence was the greatest—in order to secure them. Our men and women on the ground, increasingly joined during the surge by their Iraqi partners, courageously, selflessly, and skillfully did what was required to accomplish this goal.

"Clear, hold, and build" became the operative concept—a contrast with the previous practice in many operations of clearing insurgents and then leaving, after handing off the security mission to Iraqi forces that proved incapable of sustaining progress in the areas cleared. Then–Lieutenant General Ray Odierno, commander of the Multi-National Corps–Iraq, and his staff developed and oversaw the execution of these and the other operational concepts brilliantly.[2] Indeed, in anticipation of the new approach, he ordered establishment of the initial joint security stations in the weeks before I arrived. His successor in early 2008, then–Lieutenant General Lloyd Austin, did a similarly brilliant job as our operational commander for the final portion of the surge.[3] On receiving the Corps' guidance, division and brigade commanders and their headquarters orchestrated superbly the implementation of these concepts. And our company, battalion, and brigade commanders and their troopers translated magnificently the new strategy and operational concepts into reality on the ground in the face of determined, often barbaric enemies under some of the most difficult conditions imaginable.

But the new strategy encompassed much more than just moving off the big bases and focusing on security of the people. Improving security was necessary, but not sufficient, to achieve our goals in Iraq. Many other tasks also had to be accomplished.

The Comprehensive Civil-Military Approach

The essence of the surge, in fact, was the pursuit of a *comprehensive* approach, a civil-military campaign that featured a number of important elements, the effects of each of which were expected to complement the effects of the others.[4] The idea was that progress in one component of the strategy would make possible gains in other components. Each incremental step forward reinforced and gradually solidified overall progress in a particular geographic location or governmental sector. The surge forces clearly *enabled* more rapid implementation of the new strategy and accompanying operational concepts; however, without the changes in the strategy, the additional forces would not have achieved the gains in security and in other areas necessary for substantial reduction of the underlying levels of ethnosectarian violence, without which progress would not have been sustained when responsibilities ultimately were transferred to Iraqi forces and government authorities.

The Sunni Awakening and Reconciliation

Beyond securing the people by living with them, foremost among the elements of the new strategy was promoting reconciliation between disaffected Sunni Arabs and our forces—and then with the Shi'ite-dominated Iraqi government. Professor Mansoor rightly highlights this critical element as ranking with the most important factors that contributed to the success of the surge.

I often noted at the time that we would not be able to kill or capture our way out of the industrial-strength insurgency that confronted us in Iraq. Hence we had to identify those insurgents and militia members who were "reconcilable," and we then had to persuade them to become part of the solution in Iraq rather than a continuing part of the problem. Reconciliation thus became a critical component of the overall strategy. We were fortunate to be able to build on what ultimately came to be known as the Sunni Awakening, the initial increment of which began several months before the surge, outside the embattled Sunni city of Ramadi in violent Anbar Province, some sixty miles west of Baghdad. There, in the late summer of 2006, during the height of the violence in Anbar, Colonel Sean MacFarland, a talented U.S. Army brigade commander, and his team agreed to support a courageous Sunni sheik and his tribal members who decided to oppose al-Qaeda in Iraq, which the tribesmen had come to despise for its indiscriminate attacks on the population and implementation of an extreme version of Islam that was not in line with their somewhat more secular outlook on life.[5] The initiative included empowering young men of the tribes who wanted to help secure their areas against al-Qaeda depredations. Ultimately, shortly after the surge of forces commenced and throughout 2007 and into 2008, this arrangement was replicated over and over in other areas of Anbar Province and Iraq. The Awakening proved to be a hugely important factor in combating al-Qaeda terrorists and other Sunni insurgents and, over time, in combating Shi'a militia in select areas as well.

Some observers have contended that we got lucky with the Awakening. Undeniably, it was fortunate that the initial development of a tribal rebellion against al-Qaeda had begun by the time the surge began. Despite this reality, however, the spread of the Awakening beyond Ramadi was not serendipity; rather, it was the result of a conscious decision and a deliberate effort. I was well aware that there had previously been reconciliation initiatives that had worked in the short term. Indeed, I oversaw the first of these initiatives, in the summer of 2003, when I commanded the 101st Airborne Division in northern Iraq and Ambassador Jerry Bremer, the head of the Coalition Provisional Authority, personally authorized me to support an Iraqi-led reconciliation effort. That effort helped make that part of Iraq surprisingly peaceful well into the fall of 2003, as the Sunni Arabs cast out of jobs and out of society by the de-Ba'athification policy still had hope of being part of the new Iraq in our area. Ultimately, however, that initiative, along with reconciliation efforts in subsequent years in western Anbar Province and elsewhere, foundered due to a lack of support by Iraqi authorities in Baghdad. I watched these initiatives during my second tour in Iraq, as commander of the Multi-National Security Transition Command–Iraq from June 2004 to September 2005.

Given my recognition of the importance of reconciliation, I was determined that we would support the nascent Awakening and then, over time, gain our Iraqi partners' support, as well. In fact, my first trip outside Baghdad, shortly after taking command on February 10, 2007, was to assess the progress of the initiative in Ramadi. After seeing the results of the Awakening up close, I quickly resolved that we would do all that we could to support the tribal rebellion there and also to foster its spread through other Sunni areas of Iraq. (Eventually, we also supported Shi'a awakenings in some of the areas troubled by Shi'a militias.) We would, in effect, seek to achieve a "critical mass" of awakenings that would set off a "chain reaction" as rapidly as was possible—initially up and down the Euphrates River Valley in Anbar Province and then into neighboring Sunni Arab areas of Iraq. Of equal importance, we would also seek the support of Iraqi Prime Minister Maliki for these initiatives. (I personally took him to Ramadi in March 2007 to speak to the tribal sheiks leading the Awakening there, and I subsequently took him to other Sunni areas for similar endeavors as well.)

The decision to support the awakening movement and, in essence, reconciliation carried considerable risk and was not initially embraced by all of our commanders. Many correctly pointed out that the leaders and members of the groups that wanted to reconcile with us—groups that might be willing to embrace the Awakening—had our blood on their hands. Beyond that, it was clear early on that Prime Minister Maliki was willing to allow us to support awakenings in strictly Sunni areas such as Anbar, but that he had understandable concerns about them when they approached areas of greater concern to his Shi'a coreligionists; moreover, he also was not at all enthusiastic initially about providing Iraqi resources and assistance for what came to be known as the "Sons of Iraq," the young men who helped augment coalition and Iraqi police and army forces in securing their tribal areas. Regardless, I was convinced that there was no alternative if we were to reduce the violence and divert key elements of the Sunni insurgency from their actual or tacit support for the actions of al-Qaeda. So we pressed ahead and dealt with the many issues that arose along the way, helped initially by superb work by my first deputy, British Lieutenant General Sir Graeme Lamb, a friend and colleague of many years, and then by the establishment of a Force Strategic Engagement Cell that was headed by a talented two-star British officer, Major General Paul Newton, and an impressive senior U.S. diplomat, Don Blume. Once again, Pete Mansoor relates all of this superbly.

Ultimately, the Awakening movement—and, in effect, reconciliation—did spread dramatically. There were many challenges as this transpired, especially when Prime Minister Maliki and other Shi'a leaders developed concerns over the spread of the movement into Baghdad and areas near predominantly Shi'a or mixed communities. Our reconciliation team—aided enormously by Emma Sky, a brilliant British woman who served as a special assistant to me during the latter part of the surge (having served as General Odierno's political adviser earlier and subsequently)—worked tirelessly to deal with the seemingly endless list of issues and with the woman appointed by Prime Minister Maliki to oversee reconciliation initiatives for the Iraqi government. And, ultimately, a year and a half into the surge, we had on our payroll more than 100,000 "Sons of Iraq" (more than 20,000 of them Shi'a), young men who lived in the areas of the Awakening movements and who then helped secure their neighborhoods from both Sunni insurgents and Shi'a militias.

In sum, the spread of the Awakening was not serendipity; it was the result of a deliberate decision I took soon after taking command. To be sure, the timing of the initiative outside Ramadi was fortuitous, but from even before taking command I knew that reconciliation had to take place if we were to reduce violence significantly by the fall of 2007. We thus were determined to capitalize on the Ramadi initiative by promoting the spread of Awakening movements and facilitating the resulting reconciliation among sects, tribes, and factions. I understood the numerous risks, and we took measures to ensure that Awakening movements and the "Sons of Iraq" did not turn into an unaccountable militia force that would cause more trouble for Iraq in the long run than they were worth in the near term. Looking back, the risks clearly were worth the resulting gains.

Targeted Special Operations

Another critical component of our comprehensive approach was an intensive campaign of targeted operations by U.S. and British special operations forces to capture or kill key insurgent and militia leaders and operatives. Although I publicly acknowledged from the outset that we would not be able to kill or capture our way to victory (hence the need to support the Awakening), killing or capturing the most important of the "irreconcilables" was an inescapable and hugely important element of our strategy. Indeed, we sought to pursue key irreconcilables even more aggressively than was the case before the surge.

Consequently, I encouraged then–Lieutenant General Stan McChrystal, commander of the U.S. Joint Special Operations Command and the Counter-Terrorism Special Operations Task Force operating in Iraq, to be relentless in the pursuit of al-Qaeda and other Sunni Arab extremist leaders, bomb makers, financiers, and propaganda cells—and to do the same with key Iranian-supported Shi'a Arab extremists as well (though the latter effort was frequently constrained by Iraqi political factors, given the proclivities of the Shi'ite-led government). As the surge proceeded, the capacity and pace of U.S.- and coalition-targeted special operations under Lieutenant General McChrystal and subsequently by then–Vice Admiral William H. McRaven increased substantially, as did the tempo of targeted operations by the Iraqi counterterrorist forces that we trained, equipped, advised, and also enabled with helicopters and various intelligence, surveillance, and recon-naissance assets.[6] The results were dramatic: the targeted operations—as many as ten to fifteen per night—removed from the battlefield a significant proportion of the senior and midlevel extremist group leaders, explosives experts, planners, fi-nanciers, and organizers in Iraq.[7] Looking back, it is clear that what the American and British special operators accomplished, aided enormously by various intel-ligence elements, was nothing short of extraordinary. Their relentless operations, employment of unmanned aerial vehicles and other advanced technology, tactical skill, courage, and creativity were truly inspirational. But by themselves they did not and could not turn the tide of battle in Iraq; once again, the key was a com-prehensive approach, in which this element, like the others, was necessary but not sufficient.

The Development of Iraqi Security Forces

Supporting the development of the Iraqi Security Forces was also vitally impor-tant—and an effort with which I was intimately familiar, as I had led the establish-ment of the so-called "train and equip" organization and commanded the Multi-National Security Transition Command–Iraq for the first fifteen and a half months of the organization's existence, during which I was also dual-hatted as the first commander of the NATO Training Mission–Iraq.[8]

Although I halted the transition of tasks from coalition to Iraqi forces shortly after I took command, we knew that ultimately such transitions would be essential to our ability to draw down our forces and send them home. As President Bush used to observe, "U.S. forces will stand down as the Iraqi forces stand up." We knew that ultimately the U.S. military could not support the replacement of the five surge brigades and the other additional forces deployed to Iraq in 2007. It thus was imperative that Iraqi forces be ready by the latter part of 2007 to assume broader duties so that coalition forces could begin to draw down and the surge forces could go home. Beyond that, Iraqi leaders, frequently with unrealistically elevated assessments of the capabilities of their security forces, repeatedly advo-cated continued transition of security and governance tasks—a desire that was commendable, if sometimes premature.

Under the capable leadership of then–Lieutenant General Marty Dempsey and his successor, Lieutenant General Jim Dubik, the train-and-equip mission steadily expanded its efforts not just to develop Iraqi army, police, border, and special op-erations units but also to build all of the institutions of the Ministries of Interior and Defense, their subordinate headquarters and elements, and the infrastructure and systems needed for what ultimately grew to a total of one million members of the Iraqi security forces.[9]

These tasks required Herculean efforts. Our programs supported every aspect of Iraqi military and police recruiting, individual and collective training, leader development (for example, the creation of basic training complexes, a military academy, branch schools, a staff college, a war college, and a training and doctrine command), equipping Iraqi forces with everything from vehicles and individual weapons to tanks and aircraft, the conduct of combat operations (with advisory teams at every level from battalion and above), development of logistical organizations and depots, construction of tactical and training bases and infrastructure, establishment of headquarters and staffs, and, as noted earlier, the development of all of the elements of the ministries themselves. Indeed, it is hard for anyone who did not see this endeavor firsthand to appreciate its magnitude. Additionally, progress required our Iraqi counterparts to replace substantial numbers of senior army and police leaders who proved to be sectarian, corrupt, or ineffective in the performance of their duties before or during the early months of the surge. Fortunately, Prime Minister Maliki and his senior military and police leaders proved willing to undertake the vast majority of the necessary changes.

Over time, we and our Iraqi counterparts achieved slow but steady progress in building the capabilities of the Iraqi Security Forces. With effective partnering of Iraqi and U.S. forces, Iraqi forces steadily shouldered more of the burdens and took over more tasks. They also increasingly bore the brunt of combat operations, with their losses totaling several times those of coalition forces. I often noted to the president, Prime Minister Maliki, and others, in fact, that as the surge proceeded, Iraqi security forces clearly were fighting and dying for their country. Progressively, over the months and years that followed, the coalition turned over responsibility for security tasks to Iraqi forces until, at the end of 2011, Iraqi elements assumed all security tasks on their own, with only a residual U.S. office of security cooperation remaining in Iraq.

The Civilian Components

The comprehensive strategy employed during the surge also had significant civilian components. Indeed, Ambassador Crocker and I worked hard to develop unity of effort in all that our respective organizations and coalition and Iraqi partners did. The campaign plan we developed in the spring of 2007, in fact, was a joint effort of my command, Multi-National Force–Iraq, and the U.S. embassy, with considerable input from coalition partners such as the United Kingdom. (This civil-military plan built on the partnership that my predecessor, General George Casey, had developed with then–U.S. Ambassador Zalmay Khalilzad, albeit with the changes in strategic and operational concepts that I have described.) And over time, our plan was also, of course, synchronized in close coordination with our Iraqi counterparts. Appropriately, the mission statement in the campaign plan we finalized in the early summer of 2007 included many nonmilitary aspects, highlighting the combined approach on which we all embarked together.

As security improved, the tasks in the civilian arena took on greater importance. It was critical, for example, that we work with our coalition and Iraqi civilian partners to help repair damaged infrastructure, restore basic services, rebuild local markets, reopen schools and health facilities, and support the reestablishment of the corrections and judicial systems and other governmental institutions. While not determinative by themselves, such improvements gave Iraqi citizens tangible reasons to support the new Iraq and reject the extremists, insurgents, and militia members who had caused such hardship for them.

To facilitate and coordinate such efforts, each brigade and division headquarters was provided an embedded provincial reconstruction team of approximately a dozen civilian and military experts (often led by retired diplomats and development specialists). The U.S. Congress also provided the units substantial funding (through the Commander's Emergency Response Program) to help with these efforts (and the U.S. embassy and some coalition nations did likewise through their sources of funding). Again, over time, progress in these initiatives proved essential to gaining the support of the Iraqi people for their government and to turning the people against both Sunni and Shi'a extremists. These tasks were huge and often expensive, but they were essential to gradually improving basic services and other aspects of life for the Iraqi people. With steadily improving security and with the U.S. Army Corps of Engineers taking on the oversight of the larger reconstruction projects for the embassy as well as for the military, the effort moved forward relatively well, although there were innumerable challenges, including security issues, corruption, design and management shortfalls, and so on. But even in the face of such obstacles, substantial reconstruction progress was nonetheless achieved.

Detainee Operations and Rule-of-Law Initiatives

Another important component of the comprehensive approach was the conduct of detainee operations. In this area, also, we had to implement significant changes. The scope of this effort was enormous. In fact, the number of detainees in U.S.-administered facilities reached twenty-seven thousand after I temporarily halted detainee releases until we could implement programs that provided a review process for the detainees in our facilities and could establish rehabilitation and reintegration programs to reduce the recidivism rate of those we released back to their communities.

Early on in the surge, it was clear to many of us that the detainee facilities we were operating had become breeding grounds for extremism. Indeed, some of our special operators, having recaptured the same individuals more than once, began calling our facilities "terrorist universities." We were, to be sure, providing humane treatment; however, we had not identified and segregated from the general detainee population the hardcore extremists. Until that was done, the extremists asserted control (often brutally) in the facility enclosures—some of which contained up to eight hundred detainees—and spread extremist thinking and expertise among the detainee population. It became clear that we had to carry out "counter-insurgency operations inside the wire" in order to identify and separate from the detainee population the irreconcilables, just as we sought to do outside the wire in Iraqi communities. The leadership of Marine Major General Doug Stone and of those who led the elements that constituted our detainee operations task force was instrumental in this component of our overall campaign. And the performance of the thousands of soldiers, airmen, and sailors who carried out the myriad duties in the facilities—individuals who often had been retrained from other specialties to augment the limited number of military police detention specialists available in the U.S. Army—was equally impressive.

Over time, Major General Stone's team also began helping our Iraqi partners as they sought to increase their own capacity and to build the prison infrastructure to conduct Iraqi corrections operations. This was another significant U.S. civil-military effort, and it was complemented by a similarly large civil-military initiative to help the Iraqis reestablish their judicial system and to rebuild the infrastructure to support it.

Then–Colonel Mark Martins led the judicial support effort on the military side, staying in Iraq for two full years—as he was later also to do in Afghanistan—to oversee it, even as he also served as my senior legal counsel.[10] The scope of this civil-military endeavor was enormous, encompassing construction of judicial facilities, training of judicial security elements, and support for reestablishment of judicial systems and structures. Partners from the U.S. State Department, Department of Justice, FBI, and other government agencies also played key roles in this substantial effort.

Another important initiative that supported the overall campaign was the effort to improve our intelligence about the various extremist elements and about what was going on in Iraq more broadly. Here again, we pursued civil-military programs to build our capabilities (including fusion cells started under General Casey at each division headquarters to bring together all elements of the U.S. intelligence community); to expand the intelligence, surveillance, and reconnaissance assets available (everything from drones to cameras on towers); to build a massive database that our analysts could use to identify correlations and linkages between individuals and organizations; and to improve intelligence sharing with coalition and Iraqi partners. We also established human terrain teams at each brigade headquarters to help our commanders understand in a more granular manner the composition, power structures, customs, and views of the Iraqi people in their areas of responsibility.[11] And we extended secure Internet access to unprecedented levels (down to most company headquarters) within our organizations, as well. Counterinsurgency operations depend on a keen understanding of the political, historical, cultural, economic, and military situation in each area, and our initiatives built on those begun earlier in the war to further our understanding of the dynamics of each province, district, and community. Truly understanding the human terrain was vital to our ability to improve its security.

The Iraqi Political Component and Strategic Communications

As Professor Mansoor explains, the heart of the struggle in Iraq was a competition for power and resources between the major factions in the country—the majority Shi'a Arabs and the minority Sunni Arabs and Kurds. (There were subfactions of each faction as well, of course, in addition to other minority sects and ethnicities such as Turcomen, Yezidis, and Iraqi Christians, among others.) Achieving enduring progress in Iraq thus required achievement of political agreements on a host of key issues that divided the various factions. Consequently, seeking to foster agreement on such issues was yet another important component of the overall approach, and it developed into one to which Ambassador Crocker and I devoted considerable focus and effort. During the course of the surge, there were important laws passed and initiatives agreed upon—for example, a provincial powers act, an elections law, a reform of the de-Ba'athification decree, an amnesty law, and so forth; however, it was in this area that the most additional progress was—and still is—needed. Nonetheless, the surge made politics once again the operative mechanism through which Iraqis would divide power and resources—even as they struggled to create the political impetus and find the common ground to seize the moment and the opportunity offered to them.

Strategic communications—public affairs—was another important element of the campaign. My guidance here was clear: we should seek to "be first with the truth," to be as forthright as possible, to provide information on all developments and not just "good news," and to avoid the practice of "putting lipstick on pigs" (trying to make bad news look good through spin). This also meant highlighting the violent acts carried out by al-Qaeda and the Sunni insurgents, as well as those carried out by Shi'a extremists. Hanging around the neck of Shi'a cleric Muqtada al-Sadr the assassination of Shi'a police chiefs and governors and the violent acts of his followers in the holy city of Karbala in the summer of 2007, for example, contributed to his decision to order his militia to stand down until the following March. (Of course, increased pressure by coalition and Iraqi forces and Prime Minister Maliki's courageous confrontation with the militia members in Karbala contributed to Sadr's decision, as well.) Clearly establishing in the eyes of the Iraqi people that Iranian elements were supporting members of the most violent Shi'a militias also helped turn some Iraqis against Iranian meddling in their country. And fostering concepts of integrity in government and pride in the Iraqi security forces, as well as awareness of what was being achieved by coalition and Iraqi efforts—even while acknowledging our shortfalls and mistakes—was all part of a comprehensive strategic communications campaign. Like most of our other efforts, this campaign was increasingly coordinated with—and, over time, replaced by—Iraqi efforts.

There were, of course, many other components of the overall campaign: engagement with religious and academic leaders, jobs programs, support for governance at all levels, initiatives to attract outside investment back to Iraq, work with countries in the region to reengage with Baghdad and to prevent their young men from traveling to Iraq to join the extremist elements, initiatives to improve security on the borders and to reestablish customs and immigrations facilities, and programs to reduce terrorist and insurgent financing. But the elements I have outlined were the major components of the comprehensive civil-military campaign plan that guided our operations and activities. Each was of central importance to the achievement of progress during the course of the surge; and, as I have noted, accomplishments in each component reinforced and made possible further steps forward in other areas, the cumulative effect of which was considerable by the end of the surge in July 2008. Indeed, the various facets of our strategy continue to contribute positively to the situation in Iraq today, even after all U.S. combat forces have left the country.

Once again, it is important to note that the surge was all of the above, a comprehensive civil-military campaign, not just a substantial number of additional forces. The extra forces were critical to achieving progress as rapidly as we did, but they would not have been enough without the other components of the campaign.

The Magnitude of the Difficulty

As I've made clear, all of this was extraordinarily difficult and carried out in an environment of tremendous violence and frustratingly difficult Iraqi political discord. Moreover, we knew—and I stated publicly on numerous occasions—that the situation in Iraq would get worse before it got better. That proved true. There was no way to stop the violence without confronting those responsible for it. And there was no way that we could do that without putting our troopers and those of the Iraqi forces on the sectarian battle lines in Baghdad and elsewhere, especially in the areas most affected by al-Qaeda terrorists and sectarian militias. When we did that, the insurgents and militia members predictably fought back. Consequently, violence rose throughout the first five months of the surge, reaching a crescendo in May and June, to well over two hundred attacks per day, before beginning to abate and then falling fairly rapidly in July, August, and September.[12]

The decline in violence overall, and the substantial reduction in car bombings in particular, as well as gradual improvements in a number of other areas of our effort made possible by the improved security, enabled Ambassador Crocker and me to report guarded progress in congressional hearings in September 2007. While highly charged emotionally at the time, those hearings gained us critical additional time and support, without which it is likely that the mission in Iraq would have failed. And, after we were able to report further progress when we testified again in April 2008, having already commenced the drawdown of the surge as well, we were able to gain still further time and support for our efforts in Iraq.

The progress continued throughout the remainder of the surge[13] and beyond, with periodic upticks in violence, to be sure, but with the overall trajectory positive, despite continued inability to resolve many of the major political issues that divided the Iraqi people. Nonetheless, the comprehensive civil-military endeavor pursued during the surge made it possible over time to transfer tasks from U.S. and other coalition forces to Iraqi soldiers and police and, ultimately, for the United States to withdraw its final combat elements at the end of 2011 without a precipitate descent back into the violence and civil conflict that made the surge necessary in the first place.[14] None of this could have been possible were it not for the extraordinary sacrifices and service of the men and women in uniform in Iraq during the surge and their diplomatic, intelligence, and development community partners.

The Decision to Surge

President Bush's decision to conduct the surge was exceedingly courageous. His advisers were split on the decision, with many favoring other approaches that in my view would have failed. And as the going did get tougher over the early months of the surge, President Bush's steadfast leadership and his personal commitment to seeing the war through to a successful conclusion (albeit one that might take many years to unfold) took on enormous significance.

I was privileged, together with Ambassador Crocker, to participate in a weekly video teleconference with the president and the members of the National Security Council. It began promptly at 7:30 A.M. Washington time each Monday, thereby ensuring that all participants were focused at the start of the week on the mission to which the president had given his total commitment. I do not believe that any battlefield commander ever had that frequency of contact with his commander in chief, and it was of vital importance to me, as was the support of Secretary of Defense Bob Gates.

I also had a weekly video teleconference with Secretary Gates, who personally drove forward a number of programs of incalculable value to our men and women on the ground, programs such as the accelerated production of mine–resistant, ambush-protected (MRAP) vehicles; a huge increase in intelligence, surveillance, and reconnaissance assets (such as Predator unmanned aerial vehicles and optics on towers, among many others); and a host of individual protective systems and enablers for our troopers—not to mention the additional forces that I requested once I got on the ground and identified additional needs beyond those addressed by the initial surge force commitment. Secretary Gates and all of us in Iraq were supported enormously, as well, by General Pete Pace and then-Admiral Mike Mullen, the two officers who served as chairman of the Joint Chiefs during the surge. General Pace and Admiral Mullen also did yeoman service in maintaining the support of the military service chiefs who were understandably under enormous strain to produce the forces that we needed, while also gradually increasing the effort in Afghanistan, as it began to go downhill. At one point, of course, this required the extension of the tours in Iraq and Afghanistan from twelve to fifteen months, an enormous sacrifice to ask of our men and women there and their families at home, but one that proved hugely important to the campaign.

President Bush's commitment had an enormous psychological effect on our men and women in Iraq, as well as on the Iraqi people. Our troopers recognized that we had a chance to do what was needed to reverse the terrible cycle of violence that had gripped Iraq in the throes of civil war. And the citizens of the "Land of the Two Rivers" realized that there was still a chance that the new Iraq could realize the potential that so many had hoped for in the wake of the ousting of Saddam Hussein and the collapse of the Ba'athist regime in 2003.

Commanding MNF-I

I recognized early on that I had become the face of the surge. I had not asked for this role, but whether I liked it or not, I had to fill it. Beyond that, of course, it was essential that I determine the right big ideas (with lots to help, to be sure), provide clear direction, communicate that direction in all possible forms, and then oversee the implementation of the resulting plans. It was also critical that I spend time with our troopers on the ground, that I share a measure of risk with them, and that I give encouragement and provide cautious optimism that we could, indeed, achieve the objectives we'd set out for ourselves and our Iraqi partners. In truth, from the beginning I believed that our approach was correct and that we would achieve progress; however, there were undeniably moments when I was uncertain whether we could achieve sufficient progress quickly enough to report that to Congress by September 2007. On more than one occasion as the early months went by, in fact, I sat alone with Ray Odierno after our morning updates and asked him when he thought the situation was going "to turn." No theater commander ever had a better "operational architect" than I had in Ray.

As the coalition commander, I also had extensive contact with the military and civilian leaders and legislators of the countries contributing forces to the coalition and also, of course, with Prime Minister Maliki and our key Iraqi partners from all sectors of the population. I had considerable interaction as well with the U.S., international, and Iraqi press. In the latter effort, as with the leaders of the coalition countries, I worked hard to avoid projecting unfounded optimism. When asked whether I was an optimist or a pessimist, for example, I typically replied, "I am neither an optimist nor a pessimist; rather, I am a realist. And reality is that Iraq is all hard, all the time." I would then note the progress we'd achieved and setbacks we'd suffered in recent weeks. I worked hard, in fact, to maintain credibility with

coalition leaders and the media, as well as with our troopers and their Iraqi counterparts. The provision of realistic assessments was hugely important and ranked
among the biggest of the many "rocks" in my personal rucksack.[15]

Needless to say, it was the greatest of privileges to serve with the selfless men
and women, Iraqi and American and those of our coalition partners, civilian as
well as military, who did the hard, dangerous work of the surge. There seldom was
an easy period; each day was tough. But those on the ground consistently demonstrated the skill, initiative, determination, and courage needed to turn the big ideas
at my level into reality at their levels and in their areas of responsibility. They also
displayed the flexibility that was required to ensure that Multi-National Force–
Iraq was a learning organization, one that could react faster and display greater
adaptability than their terrorist, insurgent, and militia opponents. As the surge
progressed, the men and women I was privileged to command continually refined
tactics, techniques, and procedures, and they ultimately defeated their enemies in
both the physical and intellectual manifestations of counterinsurgency battle.

Because of the complexity of counterinsurgency operations and the mixture
of military and civilian tasks that they entail, it is sometimes said that counterinsurgency is the graduate level of warfare. The men and women of the surge demonstrated a true mastery of all that was required to conduct such operations. As I
often noted in later years, they earned the recognition accorded them as "America's New Greatest Generation."[16] It was the greatest honor of my life to lead such
wonderful Americans and their coalition partners during the surge.

About the Author

As I noted at the outset, Pete Mansoor is uniquely qualified to write a history of
the surge. Indeed, he possesses an unequaled combination of impressive scholarly
achievement, military service, experience in the early days in Iraq, and participation in key events during the surge. A U.S. Military Academy graduate who was
first in the class of 1982, he later earned a Ph.D. in history from Ohio State University and served a tour with the History Department at West Point. Pete also
commanded armor and armored cavalry units from company to brigade levels,
including command for more than a year of a brigade combat team deployed in
central and northeast Baghdad during the first year of the Iraq War (an experience
he relates in his 2008 book *Baghdad at Sunrise*).

I first observed Pete in the Kuwaiti desert in August 1999, when I was deployed
there briefly as a promotable colonel[17] and he commanded an armored cavalry
squadron there for four months on Operation Desert Spring. I quickly developed
respect for him and kept track of him thereafter, watching with admiration during the first year in Iraq when he commanded a brigade in Baghdad. And, when
in the fall of 2005, at the end of my second tour in Iraq, I was selected to command
the U.S. Army's Combined Arms Center at Fort Leavenworth, Kansas, I sought

out Colonel Mansoor to help us establish a new Army/Marine Corps Counter-insurgency Center. In that capacity he laid the foundation for an organization that would contribute to the changes to Army-wide training scenarios for units prepar-ing to deploy to Iraq and Afghanistan and to the revised counterinsurgency cur-ricula for various commissioned, warrant, and noncommissioned officer courses throughout the Army. During his time at the Counterinsurgency Center he also contributed at important junctures during the editing of the Army/Marine Corps field manual on counterinsurgency, which contained virtually all of the concepts that we sought to implement during the surge.

Subsequently, in the late summer of 2006, when the chairman of the Joint Chiefs of Staff sought bright colonels who had served in Iraq to conduct a review of the situation there and to lay out alternative ways forward, I nominated Pete and then-Colonel H. R. McMaster, and both were made part of the chairman's "Coun-cil of Colonels." Then, when I was selected at the end of 2006 to command Multi-National Force–Iraq, I asked Pete to lead my transition team and to return to Iraq with me as my executive officer—essentially as the chief of staff of my personal staff, which he helped to recruit and put together. He served in that role from my assumption of command in early February 2007 until his departure in May 2008 and was a tremendous source of wise counsel and an integral part of all that we did during that time.

This background makes Pete uniquely qualified to write about the surge. I am confident that this book will contribute immensely to the understanding of what our military men and women—and their coalition, Iraqi, and civilian partners—did in Iraq in 2007 and 2008. Those selfless individuals were extraor-dinary throughout our time in Iraq, but never more so than during the surge. It is gratifying to see their accomplishments recounted by one who was there and who has the academic expertise and military understanding to provide context to their endeavors and achievements and depth and understanding to their sacrifices.

David Petraeus, General, U.S. Army (Ret.)

Preface

I have recorded these events in the hope that the readers of this history
may profit from them, for there are two ways by which all men may reform
themselves, either by learning from their own errors or from those of others; the
former makes a more striking demonstration, the latter a less painful one.
—Polybius

In the summer of 2008 I hung up the U.S. Army uniform I had worn for twenty-
six years to don mufti as the General Raymond E. Mason Jr. Chair of Military
History at the Ohio State University. I had just finished my second extended
combat tour in Iraq, the latter one a fifteen-month stint as executive officer to
General David Petraeus, commander of Multi-National Force–Iraq. Although at
the time I was tempted to write an account of what had transpired during my tour
in Iraq, I knew the time was not yet right. The nation needed more distance from
the events in question to provide proper perspective on them. More important, I
was determined to wait until the primary sources that Captain Kelly Howard had
assembled for General Petraeus in Iraq were declassified and made accessible to
historians. I moved on to other projects.

Two summers later I attended a conference in Basin Harbor, Vermont, a wonderful vacation getaway on the shores of Lake Champlain. The main topic of the
conference was the war in Afghanistan, and what could be done to turn around
the situation there—or whether it was even possible to do so. The attendees were
a veritable "Who's Who" of counterinsurgency experts. As the day wore on, the
discussion invariably turned to the surge in Iraq and its applicability to the war in

Afghanistan. The use of the analogy was not surprising, but the lack of insight into what made the surge in Iraq work was truly astonishing. Here were the foremost experts in counterinsurgency warfare in the United States, I thought, and not one of them had the holistic insight to understand why the war in Iraq turned out as it did. I resolved right then and there to write a book on the surge. This book is the result of that pledge to myself three years ago.

The misinformation and ignorance—among the general public, in the historical community, within the halls of government, and even in the military—about why the surge in Iraq succeeded is somewhat disheartening. Indeed, a number of pundits still refuse to admit that the surge had anything to do with the reduction of violence in Iraq. The American people need a more comprehensive account of the Iraq War during the years of the surge, one written from the inside perspective of a member of General Petraeus's team. This is the first such account, and it serves accordingly as a landmark in the historiography of the Iraq War.

The Iraq War has generated a substantial corpus of literature covering a broad swath of topics. The surge of U.S. forces into Iraq in 2007–2008, in particular, has already been the focus of a number of books. In *The War Within: A Secret White House History, 2006–2008,* Bob Woodward covers the policy discussions in Washington that resulted in a change in strategy in Iraq in 2006. His coverage of the resulting execution of the surge in Iraq is fairly weak and primarily based on secondary sources, mainly because Woodward never traveled to Iraq to conduct research there. His conclusion—that the primary reason for the success of the surge was improved intelligence that resulted in more effective special operations—is indefensible. Tom Ricks has provided a better account of the surge itself in *The Gamble: General David Petraeus and the American Military Adventure in Iraq, 2006–2008.* Although his is an excellent account, Ricks (like all journalists) is a prisoner of his sources—the vast majority of which are oral interviews he conducted in 2007 and early 2008 while writing the book. While Ricks did travel to Iraq on several occasions to conduct research and interviews, his assertion that Lieutenant General Raymond Odierno was the primary author of the surge strategy is flawed. Linda Robinson has written an account of the surge focused on General Petraeus and his leadership entitled *Tell Me How This Ends: General David Petraeus and the Search for a Way Out of Iraq,* but she gives too much credit to General Petraeus for the success of the surge and ignores other factors—many Iraqi in origin—that help to account for the reduction in violence in Iraq. Bing West has written *The Strongest Tribe: War, Politics, and the Endgame in Iraq,* which is a Marine-centric account of the events in Iraq from 2003 to 2008; while useful, it suffers from the lack of a broader perspective. All of these books were rushed into print to coincide closely in time with the end of the surge in 2008. As a result, they lack the perspective that time alone can provide. Perhaps the best account of the Iraq War to date is Michael Gordon and Bernard Trainor's *The Endgame: The Inside Story of the Struggle for Iraq, from George W. Bush to Barack Obama.* This excellent, well-documented history nevertheless lacks an insider's perspective on the events in question. These works have one thing in common: They were all written by journalists looking from the outside of the institution inward—as through a glass, darkly.

I was both an observer and a participant in the events leading up to the adoption of the surge strategy in 2006 and its subsequent implementation in 2007–2008. As a member of the Council of Colonels that assisted the Joint Chiefs of Staff in rethinking the strategy for the Iraq War in 2006, I had an intimate look at the deliberations that resulted in the adoption of the surge by the Bush administration. My subsequent assignment as executive officer to General David Petraeus provided me unparalleled access during the execution of the surge strategy in Iraq. I sat in on the fringes of most of the key meetings between administration officials and General Petraeus and participated in all of the important gatherings of military officers in Multi-National Force–Iraq. My personal notes and recollected insights from these events have provided a strong foundation for a comprehensive account of this period in history. Furthermore, I requested the declassification of certain records from General Petraeus's personal papers stored at the National Defense University, a request that was granted. The redacted version of these papers, along with the declassified documents in the General George Casey Papers at the National Defense University, have proved most helpful in documenting the progress of the war in Iraq, and in particular the course of the surge in 2007–2008.

This book also serves as a second personal memoir of the Iraq War, a bookend of sorts to *Baghdad at Sunrise: A Brigade Commander's War in Iraq,* in which I recounted the history and exploits of the Ready First Combat Team, which I commanded, in Baghdad and Karbala in 2003–2004. This second account, however, has much less of "me" in it. The surge revolved around other people, primarily, from my perspective, General David Petraeus. He is therefore the focus of much of what I write. Furthermore, this is an account of the surge, not a comprehensive history of the Iraq War. I do not examine the controversies surrounding the decision to go to war in Iraq, the planning and execution of the invasion, or the endgame during the Obama administration. Rather, I attempt to explain how those of us on the ground and in the halls of government tried to salvage U.S. national security objectives in Iraq given the dire situation as it existed at the end of 2006.

Consider this book, therefore, the second draft of history, one that follows the journalistic accounts that have been written to date. I am positive it will not be the last word on the topic of the surge, but I hope its contribution will be enduring nevertheless.

Acknowledgments

Perhaps the most gratifying aspect of finishing a book manuscript—besides finally getting it out of the house—is in recalling all of the people who assisted in bringing it to fruition along the way. Indeed, I am indebted to a number of friends and colleagues for helping to research and shape this manuscript and see it through to publication.

Despite his incredibly busy schedule, General (Ret.) Dave Petraeus read through the entire manuscript, chapter by chapter as I drafted them, and gave me valuable input and additional insights into his role in the surge. We had a refreshing give-and-take over e-mail and phone regarding numerous topics, and although we did not always agree on every issue, we arrived at a consensus on most. The end result, with the exception of the Foreword, remains my work, but it is better for General Petraeus's contributions to it.

General Ray Odierno provided me with a copy of a lengthy, unpublished article he wrote explaining the surge from his viewpoint. It is an important part of surge documentation, and I am grateful for his sharing it with me. Likewise, Colonel (Ret.) Jim Hickey provided valuable material on his role in Multi-National Corps–Iraq and the counter-IED effort in Iraq, and Colonel Richard Iron of the British Army allowed me access to his draft manuscript on U.K. operations in southern Iraq. Their unmatched insight into various facets of the struggle in Iraq have made clear much of what was opaque in existing accounts of the war.

Several people assisted with the research for this book. Major (then Captain) Kelly Howard and Captain Haley Dennison-Uthlaut archived General Petraeus's papers in Iraq. Kelly also provided me with copies of General George Casey's declassified records from 2004 to 2006. (I will always be indebted to her and Major Hanna Mora as well for fresh coffee and muffins on Saturday mornings in Iraq—

they made the end of every long week just a bit brighter.) Scotty Dawson, a product of the Ohio State military history program and head of the historical office at U.S. Central Command, worked with the declassification team at the National Defense University to provide me copies of General Petraeus's weekly reports to the secretary of defense in 2007–2008. Conrad Crane at the U.S. Army Military History Institute provided his unmatched insight into the creation of the counterinsurgency field manual. At the Ohio State University, research associate Ryan McMahon assisted in gathering and evaluating sources on the Awakening.

I reached out to members of General Petraeus's personal staff for recollections and photos, and as usual they did not disappoint. In particular I appreciate the assistance and input provided by Major General Bill Rapp, Colonel (Ret.) Steve Boylan, Colonel Everett Spain, Major Kelly Howard, Major Hanna Mora, and Heather Wiersema. They were stars in Iraq, and they continue to shine brightly today.

Several colleagues read all or portions of the manuscript and provided valuable feedback, among them John Nagl, Conrad Crane, Williamson Murray, and Sandy Cochran (who as chief of the U.S. Army Historical Office in the Pentagon helped General Casey write an account of his time in Iraq). I also appreciate the support from my colleagues in the History Department and at the Mershon Center for International Security Studies at the Ohio State University. They are arguably the most formidable group of diplomatic-military history scholars in the United States today, and I am a better scholar because of them.

Chris Rogers and his team at Yale University Press have as usual been most helpful and supportive throughout the editing and publishing process. I greatly appreciate the relationship we have established over the years and the care with which they have handled my intellectual work. Dan Heaton, the pride of the Illini, worked his usual magic with the manuscript as editor. Joe LeMonnier produced the excellent maps.

Finally, my wife, Jana, daughter Kyle, and son J.T. have remained my staunchest supporters over the years. They have been incredibly supportive of my extended absences in the home library, accompanied usually only by my faithful Siberian husky, Cisco—now departed to the great sled run in the sky. Writing is always easier when the home fires burn brightly. Ours thankfully always have.

Abbreviations

AEI	American Enterprise Institute
AQI	al-Qaeda in Iraq
BAT	biometric automated toolset
BCT	brigade combat team
BOC	Baghdad Operations Command
BRT	brigade reconnaissance troop
BUA	battlefield update and assessment
CENTCOM	United States Central Command
CERP	Commander's Emergency Response Program
CIA	Central Intelligence Agency
CIG	Commander's Initiatives Group
CJTF	Combined Joint Task Force
CODEL	congressional delegation
COIC	Counter-Improvised Explosive Device Operations Integration Center
COIN	counterinsurgency
COP	combat outpost
CPA	Coalition Provisional Authority
CT	counterterrorism
EFP	explosively formed penetrator
FOB	forward operating base
FSEC	Force Strategic Engagement Cell
HIIDE	handheld interagency identity detection equipment
HMMWV	high mobility multipurpose wheeled vehicle, Humvee
HUMINT	human intelligence
IA	Iraqi Army

IED	improvised explosive device
IFCNR	Implementation and Follow-Up Committee for National Reconciliation
IGC	Iraqi Governing Council
ISF	Iraqi Security Forces
JAM	Jaish al-Mahdi
JSAT	Joint Strategic Assessment Team
MAC-V	Military Assistance Command-Vietnam
MEK	Mujahedin-e Khalq
MiTT	military transition team
MNC-I	Multi-National Corps–Iraq
MND-B	Multi-National Division–Baghdad
MND-C	Multi-National Division–Center
MNF-I	Multi-National Force–Iraq
MNSTC-I	Multi-National Security Transition Command–Iraq
MRAP	mine resistant ambush protected vehicle
NATO	North Atlantic Treaty Organization
NIE	National Intelligence Estimate
NSC	National Security Council
OCINC	Office of the Commander-in-Chief
OMS	Office of the Martyr Sadr
OP	observation post
ORHA	Office of Reconstruction and Humanitarian Affairs
PAO	public affairs officer
PCNS	Iraqi Political Committee on National Security
PKK	Kurdistan Worker's Party
PRT	provincial reconstruction team
RAID	rapid aerostat initial deployment
RCT	regimental combat team
ROTC	Reserve Officers' Training Corps
RFF	request for forces
RPG	rocket-propelled grenade
SCIF	sensitive compartmented information facility
SEAL team	Sea, Air, Land team
SECDEF	secretary of defense
SG	Special Group
SIGINT	signals intelligence
SIPRNET	secure Internet protocol router network
SOI	Sons of Iraq
SUV	sport utility vehicle
SWAT	special weapons and tactics
T&FF	terrorists and foreign fighters
UAV	unmanned aerial vehicle
UNSCR	United Nations Security Council Resolution

Maps

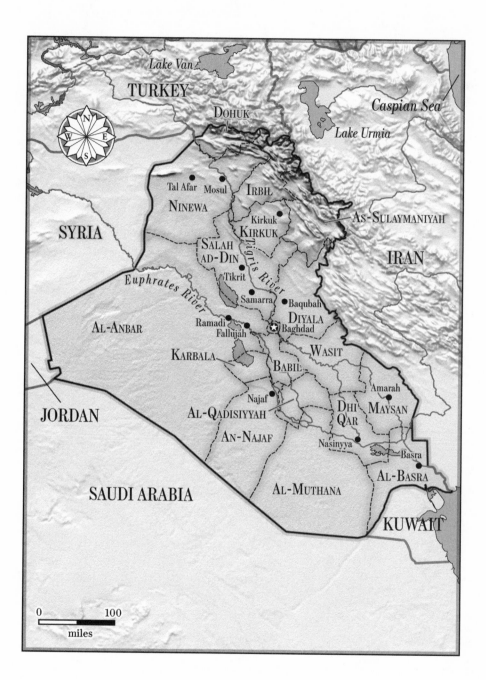

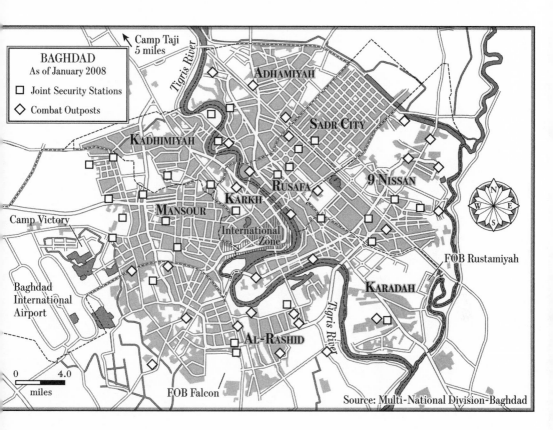

BAGHDAD
As of January 2008
□ Joint Security Stations
◇ Combat Outposts

Camp Taji
5 miles

Tigris River

ADHAMIYAH

SADR CITY

KADHIMIYAH

RUSAFA

9 NISSAN

Camp Victory

MANSOUR

KARKH

International
Zone

FOB Rustamiyah

Baghdad
International
Airport

KARADAH

0   4.0
miles

AL-RASHID

Tigris River

FOB Falcon

Source: Multi-National Division-Baghdad

SURGE

PROLOGUE

Baghdad, February 11, 2007

T he Humvee column kicked up a cloud of dust as it crawled out of Camp
Liberty, the sprawling coalition base near Baghdad International Airport,
on a cool, clear morning in February 2007. The massive facility was home
to thousands of soldiers in the 1st Cavalry Division, a Texas-based unit now responsible for security in the Iraqi capital city. Only a day before General David
Petraeus had taken command of the 140,000-plus troops in Multi-National
Force–Iraq (MNF-I), the coalition forces in Iraq. Accompanied by Major General
Joe Fil, the division commander, as well as a sizable security detachment, Petraeus
was intent on seeing for himself the carnage wrought by the brutal sectarian strife
of the previous twelve months since the terrorist bombing of the al-Askari shrine
in Samarra. After leaving the relative safety of the forward operating base, the
truck column headed for Ghazalia, a largely Sunni district in the western part of
the city. For Petraeus this area, along with Sunni Amiriyah and the mixed Sunni-
Shi'a-Christian neighborhood of Dora in south-central Baghdad, would act as the
proverbial "canary in the coal mine"—an indicator of the vitality of the city, or the
lack thereof.[1]

The column moved along roads pockmarked from previous roadside bomb
explosions. As I sat in the back of the vehicle belonging to Colonel J. B. Burton, the
commander of the brigade in whose zone we now traveled, I listened to the crack-
ling of radio traffic from subordinate units. Insurgents had detonated a roadside
bomb somewhere in the brigade's zone of action, which caused more than a bit of
consternation, given the high-ranking passengers in the column now traversing
the area. As we passed into Ghazalia, there were few signs of activity. Shuttered
businesses lined the lifeless route. Banks were closed. Tumbleweeds blew down the
streets. Traffic was nonexistent. Garbage piles with their ubiquitous smell domi-

nated the dingy scene. In an instant it was clear to me that insurgent intimidation and sectarian violence had sucked the life out of the community, which both General Petraeus and I recalled from earlier deployments (in his case just a couple of years previously) as an upscale and vibrant neighborhood. Al-Qaeda in Iraq operatives, Sunni insurgents, and Shi'a death squads had all taken their toll since then, and utter devastation was the result.

In a few minutes we arrived at our destination—a newly constructed joint security station housing an American infantry company and its Iraqi counterparts. The facility was spartan. Inside a wall of tall blast barriers, a nondescript building housed a small command post and soldier billets. As the outpost lacked running water, along with many other amenities, soldiers relieved themselves in simple plywood outdoor latrines; during our stay a plume of smoke rose from the area as soldiers set fire to a stinking mixture of fuel and human refuse.[2] Soldiers ate food trucked in from Camp Liberty, or made do with prepackaged field rations. Absent were the numerous morale, welfare, and recreation opportunities afforded by the larger forward operating base—television, movies, fast food outlets, Post Exchange, and occasional concerts. For these soldiers, life had returned to the expeditionary nature of existence in the spring and summer of 2003, when the U.S. Army was newly arrived in Iraq.

General Petraeus and as many others as could fit entered the command post to receive a briefing from the U.S. and Iraqi commanders. Instead of the high-tech plasma monitors present in command post facilities on Camp Liberty, these junior officers used a simple map, radios, and a written log to track activity in their neighborhood zone. They had been in this location for only a week or so, but already their situational awareness had increased by several orders of magnitude. Instead of periodic mounted patrols through the neighborhood, U.S. and Iraqi soldiers were now conducting joint foot patrols along the streets. When they were finished with their patrols, they returned to the relative safety of the outpost to rest, maintain their equipment, and plan future operations. But they remained in the neighborhood as a physical presence to dominate the urban landscape. Equally important, the Iraqis who remained in the area were already seeking them out and providing increasingly useful intelligence.

The U.S. commander reported, in fact, that for the first few days, the local inhabitants acted cautiously, unsure of the permanency of the outpost and its defenders. As time went by, neighborhood residents ventured forth to provide information on their tormentors. For months this company had operated intermittently in the area with an information deficit; now, in just a few short days, that scarcity had turned into a torrent of intelligence that enabled the soldiers to begin chipping away at the enemy. But progress was slow and uncertain. Time would tell how successful they would be in providing security to and relieving the suffering of the beleaguered Iraqis in Ghazalia.

Our short visit over, we returned to Camp Liberty to prepare for our next patrol. There we boarded UH-60 Blackhawk helicopters that ferried us to Forward Operating Base Falcon in the southern part of Baghdad. After touring the joint U.S.-Iraqi base and receiving a patrol briefing, we mounted a number of the U.S. Army's new Stryker combat vehicles and set out for the religiously mixed neighborhood of Dora. Riding in the back of one of the Strykers and armed for this journey with an M-4 carbine, I scanned the rooftops and alleyways for snipers. After a short drive, we entered the Dora market. Here, too, the evidence of the sectarian bloodletting of 2006 was unmistakable. By December of that year, Dora was the scene of one-third of all killings in the Iraqi capital.[3] We drove past a former police station that had been blown up by a suicide car bomb. In the market area, buildings bore evidence of rocket and mortar strikes, their blackened sides a grim reminder of the task before us. The few Iraqis in the market moved cautiously, aware of the many dangers that jeopardized their lives. As with Ghazalia, the Dora area was largely a ghost town.[4]

Al-Qaeda terrorists, Sunni insurgents, and Shi'a militiamen had intimidated the population of Baghdad into submission. The colorless reports and operational summaries that General Petraeus and I had read before departing the United States did not do justice to the extent of damage to the Iraqi capital, its inhabitants, and the Iraqi psyche. The severity of the situation hit us like a ton of bricks. The situation in Iraq had spiraled rapidly downward, and U.S. forces and their Iraqi partners had a limited amount of time to reverse the momentum before the clock ran out. The political battles that had attended General Petraeus' confirmation hearings in Washington receded into the distance as the full magnitude of the task ahead of us became apparent.

We returned to Forward Operating Base Falcon in a somber mood. After a short helicopter flight, we arrived back at Camp Victory to take stock of what we had seen during the day. We drove to MNF-I headquarters in the al-Faw palace to attend to the e-mail traffic and other business that had piled up during our absence. As General Petraeus withdrew into his office for an evening of work and private deliberation, his aide de camp, Major Everett Spain, showed me a note that a soldier in the Ghazalia joint security station had handed him during our visit. The soldier wrote simply, "What are we doing here?" The answer to that question was both simple and complex, but a full response requires a recounting of the first several years of the Iraq War and an assessment of the security situation in Iraq at the end of 2006.

CHAPTER 1

A War Almost Lost

The first, the supreme, the most far-reaching act of judgment that the
statesman and commander have to make is to establish . . . the kind of
war on which they are embarking; neither mistaking it for, nor trying to
turn it into, something that is alien to its nature.

—Carl von Clausewitz

By the end of 2006, the United States, its coalition partners, and its indigenous allies were well on their way to losing the war in Iraq. By December
of that year, more than three thousand Iraqis were dying violently every
month.[1] Terror gripped the Iraqi people, many of whom suffered from a lack of
basic services and employment. The fabric of Iraqi society had been torn by a nascent civil war that featured ethnosectarian struggles for control over state power
and resources. Sunni insurgents attacked U.S., coalition, and Iraqi security forces
with roadside bombs, mortar and sniper fire, and occasionally direct assaults on
isolated positions. Al-Qaeda-affiliated terrorists preyed on Shi'a Iraqis by using
massive car bombs and suicide bombers that killed dozens and sometimes hundreds of people with each explosion. In return, Shi'a militias roamed into religiously mixed communities in Baghdad and elsewhere to cleanse them of their
Sunni inhabitants. The bound-and-gagged bodies of young Sunni males turned
up on Baghdad's streets each morning, often displaying such grisly signs of torture as holes drilled into their skulls. To make matters worse, local security forces,
particularly the Iraqi National Police, were implicated in this sectarian violence.
Sunni communities under violent siege rallied around their defenders of last re-

sort—insurgents and al-Qaeda operatives who intimidated the local inhabitants, preyed upon them for sustenance, and brutalized those who failed to provide support. By the end of 2006 more than 1.6 million Iraqi Sunnis had fled the country, largely emigrating to Syria and Jordan, and an additional 1.5 million—70 percent of whom originated from Baghdad—were internally displaced within Iraq.[2] Iraq was coming apart at the seams, beginning with its capital city, Baghdad.

This dire situation had been building ever since the start of the U.S. invasion of Iraq in the spring of 2003. The rapid victory of U.S. forces in toppling Saddam Hussein's Ba'athist regime masked fundamental issues that haunted the subsequent occupation of the country.[3] Absence of planning for the aftermath of major combat operations—a shortfall in large part predicated on the assumption that Iraqis would view American troops as liberators and would cooperate to quickly take charge of their own destiny—resulted in a chaotic occupation that failed to deliver enough security, jobs, and essential services to instill hope in the Iraqi people that a better life lay ahead. To the Iraqi people, the 2003 war was a continuation of the war that began in 1991 and continued via the United Nations sanctions regime. The sanctions depleted Iraq's resources, deeply frayed the social fabric of the country, and all but destroyed the welfare state that had been able to care for Iraq's citizens (at least those who did not cross Saddam Hussein) before the Gulf War.[4] The Iraqi people needed a great deal more help than U.S. planners envisaged.

What was supposed to be a difficult stability operation in postconflict Iraq instead turned into a vicious counterinsurgency fight in an environment in which the Iraqi government and law and order had completely collapsed and the Iraqi economy at first sputtered, then stalled. When the rosy assumptions that underpinned the invasion proved flawed, there was no branch plan to fall back upon, and the hoped-for liberation soon turned into an arduous occupation governed by a series of improvisations. Despite widespread relief at Saddam Hussein's downfall, the majority of the Iraqi people were unwilling to risk their lives by cooperating with coalition forces for the sake of an uncertain future.

Temporal and conceptual shortfalls hampered postwar planning. Bush administration officials viewed the takeover of Iraq in much the same light as the Allied occupation of Germany or Japan after World War II, an analogy that was both inaccurate and inappropriate. To begin with, General George C. Marshall, the U.S. Army chief of staff in World War II, began preparation for the occupation of Germany on January 6, 1942, only one month after the Japanese attack on Pearl Harbor, when he authorized the creation of a school to train officers in military government functions.[5] By the end of 1943, the foundation had been laid for a military government in Germany, nearly eighteen months before this goal became reality.[6] Serious planning for the occupation of Iraq, on the other hand, did not begin until January 20, 2003, only two months before the beginning of the invasion, when Secretary of Defense Donald Rumsfeld tasked retired Lieutenant General Jay Garner with establishing the Office of Reconstruction and Humanitarian Affairs (ORHA). The amount of time devoted to planning for regime replacement was woefully insufficient given the huge task ahead.[7] Much of the substantive planning that was accomplished focused on humanitarian issues, and indeed these efforts helped to forestall a humanitarian crisis in Iraq in the spring of 2003.[8] Planning for regime replacement, on the other hand, was disjointed, fragmented, chaotic, and riven with bureaucratic rivalries that dissipated the U.S. effort to create a stable Iraq following the conclusion of major combat operations. The result was a catastrophic failure of American policy and strategy, the results of which still resonate to this day.[9]

Ironically, the Allied experience in liberating and occupying nations during World War II was applicable, but the Bush administration chose the wrong examples. Instead of Germany or Japan, the occupations of Italy in 1943 and Korea in 1945 were better guides to the liberation of Iraq in 2003. The Allied treatment of Italian fascists was both pragmatic and reasonable, compared to punitive de-Nazification efforts in Germany. The experience of controlling Korea from 1945 to 1950 with a corps headquarters instead of a larger and more capable army headquarters provides a useful lesson in how not to manage a military occupation. Had Department of Defense and other interagency officials understood and learned from the history of the U.S. armed forces in occupation duties, they could have avoided many of the mistakes that soon turned the Iraq War into a strategic nightmare.[10]

The efforts of Garner and his team to stabilize Iraq after the fall of Baghdad were well intentioned but dysfunctional. Inadequate communications, poor coordination, and personal rivalries hampered the best efforts of those involved in the process. In response, on May 11, 2003, Rumsfeld established a new headquarters, the Coalition Provisional Authority (CPA), to govern Iraq. The ensuing transition between ORHA and CPA created even more turmoil. When Ambassador L. Paul Bremer III arrived in Baghdad to assume duties as the head of CPA, he largely ignored the advice and understanding of Iraqi institutions offered by Garner and his team.[11] Bremer had served as ambassador to the Netherlands in the 1980s, but he had little experience in the Middle East, did not speak Arabic, and lacked a thorough knowledge of the history, politics, social composition, and psyche of the Iraqi people. His decision making and handling of the transition in just his first three weeks in Baghdad arguably set the stage for a lengthy and virulent insurgency.

Bremer's first major decision was to de-Ba'athify Iraqi society. Saddam Hussein and the Ba'ath Party had controlled Iraq for more than three decades with an iron fist and brutal resolve. By 2003 Iraqi society was highly traumatized, with sectarian and ethnic tensions lingering just below the surface. Senior Ba'athist leaders had to be removed from their positions and those implicated in criminal activity put in prison to await trial for their misdeeds. How deep to extend de-Ba'athification, however, was an open question.

The Iraqi Ba'ath Party was a hierarchical organization with a half-dozen layers. At the top were Saddam Hussein, his immediate family, and his closest advisers; just beneath them were other key regime officials, and so on. Had Bremer decided to disenfranchise the top three levels of the Ba'ath Party—perhaps one thousand or so of the highest-ranking Ba'athists—few Iraqis would have objected. But such action was not decisive enough for the America's new viceroy in Iraq. Influenced by Douglas Feith and the Pentagon's Office of Special Plans, Bremer decided that de-Ba'athification would extend to the fourth, or *firqah*, level.[12] This decision put out of work not just Saddam Hussein, his immediate family, and their closest compatriots, but tens of thousands of ordinary Iraqis—most but not all Sunni—who had joined the party in order to obtain better jobs (Ba'ath Party membership being a requirement for the best positions in Iraqi society). These were professionals, doctors, engineers, university professors, and civil servants—many of them the same people that U.S. war plans had assumed would remain in their positions to enable Iraq to function after regime change occurred.[13] Instead, CPA Order Number 1 (May 16, 2003) put these Iraqis out of work, denied them their livelihood and pensions, and removed any chance of a political future.[14] In short, de-Ba'athification took hope away from much of Iraq's Sunni elite class, which viewed de-Ba'athification as de facto "de-Sunnification" of Iraq.[15] One could hardly fault the Sunnis for rejecting the future vision of Iraq put forward by America and its allies. For all of its faults, and they were many, the Ba'ath Party was an equal-opportunity oppressor. U.S. policy opened the door to a sectarian Iraq. ORHA administrator Jay Garner later told journalist George Packer that he woke up the day after Bremer issued the de-Ba'athification decree to discover "three or four hundred thousand enemies and no Iraqi face on the government."[16] In a single stroke of the pen, Bremer had created the political basis for the Iraqi insurgency.[17]

Bremer's second major decision compounded the errors of his first. CPA Order 2, again influenced by Deputy Secretary of Defense Paul Wolfowitz and Undersecretary of Defense for Policy Douglas Feith, disbanded all Iraqi government departments that had a role in security or intelligence—the Republican Guard, the Special Republican Guard, paramilitary organizations created by Saddam Hussein as instruments of regime control, and, most critically, the Iraqi Army, Air Force, Navy, Air Defense Force, and other regular military services.[18] Clearly, CPA had to dissolve those entities developed by Saddam Hussein and the Ba'ath Party for regime control, many of which were implicated in horrific acts of violence against the Iraqi people. The decision to disestablish the regular armed forces of Iraq was much more troubling and harder to justify. The U.S. military's own war plans called for using the Iraqi Army to help stabilize postwar Iraq.[19] While the Republican Guard and other instruments of regime control were understandably unpopular, the Iraqi people viewed their armed forces as national institutions, which "generated considerable sympathy and respect throughout Iraq."[20] With the exception of the Kurds, most Iraqis wanted the armed forces retained intact, albeit shorn of their Ba'athist ideology.

In his memoirs, Bremer insists that recalling the Iraqi Army would have been logistically difficult since the Iraqi soldiers had fled home, their barracks and camps thoroughly looted and uninhabitable. He also equates the regular Iraqi Army with the worst of abuses committed largely by other security organizations during Saddam's regime.[21] His arguments ignore several basic facts. Iraqi soldiers may have gone home, but they had also taken their weapons with them. It would have been possible to call them back to the colors (jobs, after all, were scarce) and reform units under new senior leadership. The reformed Iraqi Army would have been capable of helping to stabilize Iraq. When CPA later offered the soldiers back pay to soften the blow to the Iraqi economy, hundreds of thousands showed up to collect. It would have been easy enough to find tens of thousands of volunteers to reform the ranks under new leadership, and put them to work on Iraq's streets to reduce looting and violence. Instead, CPA Order Number 2 put out of work hundreds of thousands of armed young men, and even more critically, tens of thousands of officers—mostly Sunni—who were stripped of their rank and denied their livelihoods, their pensions, any hope of a political future, and perhaps most important in Iraqi society, deprived of their honor.[22] Many of these men, willing enough at first to cooperate with American forces and their allies, took their not inconsiderable military skills with them into what they viewed as honorable resistance to the occupation of their homeland.[23] In a second stroke of the pen, Bremer had created the military basis for the insurgency.[24]

The isolation of the Sunni elite from Iraq's political future deepened when Bremer formed the Iraqi Governing Council (IGC) in July. Politicians who had spent much of the past three decades in exile, some of them highly sectarian in outlook, dominated the body. The Sunni elite were largely shut out of the council, as were the Shi'a underclass, whose champion was the fiery cleric Muqtada al-Sadr. The twenty-five members of the council lacked any real authority, other than to parcel out jobs in the ministries they dominated. In fact, the council members could not agree at first as to how to allocate the twenty-one ministries among themselves, so they created four new ministries to allow each council member to select one minister. The council members did not even hide their agenda, telling Bremer the apportionment was simply designed to create "jobs for the boys."[25] Government services, already critically degraded by the loss of expertise due to de-Ba'athification, suffered even further when technocratic managers were replaced by political hacks in many of the key ministries. The creation of the IGC began the polarization of Iraqi politics based on sect—an outcome that was not necessarily a given after the fall of the Ba'athist regime. Furthermore, the IGC neither convinced the Arab "street" that Iraqis were in charge of their own destiny nor served to increase the legitimacy of the occupation authority among Iraqis.[26] CPA and the IGC would clash on a number of issues in the months ahead, and their tenuous relationship would reach a breaking point during the crisis brought about by the uprisings of April 2004.

De-Ba'athification, the disbanding of the Iraqi Army, and the creation of the sectarian Iraqi Governing Council were disastrous decisions that would lead to years—and perhaps generations—of bloodshed in Iraq. These decisions turned what would probably have been a minor Ba'athist guerrilla movement into a widespread Sunni nationalist insurgency. Historian Andrew Terrill, who has written perhaps the best analysis of de-Ba'athification to date, writes, "In particular, it is now understood that loyalty commissions led by politicians and set up to identify internal enemies can take on a life of their own and become part of a nation's power structure. Once this occurs, such organizations are exceedingly difficult to disestablish. Likewise, the basic unfairness of collective punishment has again been underscored as an engine of anger, resentment, and backlash. Conversely, the importance of honest and objective judicial institutions has also been underscored, as has the importance of maintaining a distinction between revenge and justice."[27] According to historian Mark Moyar, Bremer and other leaders who made these decisions "lacked empathy and judgment, as well as historical knowledge."[28] In Moyar's view, reconstruction in the South after the American Civil War was a much closer analogue to Iraq in 2003 than Germany after World War II. Had American leaders possessed better historical sense, they would have realized "that disfranchising entrenched elites and transferring political power to a new group of uncertain character via elections would drive the old elites into rebellion."[29] Indeed, according to historian Mark Grimsley, radical reconstruction in the American South led to a protracted war that pitted "the forces of white supremacy against the forces of black liberation" and took nearly a century to resolve.[30]

The dysfunction of the occupation during the first crucial year after the fall of Baghdad to U.S. forces in the spring of 2003 is best illustrated by CPA's approach to reconstruction and tribal engagement. Extensive looting of Iraqi infrastructure in April 2003 and widespread unemployment should have made reconstruction an important priority. In some areas, such as northern Iraq (an area under the command of Major General David Petraeus and the 101st Airborne Division), reconstruction and other activities aimed at putting the Iraqi people back to work and improving their lives took top priority. Petraeus understood that time was of the essence in this regard, since, in his words, "every Army of liberation has a half-life beyond which it turns into an Army of occupation."[31] He viewed money as important as ammunition in the struggle to stabilize the situation in Iraq in the spring and summer of 2003.[32]

To assist commanders in reconstruction activities, CPA authorized the use of captured Ba'athist funds for the Commander's Emergency Response Program, or CERP. This program gave unit commanders the wherewithal to fund local projects in their areas. Military commanders on the ground had a much closer connection to the Iraqi people than CPA administrators holed up behind blast barriers in the Green Zone. They better understood the needs of the people and could discuss potential projects with neighborhood and district governing councils in their areas, thereby providing local Iraqis some input into the governing process. Low-cost, high-impact projects funded by CERP were critical to bringing hope to the Iraqi people for a better life ahead.

Bremer, who was, in the words of his old boss Henry Kissinger, a "control freak," preferred to centralize reconstruction planning at CPA.[33] When CPA submitted a request through the Office of Management and Budget for appropriated funds for reconstruction, the U.S. Agency for International Development was shut out of the process.[34] After Congress appropriated $18 billion for Iraqi reconstruction, the vast majority of the money went into projects centrally planned by CPA, which ignored such critical areas of the economy as agriculture. Management of a myriad of small projects by CPA administrators was impossible; instead, the bulk of the money went into large, overambitious reconstruction projects that would take years to complete and that would be undertaken by multinational corporations. This meant that the Iraqi people would not see an improvement in their condition for many months or years, and that a sizable chunk of the reconstruction aid would end up as company profits or would be consumed in administrative and security overhead. CERP funds expended by brigade and battalion commanders mostly went into the pockets of Iraqi small businessmen, who hired Iraqi laborers to work on their projects with minimal overhead for security (they were working in their own country, after all). Bremer and CPA viewed reconstruction as a catalyst to long-term economic growth; U.S. military commanders viewed it as an extension of their counterinsurgency campaign. The amount of money expended on CERP was dwarfed by the reconstruction funds dominated by CPA—the largest U.S. foreign aid program since the Marshall Plan.[35] The result was Iraqi disillusionment at the pace of reconstruction, along with the mismanagement and waste that attended to CPA's efforts.[36]

CPA's policy toward Iraqi tribes showed its lack of cultural awareness and understanding of the complex relationships that existed in Iraqi society. Iraqi tribes represented civil society in the Arabic tradition, yet for nearly a year CPA ignored the tribes as an anachronism in Iraq's modern political future. Some unit commanders engaged tribal sheiks on their own accord, but CPA did not convene a gathering of tribal sheiks until May 2004, far later than advisable to engage their support for the way ahead in Iraq. In CPA's view the tribes were part of Iraq's past and had no place in its present or future. Ironically, the tribes turned out to be a major part of the solution to stemming the insurgency and destroying al-Qaeda in Iraq when all seemed lost in 2006.[37]

CPA was an ad hoc organization created by necessity when the initial plan to stabilize Iraq, based on overoptimistic assumptions that had no basis in reality, failed in the looting and chaos of the spring of 2003. Part of the problem with the organization was its leadership, as Bremer and others sought to apply neo-conservative ideological principles to a situation that demanded a more nuanced understanding of Iraqi history, culture, economics, and psychology. But management shortfalls also contributed to its dysfunction. CPA never operated with more than two-thirds of the required personnel, lacked expertise in crucial areas, and battled constant turnover. During the fourteen months of CPA's existence, only seven people served with the organization from start to finish.[38] The astonishing reality is that the largest foreign assistance effort ever undertaken by the United States was managed by an ad hoc organization created as an improvised solution to a crisis of America's own creation.[39]

Despite these egregious strategic errors, the occupation of Iraq could have succeeded had the U.S. and coalition military forces been able to bring security to the streets of Baghdad and to the remainder of the country. Lack of troops significantly lessened the chances for a successful outcome in that regard. Fewer than two weeks after the fall of Baghdad, Secretary of Defense Rumsfeld canceled orders that would have deployed the 1st Cavalry Division and its sixteen thousand soldiers to Iraq.[40] The remaining troops in the newly renamed Combined Joint Task Force (CJTF) 7 were too few to secure Iraq without assistance from Iraqi police and military forces, which in the case of the former were corrupt and highly incompetent, and which in the latter case CPA had dissolved. Would-be insurgents and criminals promptly looted unguarded ammunition depots, which provided the wherewithal for the insurgency in the months and years ahead. The Pentagon put CJTF 7 under the command of newly promoted Lieutenant General Ricardo Sanchez, the most junior three-star general in the U.S. Army. The situation called for a more robust headquarters led by a more seasoned and capable leader. But the belief that the war in Iraq was essentially over led to the decision to underresource the stabilization effort and place it in the hands of the most available person, rather than the most capable.

Over the course of the summer and fall of 2003, security deteriorated as a growing insurgency began to contest control of portions of the country. During the Ramadan observance in October–November 2003, the 1st Armored Division suppressed the first of a series of urban uprisings in Baghdad by newly formed insurgent organizations.[41] Yet even in the midst of this guerrilla conflict, the administration refused to acknowledge reality. "I don't want to read in *The New York Times* that we are facing an insurgency," President Bush announced in a meeting of the National Security Council on November 11, 2003. "I don't want anyone in the cabinet to say it is an insurgency. I don't think we are there yet."[42] Secretary of Defense Rumsfeld that month requested briefings on historical insurgencies and successful methods to counter them, but he continued to argue publicly that U.S. forces were merely up against Ba'athist "dead enders."[43]

U.S. Army and Marine Corps units on the ground in Iraq did not have the luxury to ignore the reality confronting them. Their preparation and training, however, had not prepared them to fight a counterinsurgency war. U.S. military doctrine in the decade leading up to the Iraq War stressed rapid, decisive operations and quick victories by high-tech warfighting forces.[44] To counter the rising insurgency now confronting them, most U.S. commanders on the ground in Iraq resorted to offensive operations such as raids and cordon-and-search missions to kill or capture insurgent and terrorist operatives. In some cases, lacking precise intelligence and deficient in cultural awareness, units did more harm than good in executing security operations to quell the insurgency.[45] Over time, unit commanders adjusted their tactics, techniques, and procedures to make them more effective for the type of conflict in which their units were engaged. They assessed the political, military, and economic situation and devised plans more in tune with the unique set of circumstances each faced in his area.[46] These adjustments, however, were far from uniform as the U.S. Army and Marine Corps slowly adapted their education and training to the new reality confronting warfighting forces in Iraq.

Tactical adjustments alone could not win the war. CJTF-7 lacked a coherent strategy and a defined operational concept to achieve the ends of policy. Indeed, even those ends were largely fluid in the first years of the war, as the hunt for weapons of mass destruction gave way to more esoteric goals, like planting democracy in the heart of the Middle East.[47] Offensive operations to kill or capture insurgent and terrorist operatives could not by themselves bring stability to Iraq. To achieve this goal, U.S. leaders needed to think more broadly about the campaign. To a certain extent, they did. As the war continued, military and political leaders added lines of operation to improve governance, bolster economic growth, provide essential services to the Iraqi people, and prosecute an information campaign to influence the Iraqi people while informing the broader American and world audiences. The execution of these tasks, however, fell far short of expectations. The poor relationship between CPA and CJTF-7 did not help matters.[48]

Nevertheless, U.S. forces enjoyed some successes in the final six months of 2003. In July the 101st Airborne Division and special operations forces in Mosul killed Uday and Qusay Hussein, Saddam's brutal and cruel sons. U.S. forces defeated the insurgent Ramadan offensive and began to chip away at the organized crime rings that had sprouted in Iraq's major cities. Finally, in December soldiers of Colonel Jim Hickey's 1st Brigade, 4th Infantry Division, along with special operations forces, captured Saddam Hussein hiding in a hole on a farm near his ancestral home in Tikrit. These achievements took the wind out of the sails of the Ba'athist-led insurgency and created the conditions for a reengagement with Iraqi Sunnis. Violent incidents dropped in the first three months of 2004 to levels not seen again until the summer of 2008, after the surge ended.[49]

A window of opportunity existed to bring Iraq's Sunni population into support for a new way ahead, but Bremer and the Bush administration failed to take advantage of it. Reconciliation with Iraqi Sunnis would have required modification of the draconian de-Ba'athification decree and dissolution of the Supreme Council on de-Ba'athification led by the Shi'a expatriate Ahmed Chalabi, an Iraqi with close ties to the Bush administration, who used the organization to hammer the Sunnis and thereby ingratiate himself with the Shi'a community.[50] Perhaps believing that without its purported leader the insurgency would simply wither away, Bremer decided instead to forge ahead with the creation of a Transitional Administrative Law (a temporary constitution) under the aegis of the Iraqi Governing Council.[51] The result was a radicalization of the leadership of the insurgency, now increasingly under the sway of Islamist extremists flowing into Iraq from outside the country.[52]

Sensing that the downturn in violence was an appropriate moment to readjust its military posture, CJTF-7 used the changeover of combat brigades in the late winter and early spring of 2004 to order its units to withdraw from their positions inside Iraq's cities and consolidate them in larger forward operating bases (FOBs)—temporary facilities housing soldiers and their equipment—on the outskirts. In Baghdad, this repositioning meant the consolidation of U.S. units into the Green Zone plus four large operating bases on the city's periphery: Camp Victory/Liberty near Baghdad International Airport, FOB Falcon in southern Baghdad, FOB Rustamiyah in southeast Baghdad, and Camp Taji north of the capital city. The decision to withdraw from inside the cities was based on the belief that U.S. forces were a virus infecting Iraqi society, and that the longer American troops remained inside Iraq's cities, the more antibodies in the form of insurgents they would create.[53] The decision was a mistake. One of the primary objectives of a counterinsurgency operation is to secure the population, thereby protecting the people from violence and intimidation and isolating the insurgents from resources and support. To protect the people, security forces must be positioned among them. Iraqi security forces were neither numerous enough nor well enough trained to secure areas vacated by the more capable U.S. Army and Marine forces. American troops, now positioned in remote operating bases, could not provide the Iraqi people adequate security against insurgents, terrorists, and militias, no matter how many patrols they conducted outside the wire. The withdrawal of U.S. forces from Iraq's cities in April 2004 coincided with a significant upturn in violence in the country. The correlation was hardly accidental.

The relative lull in violence would not last. On March 31, 2004, four Blackwater contractors took a wrong turn and drove their SUVs into Fallujah, where armed militants ambushed and killed them. Enraged Iraqis then dragged two of the mutilated corpses to the city center and hung them from a bridge spanning the Euphrates River. U.S. Marines surrounded the city and installed a dusk-to-dawn curfew, but Bush and Rumsfeld demanded quick action to apprehend the perpetrators and bring Fallujah under control.[54] Administration pressure led to a premature assault on the city with two thousand Marines, an inadequate force for the difficult mission. Arabic media portrayed the assault inaccurately as a civilian bloodbath, and members of the IGC threatened to resign their positions if the attack continued.[55] The insurgents resisted fiercely, but after four days of fighting, the Marines neared their objectives in the city center. On the verge of defeat, the insurgents were saved when Bremer (with the concurrence of General John Abizaid, head of U.S. Central Command) bowed to Iraqi Governing Council pressure and agreed to halt the offensive.[56] Two weeks later the offensive was canceled altogether. The United States had suffered the worst of all outcomes—a potential military victory was forsaken due to political spinelessness; the Arabic media painted U.S. forces as war criminals despite the decision to retreat; and Fallujah remained in the hands of Sunni insurgents, who claimed victory against U.S. forces.[57]

Elsewhere in Iraq, the Shi'ites were also stirring. The U.S. invasion had lifted the lid on sectarian passions and the Shi'ites, long denied political power in Mesopotamia, were determined to seize the opportunity to establish their dominance. Some groups, such as the Supreme Council for the Islamic Revolution in Iraq (SCIRI) and the Dawa Party, cooperated with the Americans and worked within the system established by CPA to gain power by co-opting the emerging political and security establishment in Iraq. The Shi'a underclass, led by the radical cleric Muqtada al-Sadr, took a different course. Sadr attempted to muscle fellow clerics aside to gain power; he had been implicated in the murder of a moderate Shi'a cleric, Abdel Majid al-Khoei, in the holy city of an-Najaf in April 2003. Sadr and his compatriots seized the opportunity in the vacuum of power formed by the collapse of the Ba'athist regime to form a militia, the Jaish al-Mahdi, composed of the dispossessed and largely illiterate male population of Sadr City and other Shi'a enclaves, with the intention of gaining control of communities across southern and central Iraq. Peeved at being left off the Iraqi Governing Council, in October 2003 Sadr openly declared the formation of a shadow government to challenge the authority of CPA. Despite this brazen challenge to their authority, Bremer and Sanchez failed to act decisively to rein in Sadr and his followers.[58]

By spring 2004, Bremer felt he could no longer ignore Sadr's challenge to Iraq's future. On March 28, CPA ordered the closure of Sadr's newspaper, *al-Hawza,* which resulted in riotous demonstrations in Baghdad by thousands of his followers. When a week later special operations forces arrested Sadr's top aide, Mustafa al-Yaccoubi, full-scale rebellion erupted. Jaish al-Mahdi militiamen attacked government and coalition facilities in an-Najaf, Kufa, Karbala, Diwaniyah, Kut, and in Sadr City in Baghdad. The newly formed Iraqi Civil Defense Corps largely dissolved, and the weak and inept police forces were either unwilling or incapable of stemming the Shi'a tide. Coalition contingents in south-central Iraq were a mixed bag and showed how desperate the Bush administration was for CJTF-7 to look like a coalition without the capacity to act like one: the Ukrainians wouldn't fight because their political leaders forbade them to leave their base; the Spanish disgracefully retreated; the Poles and Salvadorians at least defended themselves, though given lack of strength and national caveats on rules of engagement, they could do little to regain control in their areas. Car bombs destroyed five bridges along Main Supply Route Tampa, the coalition lifeline that ran from the port in Kuwait to Baghdad. For several days, supply convoys were unable to move north. The uprising created a serious political crisis for CPA and a logistical crisis for CJTF-7.[59]

American political and military leaders moved decisively to rein in Sadr and his militia. Rumsfeld recalled the 1st Armored Division and the 2nd Armored Cavalry Regiment, which were en route home after a year in combat, and ordered the units back into Iraq to help restore order. Task forces from the 1st Armored Division attacked to regain control of Kut, Kufa, Najaf, and Karbala, while a brigade of the 1st Cavalry Division fought militants in Sadr City, the Shi'a slum that dominated eastern Baghdad. After several weeks of tough fighting, the superior discipline and firepower of the U.S. forces prevailed. Sadr and his militia were on the ropes; it but remained for Bremer and the Iraqi Governing Council to complete the military victory by arresting Sadr for instigating the violence or sending him into exile. Early in the crisis, it seemed Bremer was willing to take decisive action. He told Condoleezza Rice, Bush's national security adviser, "We need to react vigorously. We must not let him get away with this."[60] But after key members of the governing council threatened to resign, Bremer balked. In early June the council convinced Bremer to offer Sadr and the Jaish al-Mahdi a cease-fire on the condition that they would pursue their agenda through the political process. Defeated on the field of battle, Sadr gladly accepted the offer. He had no intention of disarming his militia, however. In succeeding months the Jaish al-Mahdi rearmed and reorganized, and in August it rose up again in an-Najaf. This time it was the turn of U.S. Marines to combat the Shi'a rebels. They defeated Sadr's forces handily, only to also see their military victory annulled by another cease-fire, this time brokered by Ayatollah Ali al-Sistani, the senior Shi'a cleric in Iraq. This time Sadr did enter Iraqi politics, but his militia continued to grow in strength, numbers, and capability, unchecked by coalition forces. Perhaps six thousand strong in the spring of 2004, the Jaish al-Mahdi had grown by several orders of magnitude by the beginning of the civil war two years later. Sadr might have been finished off as a political and military force in Iraq, but instead, U.S. and Iraqi fecklessness had strengthened his hand and allowed him to claim the mantle of resistance against a foreign occupier of Islamic land.

CPA and coalition forces had missed major opportunities to bring the Sunnis back into the political process, to stem the growing insurgency, and to check the rise of Shi'a militias. The successes of the 1st Armored Division in defeating the Shi'a uprising across south-central Iraq, along with the Marine offensive in Fallujah, could have led to a resounding military success even as the political process faltered. Instead, these accomplishments were wiped out by weak political leadership that halted the attack in Fallujah just when it showed promise, and likewise allowed Muqtada al-Sadr to escape the consequences of his reckless and irrespon-

sible actions. Sadr—the one Iraqi leader who had stood up to the American occupiers—emerged strengthened as a hero to the Shi'a underclass. Not only the
Americans but also his fellow Iraqis had misjudged his political savvy and staying
power.

On June 28, 2004, the United States returned sovereignty to an Iraqi government
led by Ayad Allawi. The Iraqi state still lacked effective security forces and therefore relied heavily on U.S. and coalition troops to stem the rising insurgency, combat terrorism, and guard its national borders. Even though Iraqi police and army
budgets were heavily dependent on U.S. assistance, and Iraqi forces lacked adequate training and leadership, American policy makers agreed to cede authority
to Iraqi leaders to recruit, promote, and dismiss military personnel. This policy
cleared the way for Iraqi politicians to fill key command and staff positions with
leaders chosen on the basis of their religious and political affiliations, rather than
on the basis of competence.[61] It was a small step from there to a situation in which
elements of the Iraqi security forces became involved in fomenting sectarian violence, rather than acting as a brake on the acceleration toward civil war.

The war in Iraq drifted, a victim of domestic politics in the United States in the
run-up to the presidential election. Internationally and within Iraq, support for
the U.S. war effort, never high to begin with, plummeted after revelations in the
spring of serious prisoner abuse at Abu Ghraib prison, west of Baghdad. Military
police soldiers on one of the night shifts had sadistically abused Iraqi detainees the
previous fall, and shocking photos of the misdeeds eventually found their way to
the media and the Internet.

The ramifications from the publication of the appalling photos were immediate and severe, but astonishingly the fallout did not include the sacking of the
secretary of defense. Rumsfeld rightly offered his resignation, but President Bush
twice refused to accept it.[62] Bush was loyal to a fault toward his subordinates. The
lack of accountability in the case of Abu Ghraib left in place a leader of America's defense establishment who had demanded a war plan for Iraq predicated on
the best-case scenario, and who then refused to admit that his assumptions were
wrong when reality hit home after the fall of Baghdad. Rumsfeld's refusal to approve more troops to secure Iraq, his insistence that the insurgent and terrorist violence was merely the work of a few "dead enders," and his denial of the existence
of an insurgency all contributed to the dysfunction of the American military effort. And now, in the words of Bing West, Rumsfeld "had lost the moral authority
to lead."[63] Despite the damage to his credibility as a senior leader, Rumsfeld would
remain at the helm of the Pentagon for another two and a half years. He would
finally resign in the wake of the 2006 midterm elections that tilted congressional
power decisively to the Democratic Party. Ironically, it was a domestic political
collapse, and not the fact that the United States was actually losing the Iraq War,
that prompted Rumsfeld's departure from the Department of Defense.

CPA gave way to an American embassy under Ambassador John Negroponte, the U.S. ambassador to the United Nations, whose distinguished foreign service career included postings in Asia, Europe, and Latin America. Negroponte was no stranger to counterinsurgency warfare or to the political struggles of weak states, having served in Saigon during the Vietnam War and Honduras during the first Reagan administration. On the military side, CJTF-7 had morphed into Multi-National Force–Iraq (MNF-I), under the command of General George Casey, a career infantry officer whose father, also an army general, had died in a helicopter crash in Vietnam.

Casey injected fresh thinking into the war effort. He brought in counterinsurgency experts such as U.S. Army Colonel Bill Hix, a Special Forces officer and the son of a CIA operative, and Kalev Sepp, a retired Special Forces colonel who had served in the advisory mission to El Salvador in the 1980s, to revamp MNF-I's operating procedures. Casey and Negroponte also codified MNF-I's strategy and operational concept in a campaign plan, something that the coalition had lacked up to this point in its existence. Together, they repaired the tattered relationship between the civil and military sides of the war effort in Baghdad.

Sepp, with a Harvard Ph.D. and field experience in counterinsurgency warfare, was the perfect person to examine what ailed U.S. operations in Iraq. He started by examining four dozen twentieth-century insurgencies to determine the best (and by extension, the worst) practices in countering them.[64] Although Sepp cautioned that "a strategic victory does not validate all the victor's operational and tactical methods or make them universally applicable," his list of the best counterinsurgency methods was a damning indictment of U.S. operating methods in Iraq in late 2004 and early 2005.[65] "The focus of all civil and military plans and operations must be on the center of gravity in any conflict—the country's people and their belief in and support of their government," Sepp wrote.[66] This was hardly the case with U.S. operations in Iraq, which focused heavily on killing and capturing insurgents and on building Iraqi security forces to assume the burden of combat over time. Effective counterinsurgents also emphasized respect for human rights (the Iraqi government and its security forces would soon be implicated in a number of abuses of the Sunni population), honest police forces and an effective judicial system (largely absent in Iraq), measures to control the population (insurgents and militias could move relatively freely), programs for amnesty and rehabilitation of insurgents (which suffered from lack of commitment on the part of the Iraqi government), an effective advisory effort for the host nation military (woefully lacking early in the war), border security to prevent insurgent and terrorist infiltration (Iraqi borders were largely unguarded), and exceptional leadership to inspire the people to resist the insurgent call to arms.[67] At the operational and tactical levels, poor counterinsurgency practices included heavy use of firepower and large unit sweeps to clear areas, rather than reliance on precision intelligence and small-unit patrolling to police neighborhoods and protect the population. Sepp ended his analysis with a stern admonition: "It is still possible for Iraqi and coalition govern-ments to adopt proven counterinsurgency practices and abandon schemes that have no record of success."[68] In part based on this analysis, General Casey ordered the creation of an academy to train leaders in counterinsurgency principles as they began their tours in Iraq.[69]

Terribly underresourced during the first year of the war, the military organiza-tion in Iraq was bolstered by the creation of a corps headquarters, Multi-National Corps–Iraq (MNC-I) to handle tactical matters, and a new organization to train and equip the Iraqi military, Multi-National Security Transition Command–Iraq (MNSTC-I). Lieutenant General David Petraeus returned to Iraq after a short stint in the United States to command the effort to build new Iraqi military forces, which the Bush administration would come to view as its exit strategy from the conflict. Petraeus replaced the civilian contractors who had been training the new Iraqi Army with U.S. Army soldiers, most of whom, regrettably, were inadequately prepared for their role as advisers. The effort improved slowly over time as the institutional training base in the United States developed programs to better pre-pare advisers for their roles, coalition partners added capability to the effort, and MNSTC-I gained experience in training indigenous forces.

In the security realm, the MNF-I campaign plan had two major lines of op-eration: isolating and neutralizing the insurgency, and creating and training Iraqi security forces.[70] Petraeus with his usual energy had MNSTC-I working hard to-ward the second goal. The first objective was more nebulous. Killing and capturing terrorist and insurgent operatives was certainly part of the equation, and indeed most special operations forces assigned to Iraq focused more intensely on that ob-jective rather than on training and advising the Iraqi military.[71] Conventional U.S. Army and Marine forces suffered from poor operational guidance that mandated, for the most part, positioning on large forward operating bases. This necessitated mounted patrols in armored Humvees, which in turn precluded close contact with the Iraqi people. The task to block insurgent and terrorist infiltration along the border with Syria was more hope than reality.

U.S. forces did not lack capability or firepower; they lacked intelligence and a political framework in which to operate effectively. A "Red Team" analysis con-ducted for General Casey on July 15, 2004, noted the criticality of precise intel-ligence in targeting insurgent and terrorist operatives. "Unless framed within a convincing political rationale and precisely targeted, the application of force strengthens the insurgency and causes it to grow," the analysts noted.[72] To meet the first challenge, the analysts devised a clever political strategy. MNF-I should encourage the Iraqi government to bring the Sunnis back into the political pro-cess; in return, rehabilitated Sunni leaders must brand as enemies of the state Abu Musab al-Zarqawi, the head of al-Qaeda in Iraq, and his organization, as well as assist in efforts to eliminate them.[73] This strategy was not dissimilar to that eventu-ally employed during the surge, when American commanders enlisted the support of Iraqi tribes to battle al-Qaeda in exchange for security assistance and recon-struction contracts.

The lack of intelligence was a challenge partly of the coalition's own making. General Casey's initial campaign plan stated that MNF-I would undertake "full-spectrum counter-insurgency operations to isolate and neutralize" the enemy, as well as organize, train, and equip Iraqi security forces to create a secure environ-ment in the longer term.[74] The goal was to drive "a wedge between the insurgency and the people of Iraq, separating them from their supporters and potential sup-porters."[75] This was a sensible concept, but the devil was in the details. How co-alition forces went about undertaking "full-spectrum counter-insurgency opera-tions" mattered a great deal. Intelligence-based, precision operations to kill and capture the enemy are a staple of effective counterinsurgency warfare. But without an enduring presence among the population, and with a number of areas of Iraq uncovered by any type of security force, the coalition suffered from a dearth of human intelligence. Its signals interception resources, which would in time add powerful capabilities to the war effort, were initially anemic. Iraqi police and mili-tary forces, which had the cultural knowledge and language capabilities necessary to communicate with the Iraqi people, were too few, too apathetic, too ill-trained and poorly equipped, and in some cases too sectarian to make up for the shortfall of U.S. and coalition forces in Iraq.

In fact, the MNF-I campaign plan acknowledged the risk of a premature com-mitment of Iraqi forces before they were prepared to operate on their own and encouraged an emphasis on quality rather than quantity.[76] This focus would work only if the Iraqi forces were given time to mature behind a shield of coalition forces robust enough to secure the country, but both time and troops were in short sup-ply. The campaign plan put forward the goal of having Iraqi forces maintain local security with limited coalition support by the end of 2004, and to take the lead in securing Iraq's eighteen provinces by mid-2005.[77] The two goals—to develop quality Iraqi security forces and to have them take responsibility for securing Iraq within twelve months—were in direct conflict. Given the challenges confronting the Iraqi government and the coalition, victory was a long-term prospect at best.

In Fallujah the insurgency metastasized. Abu Musab al-Zarqawi, the head of al-Qaeda in Iraq, installed a reign of terror in the city and instituted a particularly severe brand of Shari'a law. In his spare time he would cut off the heads of selected prisoners and then post the video on the Internet. Fallujans were cowed into sub-mission. The Marines, isolated from the people in their base outside the city, could do little to turn the situation around. Roadside bomb explosions, rocket strikes, and suicide attacks increased. Imams and tribal sheiks, upset at the treatment of the Sunni elite by the United States and its chosen Iraqi government, sided with the insurgents.[78] Al-Qaeda had approached these leaders with a simple message— Sunnis needed to band together to fight the American invaders and their "Persian"

(Shi'a) lackeys. For now, the message resonated with the Sunni people, particularly in al-Anbar province in western Iraq.

Insurgent control of Fallujah was a direct challenge to Iraqi sovereignty; Allawi and the coalition could not allow the insurgents to retain control of the city. The Iraqi prime minister attempted to negotiate a deal with the insurgents, but without success. By the first week in November, General Casey had assembled five Marine battalions and a U.S. Army armored brigade, along with two Iraqi Army infantry battalions, in the vicinity of Fallujah. To prevent inaccurate civilian casualty counts from leaking out of the city, which the residents largely abandoned in the run-up to the assault, the coalition began the operation by seizing the city hospital, from which had emanated highly inaccurate civilian casualty statistics during the hostilities the previous April. Beginning on November 8 the Marines and soldiers went house to house, cleared roughly thirty thousand buildings, and in the process killed the two thousand insurgents who stayed to defend the city, at the cost of seventy American lives. Zarqawi and other leaders, dressed as women, sneaked away before the attack began and left their foot soldiers behind to die. It was the first attempt by the insurgency to hold ground, and it failed dramatically. After a six-week battle, the city lay in ruins.[79]

Fallujah was the end of the kinetic road for MNF-I. The coalition could not afford to move battalions around Iraq to demolish one city after another in the quest to destroy insurgent forces. The fighting was also hardening Sunni public opinion against the Iraqi government and the coalition that supported it. After the fighting ended in Fallujah, the MNF-I assessment of its campaign plan concluded, "There is little objective evidence that a wedge is being driven between the insurgents and the population of Iraq."[80] Absent the ability to hold areas once cleared of enemy forces, General Casey correctly viewed Fallujah-style attacks as a dead end.[81] There had to be another way.

The "other way" adopted in 2005 was to begin to turn the war over to the Iraqis. U.S. military leaders understood that insurgencies were typically long-term affairs, with the average insurgency lasting a decade or longer. With some justification, they did not think Americans would support an extended war in Iraq—at least not at a significant cost in blood and treasure. Accordingly, the coalition would continue to battle insurgent and terrorist forces while supporting newly created government institutions, helping to create military and police forces, doing whatever they could to energize the economy, and encouraging Iraqis to take the lead in securing their homeland.[82] More than two years into the war, many U.S. units had adopted a number of the more important tenets of counterinsurgency warfare, such as the need to structure raids and other offensive missions on precise intelligence, but the application of counterinsurgency principles across the force was uneven.[83] While U.S. military forces hunted down insurgent and terrorist leaders and conducted other counterinsurgency tasks, Multi-National Security Transition

Command–Iraq became the main effort to train and equip Iraqi security forces capable of stabilizing Iraq and fighting the insurgency over the long haul. U.S. units
would partner with Iraqi forces in their areas to help them build their capacity to
conduct security operations, while advisers (euphemistically and tellingly called
"transition teams") would embed within Iraqi security organizations to provide
advice and assistance. General Casey optimistically set November 30, 2005, as the
date for transition of security responsibilities at provincial level to Iraqi control
and for reestablishment of security along Iraq's borders.[84]

If MNF-I could reduce the insurgency's strength to a level Iraqi forces could
handle on their own within the allotted time frame, then this strategy made sense;
if not, it was a recipe for failure. General Casey's planners understood the risks.
In the April 2005 contingency plan that governed coalition force operations, the
planners wrote that "in the face of a coup, factional violence or the beginnings of
a civil war, it is doubtful that over the next two years ISF [Iraqi Security Forces]
would be able to respond effectively as tribal, factional, and ethno-religious loyalties prevail over those to the nation."[85] Other than a promise to closely monitor
these threats, the document remained silent on what measures would be taken
were one of these risks to emerge as reality—as indeed would happen less than
ten months later. The planners put forward a requirement to maintain three brigades in operational or theater reserve to mitigate risk, but given the already over-
stretched U.S. Army and Marine Corps, these reserves existed only on paper as the
implementation date (spring 2006) came and went.[86]

In a radio address to the nation on August 27, 2005, President Bush clearly
laid out his strategy to the American people. "American and Iraqi forces are on
the hunt side by side to defeat the terrorists," the president stated. "As we hunt
down our common enemies, we will continue to train more Iraqi security forces.
Our strategy is straightforward: As Iraqis stand up, Americans will stand down.
And when Iraqi forces can defend their freedom by taking more and more of the
fight to the enemy, our troops will come home with the honor they have earned."[87]
America was in the war no longer to win it but to hand it over to the Iraqis as soon
as possible and then head for the exits.

As 2005 came to a close, General Casey remained optimistic that the strategy would pan out.[88] The Iraqis had held three relatively violence-free elections
that year and had adopted a constitution, however imperfect, that created a representative government. The December elections and various amnesty proposals
being debated had the potential to bring the Sunnis back into the political process. Special operations forces were disrupting al-Qaeda networks, and increasing
numbers of Iraqi border forces promised to retard the flow of terrorist recruits
into the country. Finally, MNF-I believed that the Iraqi Army was increasingly
capable of taking the lead in securing Iraq. The next year would be the "Year of the
Police." MNF-I leaders believed that by the end of 2006 the Iraqi police would be
in a position to begin to take the lead in counterinsurgency efforts, the start of a

transition to a state once again subject to the rule of law.[89] U.S. Ambassador Zalmay Khalilzad and General Casey signed a mission statement at the end of 2005 that declared, "The Coalition is entering the decisive phase of our involvement in Iraq."[90] They were right, but for the wrong reasons.

Other strategic and operational options existed, but they required a rethinking of the war and the doctrine used to wage it. In the heart of the insurgency in al-Anbar province, Marines were learning to move beyond their traditional penchant for offensive operations to kill or capture the enemy. Marine commanders soon discovered that combating an insurgency was as challenging in its own right as launching an amphibious invasion. Insurgents attacked via ambush using roadside bombs, mortars and rockets, and snipers, and then blended into the population to evade counterstrikes. To come to grips with this shadowy enemy, the Marines had to make inroads into the population. That was easier said than done in al-Anbar, where the predominantly Sunni population felt deeply dispossessed by the American invasion and the installation of a Shi'a-Kurdish government in Baghdad.

The Marines of Regimental Combat Team 2, stationed in western Iraq and led by Colonel Stephen Davis, were among the first to change their operating methods to fight and win a counterinsurgency campaign. Davis began by finding a wedge he could exploit. Al-Qaeda was in Iraq to kill Americans and establish a terrorist safe haven, while the nationalist insurgents were fighting for their homes, their families, and their tribes. Al-Qaeda had muscled in on the ages-old trading business along the upper Euphrates River to fund its operations, thereby denying the profits to the tribes that depended on smuggling for their livelihood. In 2005 Lieutenant Colonel Dale Alford, commander of the 3rd Battalion, 6th Marines, was able to exploit these differences to ally with the Abu Mahal tribe in the al-Qaim region along the Iraqi-Syrian border. To succeed, the tribe needed help fighting the well-armed terrorists, but it also needed security to ensure that its people would not be subject to murder and intimidation in retaliation for their alliance with the Marines. Alford divided his battalion and established more than a dozen combat outposts in the region, each of them supported by available Iraqi security forces. The tribe provided young men for the police and army, along with hundreds of others to act as the eyes and ears of the better-armed Marines. Together they squeezed al-Qaeda out of the area.[91]

Colonel H. R. McMaster, commander of the 3rd Armored Cavalry Regiment based in the vicinity of Tal Afar in northwestern Iraq, also decided to depart from prevailing policy and based his forces in small combat outposts inside the city. Positioned along the transit corridor between Syria and Mosul, Tal Afar had evolved into a major al-Qaeda base in the wake of the elimination of Fallujah as a terrorist safe haven. To combat this lethal threat, McMaster understood he could not simply patrol into the city from the periphery and expect to control it. After spending three months clearing insurgents from surrounding villages, McMaster enclosed Tal Afar with an earthen berm and then proceeded to clear the town itself with several thousand Iraq soldiers and the thirty-eight hundred cavalry-men of his regiment. The insurgents resisted fiercely but in the end succumbed to superior numbers and firepower. To hold Tal Afar, Lieutenant Colonel Chris Hickey's armored cavalry squadron established thirty combat outposts within the city's neighborhoods, one every five to six blocks. While his troopers established control of the city, McMaster and his officers worked with local Iraqis to cleanse the government and the police force of the worst sectarian actors. By the end of 2005 life had returned to Tal Afar, a small beacon of hope in a wider sea of troubles in Iraq.[92]

The Bush administration seized on the success of McMaster's counterinsur-gency operations in Tal Afar to put forward a new political-military concept for the war in Iraq—clear, hold, and build.[93] Billed as a new strategy by Secretary of State Condoleezza Rice in testimony before the Senate Foreign Relations Com-mittee in October 2005, the concept involved clearing areas of insurgent forces, holding them to secure the population, and building institutions of governance and providing essential services to enhance the long-term legitimacy of the gov-ernment.[94] Rice also announced the extension to Iraq of provincial reconstruc-tion teams, a concept first used in Afghanistan. These teams would finally provide a civil-military interface to coordinate reconstruction efforts at the local level. Rumsfeld complained that the new concept had not been coordinated with the Pentagon or the commanders in the field, an indictment of the poor interagency coordination process in the Bush administration.[95]

McMaster's success in Tal Afar obscured some fundamental issues with pros-ecuting a counterinsurgency campaign along similar lines in the rest of Iraq. The 3rd Armored Cavalry Regiment and its Iraqi allies had nearly 9,000 soldiers to protect a city of 200,000 people, or 1 soldier for every 22 Iraqis. This figure, along with Tal Afar's compact geography, enabled McMaster to secure the population by establishing numerous combat outposts within the city. They could literally see just about every part of the city, a luxury that U.S. and Iraqi forces in the massive Iraqi capital could never enjoy.[96] To apply the same template to the remainder of Iraq would require tens of thousands of additional soldiers. On the other hand, Multi-National Force–Iraq could have applied the concept in the most important neighborhoods of Baghdad, but chose not to do so. Experimentation with popula-tion protection was fine in more remote areas of Iraq, but in Baghdad, where the war would be won or lost, the focus on transition of security responsibilities to the nascent Iraqi security forces would not be interrupted by such notions.

The more important lesson was political. McMaster realized that the insur-gents were exploiting the sectarian divisions within the largely Turkoman popula-tion of Tal Afar. Three-quarters of Tal Afar was Sunni, but the police were led by a Shi'a commander appointed by the government in Baghdad. His force consisted largely of fellow Shi'a, who feared the Sunni community and preyed upon them through arrest (little more than kidnapping, often followed by torture) and mur-der. The Sunni mayor, Najim Abdullah al-Jibouri, had lost his career when Bremer dissolved the Iraqi armed forces and was initially sympathetic to the national-ist insurgency. Together, McMaster and Hickey persuaded Najim and the local tribal sheiks to turn from fighting one another to cooperating in a common cause against al-Qaeda. The *takfiris*—hardline Muslims who believe in an extremely strict interpretation of Islam—had descended on Tal Afar and had made everyone's lives miserable with their extremist brand of Shari'a law and brutal terror. McMaster was able to reform the police force to make it more balanced, in the process defy-ing decrees from Prime Minister Ibrahim al-Ja'afari's government in Baghdad that would have continued policies that had contributed to the sectarian struggles in Tal Afar in the first place. The democratically elected government in Baghdad was part of the problem, which could be defined in a single word—sectarianism.

The Bush administration believed that elections were the solution to ending the insurgency. The election of a more broadly based and legitimate government, the thinking went, would result in a lessening of support for armed conflict.[97] The faith in democracy in Iraq at this point in time was misplaced. What the adminis-tration failed to realize is that democracy works only when a social compact exists as its foundation. Sectarian and ethnically based political parties and agendas that ensure bloc voting are hardly the basis for successful representative government. The foundation for democracy in the United States rests in large part on a viable middle class, freedom of expression, freedom of the press, freedom of assembly, and respect for minority rights. Americans may not like the results of a given elec-tion, but with the one exception of the election of 1860, they don't pick up rifles and take to the barricades to protest when a vote fails to go their way. The lack of a strong civil society, a vibrant middle class, and a historical tradition of democracy in Iraq made the institution of a representative government there an uphill climb at best.

Furthermore, the Transitional Administrative Law had created a single elec-toral district in Iraq in lieu of creating local districts (such as the congressional districts in the United States). This system benefited the parties that could collect the most votes but worked against the interests of more remote areas of the coun-try. It also ensured that the members of the Council of Representatives would be beholden to party bosses rather than to local constituents, since there were none of the latter. As a result, some members of the Iraqi Council of Representatives did not even reside the majority of the time in Iraq.

In any case, the hopeful sign of purple fingers waving in the air masked a darker reality. In Iraq in 2005, insurgents intimidated most Sunnis into staying away from the polls. Iraqis had voted largely along sectarian and ethnic fault lines; Arab Sunnis, who represented roughly one out of every five Iraqis, ended up with only 8 percent of the seats in the Council of Representatives.[98] The United Iraqi Alliance, a grouping of Shi'a parties backed by the clerical establishment in Najaf and in part funded by Iranian money, dominated at the polls.[99] The result of the elections was the installation of a largely Shi'a-Kurdish government and the approval of a constitution validating its control, which fed the perception among the Sunnis that the United States was shutting them out of power—power that they had enjoyed for more than a millennium. The Shi'ites of Iraq had finally seized the reins of political authority, and the more extreme among the faithful were ready to pay the Sunnis back for decades of oppression. Rather than a salve to heal the wounds of conflict, the elections of 2005 became a catalyst to increased sectarian violence and civil war.[100]

Classic counterinsurgency theory, such as the writings of French Army colonel and counterinsurgency theorist David Galula, posits that the key to prevailing in counterinsurgency warfare is to establish the legitimacy of the government and make certain its ability to protect the population from insurgent intimidation and violence. Insurgents rely on the people for sustenance and support and hide among them in plain sight. By severing the link between the insurgents and the people, the counterinsurgent can remove the essential prerequisite for insurgent success. The insurgency will not be destroyed; it will simply dry up.[101] The Galula model, however, applies principally in those cases where the population of a country is primarily concerned about the effectiveness and legitimacy of its government, rather than in its sectarian or ethnic makeup. Counterinsurgency efforts to improve the legitimacy of a government and protect the population are then operative. But when sectarian or ethnic identity trumps other factors, protecting the people without political reform will avail the counterinsurgent little in the way of gaining their trust and confidence.[102] In these cases, the counterinsurgent must work to broaden the composition of the government to enable all groups to have a stake in it. Doing so while protecting the people to alleviate the security concerns that prevent them from reaching common ground with one another can then have a substantial impact and provide a way forward.

By 2005, violence had started to cause Iraqi society to facture along sectarian and ethnic fault lines. When security is tenuous, basic services are interrupted, and physical survival is in question, people rely on those who are closest to them or who share common physical or cultural bonds: family, tribe, sect, and ethnicity. In such circumstances, more esoteric notions, such as "nation," often fall by the wayside. The assumption behind U.S. efforts was that since the Iraqi government was democratically elected, it was legitimate. American efforts to raise, train, and equip Iraq security forces would provide the regime the wherewithal to combat the threat to its integrity and secure a monopoly of violence for the state. If, however, the Iraqi government used its military and police forces to suppress the Sunnis and ensure that power and resources flowed to certain groups, then the United States was guilty of supporting the Shi'ites and Kurds in a civil war partly of its own creation.

There was evidence to support the latter theory. On November 13, 2005, U.S. forces acting on a tip raided an Iraqi prison (the "Jadriya Bunker") in Baghdad and discovered 169 emaciated prisoners—166 of whom were Sunni—in squalid conditions, many exhibiting visible signs of torture. American military and diplomatic leaders decried the abuse, while the Iraqi government tried to deflect charges of sectarianism. Bayan Jabr, the Iraqi minister of the interior responsible for the facility, sought to downplay the discovery by stating, "There has been much exaggeration about this issue. Nobody was beheaded or killed."[103] Other Iraqi officials blamed the Badr Organization, an Iranian-trained militia affiliated with the Supreme Council for the Islamic Revolution in Iraq, for operating the facility. Indeed, many Badr Organization personnel had joined the Iraqi security forces, and although they now wore Iraqi Army or police uniforms, their allegiances were still tainted by their association with the sectarian organization. Although Jabr denied militia involvement, the incident was a clear indication—if one were needed—that all was not well with the new Iraqi government.

The slide into civil war had begun two years earlier. Zarqawi had ordered his followers as early as 2004 to attack Shi'ites with the intention of igniting a sectarian civil war. During the Shi'a religious celebration of Ashura in March 2004, suicide bombers and mortars targeting the faithful in Kadhimiyah (a district in northwest Baghdad) and the holy city of Karbala killed 181 people and wounded several hundred more.[104] Attacks on Shi'a civilians accelerated from that point onward, as did the response by Shi'a militias and Iraqi security forces against Sunnis for their assumed complicity in the bombings. With the installation of a Shi'a government led by Prime Minister Ibrahim al-Ja'afari in early 2005, Shi'a retaliation, carried out by the Shi'a-dominated police, grew in scale and intensity.[105] Zarqawi's logic was sound, if murderous. As the Iraqi government took reprisals against the Sunni population, fearful Sunnis would have little choice but to support Zarqawi's fighters against the government and its security forces. Al-Qaeda could then take advantage of the ensuing chaos to carve out a safe haven in the "Sunni Triangle" in Iraq as the basis of a new caliphate, dominated by al-Qaeda and its leaders. As for instigating bloody fighting among Muslims, Zarqawi was unapologetic. "The Shi'a destroyed the balance," Zarqawi declared. "Until the majority stands up for the truth, we have to make sacrifices for this religion, and blood has to be spilled. For those who are good, we will speed up their trip to paradise, and the others, we will get rid of them."[106]

Sectarian cleansing of Baghdad neighborhoods began after the battle for Fallujah ended. Sunni refugees from the fighting settled in the western Baghdad neighborhoods of Ghazalia and Amiriyah, where they helped to evict Shi'a residents. Shi'a death squads cleansed Sha'ab, on the northern border of Sadr City, of its Sunni residents. And so it went, day after day, week after week, as Arabs fought each other over professions of faith going back more than thirteen hundred years.[107] In the meantime, U.S. forces, having relocated to large bases on the out-skirts of Iraq's cities, lost touch with the people. The June 2005 campaign assess-ment concluded, "Insurgent attacks—particularly suicide attacks—and the force protection measures required to prevent them, have separated Coalition soldiers from the population."[108] Increasingly, coalition forces were blind to the sectarian violence occurring on their watch.

The trigger that fanned the flames of sectarian hatred was the destruction of the al-Askari shrine, the "Golden Dome" mosque in Samarra, the fourth-holiest shrine in Shi'a Islam. It housed the tombs of the tenth and eleventh imams in line of succession after the founder of Shi'a, Ali (who is buried in the holy city of Najaf). Also buried in the shrine was the mother of Imam Muhammad al-Mahdi, who the Shi'ites believe will reappear at some point in the future to bring justice and peace to the world. By 2006 Samarra was a city composed almost entirely of Sunni residents. The destruction of the shrine, then, would appear as a direct attack by Sunnis on the Shi'ites. Early in the morning on February 22, 2006, a small group of men wearing Iraqi military uniforms entered the shrine, tied up the guards, and planted explosives that destroyed the shrine's golden dome. Sub-sequent investigations confirmed al-Qaeda's responsibility for the bombing.[109]

Al-Qaeda wanted a reaction; it got one. The bombing of the holy shrine un-leashed widespread outrage and a wave of reprisal attacks across Iraq that let loose the passions of sectarian hatred and civil war. "This is as 9/11 in the United States," said Iraqi Vice President Adel Abd al-Mehdi, a member of the Supreme Council for Islamic Revolution in Iraq.[110] The senior Shi'a cleric in Najaf, Ayatollah Ali al-Sistani, who had done so much to tamp down violence since the invasion of the country in 2003, signaled his willingness to take the gloves off. He released a state-ment that read, "If the government's security forces cannot provide the necessary protection, the believers will do it."[111] The Shi'a faithful needed no further encour-agement. Across Iraq mobs took to the streets chanting their desire for revenge. Iraqi security forces stood by while militiamen shot rocket-propelled grenades and machine guns at Sunni mosques. Scores were torched and several imams killed. The civil war had begun.

Iraqi and U.S. leaders appealed for calm, as they understood the danger inher-ent in the situation. General Casey issued an order directing his forces to sup-port Iraqi efforts to stabilize the country, including deterrence of ethnosectarian violence in ethnically and religiously mixed areas of Baghdad. "This is not about framework operations, nor is it business as usual," Casey wrote.[112] But the order was to little avail; the genie was out of the bottle. Even Muqtada al-Sadr called for an end to the sectarian fighting, but the extent to which he was in control of his organization at this time is unclear. The Jaish al-Mahdi was ill-disciplined and loosely organized. By 2006 it served as a cover for a large number of Shi'a militia groups, some of which were armed and trained by Iran. In the days after the al-Askari shrine bombing, the Jaish al-Mahdi was unleashed as sectarian violence swept through Baghdad. In the next few days, more than thirteen hundred Iraqis died as a result of the sectarian bloodletting.[113]

Baghdad's neighborhoods girded themselves for war, a sectarian battle for survival. Residents cordoned off streets with hasty barricades made from old vehicles, concertina wire, and concrete. If the Iraqi government could not provide security, the insurgents and militias could and would—for a price. In the atmosphere of pervasive fear that gripped Baghdad, Iraqis were willing to pay for what amounted to nothing more than a protection racket. Al-Qaeda suicide bombers targeted Shi'a marketplaces and other community centers, while Shi'a death squads roamed the streets, bent on cleansing Baghdad's mixed neighborhoods of their Sunni inhabitants. Young Sunni men caught at legal or illegal checkpoints manned by Shi'a police or militias were often kidnapped, tortured, and killed, their bodies dumped unceremoniously on the streets. Sheer numbers gave a decided advantage to the Shi'ites. The Jaish al-Mahdi had dominated Sadr City since the summer of 2003; now it controlled Kadhimiyah, and was making inroads elsewhere as well. By the summer of 2006, the Jaish al-Mahdi was winning the battle for the streets of Baghdad, while the Sunni insurgency was dominant in many of the rural areas surrounding the city.[114]

Political stalemate in Iraq did not help matters. The elections of December 2005 resulted in another sweeping victory by the Shi'a list, but the various parties could not come to consensus on who would lead the next government. Ja'afari wanted another term as prime minister, but his candidacy was blocked by opposition from the Kurds, SCIRI, and President Bush, who viewed him as a weak, divisive, and ineffective leader. The political stalemate dragged on while Iraq disintegrated. After four months of wrangling, Nouri al-Maliki from the Dawa Party emerged as a compromise choice to lead Iraq's first "permanent" government, which was sworn in on May 20.[115]

Maliki was an interesting choice to lead a national-unity government. He had spent much of his exile from Iraq as the Dawa Party representative in Damascus. He was distrustful of American intentions, and a diehard opponent of the Ba'ath Party. As the deputy on the De-Ba'athification Commission, Maliki displayed an uncompromising attitude toward the former rulers of Iraq and what in his view was their continuing manifestation in the insurgency. In large measure, he was an enigma to American military and political leaders. His strength, in the eyes of many Iraqi political leaders, was his perceived weakness. Since the Dawa Party from which he emerged lacked an armed militia and Maliki was a second-tier leader of the party, other Iraqi politicians saw little threat in his candidacy. For better or worse, the war now rested on his shoulders.[116]

Maliki was inexperienced and ill-prepared for his ascension to the top political post in the Iraqi government. He had spent much of his adult life in opposition to Saddam Hussein and the Ba'ath Party and approached politics with a conspiratorial outlook. He was also in a difficult position politically. To stem the civil strife in Iraq, Maliki needed to rein in the Shi'a militias, but the two largest groupings, the Jaish al-Mahdi and the Badr Organization, belonged to parties (SCIRI and the Office of the Martyr Sadr, or OMS) that formed the core of his political support. Additionally, many Shi'ites viewed the militias as a hedge against Sunni resurgence or American perfidy. Maliki trod carefully and charted a middle course, a position that pleased no party fully, particularly the United States. Ambassador Khalilzad continually pressed Maliki to disband the militias, to no avail.[117]

On June 14, Maliki announced a new plan to improve security in Baghdad, "Together Forward." The plan entailed more security forces on the streets, increased vehicle checkpoints, a curfew, and more raids against suspected terrorist and insurgent hideouts. With only fifty-seven thousand coalition and Iraqi security forces in the city (approximately one for every one hundred citizens, or half the number recommended by doctrine), there were not enough forces to hold areas that were cleared of insurgent and militia operatives. As a result, the operation failed to stem the sectarian violence in Baghdad. The reluctance of the Iraqi government to confront extremists on all sides was also an issue. Sadr City was off limits to coalition operations unless cleared through Maliki's office and many other Shi'a areas were left untouched by the operation.[118] Unless the Iraqi government and MNF-I confronted the Shi'a militias as well as the Sunni insurgents and al-Qaeda terrorists, the plunge into civil war would continue. Even the death of Zarqawi to a U.S. air strike in early June failed to stem the violence. He was replaced as head of al-Qaeda in Iraq by an expert bomb maker, Abu Ayyub al-Masri, who continued to stoke the fires of civil war with lethal car bombs and suicide attacks. As U.S. commanders were beginning to learn, al-Qaeda in Iraq had a deep bench.

Nevertheless, the formation of an Iraqi government and the death of Zarqawi brought hope to American leaders. After having expressed concern over the destruction of the al-Askari shrine in February, civil and military officials expressed optimism that the worst was behind them. This optimism—however guarded—at times bordered on the surreal. The updated MNF-I campaign plan that spring listed various "Wild Cards" for 2006, among them an event that had already occurred: "A trigger event sparks widespread sectarian violence which spirals into civil war. Potential trigger events include a desecration of a Shi'a religious symbol, a mass casualty attack against Shi'a civilians, or an assassination of a key Shi'a leader by Sunnis."[119] Given the magnitude of the violence following the destruction of the al-Askari shrine, the ignorance of events outside the confines of the MNF-I planning cell embodied in this statement is truly astonishing.

Despite the increased ethnosectarian violence in Iraq, MNF-I's goals remained unchanged. "We are entering the decisive phase of the campaign to bring security and stability to Iraq," the campaign plan stated. "Our actions during liberation, occupation and partnership have enabled the coalition and successive Iraqi governments to set the conditions for the stabilization of Iraq and for the transition to

Iraqi self-reliance. Completing this transition during the tenure of this constitutionally-elected government is the focus of the Campaign Plan."[120] Absent from the intent statement was any discussion of the enemy and the Iraqi people. Transition was not a focus, but *the* focus, of the campaign plan. The plan went on to state that the primary goal for 2006 would be to secure Baghdad, but it emphasized the primacy of the Iraqi security forces in this effort, supported by improvements in governance and the economy.[121]

The emphasis on transition rippled throughout the force. At Multi-National Force–Iraq, General Casey overruled a request by the Multi-National Corps–Iraq commander, Lieutenant General Peter Chiarelli, to retain the 2nd Brigade, 10th Mountain Division, in Baghdad. Its departure left a void in Kadhimiyah and Ghazalia to be filled by the Jaish al-Mahdi and Sunni insurgents. Casey was adamant that withdrawing U.S. combat forces from Iraq was the right thing to do. In his eyes, a lighter U.S. footprint would force the Iraqi government to reconcile with its opponents, rein in the militias, and prod the Iraqi security forces to take the lead in counterinsurgency operations.[122] Regrettably, it did none of the above.

Up until the bombing of the al-Askari shrine, one could make a case that the strategy of transition to Iraqi control was the correct one. That strategy was much harder to justify in the wake of the increasing sectarian violence of 2006. There was too large a disconnect between MNF-I's stated priorities—secure Baghdad, defeat al-Qaeda in Iraq, neutralize the insurgency, defeat Shi'a extremists, and deny Iranian influence—and the goal of handing over the lead in security operations to Iraqi control by the end of the year.[123] Between 2004 and 2006 MNF-I had killed more than six thousand insurgents and detained twelve thousand others, yet violence in May 2006 hit a record high of 3,196 attacks, a third of them in Baghdad.[124] By July, Casey, who only a few weeks earlier had decided to reduce the number of U.S. brigades in Iraq by the end of the year to ten, belatedly recognized the need to retain more forces to curtail the violence that was tearing Iraq apart.[125] He contacted Secretary of Defense Rumsfeld and requested the retention in Iraq of the 172nd Infantry Brigade, which was already on its way back to its home station in Alaska. As had been the case with the 1st Armored Division during the crisis of April 2004, Rumsfeld recognized the need to retain more forces to combat the growing tide of violence. The Strykers stayed in Iraq and went to Baghdad. Despite this tactical adjustment, Casey clung to his chosen strategy with its heavy emphasis on transferring security responsibilities to Iraqi forces.[126]

In August the Iraqi government and MNF-I tried again to secure Baghdad with Operation Together Forward II. It failed just as miserably as the first iteration. The Iraqi government remained riven by sectarianism, a number of ministries acting as little more than extensions of the political parties that controlled them. Available Iraqi forces could not hold cleared areas, and U.S. forces remained housed in large forward operating bases on the periphery of the city. The Iraqi National Police performed so poorly and were so riven by sectarianism (in some

cases National Police units functioned as little more than Shi'a death squads) that
they had to be pulled off duty for retraining.[127] The root of the problem continued to be the inability of the Iraqi and coalition security forces to contain the
ethnosectarian violence in Iraq. The campaign plan had acknowledged the risk
of sectarian violence overwhelming the immature Iraqi army and police forces.[128]
This danger was in fact now playing out on the ground in Baghdad. Regrettably,
General Casey and other senior commanders did not believe Iraq had yet crossed
the threshold into civil war, and so they remained cautiously optimistic that the
strategy was succeeding—albeit more slowly than desired—despite clear evidence
to the contrary. General John Abizaid, head of U.S. Central Command, went so far
as to tell Secretary of Defense Rumsfeld, "The level of violence isn't the measure
of success."[129]

As 2006 wore on, MNF-I tried to wage the war with inadequate resources and
by means of an increasingly inappropriate strategy of transferring security responsibilities to Iraqi security forces that were fundamentally unprepared to accept
them and in some cases were complicit with the sectarian violence now tearing
the country apart. Violence in Baghdad jumped 43 percent from the summer to
October 2006, and the killing did not stop there.[130] By December, more than three
thousand Iraqis were dying every month in ethnosectarian violence.[131] The Joint
Campaign Progress Review that month forthrightly addressed the implications of
the violence in stark terms:

> The situation in Iraq has changed considerably since the Joint Campaign Plan
> was written. Many of the risks identified within the Campaign Plan have ma-
> terialized. Many of the assumptions did not hold. We are failing to achieve
> objectives in the Economic Development, Governance, Communicating, and
> Security lines of operations within the planned timeframes.[132] It is extremely
> unlikely that the End State will be achieved by 2009. Improvements in bring-
> ing all the elements of national power to bear are necessary. In particular, eco-
> nomic development that improves the lives of all Iraqis, effectively establishing
> the rule of law, and achieving reconciliation among the Iraqi parties are criti-
> cal. However, the prerequisite to success in these areas will be protecting the
> Iraqi population from the sectarian violence that has been spurred on AQI and
> extremist organizations such as JAM.[133]

The realization that ethnosectarian violence lay at the heart of the problem and
that protecting the Iraqi people to enable them to find common political ground
had to be the primary goal of the campaign had come much too late, as did the realization that MNF-I needed more resources to accomplish its mission. "Thus the
unifying deduction from this analysis of the Campaign is that its ends, ways, and
means are out of alignment," the Campaign Progress Review in December 2006
concluded. "If the risk is constant or even increasing, and the ends remain constant, then the means need to be increased, in addition to adjusting the ways."[134]

That month the Iraq Study Group sadly concluded, "Because none of the operations conducted by U.S. and Iraqi military forces are fundamentally changing the conditions encouraging the sectarian violence, U.S. forces seem to be caught in a mission that has no foreseeable end."[135]

The statement was the uncomfortable and disheartening truth of a war that by the end of 2006, despite the well-intentioned and at times heroic efforts of those waging it, was all but lost.

CHAPTER 2

Designing the Surge

This is not double down. This is all in.
—General David Petraeus

T he new strategy for reversing Iraq's death spiral, subsequently known as the surge, was the result of collective and individual deliberation on what went wrong in Iraq and how to fix it. Groups working for the National Security Council, the State Department, and the Joint Chiefs of Staff all wrestled in the fall of 2006 with the deteriorating situation in Iraq and what to do about it. A congressionally appointed Iraq Study Group also examined the state of affairs in the country and provided its own recommendations to the administration by the end of the year. These groups were all important in deliberating the change in strategy that would change the course of the war. Individuals also made a huge difference. Retired General Jack Keane, working as a member of a team assembled by the American Enterprise Institute, gained entrée to the Oval Office and advised President Bush to reinforce the effort in Iraq to forestall defeat and achieve victory. Most important, the president refused to give in to his many critics, who were all too quick to declare the war lost. Swimming against every political tide in the United States and the world, Bush decided to send tens of thousands of additional troops to Iraq and to alter the priorities of U.S. forces there in accordance with a new counterinsurgency doctrine published in December 2006. His leadership and personal involvement in the details of strategic decision making, regrettably lacking in the early years of the war, made the critical difference when it mattered most in 2007 and 2008.

∎

My role in the surge evolved via a circuitous route. I left Iraq after my first tour as a brigade commander in July 2004 both gratified that I had had the opportunity to lead American soldiers in combat and frustrated that we could not do more to stem the rising tide of violence. A year later I was posted to the Council on Foreign Relations in New York City as a senior military fellow. There I had the opportunity to reflect on my experiences, to research and study counterinsurgency warfare, and to meet and discuss the war with a number of perceptive observers and participants with extensive understanding of the conflict. Among others whom I met and held discussions with were Max Boot, a perceptive thinker, author of two excellent books on military history, and a columnist for the *Los Angeles Times;* Jane Arraf, a reporter who had extensively covered the Iraq War from inside the country; George Packer, journalist and author of *The Assassin's Gate,* an excellent book on the origins and early months of the Iraq War; and Michael Gordon, *New York Times* reporter and coauthor of *COBRA II,* the best book on the development of the Iraq war plan. I was able to travel as well, and several of my trips took me to Washington, D.C., where I was able to meet and discuss Iraq issues with a number of friends and colleagues, including Eliot Cohen at the Paul H. Nitze School for Advanced International Studies, Williamson Murray at the Institute for Defense Analyses, and my good friend Colonel Jim Hickey, also at the Institute for Defense Analyses. This period of reflection sharpened my thinking on counterinsurgency operations and the Iraq War and prepared me well for the storms to come.

In the midst of this enjoyable assignment, little did I know how dramatically my life was about to change. In January 2006 I received a call from Bob McClure, a fellow West Point alumnus who was then serving as the executive director of the Business Executives for National Security. His group was hosting Lieutenant General David Petraeus, the commander of the U.S. Army Combined Arms Center at Fort Leavenworth, for a breakfast meeting in a couple of weeks. Petraeus was heading up to West Point for a speaking engagement later in the day, but he had an open afternoon. Would I be willing to host a roundtable for him at the Council on Foreign Relations? I absolutely would. Council members—a mixture of businessmen, academics, government officials, and other professionals—were deeply interested in the Iraq War. Lieutenant General Petraeus, with his widespread knowledge of Iraq garnered from his two tours in the country, was a perfect fit to speak to the group. I made the arrangements.

I had met Petraeus on only one other occasion. In the fall of 1999 as part of an ongoing series of deployments to deter adventurism by Saddam Hussein, I deployed with the 1st Squadron, 10th Cavalry to Kuwait. The U.S. military did not want to assign a general officer on a permanent basis to command the forces in Kuwait, so every month a new brigadier general or promotable colonel rotated into command at Camp Doha. Colonel Petraeus was one of the officers who commanded the post during our four-month tour in the country. We briefed him on our contingency plan for defending Kuwait, took him on a staff ride of our battle positions, and invited him to selected training events. I remembered him as an intelligent and perceptive officer with practically unlimited energy.

Six years later we met again in New York. He had not changed a great deal, other than having expanded his store of knowledge and experience during a tour in Bosnia hunting war criminals and two tours in Iraq, first as the commander of the 101st Airborne Division and then as commander of the Multi-National Security Transition Command–Iraq. After a brief introduction, Lieutenant General Petraeus launched into a thorough discussion of the Iraq War and where, from his viewpoint, it stood. After he ended his talk, as the panel chair I took the liberty of asking the first question. "You have described the creation of Iraqi security forces that are growing numerically according to plan," I began. "But what steps have we taken to ensure those forces are not used in a sectarian manner by the Iraqi government?" It was a high, hard, inside fastball and probably not what he expected from a serving colonel. Petraeus answered the question by describing MNSTC-I's efforts to pair advisers with Iraqi military leaders, although lack of personnel left the police advisory effort short of its goals. He also made a mental note to check up on me later.

After the meeting broke up, Petraeus asked me what I was doing at the Council. I told him that I was researching counterinsurgency operations and in particular studying the Iraq War. He thanked me for hosting the roundtable and departed for West Point. Later his staff briefed Petraeus on my background: first in the class of '82 at West Point, Ph.D. in military history from the Ohio State University, brigade commander in the 1st Armored Division in Baghdad during the first year of the war. It was the sort of résumé bound to spark his interest. Petraeus made another mental note. A few weeks later I received a call from my personnel manager at the U.S. Army Human Resources Command. Lieutenant General Petraeus had asked for me to come to Fort Leavenworth to stand up a new organization—the U.S. Army/Marine Corps Counterinsurgency Center. Was I interested in the job? Lieutenant General Petraeus later called me directly and noted that the position would not be as prominent or career-enhancing as being an executive officer to a four-star general (a position for which I was being considered), but it would probably be more significant in terms of potential contributions to the fight. I gladly accepted the post.

In late June 2006 my family and I moved to Fort Leavenworth, Kansas. While my wife, Jana, and our daughter Kyle and son J.T. settled into post housing, I attended to the task of establishing the counterinsurgency center. Lieutenant General Petraeus and Lieutenant General James Mattis, the head of the Marine Corps Combat Development Command at Quantico, Virginia, established the center as an integrating agency that could coordinate the various aspects of counterinsurgency doctrine, training, and education in the U.S. Army and Marine Corps. To say we were a small, flat organization would be an understatement. The deputy director was Marine Colonel Mark Olson, a reservist with civil affairs experience in Iraq who was now on full-time active duty. The third member of the team was Major Mark Ulrich, a Special Forces officer with extensive experience working with indigenous military forces in Colombia. He had once been kidnapped by a criminal gang in Bogotá and had killed two men to escape captivity—one of them with his bare hands. The two colonels were suitably respectful around him.

For the first few days we put our heads together to discuss a vision for the organization and what it could accomplish. We decided the center should focus on six areas: development, improvement, and implementation of counterinsurgency doctrine and best practices; integration of counterinsurgency principles within and among the services; historical and present-day research into and publication on counterinsurgency topics; advice to leaders and organizations; improvement of professional military education; and outreach to the media, think tanks, and government organizations with a shared interest in insurgencies and how to counter them. It was an ambitious agenda. With limited manpower, we would obviously have to pick and choose our spots carefully.

A week later I met with Lieutenant General Petraeus to brief him on the center's concept and to get his feedback. He was open to our ideas—the white lines were fairly wide and he would let us know if we strayed too far outside of them. Until then, we should take the initiative and proceed along our chosen focus areas. I was impressed by the latitude he was giving us to accomplish our mission.

At the end of the briefing, I voiced a personal concern. Petraeus had long been known for his excellent physical condition and demanding workout regimen. He would routinely challenge officers and soldiers to push-up contests (which he would just as routinely win). He also was known for taking new staff members on the "Ridge Run" at Fort Leavenworth, a several-mile course along the bluffs overlooking the Missouri River. I had thrown out my lower back eighteen months earlier and as a result now had a permanent physical profile; I knew there was no way I could keep pace with the general. "If you expect me to keep up with you on your runs, sir," I told him, "then you better find a new director for the COIN Center." Petraeus laughed and replied, "Don't worry, Pete. I didn't hire you for your body." I laughed, heaved a sigh of relief, smiled, and bid him good day.

Mark Olson, Mark Ulrich, and I began our mission by reading the draft counterinsurgency field manual, FM 3-24, cover to cover and providing input to its principal author, Conrad Crane. "Con" had a Ph.D. from Stanford University and was a 1974 West Point classmate of Petraeus's. I had worked with him during my tenure as an assistant professor of military history at West Point from 1992 to 1994; he had since retired to assume the directorship of the U.S. Army Military History Institute at Carlisle Barracks, Pennsylvania. Some military analysts, such as Ralph

Peters, were highly critical of the early draft manual for what they viewed as its focus on a "hearts and minds" approach to counterinsurgency in an era when religious-based insurgencies are immune to such a soft approach.[1] Although the drafters focused on protecting the population against insurgent intimidation and violence, they did not use the term "hearts and minds," and in fact their approach to counterinsurgency was not as soft as some critics contended. But I agreed that the manual needed to be edited to make that difference more explicit. Indeed, Lieutenant General Petraeus was already "taking control of the electrons"—our phrase for assuming the primary editing role—and was doing just that.

I met Peters and another of the manual's authors, Lieutenant Colonel John Nagl, to hash out the differences in a heated meeting at Fort Leavenworth arranged by Lieutenant General Petraeus. I agreed wholehearted with Peters that counterinsurgency is more than passing out soccer balls to kids and otherwise trying to win over the hearts and minds of the people through good deeds; my experience in Baghdad and Karbala in 2003–2004 showed me that there was plenty of killing involved, and that earning the trust and confidence of the population by providing security was far more important than winning its gratitude through nation building. But the United States does not have the leeway, as some pundits advocate, to undertake counterinsurgency operations focused on killing the enemy regardless of the collateral damage caused to civilian lives and property. The American people would not put up with such brutality. The modern media environment ensures that any excesses would immediately be broadcast to a shocked public. We had to find a more suitable way to win these types of wars than to create a desert and call it peace.[2]

Lieutenant General Petraeus read every word of the manual and personally edited and reedited key sections of it—thirty drafts of the first two chapters alone. He hedged the more assertive statements in the initial draft. Petraeus rewrote a sentence that read, "The best weapons for counterinsurgents do not shoot," for instance, to "Some of the best weapons for counterinsurgents do not shoot," since, as he told me on a number of occasions, the infantryman in a firefight with insurgents is not going to throw money at them. The major tenets of the proposed doctrine, however, remained unchanged. Counterinsurgency warfare is a mixture of offensive, defensive, and stability operations. The population is the key to winning or losing these types of wars, in which the battle over legitimacy is the determining factor in victory or defeat. The most important determinant of legitimacy is the ability to provide security for the population. We had all read the axiom that "insurgencies are 80 percent political," but as Con Crane (mimicking U.S. counterinsurgency adviser John Paul Vann) pointed out, even if security is only 20 percent of the equation, it is the first 20 percent. The counterinsurgent needs to understand the insurgent, his strategy, and his motivation, as well as the cultural milieu in which the war takes place. But in the end, control of the population is far more important than winning its hearts and minds, for effective control of the people isolates the insurgents from their support base. Counterinsurgents also have to be prepared for a long-term commitment, a tough proposition for democracies in which the voting public can in part determine the scale, scope, and length of any such undertaking.[3]

In November, just a month before the manual went to publication, Lieutenant General Petraeus handed me chapter 1 and told me to look it over one more time for any changes I felt were needed. The manual had gone through extensive revisions by that point and was greatly improved from the draft prepared in June. I was still concerned about the absence of any declarative statement about troop numbers in the current version of the manual; it merely stated that counterinsurgency is "manpower intensive." In my view the United States had gone into Afghanistan and Iraq without enough troops to secure the population after major combat operations ended, a shortfall that in part fed the growing insurgencies in both countries. I felt it important to provide some sort of rule of thumb to future planners in this regard; while not definitive, such a doctrinal statement could provide support for adequate resources to stabilize future conflict zones. If political or military leaders believed that an operation could succeed with fewer troops, then they would have to provide their reasoning as to why that would be the case. Otherwise, it was too easy to declare that technology could substitute for boots on the ground, a case made by Secretary of Defense Donald Rumsfeld in both wars.

Petraeus had also already identified this shortcoming and agreed with my reasoning. He directed Crane to revise the section of the manual regarding force density. The revised section stated that while "no force level guarantees victory for either side" and any calculation on troop density is dependent on the circumstances in a given situation, the history of these types of conflicts suggests that a ratio of twenty counterinsurgents for every one thousand residents in an area is the minimum required for effective counterinsurgency operations. These operations are manpower intensive because the counterinsurgent has to secure the population wherever the people live, while insurgents can pick and choose their points of attack.[4] Since it brought to light the very difficult but realistic costs of ongoing counterinsurgency wars in Iraq and Afghanistan, the revised section became one of the most contentious parts of the manual, but Lieutenant General Petraeus overrode the objections of the critics on this issue. The troop density ratio became part of published doctrine.[5]

With the editing of the counterinsurgency field manual proceeding apace, the two Marks and I decided to focus some energy on another part of our mission. Every unit in the U.S. Army conducted a rotation at one of three combat training centers before deploying to Iraq or Afghanistan. Army officers and noncommissioned officers assigned to these centers supervised this training. These observer-controllers, as they were called, were a vital part of the institutional training base and provided much-needed advice to units about to deploy to war zones. But who,

I wondered, ensured that they understood counterinsurgency doctrine before su-
pervising units in training? U.S. Army Training and Doctrine Command lacked a
system to certify observer-controllers, other than the local training they received
upon arrival at Fort Irwin, California; Fort Polk, Louisiana; or Hohenfels, Germany. We decided the U.S. Army/Marine Corps Counterinsurgency Center could
play a useful role as a "train the trainer" organization. I made contact with the
National Training Center at Fort Irwin and the Joint Readiness Training Center
at Fort Polk and arranged to hold two-day seminars at their locations to educate
observer-controllers in counterinsurgency doctrine and principles. Our first trip
in September to Fort Polk at the invitation of Brigadier General Dan Bolger was
very successful, and we looked forward to expanding our offerings in the future as
time and manpower allowed.

On Saturday, September 16, 2006, about three months into my tenure as the
founding director of the Counterinsurgency Center, Lieutenant General Petraeus
sent me an e-mail with an interesting request: "Pete, need by noon tomorrow, if
you can, the top ten changes/adjustments you'd make in/with respect to Iraq if you
were the SECDEF." I took some time to reflect on my hypothetical appointment
as defense secretary, then typed a memo with my response. This was typical of the
type of open-ended dialogue that Petraeus valued, and I was happy to oblige.
    My top recommendations were to increase the size of the Iraqi Army and to
staff the U.S. advisory effort with quality personnel. The number and quality of
the Iraqi security forces were simply insufficient to subdue the insurgency or provide security to the people, which was the most important factor in increasing
support for the Iraqi government. I stressed next that we needed to forget the
"ramp-down" plan and keep U.S. forces in Iraq at current levels for the foreseeable
future. "Rather than looking for a way out," I wrote, "we should be preparing for a
long-term commitment." To ensure that enough forces were available to prosecute
the war at this level without breaking the force, I argued for an increase in the size
of the U.S. Army. At the operational level, I argued that Multi-National Force–
Iraq needed to focus its efforts on securing Baghdad—the political, economic, and
cultural heart of Iraq. "Send another three U.S. brigades into the city to help the
Iraqi Army gain control of the situation, and then hold the city against terrorist
and militia threats," I wrote. After securing Baghdad, these forces could help to
accomplish another important objective—the destruction of the Jaish al-Mahdi.
Sadr's organization was one of the driving forces behind the descent of Iraq into
civil war, and until it was destroyed or neutralized, the Sunnis would not come to
the table to negotiate an end to the conflict. I also argued for getting the remainder
of the U.S. government to assist the military's efforts in Iraq in order to overcome
a deficit of support that had hampered counterinsurgency operations in the first
few years of the conflict. My final three recommendations were to reposition U.S.
forces over time to confront the strategic threat posed by Iran, to create a wartime

budget that fully funded professional military education and U.S. Army training institutions, and to take a meat cleaver to weapons-procurement programs (such as the Future Combat System) that lacked relevance to the wars the United States was likely to fight in the next couple of decades.[6] In a war where engagement ranges tended to be less than one hundred yards, we needed a replacement for the uparmored HMMWV much more than we needed a tank that could engage targets at a range of six miles.[7]

I have no idea what happened to my recommendations (though I later discovered that Secretary of Defense Rumsfeld called Lieutenant General Petraeus to the Pentagon periodically for informal discussions of the activities he was overseeing), but they must have struck a chord. A week later I was sitting at home on a Saturday evening watching college football when I again checked my e-mail. Lieutenant General Petraeus wrote that I was to be temporarily assigned to the Pentagon to serve on a group being formed by the Joint Chiefs of Staff. He could not share any further information as to the group's purpose, but I was to be in Washington by Tuesday for an assignment up to ninety days in duration. I informed my wife and kids of the news, which they took in stride, as army families normally do. Little did any of us know that this three-month assignment away from home would be followed by a fifteen-month deployment to Iraq. A long road lay ahead.

I quickly packed and made arrangements to live with my cousin, Mary Jane Barrow, and her family in Silver Spring, Maryland. I figured if I were to be gone for three months, it was better to be with loved ones in a spare bedroom and endure a longer commute than to camp out alone in a hotel room closer to the Pentagon.

The group that came to be known as the Council of Colonels convened on Wednesday, September 27, 2006, in the basement of the Pentagon underneath the offices of the Joint Staff. It was the brainchild of the chairman of the Joint Chiefs of Staff, Marine General Peter Pace, who had been prodded by retired Army General Jack Keane to delve more deeply into the wars occurring on his watch.[8] There were sixteen members handpicked by their service chiefs: four Army colonels, three Marine colonels, five Air Force colonels, and four Navy captains, one of whom, Mike Rogers, was General Pace's executive officer and therefore the acknowledged leader of the group. A minority had on-the-ground experience in Iraq. Three of us had command experience in country: H. R. McMaster (another officer nominated to serve on the group by Lieutenant General Petraeus) had commanded the 3rd Armored Cavalry Regiment in Tal Afar, Tom Greenwood had commanded a Marine Expeditionary Unit, and I had commanded the 1st Brigade, 1st Armored Division, in Baghdad and Karbala.

The Council of Colonels had an expansive charter: Did the U.S. military have the right strategy to win the war against global terrorism? Did we need to revisit the assumptions underpinning that strategy? What were the impediments to achieving our objectives worldwide, and more specifically in the Central Command area of operations? Was there a match among ends, ways, and means? We were to conduct research, invite subject matter experts to share their views, and discuss the issues among ourselves. We would meet with the Joint Chiefs weekly in their Pentagon conference room (known as the Tank) to brief them on our findings, energize their deliberations, and receive guidance. The idea was to feed ideas and options to the chiefs, not to present them with finalized strategic plans.

For the first time in the history of the Joint Chiefs of Staff, a group of colonels would convene with the chiefs in the Tank to discuss matters of major national importance. We sat on the side of the room like a courtroom jury ready to provide judgment on their proceedings. The Air Force chief of staff, General T. Michael "Buzz" Moseley, would enter the Tank, nod to the assembled colonels, and greet us with a lighthearted, "Colleagues." To General Pace's credit, he allowed anyone in the room to speak if he felt the need to contribute to the proceedings. On several occasions I found myself locked in discussion with the chairman or another of the chiefs regarding strategic issues. Our independence from the day-to-day drudgery of the military bureaucracy would give the chiefs a fresh viewpoint they would not receive from their own staffs. Once more I found myself part of a team that had been given a broad mandate, and the white lines were again painted fairly wide.[9]

The United States was facing an uncertain, ambiguous strategic environment not confronted by American policy makers since the turn of the twentieth century and the unexpected dawn of the American empire.[10] There were no simple strategies for this conflict, which was in essence a "wicked problem." These types of problems involve complex systems where a change to one part of the system not only changes the outcome but changes the system itself. Any action or strategic choice creates effects that are predictable only to maybe the second or third order. Beyond that, the effects are unknowable. Wicked problems might have no solution at all; often they can only be managed. Dealing with them requires insight, discernment, and a multidisciplinary approach.

The Council of Colonels began by examining the threat, which was much more complex than commonly believed. Terrorist groups were not all created equal; we needed to view them in their local contexts. By defining the threat broadly after 9/11, the United States had given disparate groups reason to cooperate. The greatest threats in the near future would come from terrorist groups taking advantage of unstable areas that lacked viable institutions, but the United States had limited current capacity to assist states in creating them. Our response to the threat since 9/11 had trapped the United States in an operational/tactical framework of military action that left out many of the other levers of national power. We needed a more holistic strategy to address these shortfalls, one that could transcend administrations.

The "Long War," as General John Abizaid at U.S. Central Command dubbed it, was in reality an intra-Islamic civil war, but how it would play out over the long term was anyone's guess. Al-Qaeda had attacked the United States, the "far enemy," in order to energize Muslims against the West. But its real goal was the establishment of a Sunni caliphate across the Islamic world, and in this regard there were other competitors for power in those lands, not the least of which were the nation states that already resided there. Al-Qaeda's strategy would inevitably pit it and its allies against other Muslims.

There were a few historical perspectives into which we could place this conflict. The most recent was the Cold War, a forty-year competition between the United States and the Soviet Union for global supremacy. The analogy was flawed. The Cold War featured competing political ideologies, use of proxy forces around the world, and "rules of the game" that prevented the outbreak of World War III. It ended with the economic collapse of the Soviet Union and the peaceful breakup of its empire. Messianic religious groups that used terrorism to achieve their goals, however, could not be contained as the United States and its allies had contained communism. There were no rules; al-Qaeda would destroy the West if it could. Most important, we realized that placing the Islamic world into the context of the Cold War would generate exactly the kind of conflict that al-Qaeda wanted—a "clash of civilizations."[11] We would be playing into the terrorists' hands if we went down that road.

A more useful context was provided by the wars of religion in Europe in the sixteenth and seventeenth centuries, a period in which Protestants and Catholics vied for supremacy in an intra-Christian civil war. The conflict featured parallels to the early twenty-first century: the rise of new political entities (states), new means of communication (the printing press), competing religious ideologies, insurgencies (the Dutch revolt), and mass destruction (such as the sack of Magdeburg, which resulted in the deaths of roughly twenty-five thousand civilians in a single day). The increasing violence culminated in the bloody Thirty Years' War, which devastated much of central Europe. The revulsion against the massive bloodshed led to the codification of rules of warfare in the Treaty of Westphalia in 1648, which placed the power of secular rulers above that of religious leaders and ultimately led to a separation of church and state in most European nations.

Pigeonholing the long war into a single historical analogy, however, could result in the creation of appealing but inappropriate strategic choices. It was counterproductive, for instance, to view the current struggles in religious terms, for doing so would provide no room for compromise. Promotion of democracy could be counterproductive as well. Many states in the Middle East lack the historical foundation and social compacts that make democracy possible; religion and politics are fused to a much greater degree than is currently the case in the West. Modernity was toxic to radical Islam; liberalization and secular education, not democracy, were what was needed to counter the extremists, but they would take generations to take root. In the end, the solution to Islamic radicalism had to come from within the Islamic tradition.

The group discussed and debated a wide variety of issues: the wars in Iraq and Afghanistan; the Israeli-Palestinian conflict; various terror organizations, including al-Qaeda; the role of Islam in fomenting extremism; rogue regimes such as those in North Korea and Venezuela; the Iranian bid for Middle East hegemony; the conundrum of Pakistan; how to accommodate a rising China; such disruptive problems as flu pandemics, cyberattacks, and water shortages; and how to keep Americans supportive of our chosen strategy over the long haul. After several weeks of work, we reached an impasse. Invariably, every discussion would circle back to Iraq and what to do about the situation there. Failure would create a disaster that would extend far beyond Iraq's borders. The impact of massive numbers of refugees, increased terrorism, radicalization of populations in the Middle East, potential intervention of neighboring states in the crisis, oil shocks, and the possible breakup of the Iraqi state would be so damaging to U.S. national security that we could not just assume it away and move on. In early November after several weeks of meetings, the chiefs agreed. They changed our mission and told us to focus exclusively on Iraq.

The group lacked consensus regarding the way forward. A number of us felt that the United States needed to stop couching its strategy in terms of actions that would allow a reduction in U.S. forces and instead refocus it on defeating the insurgency. Others believed the time had come to withdraw U.S. forces, either in part or in whole. Most of the group understood the likely consequences of a complete withdrawal from Iraq: full-blown civil war, a spike in oil prices, massive sectarian cleansing, the withdrawal of the international community, loss of U.S. credibility in the region, creation of al-Qaeda sanctuaries in ungoverned areas, and the ascendancy of Iranian power across the "Shi'a Crescent." Baghdad would come to resemble Mogadishu. It was not a pretty picture to contemplate.

We began to brainstorm ideas for reversing the downward spiral in Iraq, or, failing that, to manage the consequences of failure. At its core the war in Iraq concerned the distribution of political power and economic resources among Iraq's various sects and ethnicities. The key issue was how to persuade the Shi'ites to enter into a political accommodation with the Sunnis and, to a lesser extent, the Kurds. Otherwise, the winner-take-all mentality stemming from the current Iraqi approach to the democratic system that we had introduced into the country would create existential threats that could not be reconciled. Some analysts raised a false dichotomy between security and economic development; in fact, the major issue was neither of these. It was politics. But the extreme violence in Iraq had frozen politics as the operative force for determining the division of power and resources among the Iraqi people. Until we could bring the level of ethnosectarian violence down, the Iraqi elites would remain entrenched in their ethnic and sectarian positions. Iraqi politicians at the time had no incentive to compromise, since our stated policy was to stand up the Iraqi security forces and then leave. They were girding for a war that would determine winners and losers after our departure, not compromise.

I argued for a doubling of Iraqi security forces, for an increase in the number and quality of embedded advisers, and for greater partnership between U.S. and Iraqi units to increase their effectiveness. To accomplish these goals, we needed to send more troops to Iraq. We needed to bring more Sunnis into the political process and into the security forces by persuading the Iraqi government to issue an amnesty decree and to modify the implementation of de-Ba'athification. We had to force the Iraqi government to rein in the militias that were engaged in the sectarian cleansing of Baghdad and other cities. We had to create more stakeholders in the government by improving its capacity to govern and deliver essential services to the Iraqi people. But most important, we had to work with Iraqi security forces to protect the Iraqi people, and that meant moving off the big forward operating bases and stationing our troops in local neighborhoods, where, hand in hand with the Iraqi Army and police, they could help to defend the Iraqi people from terrorists and militias alike.

Others had alternate proposals. McMaster proposed an even larger reinforcement of our war effort in Iraq, on a scale that would have required a significant increase in the size of the Army and Marine Corps or the mobilization of reserve forces, which had already been heavily used in the war to date. A number of Air Force and Navy officers advocated a phased drawdown of the U.S. ground presence, with the eventual goal of creating "enclaves" elsewhere in the Gulf Region to deter Iran and to prevent the violence in Iraq from spilling over to neighboring states.[12]

After a lengthy debate, I felt we needed to bring clarity to our various proposals. I got up, walked over to the white board, and picked up a marker. I termed the heavy reinforcement of Iraq "Go Big." I labeled my suggestion, which focused on remaining engaged to win the war over the long haul, "Go Long." As for a phased withdrawal, I wondered aloud what we should call that strategy. "Go Home," someone shouted. Everyone laughed, but the label—albeit inaccurate—stuck.[13] One thing we could all agree on. Iraq was in a civil war, and we were on the road to defeat. As we put it to the chiefs, "We are losing because we are not winning, and time is not on our side." That dose of reality got their attention.

While the Joint Chiefs of Staff reconsidered options for the Iraq War that fall, other individuals and groups were also considering a new way forward. President Bush, who wanted to give the generals the leeway that they lacked during the Vietnam War, had remained too detached from important strategic details to this point. In the wake of the sectarian violence that erupted in the winter and spring of 2006, he was now one of the first to sense something amiss. Rumsfeld, Abizaid, and Casey all subscribed to the theory that the insurgency was in large part a result of Iraqi rejection of the U.S. occupation of their country, and therefore withdrawing American troops from Iraq's cities would help to reduce violence.[14] After the Samarra bombing, they failed to adjust their thinking on the issue. The president was more perceptive. "The sectarian violence had not erupted because our footprint was too big," Bush later wrote. "It had happened because al-Qaeda had provoked it."[15] Bush realized the current strategy was not working. He directed National Security Adviser Steve Hadley to undertake a review of the war effort. Unfortunately, without a stated deadline, the assessment drifted.[16]

Hadley decided the president should hear the views of selected experts from outside government. In June 2006, Bush met with several of them at Camp David: Fred Kagan of the American Enterprise Institute, journalist Robert Kaplan, former CIA operative Michael Vickers, and distinguished scholar Eliot Cohen of the Paul H. Nitze School of Advanced International Studies. They advocated for more troops, a shift in operational focus to a more appropriate counterinsurgency effort, and holding the commanders in Iraq and Tampa accountable for results.[17] The president also flew to Baghdad that month to meet Prime Minister Nouri al-Maliki and to encourage him to tackle the tough issues confronting his young administration. These meetings did not result in changes to the strategy, but were added confirmation in the president's mind that change was required.

On August 17, Bush convened a national security meeting with Abizaid, Casey, and Ambassador Zalmay Khalilzad attending via video teleconference.[18] Operation Together Forward had failed; Iraqi forces proved incapable of securing Baghdad's neighborhoods on their own. The president asked for options but received the same answer from his commanders—transfer control to Iraqi forces even faster. Bush left the meeting convinced that if a new strategy were to emerge, it would have to originate elsewhere. He assigned Hadley to gather his Iraq team and to conduct a thorough review, revisit assumptions, and generate new strategic options.[19] With the midterm elections less than three months away, however, any hint that the administration was having second doubts about Iraq was politically radioactive. Although the National Security Council, the Joint Chiefs of Staff, and the State Department were all now conducting reviews of Iraq strategy, they remained disconnected due in part to the risk of a leak that would warn the American people that the Bush administration was second-guessing the way ahead in Iraq. The National Security Council and State Department teams shared papers and views due to the good relations between Secretary of State Condoleezza Rice and her onetime deputy at the National Security Council, Steve Hadley. But there was no chance of gaining Rumsfeld's cooperation to review a failing strategy he had championed for more than three years.[20] Serious debate on changing course would have to wait until the voters had had their say.

The National Security Council review in the fall of 2006, which proceeded without input from the Office of the Secretary of Defense or the Joint Chiefs of Staff, focused on three options. The first was to accelerate the training of the Iraqi security forces. This was essentially the same course of action then in effect and was supported by the Department of Defense, U.S. Central Command, and Multi-National Force–Iraq. The second option was to pull U.S. military forces out of

Baghdad to allow the sectarian fires to burn themselves out within the city. Sunni and Shi'a insurgent and militia groups would eventually settle their scores, with Baghdad as the ultimate prize. U.S. forces would contain the spillover of the violence outside the city and continue to target al-Qaeda operatives in Iraq. This course of action would reduce U.S. casualties, but the death toll among the Iraqi people would be grim, and there was no guarantee that the violence could be contained. The final option was to conduct a fully resourced counterinsurgency campaign to secure the Iraqi people—especially in Baghdad—and to reduce the violence that was tearing the country apart. This course of action also entailed a large measure of risk and would require increased sacrifice of American blood and treasure to implement. Given the deteriorating situation in Iraq, there were simply no easy options that did not entail a great deal of risk or significant consequences.[21]

Lieutenant General Petraeus discussed the three options with Meghan O'Sullivan, the special assistant to the president and deputy national security adviser for Iraq and Afghanistan. She asked Petraeus for his recommendation, and he indicated that he favored the final option—a fully resourced counterinsurgency strategy. When asked what would be needed in terms of forces, Petraeus was explicit. "Everything you can get your hands on."[22]

The American people went to the polls on November 7, 2006, and delivered a resounding rebuke to the Bush administration. Antiwar sentiments played prominently in the voters' anger toward incumbent Republicans. The Republican Party lost control of both houses of Congress, which meant that over the next two years the president could expect a continuous stream of congressional hearings into the Iraq War and enormous political pressure to cut America's losses and withdraw. Secretary of Defense Rumsfeld, understanding the reason for the electoral defeat and the need for a change in leadership in the Department of Defense, submitted his resignation, which President Bush, who had already decided to make a change at the Department of Defense in any case, immediately accepted.[23] Belatedly, the administration would bring in new leadership to oversee the war effort.

The president's choice as the new secretary of defense, Robert Gates, was inspired. Gates was a twenty-six-year veteran of the Central Intelligence Agency who had served key roles in the George H. W. Bush administration as deputy national security adviser and as CIA director. Now retired from government service, the sixty-three-year-old Gates was the president of Texas A&M University. He was also a member of the Iraq Study Group, which meant that he was abreast of the latest intelligence and policy deliberations concerning the war in Iraq. This combination of government experience at the senior executive level and recent study of the major problem confronting the Department of Defense meant that Gates was uniquely positioned to contribute immediately upon being sworn in. Unlike Rumsfeld, Gates held no illusions about where the United States stood in Iraq. He told Senator Carl Levin during the Senate Armed Services Committee hearings on his confirmation that the United States was not winning in Iraq. That recognition would bring a radically different atmosphere to the Office of the Secretary of Defense.

The end of the electoral campaigning season also brought greater clarity to the efforts of the NSC, State Department, and the Joint Chiefs of Staff to redefine the core U.S. interests in Iraq and the strategy for achieving them. With the midterm election over, the barriers to cooperation among the various groups examining the Iraq War were now gone. After several months of disparate efforts to review the options for the way ahead, President Bush finally designated the NSC as the lead agency for a formal review of Iraq strategy.[24] He also made the key decision that population security in Baghdad would henceforth be the top priority for U.S. forces.[25] The surge strategy logically flowed from this firm and courageous decision.

The willingness of the Iraqi government to cooperate with a new strategy was also in question. On November 8, National Security Adviser Stephen J. Hadley sent a memo to President Bush summarizing the results of his recent visit to Baghdad and outlining policy options for the way ahead.[26] "We returned from Iraq convinced we need to determine if Prime Minister Maliki is both willing and able to rise above the sectarian agendas being promoted by others," Hadley wrote. "Do we and Prime Minister Maliki share the same vision for Iraq? If so, is he able to curb those who seek Shi'a hegemony or the reassertion of Sunni power? The answers to these questions are key in determining whether we have the right strategy in Iraq."[27] In private Maliki reassured American leaders of his good intentions, but the actions of his government could be construed otherwise. Members of the prime minister's office would intervene to prevent detention of Shi'a hardliners, the leadership of the armed forces was being stacked with Shi'a commanders, and the government was doing little to provide essential services to Sunni areas. The question was whether Maliki was just too weak to prevent such actions, or whether he was a willing participant in a Shi'a bid for domination. Maliki's reliance on political support provided by the Office of the Martyr Sadr and its militia extension, the Jaish al-Mahdi, constrained his options. "His intentions seem good when he talks with Americans, and sensitive reporting suggests he is trying to stand up to the Shi'a hierarchy and force positive change," Hadley concluded. "But the reality on the streets of Baghdad suggests Maliki is either ignorant of what is going on, misrepresenting his intentions, or that his capabilities are not yet sufficient to turn his good intentions into action."[28] The national security adviser went on to outline steps the Maliki and Bush administrations could take to reduce sectarianism and strengthen the Iraqi government, but until the fundamental issue of Maliki's intentions was resolved, any actions to improve the political situation in Iraq would remain stillborn.

President Bush decided that he needed to meet Maliki to discuss matters face to face. On November 30 the president met the prime minister in Amman, Jordan, to discuss the way forward in Iraq. Publicly, the two leaders agreed to accelerate the training of Iraqi security forces and the transition of security responsibilities to them.[29] Privately, Maliki agreed to commit more Iraqi forces to secure Baghdad, to allow coalition military operations in Shi'a neighborhoods and against Shi'a militia leaders without political interference, and to rein in the Jaish al-Mahdi and other Shi'a militias. The Iraqi prime minister also agreed to pursue political reconciliation among all sects and factions as security improved. For his part, Bush reiterated American support for the Iraqi government, and he would soon make a decision on providing additional resources—including tens of thousands of additional troops—to the war effort.[30] The public emphasis on transition did not make sense in the current security environment (and given the president's upcoming decision on committing more troops to Iraq), but it is likely that President Bush agreed with Prime Minster Maliki's emphasis on transition to keep him on board with the surge. In any event, the private deals were more important than the public ones. Ambassador Khalilzad and General Casey worked with Maliki over the next month to gain his consent to the introduction of additional U.S. forces into the conflict and to gain public support from the Iraqi government for the next plan to secure Baghdad, whatever it might be.[31]

While military and civilian officials in the administration discussed options for the way ahead in Iraq, other groups outside government were also examining the future of the conflict. Led by former Republican Secretary of State James A. Baker III and former Democratic Congressman Lee H. Hamilton, the congressionally sponsored Iraq Study Group was an attempt to build a new Iraq policy with a broader, bipartisan mandate. The group began its deliberations in a meeting on Capitol Hill on March 15, 2006, with members of both political parties in attendance. Four working groups consisting of forty-four Iraq and foreign policy specialists analyzed the strategic environment, military and security issues, political development, and the economy and reconstruction. The working groups consulted outside experts and retired military officers, intelligence community personnel, serving government and military officials, foreign officials, and Iraqi leaders. Members of the study group made one short visit to Iraq from August 30 to September 4. The group's assessment was wide ranging; regrettably, its findings were not.[32]

The Iraq Study Group released its report on December 6, 2006, to an expectant public. The document accurately described the central problem in Iraq. "Sectarian conflict is the principal challenge to stability," the report stated. "The Iraqi people have a democratically elected government, yet it is not adequately advancing national reconciliation, providing basic security, or delivering essential services."[33] Yet the report missed the connection among these problems. "Sustained increases in U.S. troop levels would not solve the fundamental cause of violence in Iraq, which is the absence of national reconciliation," the report stated.[34] The authors missed the point that in view of the high levels of ethnosectarian violence then tearing Iraqi society apart, political reconciliation was impossible. Instead of dealing with this root cause of the violence, the report's two major proposals focused on how to limit U.S. liabilities in Iraq.

There were members of the study group—former senator Chuck Robb and Bob Gates among them—who supported a temporary reinforcement of U.S. troops in Iraq. They persuaded their colleagues to add a section in the report dealing with a potential increase in forces:

> Because of the importance of Iraq to our regional security goals and to our ongoing fight against al-Qaeda, we considered proposals to make a substantial increase (100,000 to 200,000) in the number of U.S. troops in Iraq. We rejected this course because we do not believe that the needed levels are available for a sustained deployment. Further, adding more American troops could conceivably worsen those aspects of the security problem that are fed by the view that the U.S. presence is intended to be a long-term "occupation." We could, however, support a short term redeployment or surge of American combat forces to stabilize Baghdad, or to speed up the training and equipping mission, if the U.S. commander in Iraq determines that such steps would be effective.[35]

The "substantial increase" of troops discussed in this section of the report mirrored the Council of Colonel's "Go Big" approach; it was rejected for the same reasons the Joint Chiefs rejected it. A temporary surge of thirty thousand to forty thousand was more realistic given the available forces in the U.S. Army and Marine Corps. However, due to the reluctance of General Casey in Baghdad and General Abizaid in Tampa to support large-scale troop increases, this part of the report drew little attention when it was released.

The study group proposed to change the primary mission of U.S. forces in Iraq. Instead of combating the insurgency, U.S. troops would train and equip Iraqi security forces as their primary mission. The U.S. government should also engage Iraq's neighbors in a diplomatic dialogue to create a regional consensus on how best to stabilize Iraq. Both of these recommendations were flawed. Neither proposal addressed the root causes of the violence in Iraq or the inability of Iraqi politicians to mitigate it given the massive bloodshed that was forcing tribes, sects, and ethnic groups to collapse in on themselves. Reconciliation among these groups was a forlorn hope unless security improved, a prerequisite that the report's recommendations did little to achieve. The report's authors acknowledged the high stakes at play in Iraq and the severe consequences that attended to the deteriorating situation, but their proposals lacked the impact necessary to reverse the war's downward spiral.

Although the recommendation to launch a diplomatic offensive to engage Iraq's neighbors seemed sensible on the surface, it missed the point that the United

States lacked the leverage to force Iran and Syria to stop their damaging actions and to persuade them to act constructively to stabilize Iraq. These countries had their reasons for supporting various armed factions inside Iraq and they were not about to change their policy in the wake of a U.S. charm offensive. Even if they had a change of heart, it was unlikely that indigenous Iraqi insurgent and militia groups would respond to their calls for peace.

The fallacy of using U.S. advisers to train Iraqi security forces and handing over security responsibilities to them without significant and extended assistance from U.S. combat forces was already apparent. Operations Together Forward I and II had shown the inability of Iraqi forces to hold Baghdad's neighborhoods once they had been cleared. Increasing the speed of this transition was likely to make matters in Iraq worse, not better. The ethnosectarian violence was too daunting for the inexperienced Iraqi troops and police to handle; indeed, it was likely to splinter the Iraqi security forces as Iraqi sects and factions girded for civil war. This had already happened with the National Police, which in many cases aided and abetted the sectarian violence in Baghdad and elsewhere.

The Iraq Study Group report was released with great fanfare, but it was dead on arrival in the administration. President Bush listened politely to the members of the study group when they presented their report to him on December 6 in the White House, then largely ignored their recommendations. The report had no impact on President Bush's decision making. The same could not be said of another study, this one by a private Washington think tank.

As the Iraq Study Group went about its business, members of the American Enterprise Institute (AEI) gathered in Washington, D.C., to analyze the war and provide input on how best to turn around a failing effort. Members of the Institute's Iraq Planning group were led by former West Point professor Fred Kagan, who wrote the group's report. Among other participants, prominent members included retired General Jack Keane, a close mentor to Lieutenant General Dave Petraeus and Lieutenant General Ray Odierno; retired Army Lieutenant General Dave Barno, who commanded U.S. forces in Afghanistan from 2003 to 2005; retired Army Colonel Joel Armstrong, who had served as H. R. McMaster's executive officer in Tal Afar; Larry Sampler from the Institute for Defense Analyses; Michael Eisenstadt of the Washington Institute for Near East Policy; Fred Kagan's wife, Kimberly Kagan, who at the time worked in the Center for Peace and Security Studies at Georgetown; and Michael Rubin and Thomas Donnelly of AEI. Kagan rolled out the group's report, "Choosing Victory: A Plan for Success in Iraq," as President Bush deliberated his choices. The report concluded that victory in Iraq was still possible, but the Bush administration needed to commit more resources to achieve it. The decisive point was Baghdad—the political and economic center of Iraq. To secure the capital city, Multi-National Force–Iraq needed to balance its need to train and equip Iraqi security forces with a commitment to secure the

Iraqi people against rising violence. To accomplish the latter goal, the group advocated a reinforcement of seven Army brigades and/or Marine regiments to the war
effort—primarily to clear Baghdad's neighborhoods and hold them against insurgents and militia forces. U.S. forces would partner with Iraqi units, which would
bolster Iraqi capabilities as they went about securing Baghdad's neighborhoods.
As security improved, reconstruction aid would improve the lives of Iraqi citizens
and thereby boost the legitimacy of the Iraqi government.[36]

The AEI report gained traction because of the influence of General Keane,
a former U.S. Army vice chief of staff and a respected voice in Washington. On
December 11, just a few days before the rollout of the AEI report to the public,
Keane met President Bush in the Oval Office to discuss strategy for the Iraq War.
The meeting also included Professor Eliot Cohen, with whom H. R. McMaster
and I had breakfasted earlier in the morning to discuss our views on Iraq; retired
U.S. Army General Barry McCaffrey, the former head of U.S. Southern Command;
retired U.S. Army General Wayne Downing, the former head of U.S. Special Operations Command; and Stephen Biddle, a senior fellow at the Council on Foreign
Relations. Cohen, author of the influential book *Supreme Command,* in which he
argued that civilian leaders should remain engaged in the crafting and execution
of strategy and not blindly defer to military judgment, called for more accountability among the senior military leaders involved in the failing war effort in Iraq.
McCaffrey wanted to increase the advisory program while slowly decreasing U.S.
troop numbers. Downing argued for a shift in the war effort to focus on special
operations forces and their kill/capture missions against terrorist, insurgent, and
militia leaders. Biddle thought that adding more forces was the only option that
could reverse the downward spiral in Iraq, but he offered no plan on how they
would be used.[37]

General Keane's role in the meeting was pivotal. He came to the Oval Office
well prepared by his own thinking on the matter and by his participation in the
study group at AEI. Keane laid out for Bush a vision for the prosecution of the Iraq
War that reinforced the president's thinking: add more troops, get them off the big
bases and into the local communities, change the priority to protecting the Iraqi
people, and focus on Baghdad—particularly the mixed Sunni-Shi'a neighborhoods where most of the violence was occurring. The current strategy had failed;
therefore, the president would have to change out senior commanders in Iraq and
Tampa to implement the new counterinsurgency campaign. Later, Keane gave a
more thorough briefing along the same lines to Vice President Dick Cheney. The
president, vice president, and national security adviser were clearly impressed, but
they had to get the Joint Chiefs on board or there would be public dissension.[38]

On December 13 President Bush, Vice President Cheney, and National Security Adviser Hadley traveled to the Pentagon to meet the Joint Chiefs of Staff in the
Tank. The president rarely met the Joint Chiefs on their own turf. The meeting was
an outreach by Bush to get the chiefs to support a changed concept for prosecuting

the Iraq War. The chiefs were not opposed to a surge of forces to Iraq per se, but they felt the additional forces should be given a finite task, rather than just be used to thicken the line. In the end, the chiefs felt the U.S. military needed to evolve to a sustainable regional presence—the sooner the better—to mitigate the risk of other potential conflicts. The chiefs were unanimous that the land components were too small for all the missions they were executing around the world. Some also argued that public support for the war would slip away before a surge of forces could take effect, a consideration clearly in the political realm of the president. The president listened as the chiefs listed their concerns, particularly the shortage of troops and the strain of the war on service members and their families. U.S. Army Chief of Staff General Peter Schoomaker was particularly concerned about the strain of repeated deployments on his service. Army brigades were being stripped of senior leaders to staff the advisory effort in Iraq. ("We don't have a fifteen-brigade effort in Iraq," he lamented at one point to the Council of Colonels. "We have closer to a thirty-brigade effort. The other fifteen brigades just don't have privates.") President Bush agreed to consider an increase in the size of the U.S. Army and Marine Corps to ease the burden of continued deployments on the services. But the president held to his position that winning the war was his top priority. "The surest way to break the military would be to lose in Iraq," he told the chiefs at the end of the meeting.[39]

"We are in a race for time," I wrote in my notes. The American people were growing tired of war, and their frustrations had begun to severely impinge on domestic politics. Whatever the president decided, it would probably be our last, best shot at salvaging victory. But my role in the discussions surrounding the drafting of the surge had come to an end. After the Tank meeting with the president, the Council of Colonels took a few days to wrap up loose ends and then disbanded.[40] I flew home to Kansas for a much-needed holiday leave with my family. I then made plans to fly to California to visit with Kalev Sepp at the Naval Postgraduate School in Monterey to discuss counterinsurgency doctrine. Before the meeting, I arranged to spend some time with my extended family in Sacramento. Little did I know that this break was just the eye at the center of the hurricane.

Sworn in as secretary of defense on December 18, Bob Gates met with Lieutenant General Petraeus at the Pentagon to sound out his views, then flew to Iraq to visit Maliki and meet with U.S. commanders and troops. The Iraqi prime minister agreed to send three additional Iraqi army brigades to Baghdad and to bolster Iraqi command and control by creating a new security command responsible for the capital. Despite the winds of change on the horizon, General Casey remained committed to transferring security responsibilities to Iraqi forces as soon as possible. He doubted that the provision of more American forces would change the situation much, other than to create a localized, temporary improvement in security. He supported the request of Major General Joe Fil, the commander of the 1st

Cavalry Division, for two more brigades in Baghdad. But beyond that, Casey was adamant that any other surge brigades should remain as theater reserves in Kuwait or as a strategic reserve in the United States, to be called forward as needed. He still believed that his strategy was working, albeit more slowly than projected.[41] He wanted to avoid having American troops do what Iraqi troops should be doing and was concerned that too many reinforcements would lower the incentive for Iraqis to take ownership of the war.[42] When Casey sent his request for more forces through Central Command to the Pentagon just before Christmas, he requested only two army brigades and two marine battalions.[43]

An essential disagreement had developed between the commander of MNF-I and his civilian superiors in Washington. General Casey firmly believed that progress in political reconciliation among Sunnis and the Shi'ites should be a prerequisite for any surge of forces into Iraq.[44] The Bush administration had come to see that lowering the levels of ethnosectarian violence by protecting the Iraqi population was a prerequisite for reconciliation to occur.[45] There was no way to square this circle without a change of commanders in Iraq.

In a visit to Camp David two days before Christmas, Gates recommended to President Bush that Lieutenant General David Petraeus take over command of U.S. forces in Iraq.[46] Casey would take over as the U.S. Army chief of staff from General Peter Schoomaker.

Inside Iraq, Lieutenant General Ray Odierno, commander of the U.S. III Corps out of Fort Hood, Texas, had already been on the ground for several weeks. His reading of the situation was radically different from Casey's. Although Odierno could not openly oppose his current boss, he maintained back-channel communications with Petraeus. Petraeus and Odierno were of one mind on the subject of a surge: they needed all the forces that they could get to have a chance of succeeding in a difficult, but not impossible, mission. All five surge brigades plus the two marine battalions needed to flow into Iraq as soon as they were available. The president agreed, although those below him in the chain of command vacillated on whether to recommend all the surge forces at once or to send two brigades initially and then make Petraeus ask for the others one at a time.[47] The latter option would have been a public relations nightmare, with the media reporting continued failure in Iraq every time another brigade was sent forward. If the United States were to surge troops in Iraq, it was best to go all in.

On January 4, 2007, I was visiting my extended family in northern California when news leaked that the administration would nominate Petraeus to be the next commander of Multi-National Force–Iraq. I did not hear the announcement, as I was hunting quail and duck with my brother John in the Sacramento Valley. Upon returning to my sister's house where I was staying, I finally turned my cell phone back on and got on the computer to catch up on e-mail. As soon as I logged in, I noticed several messages waiting for me from Lieutenant Colonel Tom Rivard,

Lieutenant General Petraeus's executive officer. I didn't even have time to open them before my phone starting beeping with unread voicemail and text messages. Before I had a chance to read them, the phone rang. It was Tom calling, frantic that I had been out of touch for the past several hours. As the director of the Counterinsurgency Center, I was hardly the center of attention in the Fort Leavenworth universe. In fact, I didn't even rate a Blackberry. That was about to change.

"I'm on leave, Tom," I said. "What's up?"

"General Petraeus has just been nominated to be the next commander of MNF-I," Tom replied. "And he wants you to lead his transition team."

The words hung in the air. My leave was clearly over and the visit to Monterey out of the question. It was a good thing I had had a nice holiday with my family, for I would not be seeing much of them again for the foreseeable future. I packed my things and caught the next plane back to Kansas.

On January 10, 2007, President Bush appeared in the White House Library to deliver one of the most important speeches of his eight years in office. For the first time in nearly four years of war, the president told the American people that he was adopting a new strategy to "change America's course in Iraq." He admitted that the elections of 2005 had failed to bring the Iraqi people together, and that the sectarian violence following the destruction of the al-Askari shrine had enmeshed Iraq in "a vicious cycle of sectarian violence." The president took responsibility for the failing war effort, stated unequivocally his view that failure in Iraq would be disastrous for the United States and the region, and announced a new strategy to restore the fortunes of the United States and Iraq. In addition to the fifteen U.S. Army and Marine brigade combat teams already in Iraq, which would remain in the fight, a surge of five brigades—twenty thousand troops—would secure Baghdad in conjunction with Iraqi forces. An additional four thousand Marines would reinforce efforts in al-Anbar province to combat al-Qaeda in conjunction with local tribal leaders.[48] U.S. trainers and advisers would help the Iraqis to expand the size and improve the quality of their armed forces. For the first time, the mission of American forces would be to partner with Iraqi units to protect the local population. U.S. commanders and provincial reconstruction team leaders would receive additional funds for economic assistance. The additional U.S. and Iraqi forces, coupled with the lifting of restrictions on operations against terrorist and militia safe havens, would make this effort different from those that had failed in the past. As security and quality of life improved, the Iraqi people would gain confidence in their military and civilian leaders, who would find the breathing space needed to make progress on the crucial issues confronting the Iraqi nation. Victory would not entail a surrender ceremony on the deck of a battleship, but victory was both possible and essential for the freedom of America, the Iraqi people, and the world. "We can, and we will, prevail," President Bush concluded.[49]

President Bush understood the risks. He was sailing against a strong tide of public opinion. Congress was largely hostile. Iraqi support was uncertain. The fighting in Baghdad would result in more bloodshed and increased casualties. But the president was determined. "The surge was our best chance, maybe our last chance, to accomplish our objectives in Iraq," he later wrote.[50]

The reaction to the surge plan was immediate and intense. Legislators from both sides of the aisle lined up to denounce the new strategy with increasing vitriol and hyperbole. But none of them was the commander in chief of the U.S. armed forces. Unless Congress was willing to cut off funding for the war—an action that would have made the legislators responsible for certain defeat—the surge would be implemented. We had at most two years, until the next presidential election, to make good on the president's belief in the new way ahead.

Various leaders and groups had examined and debated the strategy for the Iraq War over the course of 2006, and by the end of the year the thinking of a few of these entities had converged in favor of a reinforcement of U.S. forces in Iraq to execute a new counterinsurgency campaign focused on securing Baghdad and protecting the Iraqi people. But in the end the surge did not belong to Steve Hadley and his staff at the National Security Council, or to retired General Jack Keane, or to the Iraqi Study Group at the American Enterprise Institute, or to General Petraeus or General Odierno. It belonged to President George W. Bush. After nearly four years of war, he decided to override the desires of his commander on the ground and change course.[51] Iraq had always been his war. Now the strategy to wage and win it was his as well.

The surge was the best of a number of bad options to revive the failing war effort in Iraq. I had learned on my first combat tour in Iraq the critical importance of positioning forces among the people in their neighborhoods. You could not simply commute to the fight from remote bases and expect to succeed in this type of conflict. Petraeus agreed. Indeed, under his command the 101st Airborne Division had executed just such a strategy with success—in northern Iraq in 2003–2004—where he also supported reconciliation, another feature of what would be his approach, as well as the strengthening of Iraqi civil and government institutions and targeted intelligence-driven military operations. It was asking a lot of soldiers and Marines, but if we were to have any chance of success, they would have to leave the relatively safe confines of their forward operating bases and move into smaller outposts positioned inside Iraq's cities.

We did not know whether the surge would work; indeed, the odds were stacked against us. But one thing was certain. If we stayed on our current course, the United States would lose the war in Iraq. "We have the right doctrine; we now have to get the strategy right," I lamented to my wife, Jana, one day in the fall of 2006. I wanted no part of an ugly defeat that would send America back into the depths of a generational malaise, the kind that had inflicted such angst on the nation in the wake of defeat in Vietnam. It was time to send U.S. troops back into the fight with a new strategy—not to buy time, but to win.

■

Petraeus preferred a small, nimble staff. I led his transition team, which included just three others: Petraeus's aide-de-camp, the hard-charging Captain Everett Spain, who had graduated near the top of his West Point class, had earned an MBA from Duke, and who was one of the few officers who could routinely beat Petraeus on his long runs; his strategic communications coordinator, Colonel Steve Boylan, whose insights and knowledge regarding the media would be severely tested in the months ahead; and, on a part-time basis, Lieutenant Colonel Chris Hickey, who had led a cavalry squadron in the battle for Tal Afar and who was now assigned to a war college fellowship at Fort Leavenworth. Early on Monday mornings we would fly in a small army jet to Washington, D.C., to begin a long week of congressional appointments, intelligence briefings, and meetings with senior civilian and military leaders. Petraeus made it a point to meet one on one with every member of the Senate Armed Services Committee, which had the constitutional responsibility to confirm his nomination as the commander of Multi-National Force–Iraq and appointment to four-star rank. He provided every senator he met with a copy of the counterinsurgency field manual, with key portions of the critical first chapter highlighted. With a few notable exceptions, the senators were skeptical of the surge strategy but ultimately proved supportive of Petraeus and his nomination to the command in Iraq.

On Friday afternoons we would fly back to Fort Leavenworth, but the weekend was hardly restful. Lieutenant General Petraeus used the time to compose his remarks for the upcoming confirmation hearing. Steve, Chris, and I drafted a series of questions that the boss was likely to face in the hearing, along with possible answers to them. Everett and I reviewed the calendar and mapped out the schedule for the weeks ahead. I spent time on e-mail with General Casey's team in Iraq discussing issues concerning the transition. I also coordinated with the personnel officer at Fort Leavenworth to provide deployment orders for members of the team. There were many other details to attend to, such as drawing uniforms and equipment, which we had to accomplish several hours away at Fort Riley, since Fort Leavenworth lacked a facility to issue gear to deploying soldiers.

The team was about to get much larger. Lieutenant General Petraeus and I discussed whom to bring onto his personal staff in Iraq. He had many ideas, primarily people who had worked for him in the past or others suggested to him by trusted contacts, while I had a few suggestions of my own. Petraeus valued three attributes above all else: intelligence, prior experience in Iraq, and commitment. He did not want people serving on the staff for three to six months and then leaving once their résumé cards were punched. The stipulation I made to potential staffers, with very few exceptions, was the expectation that they would remain in Iraq for a minimum of twelve months.

We assumed that after the transition was complete, I would serve as chief of the commander's initiatives group (CIG), an in-house think tank that handled a variety of strategic planning and speechwriting tasks. Lieutenant General Petraeus had another officer in mind to be his executive officer, who would serve as his personal chief of staff. When that officer declined the position for personal reasons, Petraeus decided to use me in that role. As executive officer I would help coordinate the general's near-, mid-, and long-range calendars, provide strategic advice, and serve as gatekeeper to ensure that only people with a bona fide need to see the commander were able to do so. The demands on the time of a four-star commander at war are significant, and it was essential to ensure that distractions were kept to a minimum.

After my role was settled, General Petraeus asked Colonel Mike Meese, the head of the Department of Social Sciences at West Point, for a recommendation on whom to assign to head the initiatives group. Mike said that Colonel Bill Rapp, an engineer with Iraq experience and an international relations Ph.D. from Stanford, would be the ideal choice. Bill had been the first captain of the West Point class of 1984 and was clearly a fast riser. The problem was that he had just finished a yearlong tour in Iraq a few months earlier; returning to the fray so quickly would be difficult on both him and his family. Petraeus called him anyway and after a telephone interview, offered him the job. Bill accepted, and his family, like so many other army families (indeed, Bill's wife was a West Point grad herself), soldiered on without complaint. Bill and I, the two officers nearest to General Petraeus during his time in Iraq, became close and trusted colleagues.

To staff the initiatives group, we reached out to Lieutenant Colonel Charlie Miller, a West Pointer from the class of 1990 with a Ph.D. from Columbia who had served as Petraeus's executive officer at MNSTC-I, along with Captain Liz McNally, a Rhodes scholar from the West Point class of 2000 who had also served in MNSTC-I. Charlie would be the deputy head of the initiatives group, while Liz assumed duties as General Petraeus's speechwriter. The war was a family affair for her. Her husband, John, was a Blackhawk pilot in the 25th Infantry Division in northern Iraq. Liz's father, Dr. Richard Young, a lieutenant colonel in the Connecticut National Guard, would volunteer for active duty and serve as a surgeon at the sprawling military base north of Baghdad in Taji. Her younger brother, Captain John Young, was an Air Force C-130 pilot who had recently returned home from a tour in Iraq. Both Charlie and Liz were young, bright officers who added a lot of energy, brainpower, and capability to Bill Rapp's team in the CIG. We later added Captain Derek Bennett to organize briefing packets to prepare General Petraeus for meetings. Waiting for us in Iraq was Captain Josh Lenzini, an operations research and systems analysis specialist whose job was to chart the metrics that General Petraeus used to track the war effort; little did we realize the firestorm that would erupt over these statistics over the course of the next year.

The next step was to draft senior personnel with specific expertise. Petraeus's classmate from the West Point class of 1974, Colonel (Ret.) J. R. Martin would come back onto active duty to serve as a senior adviser without portfolio. In time, J.R. would tackle a variety of issues, including acting in a "Red Team" capacity to consider MNF-I strategy from a contrarian viewpoint and find potential weaknesses the enemy could exploit. Derek Harvey, a gifted retired military intelligence colonel who had served as a literal one-man red team for much of the Iraq War (even at times providing briefings to the highest levels of the U.S. government to counter the rosy assessments emanating from Multi-National Forces–Iraq headquarters), and whom I had met while serving on the Council of Colonels, would become the senior adviser for intelligence. Mike Meese and Colonel H. R. McMaster, the talented officer with a Ph.D. in military history from North Carolina who was both well known to Petraeus and a good friend of mine, would serve periodically in Iraq to tackle specific issues but would not be permanently assigned to the staff.[52] Finally, I suggested bringing in David Kilcullen, an Australian infantry officer with a Ph.D. in political anthropology from the University of New South Wales and experience in East Timor, the Middle East, and South Asia, as the senior adviser for counterinsurgency. Dave was currently assigned to the U.S. State Department, so we would have to negotiate his release with a number of interested parties. Regrettably, the demands of his other duties would ultimately limit Dave's time on General Petraeus's staff to just four months.

Perhaps the most interesting pick was Sadi Othman, who would serve as Petraeus's senior adviser for political and cultural affairs. Like me, Sadi was a Palestinian-American. He had grown up in Jordan, and due to his six-foot, seven-inch frame and physical skills, played for a time on its national basketball team—leading Jordan to its first victory against Syria, scoring sixty-six points in the process! He was schooled in Jordan by Mennonite missionaries and then attended Hesston College, a Mennonite institution, in Kansas. A naturalized American citizen, Sadi was driving a taxi in New York City when terrorists attacked the World Trade Center, an event that later caused him to offer his services to U.S. military forces in Iraq. Petraeus met Sadi in Mosul in 2003 and assigned him as his personal interpreter. From there the relationship grew, continuing through Petraeus's days as commander of the 101st Airborne Division and later as head of MNSTC-I.[53]

Sadi had done little to ingratiate himself with General Casey and his team, so when word arrived in MNF-I headquarters that Petraeus wanted Sadi assigned to his office, I soon received a call from a Casey staffer. He relayed concerns about Sadi's personal and professional conduct and recommended that we not take him on board. I thanked the officer for his input and concern. Petraeus understood that Sadi was not always a paragon of virtue, but he had many exceptional qualities that would serve the mission well in the months to come. Sadi became the Arabic extension of General Petraeus. Since most Iraqis could not speak English, when Petraeus spoke to them, the voice they heard was Sadi's. He was constantly on the phone to Iraqi government officials, often late at night, acting as a two-way conduit of information. Sadi smoked constantly and slept little; his personal conduct would also occasionally land him in hot water with the authorities that governed the Green Zone. Sadi's desk in the U.S. embassy complex was adjacent to mine, and we often engaged in passionate discussions about Iraqi and Middle East politics.

Several other people who would end up on the staff were also already in Iraq. Mary Kohler was a Department of the Army civilian who had served with Petraeus as his protocol coordinator in the 101st Airborne Division at Fort Campbell, Kentucky. I assigned her to the MNF-I office at the U.S. embassy as his executive assistant. Her involvement in office management and the coordination of VIP lunches, dinners, congressional meetings, and other events requiring the savvy touch of a seasoned protocol officer was essential to the smooth functioning of the embassy office. Sergeant First Class Lasharon Taylor would serve as the commanding general's administrative assistant at Camp Victory. When Sadi pleaded that we hire a simultaneous translator so that he could focus on advising General Petraeus rather than translating for his many meetings, we found a unique and eminently qualified individual to fill the role. Heather Wiersema had been taken by her parents to the Gulf countries as a young child, where she grew up in the tribal culture speaking fluent Arabic. She returned to the United States as an adult to attend the University of Arizona and earn a degree as a medical technologist. Like Sadi, after 9/11 she offered her services to the U.S. military as a translator. Heather was the best simultaneous translator in Iraq, and I appreciated her keen insights into Islamic culture and current affairs as well. When she was otherwise unengaged, I would have her troll the Internet for news on Iraqi politics as well as snippets from insurgent and jihadist Web sites. Occasionally I would share these insights with General Petraeus and other members of the team to keep them informed on what the Arab "street" was thinking.

The final two members of the team, Captain Johanna Mora and Captain Kelly Howard, were carryovers from General Casey's staff. We could not have hoped for two finer officers to fill their positions. Hanna, who had joined the army at age seventeen as a medic and earned an officer's commission through the Green to Gold program, was the adjutant and scheduler. In this position, she managed the commander's calendar, which changed constantly and required a detail-oriented person to ensure that everyone was kept abreast of the changes to it. Nothing went onto the calendar without General Petraeus's or my permission, so Hanna and I would talk face to face or by phone several times a day. Hanna's husband, Alex, served on a National Police transition team in some of the toughest neighborhoods in Baghdad, including Sadr City. Kelly, serving her second tour in Iraq, was a member of the West Point class of 2002. As the operations officer, she was responsible for coordinating all of the trips for the command group, both within Iraq and overseas. It was a huge responsibility, and she executed the task flawlessly. We were fortunate to have them both on the staff.

Much was made at the time of the unique makeup of the staff. "Essentially, the Army is turning the war over to its dissidents, who have criticized the way the service has operated there the past three years, and is letting them try to wage the war their way," asserted journalist Tom Ricks.[54] Babak Dehghanpisheh and John Barry wrote in *Newsweek*, "As he began putting his staff together late last year, the joke inside the Pentagon was that no one without a Ph.D. would be eligible. 'Commanders haven't [traditionally] tried to reach out and just pick the best minds— not the guys on the fastest track for promotion, not the "best" soldiers, but the best minds with relevant experience,' says Fred Kagan, a West Point graduate and sometime teacher there, who's now at the American Enterprise Institute. 'It was wonderful to see that.'"[55] With so many highly educated and accomplished people on the team, some friction was inevitable. Another of my duties, then, unstated but real enough, was to manage egos and ensure the smooth operation of the franchise. I also cracked heads when necessary to maintain discipline and professionalism, provide focus, and keep the team working toward common goals. Coupled with my ability to "get shit done" by goading the broader MNF-I staff into action when needed, these attributes earned me the quirkily endearing and apt nickname "Hatchet Man."

On the morning of Tuesday, January 23, Lieutenant General Petraeus appeared before the Senate Armed Services Committee. Reporters and photographers filled the hearing room. The furious clicks of camera shutters were a bit unsettling to those of us not used to these events. Petraeus, calm as ever, remained unfazed.

Petraeus delivered a frank assessment of the situation in Iraq, followed by an abbreviated version of the strategy to restore America's fortunes in the war and his vision for the way ahead. The elections of 2005 had intensified sectarian divisions, while the escalation of sectarian violence after the bombing of the al-Askari shrine in February 2006 had "raised the prospect of a failed Iraqi state." The reinforcements on the way to Iraq would empower a new strategy, with the focus of the military effort shifting to protecting the Iraqi people, particularly in Baghdad. Persistent presence in the most violent neighborhoods would be an essential part of the plan. The ultimate goal was to provide the Iraqi government the space and time necessary to allow it to come to grips with the tough issues facing the Iraqi people. While there was no military solution to the conflict, improved security was essential to empowering a political solution. To assist the Iraqi government in increasing its capacity to govern and provide essential services to the Iraqi people, interagency cooperation was also critical to the way ahead.[56]

The new strategy would not change the situation in Iraq overnight. "In fact," Petraeus stated, "the way ahead will be neither quick nor easy, and there undoubtedly will be tough days. We face a determined, adaptable, barbaric enemy. He will try to wait us out. In fact, any such endeavor is a test of wills, and there are no guarantees." The general finished on a realistic but upbeat note. "In closing, the situation in Iraq is dire. The stakes are high. There are no easy choices. The way ahead will be very hard. Progress will require determination and difficult U.S. and Iraqi actions, especially the latter, as ultimately the outcome will be determined by the Iraqis. But hard is not hopeless, and if confirmed, I pledge to do my utmost to lead our wonderful men and women in uniform and those of our coalition partners in Iraq as we endeavor to help the Iraqis make the most of the opportunity our soldiers, sailors, airmen and Marines have given to them."[57]

Most senators appreciated Petraeus's candid remarks but remained skeptical about the new strategy. They generally split along party lines, Republicans in the main supportive of adding more troops to the conflict, most Democrats (with the notable exception of the nominally independent Senator Joe Lieberman) adamantly opposed. Senator Carl Levin, the ranking member of the committee, expressed skepticism that the Iraqi government would live up to its commitments. Senator Hillary Rodham Clinton spent her entire eight minutes decrying the surge without asking a single question. Senator John McCain wondered whether the administration was sending enough reinforcements to Iraq, given the shortfalls in reaching the ratio of counterinsurgents to population written into U.S. Army and Marine Corps doctrine. He had a point. Even with the U.S. and Iraqi reinforcements headed to Baghdad, the 83,000 or so troops on the ground there would not reach the 120,000 needed to meet the 1:50 security force–to–population ratio recommended by our new counterinsurgency doctrine. Private security contractors filled part of the remaining gap, a stopgap measure which I personally opposed.[58] General Petraeus acknowledged the shortfall, but believed we could nevertheless make sufficient headway in protecting the population with the forces on hand or in the reinforcement pipeline. Despite these doubts, the committee unanimously forwarded Petraeus's nomination to the full Senate, which three days later confirmed him as commander of Multi-National Force–Iraq and approved his promotion to full (four-star) general by a vote of 81–0.

After the hearing, Petraeus met with President Bush in the Oval Office. The president offered that with the surge, he had doubled down on the U.S. war effort in Iraq. "This isn't double down, Mr. President," Petraeus replied. "It's all in."[59]

It was time to pack our bags and get to Iraq. Before departing the United States, we spent one last weekend at home with our families. I took Jana, Kyle, and J.T. bowling for some family fun time. On the way out of the bowling alley, I bought each of us a trinket from a grab-bag machine. Mine turned out to be a poker chip displaying a royal flush on both sides attached to a cloth necklace. It was an appropriate symbol, I thought, for the luck we would need in the months ahead.

On Monday, February 5, after teary goodbyes with our families, General Petraeus and a small traveling contingent departed from Kansas City International Airport in a U.S. Air Force Gulfstream G-5 for a nine-hour flight to London. The ride in this beautiful aircraft was terrific, a far cry from the much more cramped jets we had gotten used to in our journeys between Fort Leavenworth and Washington, D.C. General Petraeus and I sat across the aisle from each other while working on various documents, including counterinsurgency guidance and a letter he would issue to the troops upon his change of command five days hence. Midway across the Atlantic, I pulled the poker chip necklace out of my pocket, got the general's attention, and remarked, "Hey, sir—all in." General Petraeus flashed a knowing smile and got back to work. A bit later, I made a more substantive comment. "The hardest thing for you to do, should it come to it, would be to tell the president and the American people that this thing isn't going to work." When questioned by the senators during his confirmation hearings, Petraeus had agreed to give his frank and candid assessment of the progress of the surge in periodic updates to Congress. We both were going to do our best to make the surge work, but I felt he needed to hear this dose of reality to temper his natural inclination to accept nothing less than 100 percent success. The general made no reply, but I know the comment registered. That was good enough.

At the direction of President Bush, in London General Petraeus held meetings with Prime Minister Tony Blair and various other civilian and military officials. The British assured us of their support in the coming months, but we understood that public pressure would sooner rather than later force the Labour government to withdraw British troops from Iraq. The short visit was our last taste of Western civilization. On February 7 we departed England on a flight to the Middle East. After stopping briefly in Kuwait to change into a smaller aircraft, we headed to Baghdad. The group was quiet during the short, uneventful flight, each one of us caught up in his own thoughts regarding the trials that lay ahead.

The transition was a rushed affair and quite frankly achieved little of substance. General Petraeus had a couple of one-on-one sessions with General Casey, but their deliberations remained a private affair. Casey's staff, immersed in the final details of the change of command and their departure from country, spent little time with the incoming team. Regrettably, a few officers gave us the cold shoulder, viewing Petraeus's staff as the guys sent from Washington to grade their homework. One of them told Hanna and Kelly that we were likely to fire them— something we had never even considered, but which kept them on edge for several days until Everett and I cleared the air after noticing their reticence. Despite these drawbacks, I absorbed as much as I could watching events from the sidelines, but had I not been immersed in the details of Iraq strategy since the previous September, I would have been completely lost. Given this awkward situation, in my view the change of command could not come soon enough.

On the morning of Saturday, February 10, a crowd of U.S. and Iraqi dignitaries gathered in the atrium of the al-Faw palace at Camp Victory, the headquarters of the Multi-National Force–Iraq. General John Abizaid presided over Petraeus's promotion to four-star rank and the subsequent transfer of command authority from General Casey to General Petraeus. In his remarks, General Petraeus was typically tactful and forthright. "The challenges ahead are substantial," he told the assembled audience. "The rucksack of responsibility is very heavy." If Iraqis and coalition forces could move forward together, then success was achievable. If not, Iraq would "be doomed to continued violence and civil strife." After thanking General Abizaid and General Casey for their service to the nation, he continued, "The situation in Iraq is exceedingly challenging. The stakes are high. The way ahead will be hard, and there undoubtedly will be many tough days. As I recently told the members of the United States Senate, however, 'hard is not hopeless.' Indeed, together with our Iraq partners, we can and we must prevail. Our job in the months ahead, supporting and working with Iraqi forces, will be to improve security so that the Iraqi government can resolve the tough issues it faces and so that the economy and basic services can be improved. These tasks are achievable. This mission is doable."[60] He then pledged his support to the Iraqi people to combat the barbaric enemies that sought to drive wedges between ethnic and religious groups that had lived peacefully together in the past. He finished with a pledge, "Together, we can defeat the enemies of Iraq."[61]

It was time to wield the mantle of power that the president and the American people had bestowed upon us. Immediately after the ceremony ended, I walked over to my desk and called the MNF-I operations division. "What is the status of the five surge brigades?" I asked. The answer was disheartening. "Just as it has always been," the colonel on the other end of the phone replied. "Two brigades heading to Baghdad, one to deploy to Kuwait as a reserve, and two to remain in the United States on prepare-to-deploy orders." I was dumbfounded. After repeated engagement with the chairman of the Joint Chiefs, including some very direct conversations in January, General Petraeus had already resolved this issue and gained a commitment to have all surge brigades committed and deploying as rapidly as was possible, one per month.[62] The word had clearly not yet filtered down the chain of command to the colonels in the Green Zone. I walked over to the reception area where General Petraeus was greeting dignitaries and senior members of the MNF-I staff. After a quick conversation, his reply was definitive: "Tell them to get all the brigades moving to Iraq now."

The surge had begun in earnest.

CHAPTER 3

Fardh al-Qanoon

Security may be ten percent of the problem, or it may be ninety percent,
but whichever it is, it's the first ten percent or the first ninety percent.
Without security, nothing else we do will last.
—John Paul Vann, U.S. military adviser in Vietnam

To prevail in the war in Iraq, U.S. and Iraqi security forces first had to win
the battle for Baghdad. This had been the goal of the failed Together Forward operations in 2006, which had lacked sufficient forces to hold areas
after they were cleared of insurgents and militiamen. In February 2007 the coalition would try again, this time with more troops and a new operational concept,
code-named Fardh al-Qanoon ("Enforcing the Law").[1] U.S. and Iraqi forces would
partner together from local bases called joint security stations, combat outposts,
and patrol bases. These forces would focus on securing the Iraqi people from
violence, regardless of where it originated. Beginning in early 2005 Sunni insurgents and Shi'a militia pursued premeditated strategies to push members of the
opposite sect out of the capital. Under Lieutenant General Ray Odierno and Lieutenant General Abud Qanbar, the commanders of Multi-National Corps–Iraq
(MNC-I) and the newly created Baghdad Operations Command, U.S. and Iraqi
soldiers would counter with a deliberate plan of their own to win back the streets
and secure the city.

The operational concept for Fardh al-Qanoon had emerged after several weeks
of deliberation. Planners from U.S. III Corps headquarters based out of Fort Hood,
Texas, had arrived in Baghdad the previous November to overlap with their pre-

decessors and get a head start on developing options for Lieutenant General Odierno. Among the officers who arrived early was Colonel Jim Hickey; he had commanded the 1st Brigade, 4th Infantry Division, in Tikrit during the first year of the war and had been instrumental in Saddam Hussein's capture in December 2003. He was now the senior military representative to the Joint Advanced Warfighting Program at the Institute for Defense Analyses, but had been assigned to MNC-I in Iraq to establish a Counter-Improvised Explosive Device Operations Integration Center (COIC). Hickey designed and built the facility from the ground up; the $20 million start-up cost was absorbed by the Joint Improvised Explosive Device Defeat Organization, while III Corps provided the seventy-plus officers and noncommissioned officers to staff the center. The COIC fused intelligence from a variety of sources and disseminated it to war fighters as low as company level via classified communications channels. The COIC also gave Multi-National Corps–Iraq an additional and very powerful intelligence and analysis capability that could help to unravel the details of insurgent, terrorist, and militia networks.[2]

Hickey and the corps planners were astonished at the level of violence in Iraq in general, and particularly in Baghdad. They were concerned that the MNC-I intelligence staff lacked a holistic understanding of the enemy, including his aims, his organization, and his concept of operations. The intelligence effort, in their view, focused too heavily on tactical level targeting. An overriding focus on transition and governance colored the thinking of the corps staff. Lieutenant Colonel Dale Kuehl, commander of the 1st Battalion, 5th Cavalry, which assumed responsibility for Amiriyah in western Baghdad in November 2006, described the situation upon his arrival: "While I am sure units were doing what they could to protect the populace, the focus upon our arrival was on transition. The transition focus seemed to be more interested in getting out of Iraq as quickly as possible regardless of events on the ground based upon the premise that our presence was the cause of much of the violence we were seeing. I believe this was a false premise based on a poor understanding of the dynamics playing out in the political and social infrastructure within Iraq. This strategy also ignored our moral responsibility as an Army and as a nation that we have for rebuilding what we tore apart."[3] There was not a lot of effort applied at the operational level toward understanding and combating the enemy; rather, the current fight was seen as a tactical problem to be handled by the multinational division commanders.[4]

Lieutenant General Odierno arrived on the ground in Baghdad on December 9 and took command of MNC-I five days later. He quickly realized that having special operations forces continue to battle al-Qaeda in Iraq without significant reinforcement from the corps was a losing proposition. The Sunni terrorists were the most dangerous enemy, and the corps had to engage and defeat them, beginning in Baghdad.[5] He put his planners to work on a course of action to secure Baghdad under the assumption that the corps would be reinforced by at least two brigades and perhaps more. He also brought Colonel Hickey into the planning effort as a trusted agent.[6]

In the midst of this planning frenzy, on December 19 a raid on an al-Qaeda safe house in Tarmiyah captured information vital to deciphering the enemy plan for Baghdad, including a stash of hard drives and a hand-drawn sketch of al-Qaeda's plan for controlling the city. The sketch, the work of Abu Ayyub al-Masri, the new head of al-Qaeda in Iraq, showed Baghdad broken into sectors, with each area under the command of a different terrorist leader. More important, the sketch showed the organization's support zones surrounding Baghdad, which made clear the importance of these areas. These support zones, or "belts," provided al-Qaeda operatives sanctuary and served as manufacturing and logistical bases for the terrorist group, from which they would inject such accelerants as car bombs and suicide bombers into Baghdad in an effort to contest control of the Iraqi capital. Insurgents would also try to squeeze Jaish al-Mahdi lines of communication from southern Iraq into Baghdad, which was why the area south of Baghdad had earned a sobering reputation as the "triangle of death."[7]

The existence of terrorist safe havens outside Baghdad went a long way toward explaining why the various operations to secure the city in 2006 failed. "The underlying logic was based on the political and social importance of Baghdad; demographics of the sects living in and around the city; and the physical reality of the terrain and lines of communication," Colonel Hickey observed. "What we learned [from the sketch] made sense. It corroborated what we were observing on a daily basis and other operational and intelligence reporting."[8] Lieutenant General Odierno agreed. "Our Iraqi allies also believed that controlling the belts was essential to securing Baghdad," Odierno later wrote. "They urged us to put the newly arriving troops into the belts, reporting that the accelerants were there and that the history of Iraq showed that whoever controlled the belts controlled the Capital."[9]

Briefed on the find, Lieutenant General Odierno gave marching orders to his staff. If this was the enemy's plan for Baghdad, then the corps would build a scheme to defeat it by securing the population in the city and by choking off the accelerants coming into the capital from the north, northwest, and south.[10] Under Lieutenant General Odierno, the corps became more operationally active in the maneuver of its subordinate units. The 1st Cavalry Division and its reinforcements, known as Multi-National Division–Baghdad, would be the corps main effort; all other divisions would support it to the limit of their capabilities. The goal would be to protect the Iraqi people, reduce the level of ethnosectarian violence, and defeat al-Qaeda and various militia groups (of all sects) that threatened the integrity of the Iraqi state. In contrast to the lack of coordination earlier in the war, by 2007 MNC-I had developed a fully integrated operations-intelligence structure in conjunction with the special operations command in Iraq, under the command of Lieutenant General Stanley McChrystal. The synergistic effects of conventional and special operations forces working together would be felt in a big way over the course of the surge.

In January 2007, Lieutenant General Odierno called Colonel Hickey into a large planning session in the corps commander's office. Hickey placed on the table a hand-drawn concept overlaid on a map of central Iraq. He advocated what became known as the "doughnut plan," which envisioned Baghdad as the center of a series of concentric rings surrounding the city. The rings, which encompassed the "Baghdad belts," would act as security zones to protect the capital. It was a cavalry approach to operations, and it resonated with the commander. Lieutenant General Odierno then made the decision to put two of the five surge brigades into Baghdad to help secure the city, while three other brigades would move into the belts to defeat al-Qaeda in its sanctuaries. Two marine battalions and a marine expeditionary unit would deploy to al-Anbar province to fight the battle against al-Qaeda in western Iraq.[11] The focus of surge brigades on the Baghdad belts was a major departure from the thinking of MNF-I and MNC-I in 2006 and caused a minor stir with some commentators and politicians in Washington, who did not understand the linkage between the rural areas surrounding Baghdad and the violence inside the Iraqi capital.

Upon his arrival in Iraq, General Petraeus was clear as to the direction he wanted the counterinsurgency campaign to head. The goal henceforth would be to secure the Iraqi people against ethnosectarian violence and intimidation, a goal wholeheartedly shared by Lieutenant General Odierno and his team already on the ground. As Petraeus accepted the mantle of command on February 10, Colonel Bill Rapp in the Commander's Initiatives Group electronically distributed a letter written by General Petraeus for the troops of Multi-National Force–Iraq. "We serve in Iraq at a critical time," the letter began. "The war here will soon enter its fifth year. A decisive moment approaches. Shoulder-to-shoulder with our Iraqi comrades, we will conduct a pivotal campaign to improve security for the Iraqi people. The stakes could not be higher." He continued:

> Our task is crucial. Security is essential for Iraq to build its future. Only with security can the Iraqi government come to grips with the tough issues it confronts and develop the capacity to serve its citizens. The hopes of the Iraqi people and the coalition countries are with us.
>
> The enemies of Iraq will shrink at no act, however barbaric. They will do all that they can to shake the confidence of the people and to convince the world that this effort is doomed. We must not underestimate them.
>
> Together with our Iraqi partners, we must defeat those who oppose the new Iraq. We cannot allow mass murderers to hold the initiative. We must strike them relentlessly. We and our Iraqi partners must set the terms of the struggle, not our enemies. And together we must prevail.

The way ahead will not be easy. There will be difficult times in the months to come. But hard is not hopeless, and we must remain steadfast in our effort to help improve security for the Iraqi people. I am confident that each of you will fight with skill and courage, and that you will remain loyal to your comrades-in-arms and to the values our nations hold so dear.

In the end, Iraqis will decide the outcome of this struggle. Our task is to help them gain the time they need to save their country. To do that, many of us will live and fight alongside them. Together, we will face down the terrorists, insurgents, and criminals who slaughter the innocent. Success will require discipline, fortitude, and initiative—qualities that you have in abundance.

I appreciate your sacrifices and those of your families. Now, more than ever, your commitment to service and your skill can make the difference between victory and defeat in a very tough mission.

It is an honor to soldier again with the members of the Multi-National Force–Iraq. I know that wherever you serve in this undertaking you will give your all. In turn, I pledge my commitment to our mission and every effort to achieve success as we help the Iraqis chart a course to a brighter future.

Godspeed to each of you and to our Iraqi comrades in this crucial endeavor.[12]

The letter resonated with many members of the force, and answered the question posed by the soldier in the combat outpost in Ghazalia the next day, "What are we doing here?"[13] The issue now was how to operationalize the strategy.

In his first meeting with subordinate commanders and key staff the afternoon of the change of command, General Petraeus reinforced the need to protect the Iraqi people in order to reduce ethnosectarian violence and provide the Iraqi government time and space to advance a political solution to the conflict. The surge was not as much about the reinforcements as it was about how they would be used. Indeed, as General Petraeus has noted on many occasions, the most important surge was the surge of ideas, not the surge in forces, though the additional forces obviously enabled implementation of the new ideas and concepts. The most important of the "big ideas" was that U.S. and Iraqi forces had to focus on securing the people—and to do it by moving off the big bases and living with them. U.S. and Iraqi forces had to be partnered on every level to make this new strategy work. It was important to allow the Iraqis to lead when possible, but not at the risk of the mission. "If we don't get a grip on the violence," General Petraeus stated, "then it doesn't matter who is in charge": We would lose. Information operations and public affairs would be adjusted as well. We would immediately push back against insurgent propaganda by making our information operations more nimble and decentralized. In the public affairs arena, we would tamp down expectations with the realization that violence was the key metric and that progress would take months. He reiterated three big points: Maliki was our guy, the time was right to move forward with the new strategy, and both the U.S. and Iraqi governments understood the surge to be the last, best chance to win the war.

A common complaint among soldiers in the early days of the surge was that the rules of engagement—the administrative and legal authorities that empower military forces to act—were too restrictive. In an effort to reduce civilian casualties, over time commanders had added greater restrictions on the use of deadly force against potential threats. While soldiers always retained the right of self-defense, the interpretation of the rules of engagement by subordinate commanders had increasingly tied their hands in combat against the enemy. One of General Petraeus's first acts was to order a review of the rules of engagement and their implementation by subordinate commands. The outcome of this investigation was the discovery that the current rules of engagement, with a few minor adjustments, were workable, but that risk-averse commanders had interpreted them in such a manner as to hamper troops in the legitimate performance of their duties. Together, General Petraeus and Lieutenant General Odierno, along with their staff judge advocates, reworked the interpretation of the rules of engagement to ensure that they would empower American forces rather than impede their ability to accomplish their missions. They then explicitly forbade subordinate commanders to further alter the rules of engagement, in order to prevent risk aversion from rearing its ugly head lower down the chain-of-command.

The first surge brigade, the 2nd Brigade, 82nd Airborne Division, arrived in Kuwait in early January to serve as the Iraqi theater reserve. It had hardly had time to unload its gear before it was committed to the fight for Baghdad. The remaining surge brigades would arrive one per month from February to May, supplemented by additional engineer, aviation, and military police forces. By June, Multi-National Corps–Iraq would be at full strength—twenty U.S. Army brigade combat teams and U.S. Marine Corps regimental combat teams, along with coalition units ranging from platoon to brigade strength from a number of countries. The remainder of the winter and the spring months would serve as a shaping period as the corps repositioned units, created smaller joint security stations and combat outposts in Baghdad, received reinforcements from the United States, and conducted operations to clear and secure selected portions of the Iraqi capital. Major offensive operations would begin in June.

The addition of two more brigades to the battle for Baghdad necessitated an adjustment of the battlefield geometry. The 2nd Brigade, 1st Infantry Division, under the command of Colonel J. B. Burton, secured northwest Baghdad (Kadhimiyah and Mansour districts); the 4th Brigade, 1st Infantry Division, under the command of Colonel Ricky Gibbs, secured southwest Baghdad (Rashid); the 2nd Brigade, 1st Cavalry Division, under the command of Colonel Bryan Roberts, secured central Baghdad (Karkh and the Green Zone); the 2nd Brigade, 82nd Airborne Division, under the command of Colonel Billy Don Ferris, secured northeast Baghdad (Adhamiya, Rusafa, and Sadr City), and the 2nd Brigade, 2nd Infantry

Division, under the command of Colonel Jeff Bannister, secured southeast Baghdad (9 Nissan and Karadah districts). Additionally, the 3rd Brigade, 2nd Infantry Division, a unit armed with Stryker combat vehicles under the command of Colonel Steve Townsend, served as the corps reserve. During the first months of the surge, Townsend's brigade acted as a strike force to assist landowning units to clear their assigned areas of insurgent and militia forces.[14]

One of the keys to securing Baghdad was the creation of joint security stations and combat outposts to allow U.S. troops to live among the Iraqi people and serve alongside Iraqi army and police forces. To secure the Iraqi people, coalition forces had to reposition from their large forward operating bases on the outskirts of Iraq's cities into the neighborhoods where the people lived, worked, and slept. Mounted patrols alone could not provide enough security to prevent insurgents, terrorists, and militias from fomenting ethnosectarian violence and driving Iraq deeper into civil war. Local outposts would enable troops to increase the number of foot patrols and provide a more lasting measure of security to the neighborhoods in which they were situated.

The Iraqi minister of defense, Abdul Qadir, had proposed the creation of joint security stations the previous fall. These small bases would typically contain a battalion command post jointly staffed by U.S. and Iraqi personnel, billeting space, an aid station and dining facility, latrine and shower units, a helicopter landing zone, and a motor park for unit vehicles. Combat outposts and patrol bases were similar but housed U.S. and Iraqi combat units at company and platoon level. They typically were large enough for a hundred or so personnel plus their equipment and vehicles. These outposts required foresight and planning, both to obtain the necessary permissions from Iraqi owners to occupy the land and to engineer the construction necessary for the facilities and force protection (blast walls, vehicle barriers, guard towers, and so on) needed to make them viable. As the surge progressed, more outposts were equipped with Rapid Aerostat Initial Deployment (RAID) towers, aerostats (helium-filled dirigibles tethered to the ground), masts, or Mobile Eagle Eye devices. These systems provided daylight cameras and forward-looking infrared (thermal) imaging to augment the organic surveillance capabilities of U.S. ground forces. The proliferation of security bases across Baghdad meant that more of the city was under continuous surveillance during the surge than ever before.

Both types of installations provided a way for the U.S. Army and Iraqi security forces to work more closely together, coordinate their efforts, and share intelligence. U.S. commanders in some cases would force the Iraqi army and police forces to cooperate with each other. "When we first moved in, nobody got along," Captain Dave Eastburn, commander of B Battery, 2nd Battalion, 17th Field Artillery Regiment, stated a couple of months into the operation. "Now they sit together, they talk, they eat together. I think the professionalism of the Iraqi army is rubbing off on the Iraqi police."[15] Iraqi soldiers brought cultural savvy and linguistic capabilities to the force mix. They knew the people. U.S. forces added professionalism, technical and tactical know-how, and firepower. The professionalism of American soldiers and Marines rubbed off on the Iraqi forces as well. Iraqi soldiers modeled their behavior after their better-trained and -disciplined U.S. counterparts and learned a great deal from them. This partnering of U.S. and Iraqi forces was one of the reasons for the ultimate success of the surge. "Iraqi soldiers want to be like you," General Petraeus would tell leaders of incoming units during his frequent visits to the Counterinsurgency Center of Excellence at Taji. "Right down to wearing their knee pads around their ankles," he would add humorously, to roars of laughter. Another valid, if tacit, purpose of joint security stations and combat outposts was to keep an eye on the Iraqi police forces to inhibit their involvement in sectarian violence.

Colonel J. B. Burton established the first combat outposts in Ghazalia, COP Casino and COP Wildcard, in January 2006.[16] The paratroopers of the 2nd Brigade, 82nd Airborne Division—the first surge brigade to arrive in Iraq—built COP Callahan and COP War Eagle in the Sunni insurgent stronghold of Adhamiya, east of the Tigris River. Others followed. On March 5 U.S. and Iraqi forces established the first joint security station in Sadr City. But to succeed, U.S. and Iraqi forces had to remain committed to protecting the local communities in which they now resided over the long haul. "We continue to stress to the Iraqis and our forces that this is going to take continued commitment, determination, time, and effort," General Petraeus informed Secretary of Defense Robert Gates early in the operation. "It is not just a few-week surge, it has to last."[17]

For a couple of weeks after the establishment of an outpost or joint security station, local civilians acted warily around the new arrivals to the neighborhood. Once they discovered that the troops were going to remain for an extended period, the floodgates of intelligence opened up as civilians stepped forward with information on extremists in their midst. "Joint Security Stations and Combat Outposts had a clear, noticeable effect on the Iraqi people both physically and psychologically," Lieutenant General Odierno observed. "Attitudes changed when the first concrete walls of a Coalition patrol base were erected. The protective barriers were an indicator of our intent to stay and conduct sustained operations among the populace. And they made a difference—to local citizens . . . and to the enemy, who recognized them almost immediately as a threat to their freedom of action and, ultimately, their existence."[18] Lieutenant Colonel Jim Crider, who commanded the 1st Squadron, 4th Cavalry, in the tough neighborhood of Dora in 2007 and 2008, commented, "To maintain a constant and close watch, and for our own protection, we decided to remain on the streets every hour of every day. We eventually learned that this relentless presence had a powerful psychological effect on the local population. The sight of our HMMWVs on the streets and soldiers engaging people in conversation all day and night sent a message to insurgents and average citizens alike. Unlike units of the past, who were forced to conduct a quick patrol and unable to engage the people, we literally never left. We were easily accessible and, therefore, began to receive more tips on insurgent activity."[19] Better information led to more precise targeting—the *sine qua non* of effective combat operations in counterinsurgency warfare.

The density of troops created by the additional surge forces made an enormous difference in the fight for Baghdad and other areas in Iraq. For instance, in 2006 only two battalions operated in the Rashid District of southwest Baghdad; at the height of the surge five battalions populated the district, augmented by increased numbers of Iraqi forces.[20] These reinforcements made a strategy of protecting the population feasible. During the course of the surge, Multi-National Corps–Iraq created more than sixty-five joint security stations and combat outposts in Baghdad.[21]

To secure Baghdad, U.S. and Iraqi security forces had to do more than just move out into the community. They also had to control the movement of the civilian population to prevent terrorists, insurgents, and militias from preying on the Iraqi people. Car bombs, suicide bombers, and insurgent and militia forces did not just magically appear; they moved on Iraq's roads. For a large, populous (some 6–7 million people) city like Baghdad, controlling the population was an enormous task. Iraqi security forces operated a large number of vehicle checkpoints throughout the city, but they were insufficient to halt the movement of car bombs, terrorists, insurgents, and militia forces. In some cases the security forces at the checkpoints were complicit in allowing the movement of contraband through their positions, and in other cases they were either incapable of discovering it or were incompetent in the performance of their duties. Savvy fighters could also bypass the checkpoints along the major roads by taking secondary routes.

The latest targets of al-Qaeda terrorism were commercial hubs, such as bus stations and large open-air markets, frequented by Shi'a patrons. On January 22 two car bombs ripped through the Bab al-Sharqi market in central Baghdad, killing 88 people and wounding nearly twice that many.[22] On February 1, two suicide bombers detonated explosives among shoppers in a crowded outdoor market south of Baghdad in Hillah; the blasts killed 73 people and wounded another 163.[23] On February 3, four days before our arrival in Iraq, a suicide terrorist detonated a truck filled with a ton of explosives in the Sadriyah market in central Baghdad. The explosion killed more than 130 Iraqis and wounded hundreds of others—making this attack the deadliest on record in the war to date.[24] The blast reduced several buildings in the area to shells. On February 12, the day the Iraqi government observed the first anniversary of the al-Askari shrine bombing (according to the Islamic calendar), three bombs exploded in the Shorja market, the capital's largest bazaar, and another at the nearby Bab al-Sharqi market. The attacks killed 67 people and wounded 155 others.[25] Most of the dead and wounded in these attacks were Shi'ites—the victims of the deliberate strategy by al-Qaeda to instigate reprisals, thereby abetting sectarian violence and civil war. In a continuous cycle of retaliation, Jaish al-Mahdi militiamen prowled neighborhoods to kidnap or kill young Sunni men and force Sunni residents out of their homes. We could not allow this carnage to continue unchecked. So Multi-National Corps–Iraq began with a simple precept: Good fences make for good neighbors.

To canalize vehicular and personnel movement, U.S. forces—with the concurrence of the Iraqi government—emplaced large blast barriers around many of Baghdad's markets and around the toughest neighborhoods, where sectarian violence was most prevalent. Iraqi soldiers and police controlled entry into these areas at designated checkpoints. Security forces searched and questioned civilians passing through these checkpoints, which significantly impeded the movement of arms and explosives around the city. Walls turned marketplaces into pedestrian zones and thereby removed the risk of massive car bombs and truck bombs, but they could not completely eliminate the danger from suicide bombers willing to sacrifice themselves in order to kill others. As the surge progressed, U.S. forces erected walls as fast as possible since they were a key to limiting the spread of ethnosectarian violence. General Petraeus called these barriers the "Arizona creeper," which grew at a steady rate of several hundred yards per day, and he noted that we were providing "gated communities" to the Iraqis at no charge. After Colonel J. B. Burton's brigade erected, at the request of local leaders, the first set of barriers in northern Ghazalia to prevent Shi'a militiamen from entering the mostly Sunni area, murders immediately dropped by 50 percent.[26] The barriers were so effective that insurgent propaganda—picked up by Western reporters—started to compare them to Israel's barrier on the West Bank—an attempt to raise the hackles of the Arab population against the walls.[27] General Petraeus and Ambassador Crocker made it clear that the barriers were meant not to segregate Baghdad's population but to improve the people's security against terrorist attacks. This was admittedly a fine distinction, since the gated communities we created did make the intermingling of the Baghdad population much more difficult. Publicly, Iraqi government officials made noisy complaints about the barriers (which were not popular since they restricted freedom of movement), but in private they told General Petraeus to "keep building."

Another important technique of population control is to conduct a census to establish the makeup of the population and to determine who belongs in a given neighborhood or village.[28] In Iraq, however, the issue of conducting a census was charged with political overtones. In areas undergoing ethnic or sectarian cleansing, a census could either advance or jeopardize a given party's claim to a particular location. Many Sunnis refused to believe that their sect constituted a minority of the Iraqi people, but they were fearful that a census might confirm their deepest fears. The Iraqi government also suggested distributing oil revenues based on population data; in this case, minority groups such as the Kurds did not want a census to reduce their purported percentage of the Iraqi population.

These obstacles to conducting a nationwide census in Iraq were, for the time being, insoluble. Nevertheless, for security purposes, understanding the composition of Baghdad's neighborhoods was critical. Commanders improvised and developed various ingenious methods to accomplish this task. One such example was the work of Lieutenant Colonel Jim Crider and the troopers of the 1st Squadron, 4th Cavalry, in Dora. This neighborhood was the scene of intense sectarian fighting in 2006 and 2007, as Sunni insurgents fought to retain it as a base from which to inject violence into Baghdad from the rural areas to the south of the city. Multi-National Force–Iraq Command Sergeant Major Marvin Hill, who experienced more than his share of combat in Iraq, put the situation bluntly, telling journalist Tom Ricks, "Doura was a meat grinder."[29] Crider positioned his forces in combat outposts and kept two of his platoons continuously on the streets, measures that had an immediate and beneficial effect on reducing violence. The Sunnis of Dora, however, remained aloof. Crider soon discovered their deep antagonism toward and mistrust of the Iraqi National Police, so he ordered the police to remain at their checkpoints on the outskirts of the district. "In their [Sunni] minds," Crider later wrote, "the National Police were Shi'a militiamen in uniform, and our joint patrols served as a means to bring that 'militia' to their doorsteps. For their part, the National Police believed that everyone in the neighborhood was a member of al-Qaeda in Iraq, so they readily accepted this temporary arrangement."[30] Yet Crider needed better information on Dora's residents, and he hit upon a clever solution to gather it.

Crider's soldiers would cordon off an entire city block and then proceed to interview every family inside their homes. People who were afraid to interact with American soldiers on the streets for fear of being fingered as informants would open up to them in private. The soldiers gathered basic personal and family information from every household, which enabled Crider's staff to map out the demographic realities of Dora. "We found that it was a tremendous source of intelligence that gave us an in-depth understanding of how people felt," Crider wrote. "We came to understand that AQI was supported only by a small minority of the population, and that most people desperately wanted things to improve. We discovered issues around which we could build an alliance based on a relationship of trust and respect. We could shape our talking points, information operations, and psychological operations to have the effect we wanted because we knew our target audience well."[31] In the first five weeks of the operation in Dora, Crider's unit developed thirty-six informants; as a result, by the fourth month the detention of insurgent operatives in Dora had increased fivefold.[32]

Even with census data, identifying individuals at checkpoints was a challenging task. There was no reliable national identification card, and such identification cards as existed were easily forged. To solve this problem, over the course of the surge Multi-National Corps–Iraq introduced biometric identity screening devices into Iraq. The Biometric Automated Toolset (BAT) is a laptop computer with identification processing software and associated devices that could scan a person's iris or read his or her fingerprints. The Hand-Held Interagency Identity Detection Equipment (HIIDE), fielded at the commencement of the surge in 2007, is a smaller, more portable biometric collection and matching device. Soldiers would collect biometric data during the normal course of operations; in addition, all local citizens who worked on coalition bases would be enrolled in the biometric identity program. Both devices compared biometric data to that stored in a central database. The systems flagged persons of interest. For instance, U.S. investigators entered into the database fingerprints lifted from unexploded roadside bombs; by the end of the surge, U.S. forces had detained more than seventeen hundred Iraqis for fingerprint matches linked to the planting of these devices.[33] As the database grew to more than 1.5 million identity markers, the increase in positive matches was dramatic and important, and helped enormously with detainee review and legal cases.[34] Nevertheless, the system was not perfect. The lack of defined standards and integration of the various systems under development hampered their overall effectiveness. Additionally, the question of whether to turn over the biometric database to the Iraqi government upon the eventual departure of U.S. forces from Iraq was an issue of some concern. Despite the manifest success of the program, biometric identity devices were at best a partial technological solution to lifting the veil of insurgent anonymity as they attempted to blend in with the local population.

The provision of three additional brigades to combat al-Qaeda in the Baghdad belts required the readjustment of unit boundaries, provision of more "enablers," such as aviation and engineer units, and the creation of a new multinational division headquarters to control operations south of Baghdad. Multi-National Division–Center (MND-C) was activated on April 1, 2007, under the command of Major General Rick Lynch, commander of the 3rd Infantry Division. Until this moment the area had fallen under the loose control of Multi-National Division–Baghdad (MND-B), then commanded by Major General Joe Fil of the 1st Cavalry Division. With eight brigades under his command, Fil's span of control was too large. The activation of MND-C would alleviate this problem and bring greater concentration of effort to eliminating terrorist and militia sanctuaries south of Baghdad in the so-called triangle of death.[35]

As U.S. forces adjusted their operations and command structure in Iraq, the Iraqi government created a new headquarters to control operations in Baghdad. Under Iraqi Lieutenant General Aboud Qanbar, the Baghdad Operations Command (BOC) was in charge of all Iraqi security forces in Baghdad as of March 1. The Iraqis divided the city into two area commands, Karkh on the west side of the Tigris and Rusafa on the east side of the river. The city was further subdivided into ten security districts, with an Iraqi brigade assigned to each one.[36] As part of the surge the Iraqi government had promised to reinforce the Baghdad command with three additional brigades—two from the Kurdish region and one from al-

Anbar province. Tracking the movement of these units into Baghdad created a bit of consternation, as various politicians and pundits in the United States accused the Iraqi government of reneging on its end of the deal. Although understrength, the brigades came to Baghdad.

General Aboud was Prime Minister Nouri al-Maliki's preference to command Iraqi forces in Baghdad, and he turned out to be an excellent choice. Aboud, a Shi'ite, had nevertheless risen to the rank of brigadier general in Saddam's military with service in the Iran-Iraq War and the Gulf War. He was cashiered for all intents and purposes when he refused to attack fellow Iraqis after the Shi'a uprising in 1991. Aboud came from Maliki's tribe and was therefore trusted by the Iraqi prime minister. He worked well with Lieutenant General Odierno and Major General Fil. He was also a good leader, and could be seen out and about Baghdad each day inspecting his soldiers and leading from the front. Colonel Bob Newman, an Arabic-speaking foreign area officer, served as his U.S. adviser and produced valuable reports on the ongoing affairs at the highest levels of the Iraqi command in Baghdad.

A more problematic development was Maliki's creation of the Office of the Commander-in-Chief, or OCINC. This small staff element, led by Iraqi Lieutenant General Farouk al-Araji and Dr. Bassima al-Jaidri, circumvented the established chain of command and provided Maliki a direct means to influence appointments, promotions, and even the targeting of suspected insurgents and terrorists. Concerned American officials believed OCINC served as a secret coordinating mechanism for the sectarian cleansing of the Iraqi security forces, and that some of the targets passed from OCINC were aimed more at Maliki's political opponents than at enemies of the state—although the two might have been intermingled in the mind of the Iraqi prime minister.[37] General Petraeus, in his usual way, did not confront Maliki directly regarding this issue. Rather, he arranged a luncheon with Lieutenant General Farouk and Dr. Bassima (who he later described as "an impressive and capable figure who stands out in what often is a sea of governmental mediocrity") and persuaded them to accept an American liaison officer onto their staff.[38] General Petraeus would bring up specific issues in his weekly meetings with Prime Minister Maliki, including suspicious personnel moves in the Iraqi armed forces that smacked of sectarianism. In this way he tried to bring a measure of transparency to the administration of the Iraqi security forces, as well as serving notice that we were watching the machinations of the Iraqi government to keep the cancer of sectarianism from spreading.

Politics in Iraq were largely frozen as a result of the ethnosectarian violence ripping the country apart. The night he took command, General Petraeus was invited to dinner at the residence of the U.S. ambassador, Zalmay Khalilzad. While there he witnessed a stand-up, face-to-face confrontation between the Iraqi minister of defense, Abdul Qadir, and the speaker of the Council of Representatives, Mahmoud Mashadani. Both were Sunni, but Mashadani accused Abdul Qadir of for-saking his coreligionists by not doing enough to protect them in his current posi-tion.[39] Mashadani and many other Sunni politicians, such as Vice President Tariq al-Hashemi, were upset that the Iraqi government had marginalized Sunni Arabs, who felt they had gotten nothing for joining the government except blame from other Sunnis for the sectarian violence sweeping the country. General Petraeus was stunned at the exchange, that two such senior leaders would nearly come to blows at his welcome dinner, and he was a bit taken aback by the fact that many Sunni politicians viewed the insurgency as principled resistance that was uphold-ing Sunni honor.

Shi'a Iraqi political leaders, on the other hand, were obsessed with issues of sovereignty—perhaps in part because they were so unused to wielding power that they were concerned about appearing weak to their people. They were also jus-tifiably worried about the tenuous foundation of the Iraqi government. An offer by the government of Georgia to send an infantry brigade to Iraq, for instance, was nearly rejected because Iraqi leaders were concerned the reinforcement would lead people to believe that the Iraqi government could not handle its problems by itself.[40] Shortly after General Petraeus took command, the Iraqi national security adviser, Dr. Mowaffak al-Rubaie, presented him and Ambassador Khalilzad with a list of demands that included accelerated transition of responsibilities to Iraqi Security Forces and what amounted to an Iraqi government veto on U.S. mili-tary operations, something that senior Iraqi government leaders believed had been agreed upon when President Bush and Maliki had met in Amman. General Petraeus was stunned at the audacity of the request and by the lack of understand-ing of reality that it conveyed. He responded that if the Iraqi government truly wanted the list of demands met, then Prime Minister Maliki should lay them out for President Bush in their next weekly video teleconference—but that General Petraeus would be on the next plane headed back for the United States after the video teleconference was over. That was the last he heard of those demands until the negotiations at the end of the year to renew the United Nations Security Coun-cil Resolution authorizing continued coalition military operations in Iraq. By that time, thankfully, the security situation had changed drastically, the focus on transition had resumed, and General Petraeus was actively consulting with Prime Minister Maliki on the conduct of sensitive operations, such as those in Sadr City, a sprawling Shi'a section of eastern Baghdad.

On the other hand, one could sympathize with Prime Minister Maliki's annoy-ance with the clunky notification procedures when Iraqi special operations forces were used to target Sunni and Shi'a extremists. In the early weeks of the surge, notification consisted of the MNF-I operations section calling me in the wee hours of the morning. I would in turn call Sadi Othman, who would then notify one of the prime minister's staff assistants. By this time cell phones were already ring-ing in the prime minister's office as various political actors complained about the impact of the raids. This convoluted system was a poor way to inform a government that its citizens were being targeted for capture or death. Within a few weeks General Petraeus placed a liaison cell at the prime minister's office, and gave it the responsibility of informing the prime minister's staff of pending operations—which among other accomplishments made me less sleep-deprived. Ambassador Khalilzad and General Petraeus spent a great deal of their time assuaging Iraqi concerns about issues of sovereignty, as well as emphasizing to elected American officials the need to respect Iraqi sensitivities in this regard.

The lack of managerial capability and strategic sense in Iraqi leaders also became readily apparent early on. Iraqi governmental meetings often wandered aimlessly, with officials delving into the tactical details of various issues, rather than focusing on the big picture and crafting guidance to steer governmental ministries in the chosen direction. In this regard dealing with the Iraqi government was often a frustrating experience. To alleviate the problems generated by the lack of Iraqi managerial experience, General Petraeus placed senior U.S. military officers with key Iraqi governmental officials such as Dr. Mowaffak and with Dr. Bassima and Lieutenant General Farouk at OCINC. In time, meetings improved somewhat with the incorporation of written agendas and the circulation of position papers beforehand.

The war raged on in sometimes dramatic fashion in the late winter and spring of 2007. Insurgents successfully downed several helicopters, a disturbing development since our forces were highly dependent on rotary wing transport and gunship support. On January 20 insurgents destroyed a UH-60 Blackhawk helicopter with heavy machine gun fire northeast of Baghdad, killing the twelve crew members and passengers on board, including Colonel (Dr.) Brian Allgood, one of my classmates from the United States Military Academy. Five days later they shot down another Blackhawk near the town of Hit in al-Anbar province, although the passengers and crew survived. On January 28 an Apache gunship was destroyed in fighting near an Najaf; on February 2 insurgents shot down another Apache just north of Baghdad near Taji. Perhaps the most spectacular attack occurred on February 7, when a CH-46 helicopter was destroyed by a surface-to-air missile near the town of Karmah, killing everyone aboard. Insurgents posted video of this attack on the Internet, which General Petraeus viewed during a morning staff update a few days later. Two more Blackhawks were hit and downed February 21–22 north of Baghdad.

These losses, had they continued, would have significantly hampered the war effort in Iraq. Aviation commanders responded by ensuring the operational readiness of antimissile defense equipment on each helicopter, providing more gunship support when possible, and avoiding those areas where insurgent machine guns and shoulder-fired missile teams were most active. These areas happened to be the same insurgent sanctuaries targeted for clearance by our ground operations. As spring wore on and more surge forces arrived in Iraq, the squeeze on insurgent sanctuaries had the beneficial effect of making the skies safer for helicopter transport as well. There were further losses of aircraft ahead, but the loss rate never approached that incurred in the first two months of the year. Although we did not know it at the time, the worst had passed.

As U.S. and Iraqi forces moved into the Baghdad belts, they began to uncover the true extent of the insurgent presence there. In places, the enemy infrastructure was massive and included bomb-making factories, command and control installations, media production rooms, and medical stations. On February 23 U.S. forces uncovered a bomb-making factory to the west of Baghdad near the town of Karmah, an area in which the brigade I commanded earlier in the war had maneuvered to battle insurgents as far back as September 2003.[41] The factory consisted of five separate areas containing numerous munitions, tools, propane tanks, chlorine cylinders, other bomb-making supplies, and numerous vehicles in the process of being outfitted as car bombs.[42] The chlorine cylinders were a new facet of the insurgent arsenal; they were used to make chemical bombs that would blind victims upon detonation. It soon became clear that the process of destroying insurgent sanctuaries in the Baghdad belts would take several months and the arrival of the full complement of surge forces, the last of which would not be in Iraq until June.

By the time the surge began, U.S. and Iraqi Special Operations Forces were hitting their stride. In preceding years they had learned valuable lessons regarding insurgent and terrorist organization and command and control structures. Special operations leaders came to realize that al-Qaeda in Iraq was not a hierarchical organization, but one arranged on the basis of shared experiences and kinship. They now put this knowledge to work. Under the capable leadership of Lieutenant General Stan McChrystal, the Joint Special Operations Task Force reconfigured itself into an agile network that understood how insurgent and terrorist networks operated and could react faster than the enemy when it mattered most.[43] "We had to figure out a way to retain our traditional capabilities of professionalism, technology, and, when needed, overwhelming force, while achieving levels of knowledge, speed, precision, and unity of effort that only a network could provide," McChrystal wrote several years later. "We needed to orchestrate a nuanced, population-centric campaign that comprised the ability to almost instantaneously swing a devastating hammer blow against an infiltrating insurgent force or wield a deft scalpel to capture or kill an enemy leader."[44]

Early in the surge I accompanied General Petraeus on a visit to Lieutenant General McChrystal's headquarters in Balad, and we both came away exceptionally impressed by his operations. Although some aspects remain classified, McChrystal publicly outlined the structure of his headquarters four years later: "The idea was to combine analysts who found the enemy (through intelligence, surveillance, and reconnaissance); drone operators who fixed the target; combat teams who finished the target by capturing or killing him; specialists who exploited the intelligence the raid yielded, such as cell phones, maps, and detainees; and the intelligence analysts who turned this raw information into usable knowledge. By doing this, we speeded up the cycle for a counterterrorism operation, gleaning valuable insights in hours, not days."[45] During our visit, McChrystal emphasized the criticality to his mission of intelligence, surveillance, and reconnaissance assets. Predator unmanned aerial vehicles, especially those armed with Hellfire missiles, were the coin of the realm. Allocation of these scarce assets gripped General Petraeus and, above him, U.S. Central Command and the Pentagon. McChrystal likened the debate to the argument over the allocation of gasoline during the breakout from the Normandy beachhead in the fall of 1944. Affecting his best Pattonesque accent, he quipped, "Give me Predators. I'll gain ground, I'll kill terrorists!" He would soon get his wish. As the surge intensified and more assets were made available (thanks to tremendous support by Secretary Gates for requests by General Petraeus), special operations ramped up accordingly, with the number of daily raids increasing by a factor of ten. Furthermore, the instances of mistaken identities and "dry holes" were reduced as well.[46] Lieutenant General McChrystal and the Joint Special Operations Task Force were firing on all cylinders.

As special operations forces came to see the value of networking, the institutional barriers between conventional and special forces began to slowly erode. Early in the war special operations forces would routinely conduct raids into areas controlled by conventional forces without informing them beforehand. These raids were often frustrating experiences for conventional force commanders, who would be held accountable by the local population for civilian deaths and collateral damage caused by forces outside their control conducting operations without their knowledge. By 2007 coordination between the Joint Special Operations Task Force and Multi-National Corps–Iraq was improving, even though special operations raids were still not fully transparent to those commanders with responsibility for the counterinsurgency campaign on the ground. In those cases where liaison and notification of operations occurred, commanders were better able to judge their effects and manage their consequences in a coordinated fashion.

The disruption of insurgent sanctuaries in the Baghdad belts by conventional operations also proved a boon to special operations forces. Insurgents and terrorists need bases from which to plan and prepare operations and in which to rest and recuperate. They cannot and do not simply exist in cyberspace. By interdicting enemy forces in their base areas, conventional units forced insurgents and terrorists to move and communicate. Both activities provided greater opportunities for Lieutenant General McChyrstal's network to find, target, and kill or capture the enemy. Conventional and special operations commanders came to realize that their forces enjoyed a symbiotic relationship.

Despite the manifest successes of the Joint Special Operations Task Force under Lieutenant General McChrystal's leadership, its operations alone were insufficient to destroy al-Qaeda in Iraq. The regenerative capability of the terrorist organization was simply too great. By the end of 2007 several thousand hardcore operatives had been eliminated from the battlefield, but even this number was insufficient to destroy the organization. The conclusion by some commentators, that the key to reducing violence in Iraq was the use by the Joint Strategic Operations Task Force of highly classified techniques empowered by new technology, is not supported by the record.[47] The capabilities brought to the battlefield by the special operations forces were both impressive and critical, but they were not the main reason for the collapse of the insurgency in 2007–2008. For the primary cause, we must look elsewhere.

Due to the sectarian leanings of the Iraqi government, it was much easier for Multi-National Force–Iraq to conduct operations against Sunni insurgents and terrorists than it was to rein in Shi'a militias. There was some concern that the Iraqi government was indirectly abetting sectarian cleansing by denying resources to Sunni areas. In many Sunni neighborhoods the government put up bureaucratic roadblocks to opening banks, failed to staff health care facilities, and denied essential services such as electricity and trash pickup. Government administrators claimed that the real culprit was not sectarianism but poor security. Sunni insurgents targeted government workers and therefore the latter were reluctant at best to enter Sunni areas. As the surge progressed and security improved, however, these excuses wore thin. The time and energy put into rectifying this situation were out of all proportion to the results achieved.

The Iraqi government also put up roadblocks when it came to targeting the leadership of the Jaish al-Mahdi, the umbrella organization under which most Shi'a militias fought. As the aftermath of the uprisings of 2004 had shown, Muqtada al-Sadr knew how to dodge a punch.[48] Bush's speech announcing the surge had a discernible effect on Sadr and the Jaish al-Mahdi. Convinced that the Americans were out to get him, Sadr went into hiding for four months and encouraged his chief lieutenants to do likewise. He ordered the Mahdi army not to put up armed resistance to the surge, probably because he believed the Shi'ites could outlast any temporary escalation by American forces in Iraq.[49] But the Jaish al-Mahdi was anything but a coherent organization; rather, it was a mosaic of various military groups operating under Sadr's loose mantle of authority. Sadr lacked firm control over the Mahdi army's constituent parts. While the majority of the Jaish al-Mahdi obeyed Sadr's orders and scaled back their activities once the surge began, rogue elements—many under Iranian control—continued their attacks against coalition forces.[50]

The most dangerous Shi'a militias were those beholden to Iran. Known as the Special Groups of the Jaish al-Mahdi, these organizations were armed, trained, equipped, funded, and in some cases directed by the Qods force, a special branch of the Iranian Revolutionary Guards Corps—the vanguard and protector of the religious regime in Tehran.[51] Led by Qassem Suleimani, the Qods force held the Iraq portfolio, including responsibility for foreign relations with Iran's neighbor to the west.[52] Iran's goal was nothing less than to create a client proxy force out of portions of the Jaish al-Mahdi, much as it had formed Hezbollah in Lebanon to do Iranian bidding in that state. Selected operatives were transported across the border from Iraq into Iran to receive training from Qods force instructors.[53] Arms and munitions, particularly the deadly explosively formed penetrators that could destroy an M1A1 tank, were smuggled the other way through loosely guarded border crossings.[54] By late 2006 Qods force personnel were plying their trade inside Iraq itself, a fact that would soon become apparent.

When the surge began, Iran's involvement in Iraq was an open secret, but the intelligence was somewhat murky. Several raids would soon make clear the full extent of Iranian penetration into Iraq. U.S. forces in late December 2006 detained two Qods force officers in a raid on the compound of Islamic Supreme Council of Iraq leader Abdul Aziz al-Hakim in Baghdad—one of whom was the third-highest-ranking official of the Qods force.[55] U.S. forces followed up this success by raiding an Iranian liaison office in Irbil on January 11, capturing five more Qods force operatives.[56] Documentation seized in these two raids began to unravel the mystery of Qods force activities in Iraq.[57] In retaliation for these raids and to gain bargaining chips to negotiate the release of Qods force personnel in U.S. custody, the Qods force designed an operation to capture a group of U.S. soldiers. On January 20, 2007 a well-trained team of special group operatives disguised as coalition soldiers and equipped with U.S. gear entered the Provincial Joint Coordination Center compound in Karbala, where U.S. soldiers were meeting with Iraqi officials. In the ensuing struggle one U.S. soldier was killed and three were wounded, while four others were taken prisoner and removed from the site. The attackers drove into neighboring Babil province and were probably headed to the Iranian border, but Iraqi police began trailing them after noticing suspicious behavior at a checkpoint. At this point the special group operatives panicked, shot the four Americans in cold blood, abandoned their bodies on the side of the road, and made good their escape.[58]

We suspected Qods force involvement in this attack, but could not yet prove it. Then an enormous break in the case occurred when on March 19, British forces in Basra raided a compound and detained several senior Shi'a militia operatives. Included in the haul were Qais Qazali and his brother Laith, leaders of one of the Jaish al-Mahdi special groups.[59] Qazali was a close confidant of Muqtada al-Sadr, but Qazali had formed his own special group, Asaib Ahl al-Haq, when disagreements between the two Shi'a leaders widened.[60] Also among those captured was an enigmatic figure who was soon christened Hamid the Mute by his interrogators, since he claimed to be unable to speak. After several weeks he began to respond to questioning. He turned out to be Ali Mussa Daqduq, a senior Lebanese Hezbollah operative who had a major role in militia training. Daqduq, a twenty-four-year veteran of Hezbollah, at one point commanded Hezbollah leader Hassan Nasrallah's security detail. Senior Hezbollah leaders directed Daqduq to work with the Qods force to train Iraqi special group operatives. In May 2006, he traveled to Tehran with Yussef Hashim, the head of Hezbollah operations in Iraq, where they met with the commander of the Iranian Qods force Special External Operations. Daqduq made four trips into Iraq in 2006 to observe special group operations, then was assigned responsibility for training special group operatives inside Iran in the use of explosively formed penetrators, mortars, rockets, and sniper rifles, and on how to conduct intelligence and kidnapping operations. To keep the special groups operating, the Iranian government provided several million dollars' worth of funding every month.[61]

The intelligence haul from the Basra raid unlocked many of the secrets of Qods force operations in Iraq. Captured documents included accounts of special group attacks against coalition forces in Iraq, including the detailed planning and preparation for the Karbala operation.[62] U.S. reconnaissance assets subsequently identified three training camps in Iran, complete with a full-scale mock-up of the Karbala Provincial Joint Coordination Center.[63] "What we've learned from Ali Musa Daqduq, Qayis Qazali and other Special groups members in our custody expands our understanding of how Iranian Qods Force operatives are training, funding and arming the Iraqi Special Groups," said Multi-National Force–Iraq spokesman Brigadier General Kevin Bergner in a press conference several months later. "It shows how Iranian operatives are using Lebanese surrogates to create Hezbollah-like capabilities."[64]

General Petraeus was of course briefed on the results of the raid immediately after it occurred. I was disgusted by the coldblooded and senseless nature of the Karbala executions and burned with a desire for revenge. I had Heather translate the captured orders to see what we could glean from them. It became immediately clear that they were the work of professionals; the Qods force fingerprints were all over the document and the operation. That potentially placed Qods force commander Qassem Suleimani in the chain of command for the operation, and he reported directly to the Iranian supreme leader, Ayatollah Ali Khamenei. Special group operations, particularly the use of Iranian-supplied explosively formed penetrators, were responsible for the deaths of hundreds of American and British soldiers in Iraq. The revelation of the full involvement of Iran in Iraqi violence was one more brick in an already very heavy rucksack carried by General Petraeus.

The Iranian Revolutionary Guards Corps did not take long to strike back. Four days after the Basra raid, Iranian forces captured at gunpoint fifteen British sailors and marines from the HMS *Cornwall* conducting a routine antismuggling patrol in Iraqi waters.[65] The media could only guess at the motive, but for those of us on the ground the possible link between the British raid in Basra and the abduction of British personnel on the high seas was disturbing.[66]

Some small measure of justice was not long in coming. On May 19 coalition forces killed Azhar al-Dulaimi, one of the leaders of the Qazali network and the mastermind of the Karbala operation, during a raid north of Baghdad.[67] As the spring and summer wore on, Multi-National Force–Iraq and Special Operations forces continued to target the Jaish al-Mahdi special groups, putting great pressure on the Qazali and Sheibani networks in Iraq. Nevertheless, Iranian involvement in Iraq remained a deeply disturbing aspect of the conflict.

Despite the Iraqi government's sectarian leanings, Prime Minister Maliki had promised President Bush in Amman the previous November that he would not discriminate by ethnicity or sect in the targeting of extremists who were tearing Iraq apart.[68] When Fardh al-Qanoon began, the floodgates did not exactly open, but it became somewhat easier to target Shi'a militia leaders as well as Sunni insurgents and terrorists. Military operations began to put a great deal of pressure on the various armed factions in Iraq, which ironically provided an opening to reach out to some of them. The Jaish al-Mahdi and various Sunni organizations began to splinter, which provided opportunities to engage some leaders in talks to end their armed opposition to the coalition and the Iraqi government.

Lieutenant General Graeme Lamb, the Scottish deputy commander of Multi-National Force–Iraq, was instrumental in leading the effort to identify leaders and groups that could be reconciled to the elected government of Iraq. A Sandhurst graduate, Lamb had served in a variety of infantry and special forces assignments since his commissioning in 1973, including a stint as the commander of a squadron in the renowned Special Air Service and later service as the director of U.K. Special Forces (during which time his units worked with a U.S. special mission unit in Bosnia of which then–Brigadier General Petraeus was deputy commander; they also served together as division commanders in 2003 in Iraq; and then later headed training commands in the United States and the United Kingdom as three-star generals). Lamb had several postings in Northern Ireland, where he experienced firsthand the difficulties of overcoming age-old animosities in the search for common ground on which to build a lasting peace. In reference to the Iraq War, Lamb stated to the media as the surge commenced, "It's hard pounding. This is as complex as . . . anything I've ever done. This is really difficult. This is three-dimensional chess in a dark room."[69]

Early on during the surge, Lamb described to General Petraeus scenes from his discussions with leaders of the Irish Republican Army. "He recalled talking to people who only a few days before had been swinging pipes at his lads," General Petraeus told me later. "He said that you don't need to reconcile with people who are on your side. They're already your friends. If you want reconciliation to occur, you need to talk to people with blood on their hands." This realization was a sea change for the way U.S. commanders viewed the war in Iraq (though Petraeus had supported reconciliation initiatives in Mosul in the summer of 2003 and believed it was imperative in 2007, too). Petraeus ordered the creation of a new staff section, the Multi-National Force–Iraq Force Strategic Engagement Cell (FSEC), of approximately thirty officers under the supervision of a general officer from the United Kingdom and a senior Foreign Service officer from the U.S. State Department.[70] The purpose of this organization would be to seek out opportunities to engage Sunni insurgent and Shi'a militia leaders deemed "reconcilable" and work to bring them into accommodation with the Iraqi government. We felt that most Iraqis belonged in this category. Perhaps this was a leap of faith, but it was a necessary one, for General Petraeus understood that, as he said on a number of occasions, "You cannot kill or capture your way out of an insurgency." If the majority of Iraqis were not reconcilable, then we were in serious trouble.

Some insurgent operatives and militia members, perhaps several thousand, fell into another category. These others, including the vast majority of foreign fighters who had flocked to Iraq to engage in an ill-conceived jihad against the United States, were labeled "irreconcilable." They would have to be killed or captured. That was the job of Multi-National Corps–Iraq and the Joint Special Operations Command, working with their respective Iraqi partners. The ultimate outcome of this effort would be to strengthen the voices of those in Iraq willing to fashion a nonviolent outcome to the ethnosectarian struggle in the county. Reconciliation was a generational project, but bringing armed factions in from the cold was a critical first step.

As Fardh al-Qanoon progressed, the pressure on insurgent and militia organizations increased, which helped to sort out the reconcilables from the irreconcilables. Intra-Sunni violence, in particular, would lead to huge defections from insurgent ranks, as many insurgents came to view "honorable resistance" as incompatible with the increasingly horrific acts of al-Qaeda terrorists with a different agenda.[71] Al-Qaeda terrorists, for example, used chlorine gas bombs against Sunni Arabs in al-Anbar province, which mimicked Saddam Hussein's gassing of the Kurds during the al-Anfal campaign in the late-1980s.[72] Al-Qaeda's actions opened up a number of information operations avenues to reach out to moderate Sunni Arabs, and we exploited them for all they were worth.

Reconciliation initiatives and outreach to insurgent and militia organizations would ultimately fail without the buy-in of the Iraq government. Maliki's government was highly suspicious of the motives of insurgent leaders—for good reason. Nevertheless, engagement with key opposition leaders was essential to create a way out of the conflict. The Force Strategic Engagement Cell continually interacted with Iraqi government officials tasked with pursuing reconciliation initiatives. In addition, General Petraeus and Ambassador Ryan Crocker worked tirelessly to convince Prime Minister Maliki that engagement with "reconcilable" elements of insurgent organizations was desirable, and that the basis for any agreements would be the recognition of the elected government of Iraq by all parties. If groups in opposition to the government could be persuaded to embrace the political process as a means of resolving their grievances, then the conflict over the distribution of power and resources could be driven into nonviolent political channels.

Reconciliation entailed not just outreach to groups outside the government but compromise on legislation by groups within the government. There were huge issues confronting Maliki's administration, among them the sharing of oil revenues, the distribution of power between Baghdad and the provinces, the revision of the de-Ba'athification decree, amnesty for reconciled insurgents and militia members, and the distribution of government revenues in the national budget. The pressure to make headway on these issues was intense. President Bush had staked his presidency on the success of the surge, and he was adamant about the need to prod the Iraqi government to action. But none of these issues could be solved easily. We likened the political negotiations on this legislation to American arguments over states' rights, taxation, civil rights, and similar historical controversies—each of which took decades or longer to resolve. Expecting rapid progress on these types of issues, particularly given the violence wracking the country and the dysfunctional nature of the Iraqi government, was unrealistic. Nevertheless, Ambassador Crocker and the U.S. embassy made valiant efforts toward this goal.

The violence had a direct impact on Iraqi lawmakers when on April 12, 2007, a suicide bomber exploded his vest inside the chambers of the Council of Representatives, housed in the Convention Center in the heart of the heavily fortified Green Zone.[73] The blast killed one member of parliament and wounded nearly two dozen other people. The Islamic State of Iraq, the front for al-Qaeda in Iraq, claimed responsibility. Given the extensive security precautions in the Green Zone, investigators suspected that the terrorist had inside help.[74] The blast made the tough work of reconciliation even more difficult; security would have to improve before frightened Iraqi lawmakers could make political progress.

The Council of Representatives was not the only target of suicide bombers. The swath of destruction caused by terrorist attacks was deep and wide. The near daily attacks since our arrival in Iraq in February included bombings in Baghdad, Ramadi, Haditha, Tal Afar, Tikrit, Karbala, Najaf, Habbaniyah, Mosul, Hillah, Balad Ruz, Kirkuk, Iskandariyah, Baquba, Fallujah, Samarra, and Muqdadiya. Many bombings were intended to stoke the fires of sectarian hatred; others were aimed at Sunnis who had thrown in their lot with coalition forces to fight against al-Qaeda. On February 25 a female suicide bomber struck the campus of the largely Shi'a Mustansiriya University in central Baghdad, killing forty-one students.[75] On March 5 a car bomb exploded on Mutanabi Street, an area renowned for its bookstalls and the intellectual heart of Baghdad that dates back to the era when the Abbasid caliphate ruled over the Islamic world. Nearly forty people were killed and more than one hundred wounded in the blast, which scattered books far and wide. Abdul Baqi Faidhullah, a poet who patronized the area, stated correctly, "Those who did this are like savage machines intent on harvesting souls and killing all bright minds."[76] In its heyday Islam had some of the most enlightened intellectuals, mathematicians, and scientists in the world. Ironically, al-Qaeda was bent on quashing the type of secular education that had once made the Islamic world the center of human civilization. Ignorance lay at the heart of al-Qaeda's program of extreme religious indoctrination.

A day after the attack on Mutanabi Street, suicide bombers struck at crowds of Shi'a pilgrims marching toward Karbala to commemorate Arba'een, a Shi'a religious observation that commemorates the martyrdom of Imam Husayn ibn Ali, the grandson of the Prophet Muhammad. Imam Husayn and 72 supporters died in the Battle of Karbala in A.D. 680, killed by an army belonging to the Umayyad Caliph Yazid. The battle effectively marks the start of the Islamic civil war between Sunni and Shi'a that continues to this day. Given its religious and political overtones (the fighting in Karbala was about who would control the Islamic empire), Arba'een celebrations have been the occasion of more than their share of violence.[77] The attacks on March 6, 2007, killed 137 people—nearly twice as many as perished in the seventh-century battle—and wounded more than 300.[78]

The suicide and car bomb attacks were building to a crescendo. In the deadliest single attack during the Iraq War to date, on March 27, two truck bombs exploded in Tal Afar, killing 152 people and wounding nearly 350, mostly poor Shi'ites.[79] Two days later suicide bombers killed more than 100 people in a market in the Sha'ab neighborhood of northeast Baghdad and in an attack on the market in Khalis.[80] The Council of Representatives was struck on April 12, the same day that a suicide truck bomber detonated his explosives on the Sarafiyah Bridge spanning the Tigris River in central Baghdad, sending the historic span and several cars plunging into the river below.[81] On April 14, a suicide car bomber killed 47 people and wounded 224 in an attack on a crowded bus station in Karbala.[82] A day later six bombs exploded in Baghdad, killing another 45 people. On April 18, multiple car bombings killed 191 people around Baghdad, most of them victims of a bomb in the Sadriyah market in central Baghdad.[83] On April 28, a suicide car bomber attacked a crowded security checkpoint outside the Abbas shrine in Karbala, killing 58 people and injuring three times as many.[84] This list does not include dozens of other attacks that collectively killed and injured hundreds of people in the first three months of the surge. Al-Qaeda's brutality knew no bounds; it sacrificed women, children, and mentally ill people in some attacks to disarm the suspicions of security personnel.

This level of carnage could not continue indefinitely without affecting popular support for the war. Political support for the surge, never strong to begin with, wavered both in the United States and in Iraq. Four days after the attack on the Council of Representatives, six Sadrist ministers (including the ministers of health, agriculture, and transportation), acting on the orders of Muqtada al-Sadr, quit the government.[85] Sadrists were upset at the continuing terrorist and insurgent provocations that were slaughtering Shi'a innocents (while not acknowledging that Jaish al-Mahdi death squads and other activities were part of the problem), and berated Prime Minister Maliki for his refusal to establish a timeline for the withdrawal of U.S. forces from Iraq. The political move made clear the fissures within the United Iraqi Alliance, the umbrella organization under which the Shi'ites had come to power in the January 2006 elections. Despite the withdrawal of the ministers from the cabinet, the thirty Sadrist representatives kept their seats in the parliament rather than boycott as they had done late the previous year. Maliki's government was slightly weakened but survived the challenge.

The Sadrist move was a serious miscalculation and ultimately proved to be one of the most important political events of 2007 in Iraq. By removing their support for Maliki, the Sadrists energized his natural instinct of political self-preservation, fed by his conspiratorial nature. If the Sadrists were not with him, then they must be against him. The result of this thinking led to Maliki's increased support for operations against Jaish al-Mahdi and special group leaders.[86] More important, it contributed the following year to Iraqi military operations against the Jaish al-Mahdi in Basra, Sadr City, and Amarah that proved decisive in solidifying the gains made by U.S. and Iraqi forces during the surge.[87]

The reaction in the United States to the continuing bloodshed was also severe. At a press conference on April 19, Senate Majority Leader Harry Reid stated, "I believe myself that the secretary of state, secretary of defense and—you have to make your own decisions as to what the president knows—(know) this war is lost and the surge is not accomplishing anything as indicated by the extreme violence in Iraq yesterday."[88] In his memoirs, President George W. Bush writes that Reid's statement "was one of the most irresponsible acts I witnessed in my eight years in Washington."[89] To those of us on the ground in Iraq doing our best to ensure the success of the surge, the pronouncement of doom and gloom from one of our nation's top lawmakers was disheartening. The fact is that when Senator Reid made this comment, the fourth surge brigade had just begun its operations on the ground in Iraq. The final surge units would not be in place until mid-June. Multi-National Corps–Iraq was conducting operations to shape the battlefield for the decisive operations that would begin in the summer. While ethnosectarian violence, Iraqi deaths, and U.S. casualties were still at high levels (in fact, the monthly rate of U.S. casualties was at its highest level of the entire war in the spring of 2007), saying that the surge had failed before it had even been given a chance to succeed showed U.S. domestic politics at their worst. America deserved better from its politicians.

General Petraeus arrived in Washington less than a week later to present classified testimony to the House and Senate. As usual, I sat directly behind him as he discussed the situation in Iraq with U.S. lawmakers. Although they were respectful to him in the closed sessions away from the glare of TV cameras and reporters, it was clear that many lawmakers, like Senator Reid, had already made up their minds concerning the fate of the U.S. war effort in Iraq. It was somewhat amusing to hear a few of the congressmen and senators give what amounted to stump speeches for or against the war, until reminded by their peers that there were no reporters present. Congress demanded another update in September—this one to be broadcast to the nation and the world. We had four months to make the surge work; otherwise, the veiled threat was that Congress would pull the plug on war funding.

After the hearings Everett Spain, Steve Boylan, and I flew back to Fort Leavenworth to spend a weekend at home with our families.[90] The break was wonderful, if all too brief. We were soon reunited with General Petraeus, and after spending a couple of days in Tampa at a U.S. Central Command coalition conference, we headed back to Iraq, steeling ourselves for the long, hot summer ahead.

CHAPTER 4

Tower 57

Irregular war is far more intellectual than a bayonet charge.
—T. E. Lawrence

In the summer of 2006, Sunni insurgents destroyed Tower 57—a large structure south of Baghdad that supported high voltage lines that transmitted electricity from the southern part of the country to the Iraqi capital. In the early days of the war, such vandalism had an economic purpose—criminals would strip electrical lines for their copper, which they would then sell on the black market. At this stage of the conflict, there was strategic design behind the attacks on the Iraqi electrical grid. Survey after survey indicated that aside from security, electricity was the most important service desired by the Iraqi people. The collapse of the Ba'athist regime had lifted most import restrictions, with the result that Iraq was flooded with air conditioners, television sets, refrigerators, and other consumer goods—all of which required electricity to run. In the battle for legitimacy, the insurgents rightly calculated that destroying the Iraqi electrical grid would further discredit the already tarnished reputation of the Iraqi government.

The importance of electricity was not lost on the commanders and staff of Multi-National Force–Iraq. General Petraeus and Ambassador Crocker focused on electricity as one of a number of essential services that would have to be improved in order to enhance the legitimacy of the Iraqi government. In this regard, the repair of Tower 57 was just another of thousands of tasks that would have to be performed as part of counterinsurgency operations during the surge. None of these tasks would be easy, but few turned out to be quite as difficult as the restoration of this particular structure to functioning condition. During the eight-month saga of its repair, Tower 57 became a metaphor for the progress of the surge. The process by which General Petraeus monitored the tower's repair also shows how he conducted himself as a leader and manager to inspire, persuade, and prod his subordinates to achieve their assigned missions.

One of the few tangible products that my predecessor left me was a copy of the "battle rhythm" used by General Casey to organize his work week. It was a twelve- to fourteen–hour-a-day, seven-days-a-week schedule that left little time for the more mundane aspects of daily life, such as crunching through a couple hundred e-mail messages, eating, or sleeping. I showed the battle rhythm to General Petraeus and recommended that we pare it back, but he decided that we would follow the schedule to the letter until we had completed a complete cycle or two before making any adjustments.

General Petraeus would wake up at 5 A.M. and soon be on the stationary bicycle or treadmill for a light workout. He would read a large binder of intelligence assessments and process e-mail while eating breakfast in his room. He would then drive into headquarters for the 7:30 A.M. battlefield update and assessment, or BUA in military terminology. The BUA was a large conference that included representatives from all the various staff sections and commands in Iraq, most of them participating via video-teleconference. Six days a week, General Petraeus would preside over the meeting from the Multi-National Force–Iraq headquarters in the al-Faw palace at Camp Victory, a sprawling coalition military base near Baghdad International Airport. On Thursdays we would fly via helicopter to the Green Zone, where General Petraeus would convene the BUA from the Republican Palace. The latter location would allow some of the U.S. embassy staff to participate in the BUA, which on this day of the week would focus largely on such nonsecurity matters as oil production, electricity, agriculture, and other governmental functions for which the U.S. embassy had the lead. Despite this division of labor, MNF-I, with its enormous capacity, assisted in efforts to improve these areas, which therefore came under the purview, if not outright control, of General Petraeus. He and Crocker created interagency fusion cells to deal with big issues of governance and economics, such as oil exports and electrical power. Four years into the conflict, the U.S. embassy and Multi-National Force–Iraq had finally integrated the nonkinetic lines of operation at the strategic level.[1]

The BUA would begin with staff updates on the events of the past twenty-four hours, including narrative and statistical summaries of insurgent and terrorist attacks, media coverage of events in Iraq, logistical statuses, progress (or lack thereof) of key pieces of Iraqi legislation, the organization and training of Iraqi security forces, the status of spraying Iraq's date palm trees with insecticide, and dozens of other topics displayed via ubiquitous PowerPoint slides on large video screens to an audience of dozens of staff members and others positioned behind desks in theater-style seating. The BUA would be broadcast via a secure communications link accessible by anyone with access to a SIPRNET (the military's secure communications network) terminal; subordinate commands such as Multi-National Corps–Iraq and Multi-National Security Transition Command–Iraq would link in via secure video teleconference. The Iraq War being the hottest topic in U.S. foreign policy in 2007, thousands of people, scattered across the globe from Iraq to Europe to Tampa to Washington, D.C., viewed the BUA each day. Since the audience was so vast and there were a number of topics that required handling with greater discretion, after the BUA General Petraeus would convene a small-group session with perhaps two dozen of his subordinate commanders and principal staff officers, along with Iraqi General Nasir Abadi, the vice chief of staff of the Iraqi Joint Forces. Bill Rapp and I would attend these small-group sessions, but even we would be excluded from the "small small group" sessions that sometimes ensued, in which General Petraeus would discuss the most sensitive matters with Lieutenant General Graeme Lamb, Lieutenant General Ray Odierno, and occasionally one or two others.

General Petraeus was an information sponge; he could quickly digest the contents of a slide while listening to the narrative commentary delivered by a field grade officer. But he understood implicitly that absorption of data did not equal understanding. Multi-National Force–Iraq had created dozens of metrics before the surge, but not all of them were useful or equal in importance. General Petraeus focused on the most important issues, particularly the rate of ethnosectarian violence that was ripping Iraq apart. He would weigh in with guidance as various topics were discussed. In some cases, the discussion would reveal the need for more information, which he would then assign to the appropriate agency in the form of a new slide. PowerPoint slides were tools to allow General Petraeus to drill down into issues, emphasize priorities, and impart guidance. This was his primary way of monitoring the broader issues affecting the command.

For example, in the spring and summer of 2007 the issue of troop requests became a critical concern. Although the president had approved the major troop reinforcements for the surge, these forces required a large number of "enablers" to support their operations—helicopters, military police, engineers, civil affairs, psychological operations, transportation, and other resources were all required to get the most bang for the buck out of the additional ground combat forces. Admiral William J. "Fox" Fallon, the new commander of U.S. Central Command, held a different view. A tepid supporter of the surge strategy, Fallon wanted to reduce the overall number of U.S. forces in Iraq. Starting in the spring of 2007, he put the brakes on further requests for forces, or RFFs. Whether it was a two thousand–soldier aviation brigade or a fifteen-soldier dog-handler detachment, Fallon personally reviewed every RFF and clogged the bureaucratic channels with queries for further information on why this particular unit was essential to the mission in Iraq.[2] Asking for more information is a typical way to stifle requests; consumed with work, it soon becomes easier for a staff to give in than to fight back. With his "snowflakes," Secretary of Defense Donald Rumsfeld was a master of the tactic.

Once General Petraeus discovered that his troop requests were being stone-walled, he monitored the progress of each RFF via a BUA slide, and became in essence the principal action officer to ensure their fulfillment. If Admiral Fallon or anyone else up the chain of command wanted to deny additional forces for the war in Iraq, fine. But in that case General Petraeus wanted it known publicly and at the White House that he was being denied the forces that he believed were essential for the accomplishment of the mission. The issue was too important to be swept under the rug; in the end, General Petraeus got the forces he requested.

Besides the BUA slides, e-mail was another major medium for the exchange of information on which General Petraeus relied heavily. He preferred e-mail to phone conversations because it was quicker, could engage multiple recipients at once, and left a written record of the exchange that could be archived for future reference. General Petraeus also used e-mail to flatten the organization. He would accept messages from anyone with something valuable to say—even occasionally from a soldier or a noncommissioned officer in the ranks. He would also cultivate bright officers who held important positions throughout the command, such as Lieutenant Colonel Doug Ollivant, the chief of plans for the Baghdad-based 1st Cavalry Division.[3] This small number of trusted, back-channel confidants acted as a feedback mechanism and enabled General Petraeus to get a feel for the thinking at lower echelons. When he retired to his quarters for the evening—a bedroom in a villa across the lake from the MNF-I headquarters that had previously be-longed to Saddam Hussein's mother—he would continue to send and receive e-mails well into the evening until he had cleared the inbox queue. (One of his pieces of advice to me is that I do the same—if not, the unread messages would still be there in the morning, along with dozens of new ones.) Upon rising in the morning, he would immediately go back to the computer and continue his myriad electronic discussions—right up until the BUA began at 7:30 A.M. sharp in the headquarters across the lake.

The "house," as we called the sizable four-bedroom villa where General Petraeus and a few selected members of his team lived, was a typical Ba'athist dwelling—gaudy and overdone with marble floors and twenty-foot-high ceilings. The entry opened into an expansive foyer. To the right were a large kitchen and two bed-rooms, which were occupied by Chief Warrant Officer 3 Tom Lebrun, the com-manding general's personal security officer; Master Sergeant Mike Waller, the commanding general's enlisted aide; Sergeant John Wilson, the commanding gen-eral's driver; and two members of the communications team, who were there to ensure that the phones and Internet in the house worked without interruption. To the left of the foyer was a room filled with exercise equipment and weights for physical training, and beyond that, the commanding general's bedroom and next to it the bedroom shared by Major Everett Spain ("Aide-Man") and me. General

Petraeus had a complete office suite in his bedroom with secure and unclassified Internet, a bank of phones, and video-teleconferencing capability, along with a bed, living area with satellite television, and an attached bathroom. Everett and I had a similar setup, with the exception of a row of wall lockers that divided the room to give us each a bit of personal space. I decorated my desk area with Ohio State Buckeyes and Kansas Jayhawks flags to give it a personal touch.[4] Beyond the foyer to the rear of the house were a great room and a large dining room, complete with a huge table that could seat fourteen people.

The house had remained untouched by the looting that had gripped Baghdad in the spring of 2003. The great room and dining areas were furnished in the original, horribly kitschy, faux French baroque style, dominated by large chandeliers and a color scheme infused with pink, turquoise, and gold. In the corner sat an unused 1960s-era console television, which made for a great conversation piece when compared with the ubiquitous LCD screens brought into Iraq by American forces. To the rear of the house was a large cement patio which we furnished with picnic tables and lawn furniture. General Petraeus would entertain VIP parties and visiting dignitaries in the dining room and would host occasional gatherings on the patio for larger groups. Some of my fondest memories from Iraq were of the get-togethers on the patio with the commanding general's personal staff and members of his security detail. We would eat barbequed meat, drink near beer and sodas, and share cigars while hitting golf balls into the lake or throwing bread to the fish, which grew to enormous size and swarmed like piranhas whenever fed.

Captain Hanna Mora and Captain Kelly Howard lived in a small building across the driveway from the main house, while the military police platoon that served as the commanding general's personal security detachment lived in a building fifty yards down the street. Despite the odd nature of the villa, it became home to us. At the end of each day General Petraeus would declaim the awaited and welcome words, "To the house!" We would then travel by SUV or helicopter back to the lakefront villa, where Master Sergeant Waller would have dinner waiting for us. General Petraeus, Everett, and I would then settle into an evening of e-mail and reading at our desks. General Petraeus would always check in before retiring for the night, hand me a pile of finished written correspondence and work, then bid Everett and me goodnight. He would then usually read a few minutes before going to sleep.

Despite long days and limited time, General Petraeus managed to read a number of books in Iraq, among them Bruce Catton's *Grant Takes Command,* Josiah Bunting's biography of Grant, and Doris Kearns Goodwin's *Team of Rivals.* He focused his study on how other military leaders such as Ulysses S. Grant (Civil War), William Slim (Burma campaign in World War II), and Matthew Ridgway (Korean War) took command in trying times and turned around flagging war efforts. His dedication to reading, even while deployed, puts him in sharp contrast with his Vietnam War counterpart, General William Westmoreland. Westmoreland, the commander of Military Assistance Command–Vietnam from 1964 to 1968, wrote in his memoir that beside his bed in his quarters in Saigon he kept, among other items, "several books: a bible; a French Grammar; Mao Tse-tung's little red book on guerrilla warfare; *The Centurions,* a novel about the French fight with the Vietminh; and several works by Dr. Bernard Fall, who wrote authoritatively on the French experience in Indochina . . . [but] I was usually too tired in late evening to give the books more than occasional attention."[5] We can take Westmoreland at his word, for *The Centurions,* after its first chapters, is about the French war in Algeria, not Vietnam, and had he read any of Bernard Fall's books about the French experience in Indochina, Westmoreland would have tempered the rosy pronouncements coming out of his headquarters in Saigon during his tenure as MAC-V commander. Unlike Westmoreland, General Petraeus was a military intellectual.

I protected General Petraeus's sleep religiously. Senior staff members understood that if they wanted to speak with him after 10 P.M., they should call me first. We would discuss the issue of concern and then decide whether it could wait until morning. I would wake General Petraeus only if the issue was urgent, if he needed to make an immediate decision concerning it, or if he was likely to receive a phone call from one of his superiors or from the Iraqi prime minister before morning. I often discussed these issues with the exceptional Multi-National Force–Iraq chiefs of staff, Marine Major General Thomas "Tango" Moore and Marine Major General John "Jay" Paxton. We would often decide to wait on the news, or encapsulate it into an e-mail that General Petraeus would see upon rising in the morning. In the entire fifteen months I was with him in Iraq, I woke General Petraeus up fewer than a half-dozen times, although he did get occasional direct calls from superiors in Washington in the middle of the night, often when they forgot the eight-hour time difference between the East Coast of the United States and Baghdad.

General Petraeus's extensive use of e-mail initially posed a serious problem for Everett and me. Because the previous command team was less reliant on e-mail than we were, the bedroom we shared had only one computer in it when we arrived. This arrangement was woefully inadequate; we could not go an entire evening sharing a single computer to look at our e-mail, and if one of us went back to the headquarters building to use another computer, he would be unavailable if General Petraeus needed to see us. The communications team quickly upgraded our systems so that General Petraeus, Everett, and I each had three computers on our desks—one for secret traffic, one for unclassified traffic, and one for coalition traffic (which was carried over a separate system from the SIPRNET). Our outstanding communications officer, Navy Lieutenant Dennis Holden, ensured that our offices in the MNF-I headquarters at Camp Victory, the U.S. embassy annex in the Green Zone, and the commanding general's quarters were identically equipped, so that we could leave one location and arrive at another with our computer screens displaying identical images. Beyond that, the communications team maintained three laptop computers for General Petraeus to work on while on lengthy flights or drives. Soon we were communicating at light speed.

General Petraeus and I both received and sent hundreds of e-mails each day on topics big and small. I was often included on the carbon copy line in e-mails sent by others to him. Since I was closer to the commanding general than anyone else in theater, many senior staff officers used me as a sounding board for ideas or to inquire what he was thinking on a given issue. General Petraeus and I worked out a system whereby when I replied to the more important messages, I would put him on the blind carbon copy line. Through this method he could stay informed of what was on the minds of the senior staff and my replies to them, stay silent if he wished, or weigh in with his thoughts as necessary. Often General Petraeus would validate my advice and amplify it with additional emphasis or guidance. The staff appreciated the feedback, which kept them from guessing about what the boss wanted. I was careful not to overstep my boundaries when answering these queries, but once again the white lines were painted fairly wide. The system, which took some of the e-mail burden off of the commanding general, was both effective and efficient.

Curiously, the general and flag officers of MNF-I often accepted my advice more readily than did some of my peers. On February 23 a U.S. Special Forces team detained Amar al-Hakim on his way back into Iraq after a visit to Tehran. Amar was the son of Abdul Aziz al-Hakim, the influential leader of the Islamic Supreme Council of Iraq, a Shi'a political party that had begun its existence as the Supreme Council for the Islamic Revolution in Iraq (SCIRI), a group founded during the Iran-Iraq War to topple Saddam Hussein and install a theocratic government in Baghdad. After the U.S. invasion in 2003, the Supreme Council folded its armed militia, the Badr Corps, into the Iraqi security forces, while supporting the creation of a representative government in Baghdad. Some analysts suspected that the party was beholden to Iranian interests and that the Badr Corps was alive and well in the guise of the Iraqi security forces, but the Supreme Council proved cooperative in the U.S. administration of post-Ba'athist Iraq. What was clear was that the Hakim family was one of the most prominent in the Iraqi Shi'a community and a force to be reckoned with; to detain the son of its patriarch was no small matter. Crowds in various parts of Iraq were already gathering to protest the incident as party spokesmen denounced the apprehension of such a notable figure in Shi'a political life.[6]

The phones were soon ringing off the hook as various Iraqi government officials demanded to know what was going on. Information slowly trickled in. The Special Forces team had acted on its own initiative to seize weapons that they believed were being smuggled by the convoy into Iraq. Even if there were illegal weapons in the convoy, the detention of Amar al-Hakim showed a serious lack of political and strategic awareness. The political support of the Supreme Council was much more important than the seizure of a small weapons cache that in any event would soon be replaced across the leaky Iran-Iraq border. After consulting with General Petraeus, I called the colonel in charge of the Special Forces team, which had taken Amar al-Hakim to a coalition military base in Kut.

"You need to release Hakim and the other detainees now," I told the colonel on the other end of the satellite phone.

"Why? They're smuggling weapons into Iraq."

"Doesn't matter. It's not worth the political shit storm this is causing."

"You don't understand who these people are. They're Iranian proxies."

"Perhaps, but that is also irrelevant. Right now what matters are the politics in Baghdad."

"I'm not going to release them."

"Listen," I tried one last time. "You can either accept my word that you need to release Hakim, or you can hear it from General Petraeus. Either way, the answer will be the same."

"Then let me talk to General Petraeus."

The resulting conversation wasn't pretty. General Petraeus, already a bit peeved at dealing with this unexpected issue, picked up the phone. He didn't give the colonel time to breathe. "Pick up your dog tags out of the dirt," he began in an unusually stern voice. After pausing for effect, General Petraeus allowed the colonel to have his say, but in the end the answer remained the same. We were operating from the same script.

I worked closely with Major General Tango Moore and then his successor, Major General Jay Paxton. As MNF-I chiefs of staff, they had an enormous and difficult job—to orchestrate the activities of hundreds of staff officers spread over several different buildings in Camp Victory and the Green Zone. I kept them informed of Gen. Petraeus's schedule and his information needs, while they would feed staff studies and other documents through me to him. I was impressed by their professionalism and, despite the pressure under which they worked, their positive demeanor. One of our first collaborative efforts was to adjust the battle rhythm to something more sustainable over the long run.

I began the process of adjusting the battle rhythm a couple weeks into the deployment, after we had gone through two iterations of the weekly cycle. The grueling days were wearing on me, and although he would never admit it, they were wearing on General Petraeus as well. He never projected anything less than an optimistic countenance—"setting the right tone," as he called it—but the combination of long days and bad news was grinding him down. The schedule was too full and left too little time for sleep or reflective thought; General Petraeus was getting perhaps six hours of sleep a night, and I was sinking fast on just four to five hours of sleep. There was no time for physical training, an essential activity for reducing stress and maintaining health and stamina, given that our activities were largely office-bound. The schedule was simply unsustainable.[7] I approached General Petraeus in his office. "Sir, I'd like your permission to relook the battle rhythm. You're not getting enough sleep to remain effective over the long haul, and at the present pace I'll be dead in a couple of months." I gave a nervous chuckle and continued, "I'd like to take a scalpel to the schedule, but let me give you some options, at the very least."

"No promises, Pete. Let's see what you come up with."

I went back to my desk outside his office and went to work. Rather than a scalpel, I took out a meat cleaver. Out went the weekly meeting with correspondents; General Petraeus would instead meet with reporters individually as time permitted. I axed various visits to synchronization cells at the Multi-National Division–Baghdad headquarters. Although visiting these organizations once or twice was important, it was not critical to have weekly meetings with them. Meetings with some staff sections were shortened; others were canceled and replaced with e-mail updates that were more efficient. At Prime Minster Maliki's request, we moved his weekly meeting from the evening to midday; we also consolidated it with the U.S. ambassador's meeting with him. It did not make sense to General Petraeus (or, for that matter, to Ambassador Crocker) that the ambassador and he had separate meetings with the Iraqi prime minister; by combining their meetings, they would speak with one voice while reducing the demands on the prime minister's time. The result of all this shuffling and cutting was to save twelve hours in the week. No routinely scheduled appointment went past 6:30 P.M., which cleared the evenings for e-mail, phone calls, reading, and rest. General Petraeus would normally end up getting nearly seven hours of sleep each night, which was sustainable over the long haul.

There were additions to the schedule as well. Twice a week I blocked out time for General Petraeus to visit units in the field. I also cleared a couple hours out of each Tuesday afternoon and Friday morning for physical training. Running outdoors was particularly grueling in the heat of the Middle Eastern summer, but General Petraeus thrived on it. I had initially meant for the Tuesday afternoon runs to cease once the summer furnace cranked up, but General Petraeus would have none of it. He continued the runs year-round. One memorable session in August 2007 clocked in at a balmy 122 degrees Fahrenheit, with 55 percent humidity; another session on a Sunday morning in December was conducted in the first snowfall in Baghdad in more than a century. I would carry a pair of two-liter bottles of water in my hands at the start of each Tuesday afternoon run; by the finish, they would either be drunk or poured over my shirt, which ended up dry as a bone anyway. General Petraeus, Major Spain, Captain Kelly Howard (and later her replacement, Captain Haley Dennison), his security detail, and other assorted gazelles and gluttons for punishment would routinely run six miles. Given my bad back I ran four miles along a different route, nevertheless finishing just in front of the fleet General Petraeus. Upon my departure from Iraq I proudly listed as one of my accomplishments the fact that I beat the commanding general on every Tuesday afternoon run by cutting two miles off the course.

General Petraeus fine-tuned the schedule, but largely accepted my suggestions. The *coup de grâce* came a couple of weeks later. We were sitting in the Saturday morning BUA on February 24 when Tango Moore announced that the next day would be the monthly "no BUA Sunday." General Petraeus glanced quickly in my direction, and I shrugged. Major General Moore, seeing General Petraeus's puzzled expression, explained that the MNF-I staff was given the last Sunday of every month off for rest, with the first meeting to begin no later than noon. It was yet another small detail that my predecessor had not passed on to me. After the meeting broke up, General Petraeus predictably told me to add a physical training session to his calendar the next morning. He got up to run at 6:00 A.M., ate breakfast, showered, checked his e-mail, and then rested before beginning the day's meetings. The effect on his demeanor was electric; you could just see him rejuvenate after a good run and some rest. That day gave me an idea. Why limit the no-BUA Sunday to just once a month? I teamed up with Tango Moore to approach General Petraeus with a proposal to eliminate the BUA on Sunday every other week. We must have hit him up in a weak moment, for he concurred, provided the staff continued to produce the BUA slides and the electronic brief was waiting on his computer by 7:30 A.M. A couple of weeks later, pressing our luck, the chief of staff and I proposed that the BUA be eliminated every Sunday. General Petraeus grumbled a bit, perhaps for effect, but ultimately concurred. The salutary effect on the staff was immediate and dramatic; you could see the rejuvenation in their eyes as they gained a half-day of rest each week.

Aside from the physical training and the rest, the schedule on Sunday was unique in other ways as well. The first meeting at noon was a ninety-minute "deep dive" intelligence session, during which selected intelligence officers were able to brief General Petraeus on important topics that could not be covered in depth at the morning BUA. General Petraeus loved these sessions and would often choose the topics to be briefed, allowing several weeks for the collection and analysis of information to ensure a thorough examination of the issues. The small conference room in the Sensitive Compartmented Information Facility (SCIF) was jammed each week with key intelligence leaders and analysts, who sat around the table and lined the walls of the room; others would pipe in via secure video-teleconference. The briefings were quite interactive, with General Petraeus engaging briefers in debate and challenging their assumptions. This format prevented "groupthink" from trapping the intelligence community into producing uniform assessments of what were dynamic and complex issues.

After the intelligence session, we would fly to the U.S. embassy in the Green Zone for meetings with U.S. and Iraqi officials. In the late afternoon, while General Petraeus, Sadi, and Bill Rapp were attending the weekly meeting of the Iraqi

Political Council on National Security (PCNS), I would mind the office and have Heather Wiersema give me some impromptu lessons in Arabic. Heather and I would also partake of the excellent Sunday buffet at the embassy dining facility, which made me feel slightly guilty every time I indulged in freshly carved prime rib or lobster tails with drawn butter. I couldn't quite understand why we needed such lavish fare, but it sure was tasty. At the end of the evening we would fly back to our quarters on Camp Victory and start the battle rhythm over again, week after week, month after month. I could sympathize with actor Bill Murray's character in the movie *Groundhog Day.*

General Petraeus wasted no minute. When he got into his armored SUV or helicopter, it took off with or without the other passengers. I found this out the hard way one day early in the deployment when I was focused on answering an e-mail and missed the convoy from the al-Faw palace to the helipad. The commanding general's personal security detachment, a group of exceptional U.S. Army reserve soldiers assigned to protect him, bailed me out by driving me to the Green Zone in a ground convoy (they had to pick up some supplies there anyway, or at least that is what they told me). From that point on the staff and I learned to run to the car or helicopter and buckle in before General Petraeus arrived. The aide and I quipped that it was just another opportunity to engage in some good physical training.

For General Petraeus, helicopter flights were often just another opportunity to work on e-mail, with one communications sergeant handing him a fully updated laptop computer upon takeoff and another downloading the laptop into the network upon landing. Bill Rapp, Everett Spain, and I would keep to ourselves or quietly converse about the day's events. General Petraeus would also sometimes order his pilots to fly over various neighborhoods in Baghdad so that he could gauge for himself such things as the disparity between Sunni and Shi'a areas, the number of civilians out shopping or at amusement parks, provision of electricity to neighborhoods, kids playing soccer, and the like. On one memorable flight I witnessed the aftermath of a car bomb explosion as we flew overhead. These flights were not a replacement for on-the-ground reconnaissance, but they were nonetheless useful as another indicator of the effect of the surge on Baghdad.

Occasionally, such as in the short car rides to and from the helipad or on a late afternoon flight heading back to the house, General Petraeus would be open to discussion. I decided not to waste these opportunities on mere impromptu thoughts. I would often refine a comment on current events or a piece of strategic advice and present it to him concisely during these moments. Bill Rapp would often chime in as well. I considered these burst transmissions some of the most important moments of my day, as they often gave General Petraeus a different take on affairs. He would listen, discuss the issue, and sometimes engage us in debate. I could occasionally see our ideas come out in subsequent guidance to the staff, after General Petraeus had time to mull them over and make them his own.

Despite the dreams of those (and there were many) who thought that if they could just land a position on General Petraeus's personal staff, they would be able to continuously whisper strategic advice into his ear, the opportunities to do so were rare. I cautioned job seekers that 98 percent of what we did was a daily grind of "breaking big rocks into small rocks." Full- or part-time staffers like Colonel H. R. McMaster, Colonel Mike Meese, Lieutenant Colonel Suzanne Nielsen, Colonel J. R. Martin, Major Joel Rayburn, Major Pat Buckley, and Ylbr Bajraktari (a Kosovar who would celebrate his nation's declaration of independence in February 2008) worked in conjunction with Colonel Bill Rapp and the Commander's Initiatives Group to prepare studies, write papers, escort visitors, engage with select Iraqis, and conduct "red team" analysis—the sort of grunt work that made a higher-level staff effective. Résumé builders, those interested in short-term stints to pad their record on national security affairs, were neither welcome nor invited.

Early on, General Petraeus decided that I needed to remain in the office while he traveled and attended meetings, other than those convened in the headquarters, in which I was expected to take part. Thus chained to my desk, I could keep the trains running on time, field queries from the staff, keep General Petraeus informed via e-mail, and handle any emergencies that arose. Bill Rapp and Everett Spain would accompany General Petraeus to attend to his needs and take notes as he traveled. His frequent visits to the field enabled Petraeus to meet and talk with every brigade commander and the vast majority of the battalion commanders in Iraq during their deployments. These trips kept him informed of the progress of the counterinsurgency campaign, gave him an opportunity to impart guidance and advice, and kept him in touch with the troops. During unit visits General Petraeus would meet privately with groups of company commanders to listen to what they had to say about their ongoing operations; he would often come away from these meetings with ideas on how MNF-I could improve its support for these small-unit leaders at the sharp end of the spear. He would also interact with the Iraqi people on market walks, engaging them in pleasantries with his limited Arabic and more in depth through Sadi or Heather, who would come along to serve as translators. These outings gave General Petraeus a more granular feel for what was happening on the ground in Iraq.

The relationship between General Petraeus and Ambassador Crocker was critical to the successful outcome of the surge. Although unity of command is the ideal for military and civilian agencies participating in a counterinsurgency operation, political considerations usually dictate division of the necessary authorities among a variety of actors. Division of civil and military power places a premium on the creation of a clear, common understanding of the political and security goals and how the counterinsurgent forces and agencies intend to achieve them. Only then does unity of effort become a viable substitute for unity of command.

During the Iraq War, the civil-military command structure divided responsibilities for security and other lines of operation, first between the Coalition Provisional Authority and Combined Joint Task Force 7 and later between the U.S. ambassador in Baghdad and the commander of Multi-National Force–Iraq. The civil-military relationship was not always a smooth one, as the personalities of various leaders created friction that occasionally hampered the relationship between the CPA, embassy, and military staffs. The civil-military relationship improved dramatically when Ambassador Crocker and General Petraeus assumed their positions as U.S. ambassador to Iraq and commander of Multi-National Force–Iraq in early 2007. General Petraeus was responsible for security matters, while Ambassador Crocker had primacy over the political, economic, and diplomatic lines of operation. Nothing had formally changed in the command and control structure from that under which previous leaders operated; however, the ability of Ambassador Crocker and General Petraeus to form a strong working partnership was essential to the creation of effective unity of effort during the surge operations of 2007–2008.

Ambassador Crocker and General Petraeus worked closely together, from shared meetings with principal Iraqi and coalition figures to the creation of civil-military working groups that hammered out the essentials of a joint campaign plan and supporting activities that chartered the way ahead in the war effort. Indeed, to prevent Iraqi officials from playing MNF-I off against the embassy, General Petraeus mandated that I include appropriate embassy staffers in his meetings with them. General Petraeus also invited embassy staffers to participate in his daily battlefield update and assessment briefings, which gave both military and civilian personnel a better grasp of each other's activities and progress (or lack thereof) in key areas. General Petraeus and Ambassador Crocker would jointly host congressional delegations, senior Iraqi leaders, and other dignitaries in both informal social settings and more formal briefings that made it clear they were of one mind on the essential issues. It is not readily apparent why their relationship worked so much better than those that preceded them, but it was clearly a more effective partnership. Personalities play a key role; in this regard, part of what made the Crocker-Petraeus relationship work was their professional and personal respect and admiration for each other. Both were avid long-distance runners, and often they went on long Sunday morning runs together before an injury sidelined Ambassador Crocker. Beyond their personal bonds, both understood the enormous stakes at risk during the surge and likewise were attuned to the need to work together to achieve the ambitious goals that the president had articulated for the war effort in Iraq. Together they achieved unity of purpose and effort despite a division of authority that precluded formal unity of command, and that cooperation made possible the manifest successes achieved by coalition and Iraqi forces during the surge.

The close relationship between Ambassador Crocker and General Petraeus extended to their staffs as well. Navy Captain Bill Cone, Ambassador Crocker's military assistant, and I worked closely together and became good friends during our time together in Iraq. We constantly shared news and information and coordinated the various meetings and activities of the senior leaders for whom we worked. These personal relationships were the lubrication that kept the embassy and MNF-I headquarters operating smoothly together at the highest levels. "By the summer of 2007," General Petraeus recalls, "Ryan and I were no longer heading two separate organizations. Rather, we were leading organizations that worked nearly as one, a joint civil-military counterinsurgency enterprise made up of diplomats, soldiers, intelligence professionals, development experts, and a host of others from across the U.S. government and the governments of our major coalition partners."[8]

One of the first cooperative activities between General Petraeus and Ambassador Crocker was the creation of a Joint Strategic Assessment Team, or JSAT, to review the strategic environment, assess the campaign plan, and recommend adjustments to it. Led by the talented Colonel H. R. McMaster and Ambassador David Pearce, the two dozen members of the team included, among others, U.S. Ambassador to Algeria Robert Ford and Molly Phee from the State Department, counterinsurgency adviser David Kilcullen, intelligence adviser Derek Harvey, Toby Dodge from the International Institute for Strategic Studies, Steve Biddle from the Council on Foreign Relations, Colonel Marty Stanton, Major Joel Rayburn from U.S. Central Command, and my West Point classmate Ricky Waddell, a Rhodes scholar and U.S. Army reservist who worked in the oil and gas industry in Brazil. For six weeks beginning on March 20, the JSAT wrestled with the key issues of the Iraq War and challenged the assumptions on which the U.S. and Iraqi governments had based their strategy. What were the root causes of the insurgency and ongoing violence? Was the Iraqi government the key to solving the ethnosectarian violence in Iraq, or as a party to the civil war was it part of the problem? Could a population-based counterinsurgency have more than a tactical effect on the more intractable issues that Iraq faced? The team debated the issues fiercely and presented its assessments to Ambassador Crocker, General Petraeus, and other senior leaders in a series of meetings as their work progressed. The team reported the situation as they saw it without embellishment or obfuscation. After the team's first briefing, General Petraeus reported to Secretary of Defense Gates that "their assessment of the situation here was accurate, forthright, and a bit disheartening."[9] They were doing their job, and doing it well.

One of the major outcomes of the JSAT was the lowering of the bar for what success in Iraq would look like. The communal struggle in Iraq had devolved into a low-grade civil war that would take a generation or more to fully resolve. Gone were visions of a Jeffersonian democracy; they were replaced by the concept of "sustainable stability," which failed as a bumper sticker but which nevertheless better reflected the possible outcome that could be achieved before the clock on U.S. involvement in the war ran out. The JSAT also emphasized reconciliation with various local groups along with creating and supporting a legitimate national government. The Iraqi people were now the primary focus of coalition operations; assisting the Iraqi government in developing its capacity to provide security and services to the people was a complementary task. The ideas were linked; sustainable security required the creation of a patchwork of localized political accommodations and then the stitching together of these patches into a larger reconciliation between the sects.

Crocker and Petraeus did not accept all of the group's recommendations; for instance, the notion that the coalition would somehow purge the Iraqi government of malign sectarian actors (Sadrist control of the Health, Transportation, and Education ministries was especially troubling) was rejected as an unworkable intrusion into a sovereign government.[10] Once the JSAT concluded its assessment, it turned its products over to the MNF-I and embassy staffs, which produced a new version of the joint campaign plan in July. By then, the contours of the new campaign were already in place; in fact, General Petraeus had changed the most important elements of the campaign plan the day after he took command, and he and Ambassador Khalilzad, Ambassador Crocker's predecessor, had formalized those changes by the end of their first week together. The publication of a new campaign plan in July 2007 was the end of the planning process, not the beginning. To ensure the execution of the campaign plan was well synchronized, every six weeks Ambassador Crocker and General Petraeus jointly chaired a Campaign Assessment and Synchronization Board, which assessed and articulated developments in each line of operation from the joint campaign plan.

Equally important to the success of the surge was the relationship between General Petraeus and Lieutenant General Odierno. They had quite different personalities—Petraeus introspective and cerebral; Odierno extroverted and outwardly emotional. General Petraeus enjoyed a good debate, while Lieutenant General Odierno could chew you out in one moment and then give you a big bear hug in the next—which could be quite an experience, given his six-foot, five-inch frame and lineman's build. They had served together as division commanders in Iraq in 2003–2004, during which time they had used radically different methods to fight the insurgency in their areas. Admittedly, Odierno's 4th Infantry Division in Tikrit faced a more violent situation than Petraeus's 101st Airborne Division in Mosul, but the contrast in their approaches was stark. Since then, they had trod different paths but had reached the same conclusion—protecting the Iraqi people was the key to winning the war in Iraq. Both were advised by unusual (and unusually talented) people; Sadi Othman's counterpart at Multi-National Corps–Iraq was the slightly built Emma Sky, a British national and committed pacifist who had served earlier in the war as the political adviser to Colonel Billy Mayville, the commander of the 173rd Airborne Brigade and my West Point roommate back in 1982. She was an Arabist who gave unvarnished advice to Lieutenant General Odierno, occasionally being thrown out of his office in the process. Not subject to General Order

#1, which forbade among other things the consumption of alcohol, Emma would come by my desk every now and then to tease me with a description of the martini she had consumed the night before at the British embassy. She was pessimistic about the future of Iraq and a contrarian thinker, but such unique viewpoints were just what the commanders on the ground needed to hear to counter their "can-do" tendencies. General Petraeus brought Emma onto his personal staff in early 2008 when Lieutenant General Odierno departed Iraq.

General Petraeus would tackle the challenges of the war from his strategic perch, while General Odierno handled the tactical and operational fight. General Petraeus worked the communications and coordination upward (with the Iraqi government, the Bush administration, the Joint Chiefs of Staff, and U.S. Central Command) and outward (with coalition military partners, NATO, and occasionally with regional countries as well), while General Odierno focused on defeating the Sunni insurgency and containing Shi'a militias inside Iraq, albeit with constant dialogue with General Petraeus, who often provided guidance as well. Their relationship was professional and based on mutual respect.

As with my relations with Bill Cone at the embassy, I worked closely with my peers in MNC-I, including my good friend Jim Hickey, the head of the Counter-IED Operations Integration Center, and Colonel Mike Murray, the MNC-I G-3 (operations, plans, and training officer). As a fellow Ohio State alumnus (Mike was commissioned through ROTC in Columbus, while I pursued my Ph.D. studies there in the early 1990s), Mike and I would often chat about the state of Buckeyes football, which at the end of the 2007 season took them to the national championship game against Louisiana State University. Jim and I had a standing date on Friday nights (while General Petraeus was in the Green Zone attending meetings of the Iraqi Military Committee on National Security) to eat together in the Camp Victory Mess Hall, followed by cigars and near beer (the best was St. Pauli Girl) on the roof of the al-Faw palace. It helped that a number of visitors, knowing that General Order #1 prohibited the consumption of alcohol but was silent about smoking, presented General Petraeus with cigars when they came to see him. Since General Petraeus didn't smoke, I took the cigars, kept a few for Jim and me, and gave the rest away to the troops. Jim and I would watch 25mm tracers arc into the night sky from the roof of the al-Faw palace, punctuated by the sound of an occasional bomb blast. The sessions allowed us to vent steam, but as important, I learned a great deal about the latest operations, concerns, and challenges of the Corps, while imparting to Jim the larger picture at Force level. It was the kind of networking that doesn't appear in line-and-staff wiring diagrams, but which makes for smoothly functioning organizations.

One of the most pressing issues facing General Petraeus and Lieutenant General Odierno early on was how to sustain the surge beyond a few months, which was not enough time to establish local bases in Iraqi urban areas, root out the insurgents by protecting the population, or have a psychological impact on the psyche of the Iraqi people. The problem was that the U.S. Army was too small for its missions, a result of the decision by the Bush administration not to significantly increase the size of the force despite the strains of fighting two wars, in Iraq and in Afghanistan. Most National Guard units had already served a tour of duty overseas since 9/11, which meant that the well of available reserve forces had run dry. There were not enough active duty units in the training pipeline back in the United States to sustain twenty brigade combat teams in Iraq for the foreseeable future without extending the length of their stay in the combat zone, which was already at twelve months, with only a year between deployments.

The Department of Defense had extended tours of units in Iraq at least twice already during the war. In the spring of 2004 the 1st Armored Division was en route back to its home stations in Germany when the uprising of the Jaish al-Mahdi in south-central Iraq caught the American command off guard. The division, a third of which was already at the port of Kuwait, was redeployed to counterattack the Shi'a militia in Kut, Kufa, and Karbala, and its tour of duty was extended to fifteen months.[11] More recently, in the summer of 2006 the 172nd Stryker Brigade's tour of duty was extended to fifteen months in order to provide more troops to combat the rising violence in Iraq in the wake of the bombing of the al-Askari shrine and the subsequent outbreak of massive sectarian violence in Baghdad.[12] These events could be seen as "one-offs" that did not affect the U.S. Army's standard tour rotation policy. If the surge were to be sustained, though, this policy would become increasingly untenable. The lack of units to replace those due to rotate back home would present Petraeus and Odierno with the unenviable task of requesting the extension of tours of duty for soldiers and units, resulting in personal turmoil for them and their families as well as the attendant negative publicity that would inevitably result.

The Department of Defense could not kick this can down the road. The first units scheduled to rotate back home, the 3rd Stryker Brigade, 2nd Infantry Division and the 2nd Brigade, 1st Infantry Division, had to be notified by mid-April if their tour extensions were to be executed in an orderly manner. Rather than face this difficult decision over and over again, Petraeus and Odierno decided it would be better to bite the bullet just once. While Lieutenant General Odierno prepared the troops for the bad news, General Petraeus wrote to Secretary of Defense Gates that if the surge were to be extended into 2008, his recommendation would be a fifteen-month across-the-board tour for all Army soldiers in Iraq. Three weeks later, Secretary Gates approved the request. It was a difficult decision for all concerned. Army soldiers, many of whom were serving on their second or third tours of duty already, were being asked to spend more time in the combat zone than at home with their families. They had been psychologically prepared for a year away from their home stations; now they would spend an additional three months in

Iraq. As Lieutenant General Odierno explained to General Petraeus after breaking the news to the soldiers, "I can tell you that in the minds to the troops, a three-month extension on top of a year tour adds up to much more than fifteen months." General Petraeus penned a note to the soldiers' families, thanking them for their sacrifices and service. Predictably, Congressional Democrats blasted the decision, calling it "a rotational scheme for an unstable and open-ended strategy."[13] Moderate Republicans pointed to the deeper problem that lay behind the decision—the inadequate size of the U.S. Army and Marine Corps.

Maintaining a larger troop basis for an extended period was critical to the success of the surge, but as General Petraeus and Lieutenant General Odierno would repeatedly explain, the "surge of ideas" in 2007 was more important than the surge of forces to Iraq. No idea was bigger than the shift away from a focus on hunting the enemy to a new focus on protecting the Iraqi people where they lived and worked by positioning U.S. and Iraqi forces among them. To codify this change, General Petraeus and Lieutenant General Odierno both crafted counterinsurgency guidance for their commands. As a precursor to his counterinsurgency guidance, on March 15 General Petraeus sent out a second open letter to the troops, in which he reiterated the need to live among and protect the Iraqi people in order to achieve the "overriding objective" of improving security. Success would take months, and there would be many tough days ahead. Counterinsurgency operations among the population were "helping restore a sense of hope to the Iraqi people, block-by-block," and by so doing would create "an opportunity to resolve the serious political challenges they confront, reconcile their sectarian issues, and forge the way ahead for the new Iraq—thereby giving all Iraqi citizens a stake in their new country." To address the concerns of those soldiers who felt unsure about why they were moving to less secure and more austere bases, General Petraeus wrote, "This approach is necessary, because we can't commute to the fight in counterinsurgency operations; rather, we have to live with the population we are securing."[14]

General Petraeus followed up this letter a month and a half later with formal counterinsurgency guidance that reflected the principles of the counterinsurgency field manual. The crafting of the guidance was a collaborative effort. Dave Kilcullen, in his capacity as the commanding general's senior adviser for counterinsurgency, made major contributions, but Bill Rapp and I each had a hand in the editing of the document. Of course, General Petraeus put his personal stamp on the product before its publication. "The war in Iraq has reached a critical stage," General Petraeus wrote. "During 2007, Coalition and Iraqi forces must work together to create security improvements and, in doing so, provide Iraqi leaders with the time and space to tackle the tough political issues that must be resolved in order to achieve national reconciliation and build a secure and stable Iraq." To achieve these improvements, "business as usual" would not suffice; we had to win the battle of perceptions, both locally and globally, that would determine the difference between victory and defeat. He then enumerated ten key requirements for the prosecution of effective counterinsurgency operations:

1. Secure the people where they sleep. Population security is our primary mission. And achieving population security promises to be an extremely long-term endeavor—a marathon, not a sprint—so focusing on this mission now is essential. Most extra-judicial killings occur at night and in people's homes, while most spectacular terrorist attacks occur during the day, where people shop, work and play—anywhere they gather publicly. These key areas must be secured. Once secured, an area cannot be abandoned; it must be permanently controlled and protected, 24 hours a day, or else the enemy will re-infiltrate and kill or intimidate those who have supported us. This protection must be kept up until the area can be effectively garrisoned and controlled by Iraqi police (ideally from the area being secured) and other security services. *We can't be everywhere—therefore you must assess your AOR, identify priority areas, work to secure them first, and then expand into other areas.*

2. Give the people justice and honor. We think in terms of democracy and human rights. Iraqis think in terms of justice and honor. Whenever possible, help Iraqis to retain or regain their honor. Treat Iraqis with genuine, not patronizing, dignity and respect; that will win friends and discredit enemies. You must act quickly and publicly to deal with complaints and abuses. Never allow an injustice to stand unaddressed; never walk away from a local Iraqi who believes he or she has been unjustly treated. *Second only to security, bringing justice to the people and restoring their honor is the key task.*

3. Integrate civilian/military efforts—this is an inter-agency, combined arms fight. Embedded Provincial Reconstruction Teams now operate directly alongside military units, adding new capabilities, skills, and funds to our counterinsurgency effort. PRTs bring political and economic expertise to the brigade and regimental combat teams with whom they serve, operate under force protection rules that allow them to accompany our military forces on operations, and conduct extended engagement with local communities. In order to exploit military and civilian capabilities to their fullest potential, we must fully integrate our civilian partners into all aspects of our operations—from inception through execution. *Close working relationships, mutual respect, and personal interaction between BCT/RCT* [Brigade Combat Team/Regimental Combat Team] *commanders and PRT* [Provincial Reconstruction Team] *Team Leaders are critical to achieving "interagency combined arms."*

4. Get out and walk—move mounted, work dismounted. Vehicles like the up-armored HMMWV insulate us from the Iraqi people we are securing, limit

our situational awareness, and drastically reduce the number of Soldiers able to dismount. Furthermore, they make us predictable as they often force us to move slowly on set routes. Meanwhile, an underbelly attack by an IED or an EFP may still damage the vehicle heavily—so we gain little in safety, but sacrifice much in effectiveness. HMMWVs are necessary for traveling to a patrol area or for overwatch, heavy equipment transportation, and communications. But they are not squad cars. *Stop by, don't drive by. Patrol on foot to gain and maintain contact with the population and the enemy.*

5. We are in a fight for intelligence—all the time. Intelligence is not a "product" given to commanders by higher headquarters, but rather something we gather ourselves, through our own operations. Tactical reporting, from civilian and military agencies, is essential: there are thousands of eyes out in your area—all must act as scouts, know what to look for, and be trained and ready to report it. Also, units should deploy analytical capacity as far forward as possible, so that the analyst is close—in time and space—to the commander he supports. Our presence, living alongside the people, will turn on a "fire-hose" of unsolicited tips about the enemy. Units must be prepared to receive this flood of information. Intelligence staffs and commanders must learn how to sort through reports, separating the plausible from the fictitious, integrating the reports with other forms of intelligence, and finally recognizing and exploiting a "break" into the enemy network. Once you make a break, stay on it until it pays off. *Most actionable intelligence will come from locally produced HUMINT* [Human Intelligence], *tactical reporting, follow-up of IED and sniper attacks, detainee interrogations, and SIGINT* [Signals Intelligence]. *Work with what you have.*

6. Every unit must advise their ISF partners. Joint Security Stations and Combat Outposts have put coalition and Iraqi forces shoulder-to-shoulder throughout the battlespace. Regular MiTTs [Military Transition Teams] can't be everywhere, so units must help the MiTTs enforce ISF standards, enable performance, and monitor for abuses and inefficiencies. Any coalition unit working with ISF will be studied, emulated and copied—for better or worse. Therefore we must always set the example. *Regardless of mission, any coalition unit operating alongside ISF is performing a mentoring, training, and example-setting role.*

7. Include ISF in your operations at the lowest possible level. As foreigners, Coalition forces lack language capacity, situational and cultural awareness, and a "feel" for what is normal in the environment. ISF possess all these abilities, but lack the combat power of coalition forces. Working together, with the ISF and the local populace, we are an extremely powerful combination; working unilaterally, we can be defeated piecemeal. Therefore, units should operate with an ISF presence at the lowest feasible tactical

level—ideally, at squad or platoon level. And when operating together, you must plan, sequence, and conduct operations together with local Iraqi commanders right from the outset. *Units should build a genuine, field-based partnership with local ISF units: move, live, work, and fight together.*

8. Look beyond the IED—get the network that placed it. Every IED provides a window into the network that placed it. If properly exploited, this window can be used to damage and roll back that network, thus ultimately defeating the threat. Of all key locations, the actual IED site is least important. Instead, units should look for early warning observation posts, firing and assembly points, and infiltration/exfiltration routes. Commanders should map IED patterns and use friendly convoy movement to trigger enemy action, having first pre-positioned SIGINT and reconnaissance assets to identify IED teams moving into position, and to listen for communications between Ops [Observation Posts] and firing teams. Lastly, use UAVs [Unmanned Aerial Vehicles] to trace enemy firing teams back to caches and assembly areas. *Over time, units that adopt a pro-active approach to IEDs will degrade enemy networks and push back the IED threat in their area. This will ultimately save more lives than a purely reactive approach.*

9. Be first with the truth. Public Affairs Officers and Information Operations organizations can help manage the message and set general themes. But what Soldiers say and do speaks louder than what PAOs say; the trooper on the spot has a thousand daily interactions with Iraqis and with the global audience via the news media. While encouraging spontaneity, commanders should also communicate key messages down to the individual level, so that soldiers know what message to convey in interactions with the population and the media. When communicating, speed is critical—minutes and hours matter—and we should remember to communicate to the local (Arabic/Iraqi) audience first—the U.S./global audience can follow. *Tell the truth, stay in your lane, and get the message out fast. Be forthright and never allow an enemy lie to stand unchallenged. Require accuracy, adequate context, and proper characterization from the media.*

10. Make the people choose. Some in the Iraqi civilian population want to "sit on the fence" and avoid having to choose between the insurgents and the government. They attempt to protect themselves by supporting the strongest local power; however, this makes them vulnerable to enemy intimidation. We must get the Iraqi populace off the fence—and on the side of the Iraqi government. To do this, we must first persuade the population to choose to support the government. Having done this, we must make this choice irrevocable by having the citizens publicly support government programs or otherwise declare their allegiance. Once the population has chosen to support the government, they will become vulnerable to the insurgents were we to leave. So, together with the ISF, we must protect the

population, where they live. *People in Iraq exercise choice collectively, not just individually; win over local leaders to encourage the community to shift to the side of the new Iraq.*[15]

These ten principles, in addition to amplifying guidance published by Lieutenant General Odierno at MNC-I, codified what was expected of U.S. soldiers and Marines as they went about their business during the surge. General Petraeus would update this counterinsurgency guidance every six months or so to add lessons learned from ongoing operations. (See Appendix 2 for the final version of this counterinsurgency guidance.)

To ensure that these principles were passed on to units rotating into Iraq, General Petraeus would talk to every incoming group of officers and senior noncommissioned officers attending the MNF-I Counterinsurgency Academy in Taji, a sprawling coalition base north of Baghdad. (Disappointed with the level of counterinsurgency understanding he perceived in the troops arriving from the training base in the United States, General Casey had established the academy back in 2004.) I enjoyed these outings a great deal, not least because I was able to meet up with some old friends during our brief visits. On one occasion I bumped into Donald Daoud, who had served as my translator back in 2003–2004 when I commanded the 1st Brigade, 1st Armored Division in Baghdad; on another I met up with Lieutenant Colonel Kevin MacWatters, commander of the 1st Squadron, 7th Cavalry, who had served as my operations officer in the 1st Squadron, 10th Cavalry, and as my deputy G-3 in the 4th Infantry Division earlier in the decade. The key leaders of every military and police transition team and brigade/regimental combat team were required to attend the weeklong course of instruction at Taji, which focused on those aspects of counterinsurgency peculiar to their areas in Iraq. General Petraeus would use the counterinsurgency principles as the basis for his address to these leaders, and then take questions from the group. Most of them were serious, but one wag asked, to peals of laughter, "Sir, can you bring Chuck Norris to Iraq?" Chuck Norris, the martial arts movie star, was the closest thing in Iraq to the World War II GI's ever-present Kilroy; graffiti featuring Norris were ubiquitous in the porta-potties across the combat zone. "There are no weapons of mass destruction in Iraq," one quip read. "Chuck Norris lives in Oklahoma." Norris visited Iraq several times; in fact, he was in country in September 2007, while General Petraeus was delivering testimony to the U.S. Congress. For the record, General Petraeus cannot bring Chuck Norris to Iraq, but Chuck Norris can bring Iraq to Oklahoma!

It would not be fair to say that the surge succeeded just because of General Petraeus's flair at politico-military affairs and Lieutenant General Odierno's expertise as a warfighter. These just happened to be the roles that they assumed during this critical period in the Iraq War in 2007 and 2008. But the nation was indeed well served by this leadership combination for the prosecution of the surge, which might have failed had less talented officers been at the helm.

The interface of politics and military operations was never far from General Petraeus's mind. This is not a sign, as some people opined, of political ambition or publicity seeking. Some Americans subscribe to the notion that once the trumpets sound, the conduct of war should be turned over to the nation's generals and admirals. During the first six years of his presidency, George W. Bush largely outsourced Iraq strategy to Secretary of Defense Donald Rumsfeld and the generals in charge of prosecuting the conflict. The result was a war that was nearly lost by the end of 2006. Only when the president became intimately involved in the design and supervision of war strategy late that year did he put the war footing on a sound basis. "Policy," military theorist Carl von Clausewitz theorizes, "will permeate all military operations, and, in so far as their violent nature will admit, it will have a continuous influence on them." He goes on state, "It is clear, consequently, that war is not a mere act of policy but a true political instrument, a continuation of political activity by other means. What remains peculiar to war is simply the peculiar nature of its means. War in general, and the commander in any specific instance, is entitled to require that the trend and designs of policy shall not be inconsistent with these means. That, of course, is no small demand; but however much it may affect the political aims in a given case, it will never do more than modify them. The political object is the goal, war is the means of reaching it, and means can never be considered in isolation from their purpose."[16] If President Bush came to understand this reality intuitively after much trial and error, General Petraeus understood it intimately from a long career of service, education, and self-directed study in military affairs and history. Their relationship, too, would determine whether or not the surge would succeed in the end.

As with President Abraham Lincoln during the agonizing trial of the American Civil War, President Bush took several years to find his general. The analogy was apt; the most important book that General Petraeus read while serving in Iraq was *Grant Takes Command,* by Civil War historian Bruce Catton, which had a huge impact on him.[17] The president knew intuitively what he wanted from the military in Iraq, but for too long he failed to articulate fully his vision to his senior military leaders. In fact, President Bush sought victory, even though he was reluctant to use this word after the "Mission Accomplished" misstep on the deck of the U.S.S. *Abraham Lincoln* in May 2003.[18] He had initially defined success in expansive terms—lofty pronouncements about bringing freedom and democracy to the Iraqi people. He was willing to back General Casey's strategy of transition ("as the Iraqis stand up, we will stand down") until it was clear that the strategy was failing. When General Casey declined to change this strategy as Iraq descended into civil war in 2006, President Bush stepped in to craft a new strategy and ap-point a different military leader to implement it. The strategy of transition was a way for the United States to gracefully exit the Iraq conflict, but this objective was not President Bush's primary concern. He wanted to win, and by doing so reshape the face of the Middle East.

One could argue that this goal was too broad and not within the capabilities of the U.S. and Iraqi militaries to achieve. But this critique is beside the point. If a military commander believes the mission is unachievable given the means at his disposal, he should say so. Secretary Rumsfeld and General Casey never asked President Bush for a large number of reinforcements, because they believed they had sufficient forces in Iraq to accomplish their mission. General Petraeus, on the other hand, believed more force was needed to win the war. He demanded the entire complement of surge forces, and indeed continued to press for additional enabling forces even as the surge progressed. He believed that his duty was to analyze the mission and then request the resources he considered necessary to accomplish it. If someone above him in the chain of command decided to withhold some or all of those resources, then his duty also compelled him to spell out the risks any shortfalls would entail. He never deviated from this belief, which led to some intense arguments with Admiral Fallon during the course of the surge.

President Bush and Secretary Gates were exceptionally supportive. They understood that additional assets were required to implement a fully resourced counterinsurgency strategy, and they were willing to commit them in the quest for victory. In weekly written reports to the secretary of defense and video teleconference meetings with the president and his war cabinet, General Petraeus also made clear that even with the additional forces allocated to Iraq, the surge was still a high-risk strategy, albeit the best one available to salvage victory from near certain defeat. The definition of victory itself needed to be reconsidered, with the focus on Jeffersonian democracy giving way to a less than ideal, but still suitable, form of representative government the Iraqis could live with and which would lead to "sustainable stability" in the near future. Reconciliation among Iraqi sects, ethnicities, and factions that would lead to a full-blown, functioning democracy was a project that would require the succession of one or more generations to implement. Nevertheless, unless the surge succeeded, any chance of setting Iraq on the road toward this goal would be stillborn.

General Petraeus's weekly reports to Secretary of Defense Gates were frank, comprehensive assessments of the status of the war in Iraq. They were a team effort, with Deputy Chief of the Commander's Initiatives Group Charlie Miller writing the initial draft, Bill Rapp editing it, and General Petraeus shaping the final product, with his speechwriter, Liz McNally, assisting in refining the prose. Once Petraeus approved the memo, Bill would e-mail it to me. I would give it one final edit before sending it on Monday morning directly to the secretary of defense, the chairman and vice chairman of the Joint Chiefs of Staff, and the commander of U.S. Central Command. Everyone might not agree with these assessments, but General Petraeus held nothing back from those above him in the chain of command.[19]

President Bush spoke directly with Ambassador Crocker and General Petraeus in Baghdad via weekly video teleconferences. Through this medium, the president was able to impart his orders and intent directly to those senior officers most intimately involved in fighting the war in Iraq, rather than having his guidance filtered (and potentially diluted) through several layers of command. Given the lukewarm support of the Joint Chiefs and U.S. Central Command for the surge, this method was both essential and appropriate. Some commentators have decried this direct communication, incorrectly claiming that the president was jumping the chain of command. In fact, the entire chain of command (along with many others) was "in the room" at these meetings: the president, vice president, secretary of state, secretary of defense, chairman of the Joint Chiefs of Staff, national security adviser, and others from the White House Situation Room, along with Admiral Fallon from U.S. Central Command in Tampa. A few senior aides, such as Meghan O'Sullivan, sat on the margins of these meetings; in Baghdad, Bill Rapp, Bill Cone, and I sat out of camera view and took notes, which Bill Rapp would then type up and share with attendees afterward.

During these weekly meetings, I found President Bush to be well prepared, engaged, and perceptive—the exact opposite of how some in the media and many of his opponents portrayed him. "The challenge for a supreme leader lies not in choosing at which level of guidance or abstraction to function, but rather in integrating the details with the grand themes, in understanding the forest by examining certain copses and even individual trees with great care," writes Eliot Cohen in his examination of supreme command in wartime.[20] President Bush had read Cohen's book earlier in his presidency; finally, with the outcome of the Iraq War on the line, he was putting its lessons to use. If during the first six years of his presidency George Bush was insufficiently engaged in the conduct of war strategy, during his final two years in office he was the paragon of a wartime commander in chief. He was swimming upstream against a heavy current of political opinion that held the surge to be a forlorn hope. Despite the naysayers, the president remained supportive of his commanders in the field. He deflected the political heat onto himself, thereby making their jobs a bit easier. But to the end he remained intensely engaged in the conduct of the surge. By questioning assumptions and vigorously debating options, the president oversaw a viable strategy process that kept everyone focused on his most important goals, and likewise ensured that hesitant subordinates could not undercut his intent.

President Bush was willing to spend the political capital necessary to make his chosen strategy work. After the testimony to Congress in September 2007, Bush told retired General Jack Keane, "Convey a message from me to Gen. Petraeus. 'I waited over three years for a successful strategy. And I'm not giving up on it prematurely.'"[21] The president also provided much-needed energy to the policy-making process. One video teleconference ended with the president saying he would see everyone the following week. When the national security adviser noted that there was no follow-on conference scheduled, the president replied, "If al-Qaeda rests, then I will rest." Everyone present got the message.

In addition to his weekly meetings with senior U.S. officials, the president also held frequent video-teleconferences (and occasional face-to-face meetings) with Iraqi Prime Minister Nouri al-Maliki. Maliki was a political novice, and President Bush intended these sessions to serve as a means to mentor and support him. "I was careful not to bully him or appear heavy-handed," Bush later wrote. "I wanted him to consider me a partner, maybe a mentor. He would get plenty of pressure from others. From me he would get advice and understanding. Once I had earned his trust, I would be in a better position to help him make the tough decisions."[22] Besides Ambassador Crocker and General Petraeus, Sadi Othman was usually the only American in the room with the Iraqi prime minister and his advisers as they met virtually with President Bush. Sadi invariably came away from these sessions impressed with the discussions between the president and the prime minister, which made clear that despite the heavy reliance of the Iraqi government on U.S. support, the two leaders were partners in the war effort.

Executive branch officials were not the only government leaders interested in the Iraq War. Ambassador Crocker and General Petraeus also received a constant stream of congressmen and senators from both parties desiring a firsthand look at the surge. The ambassador and commanding general would personally brief each delegation of visitors, arrange for meetings with high-ranking Iraqi officials, and coordinate visits to meet with the troops at their bases or, occasionally, on the streets of Baghdad. Given the high profile of some legislators, these visits and the subsequent press conferences would sometimes make national news.

On April 1, 2007, Senator John McCain (R-AZ), Senator Lindsey Graham (R-SC), Representative Mike Pence (R-IN), and Representative Rick Renzi (R-AZ) toured the Shorja market in central Baghdad, which had been the scene of a horrific suicide bombing only seven weeks earlier. General Petraeus led them through the market, stopped occasionally to chat with vendors in his rudimentary but serviceable Arabic, and even sipped some tea. The congressmen purchased a few carpets to take home as souvenirs. Sadi accompanied the group to translate, and Bill Rapp, Everett Spain, and I went along as well. Security was tight. We were guarded by a company of U.S. and Iraqi infantry, as well as two Apache helicopters that circled overhead—standard security measures whenever General Petraeus or another high-ranking official left the protection of a coalition base. The forty-five-minute tour passed, thankfully, without incident.

At his press conference that day, Senator McCain—a high-profile presidential candidate—commented favorably on his impression that the surge was making a real difference in improving security and said that he believed the American people were not getting a complete picture of what was happening in Iraq.[23] A week later he wrote an op-ed piece in the *Washington Post* that extolled the progress being made by U.S. and Iraqi forces in Baghdad and al-Anbar province. The trip had been his fifth since the war started and his first since the start of the surge. For the first time, Senator McCain was able to ride in a vehicle from the airport rather than flying to the Green Zone in a helicopter. He consulted with Sunni tribal leaders in al-Anbar province who had turned against al-Qaeda. He met with U.S. and Iraqi troops in a joint security station and saw firsthand the difference they were making in security Baghdad's neighborhoods. "Despite these welcome developments, we should have no illusions," McCain wrote. "This progress is not determinative. It is simply encouraging. We have a long, tough road ahead in Iraq. But for the first time since 2003, we have the right strategy. In Petraeus, we have a military professional who literally wrote the book on fighting this kind of war. And we will have the right mix and number of forces."[24]

Predictably, despite Senator McCain's calls for bipartisan support of the new strategy to give it time to succeed, his observations were roundly criticized by left-wing bloggers and Democratic politicians, who implied that he deliberately downplayed the fact that he could travel in Baghdad only under an umbrella of tight security.[25] American casualties were on the rise; in fact, April, May, and June 2007 brought the most American deaths of any three-month period in the Iraq War. What these commentators could not see was the underlying reason for the increased violence against U.S. forces. In conjunction with Iraqi security forces, American troops were taking back control of Baghdad's streets and other areas across Iraq, thereby endangering the base of support for the insurgency, al-Qaeda, and the Jaish al-Mahdi. Those elements threatened by the surge were fighting back. The strategy was not, as Senator Harry Reid had pronounced, a failure. It was in the balance.

General Petraeus did not spend all of his time with senior leaders; he also felt it was his duty to communicate with the American people and other audiences (and indeed President Bush encouraged him to do so). This imperative required a deft public affairs touch, which General Petraeus had developed over the years. To aid him with this task, the MNF-I public affairs officer, Colonel Steve Boylan, and his small staff would handle requests for interviews, public appearances, or other media matters that directly involved General Petraeus. (The Strategic Communications division of the Multi-National Force–Iraq staff handled the broader information effort.)

Transparency drove the public affairs effort. General Petraeus stressed the need for speed to beat the insurgents to the headlines—to be the first with the truth. Boylan and his team relentlessly monitored the media to gauge reporting on three elements: accuracy (were the facts correct?), context (was the broader context presented, or did the story report events out of context?), and characterization (did the reporter characterize the issues fairly?). If the story had those three elements correct, then we had no issue with the product. If not, Steve would engage the reporter and/or editor to inform and educate, or, if the fault was egregious enough, to demand a correction.

Battlefield visits were a cornerstone of the media engagement program. General Petraeus wanted the media to see what he was seeing, hear what he was hearing, and experience what he was experiencing, within the bounds of operational security. He had only two rules in this regard: he would not encourage personality profiles devoted exclusively to him, and he would not allow extended embedded time for reporters with him. He wanted the media to focus on what was happening on the ground and not on him.[26] Steve and his team also planned extensively for media engagements when we traveled back to the United States for congressional testimony, in order to give General Petraeus a chance to answer more fully questions from all sides of the political spectrum.

There were times when Steve presented proposals for interviews to General Petraeus and was told no. Steve would gently back off and then reengage later in the week. He would remind General Petraeus of his own guidance regarding public affairs, "If you don't play, you can't win." Petraeus enjoyed those interviews with reporters who did their homework and asked thoughtful, relevant, and probing questions; he endured the others, even though he doesn't suffer fools gladly. It was the quality of intellectual discussion that he enjoyed in these moments, rather than the sure knowledge that he would once again be the focus of yet another article on the Iraq War.[27]

General Petraeus had prepared personally, professionally, and, perhaps most important, intellectually his entire career for the moment when he would be called upon by the president to lead American forces as a four-star commander. He was the right person for the difficult job of commanding U.S. and coalition soldiers during the critical period of the surge. On emotionally draining days when several soldiers were killed or when terrorists slaughtered large numbers civilians, Petraeus would recall Grant's reply to Major General William Tecumseh Sherman after the particularly rough first day at the battle of Shiloh in April 1862. Late at night under a tree in pouring rain, Sherman found Grant chewing on a cigar. "Well, Grant," Sherman intoned, "we've had the devil's own day, haven't we?" "Yep," Grant replied. "Lick 'em tomorrow, though." Grant's response became our rallying cry as coalition forces absorbed difficult blows, recovered, and took the fight to the enemy. By the force of his energy, his will, and his intellect, General Petraeus turned around a flagging war effort. There were indeed tough days ahead, but he never projected anything other than a confident outlook to the officers and soldiers under his command. In setting the right tone, he made those around him believe that victory was indeed possible.

Ten days after General Petraeus and Ambassador Crocker's testimony to Congress in September 2007, Tower 57 was repaired. The road to the completion of this task had been long and winding. An initial effort by the U.S. Corps of Engineers to outsource the repair to an Iraqi civilian company went nowhere when insurgents threatened the management. The basic problem was security; Tower 57 was in a rural area (known as the triangle of death) that was rife with roadside bombs and easily targeted by mortars and snipers. Multi-National Corps–Iraq could have accomplished the mission by itself, but senior leaders rightly concluded that it would be best to force the Iraqi government to take charge of the repair effort. The effort languished as the Iraqi bureaucracy argued over which agency should accomplish the job. Three times the Iraqi Army sent a platoon of soldiers to protect the work crew assigned to fix the tower, but each time insurgent fire led the civilians to flee the scene. Frustrated senior leaders amped up the pressure, which led the Iraqi Ministry of Electricity to demand that American leaders guarantee complete security for its repair crews. In the end the repair effort took the combined labors of a battalion of Iraqi infantry supported by a platoon of Apache helicopters, an engineer team with special equipment to detect and clear roadside bombs, and a ten man repair crew. Eleven Iraqi soldiers were wounded in the operation, which took four and a half days to complete.[28]

General Petraeus had used the morning updates to emphasize the priority of this operation and to track its progress, day after agonizing day. Although some officers deride PowerPoint slides as an ineffective management tool, the problem is not the slides but rather how leaders use them. General Petraeus used the BUA slides to drill down into issues, not for the sake of micromanaging events, but to extend priorities and guidance to his subordinates (indeed, his guidance was captured by Charlie Miller in the Commander's Initiatives Group and shared via the secure Internet to brigade level). The addition of key U.S. embassy staffers in these morning briefings also led to increased cooperation between the civil and military leaders of the counterinsurgency effort in Iraq.

The significance of the repair of Tower 57 went well beyond the restoration of a four hundred–kilovolt electrical line from southern Iraq to Baghdad. Tower 57 had become a symbol of U.S. and Iraqi determination to defeat the insurgency and a metaphor for General Petraeus's resolve. It would have been easy enough to reroute the power grid around Tower 57 (which was done) and leave it at that. But by forcing the issue, General Petraeus was sending a message to Americans and Iraqis alike: We would not forgo doing difficult things just because they were hard. Hard, after all, was not hopeless.

CHAPTER 5

The Awakening

You Americans couldn't convince us [to fight al-Qaeda].
We Sunnis had to convince ourselves.
—Sheik Abdul Sattar Abu Risha al-Rishawi

The tribal rebellion against al-Qaeda in Iraq, known as the Awakening, was as unexpected as it was welcome. It predated the surge by several months, but its ultimate success and expansion outside the boundaries of al-Anbar province were uncertain when General Petraeus took command of Multi-National Force–Iraq in February 2007. By the summer of that year, the surge had acted as a catalyst for the spread of the tribal rebellion across much of western and central Iraq. The Awakening was based in large part on a political calculation among Sunni tribal leaders. They had experienced a taste of what life was like under the control of al-Qaeda, and life was not good. After al-Qaeda assassinated one too many sheiks, surviving tribal leaders realized that their alliance with the jihadists was a path to defeat. It was better to ally with Americans—a relatively neutral but very powerful tribe in their eyes—both to battle al-Qaeda and as a hedge against consolidation of Shi'a power in Baghdad. This political transformation changed the complexion of the Sunni insurgency, and with it, the entire Iraq War.

No one saw it coming. To be sure, some commanders had pursued reconciliation initiatives with former members of the Ba'ath Party in the wake of Ambassador Bremer's de-Ba'athification decree in 2003. In fact, General Petraeus had led the way in the summer of 2003, when he commanded the 101st Airborne Division, with special authority from Ambassador Bremer to pursue reconciliation. But the results there—and in western al-Anbar province in 2004 and in subsequent years—had never been supported by the Iraqi leaders of the De-Ba'athification Commission in Baghdad and thus never achieved lasting effects.

In mid-August 2006 Marine Colonel Peter Devlin, the I Marine Expeditionary Force G-2, wrote an intelligence assessment that all but conceded defeat in al-Anbar province. "The social and political situation has deteriorated to a point that MNF [Multi-National Forces] and ISF [Iraqi Security Forces] are no longer capable of militarily defeating the insurgency in al-Anbar," his report read. The tribal system in the province had collapsed; violence and criminality ruled people's lives. Sunni perceptions were that the Shi'a government in Baghdad was controlled by Iran and was deliberately marginalizing Iraqi Sunnis, particularly by cutting them out of the proceeds garnered from the sale of Iraqi oil abroad. The provincial economy remained depressed; Anbaris, except for those enriched by criminality and corruption, lived largely hand to mouth. Anbaris on the whole detested al-Qaeda but viewed the organization as their defender of last resort against a potential campaign of sectarian cleansing by the central government in the province. In short, al-Qaeda presented an "intractable problem" that Multi-National Force–Iraq could do little to solve, short of fostering an unlikely reconciliation between Iraqi Sunnis and the Shi'a government in Baghdad. "Barring the deployment of an additional MNF division and the injection of billions of dollars of reconstruction and investment money into the Province, there is nothing MNF can do to influence the motivations of al-Anbar Sunni to wage an insurgency."[1] Despite impeccable logic, the assessment was dead wrong.

General Casey and his planners at Multi-National Force–Iraq conceded Devlin's point. In the strategic assessment of May 2006, they wrote, "Economic development and governance capacity will defeat AQI [al-Qaeda in Iraq] and its facilitation network in Al Anbar. . . . It is the focus on the 'soft' elements of power (principally economic and governance) supported by the development of a consistently more capable ISF presence, that will ultimately collapse the insurgent infrastructure and create the conditions where AQI and associated T&FF [terrorists and foreign fighters] lose the capability to hinder Iraqi economic and political development, ultimately rendering them defeated in Iraq, supporting the conditions for turnover of additional security responsibilities to the ISF."[2] It was a classic "hearts and minds" approach to winning the war and it, too, was wrong.

At the time, Colonel Devlin's assessment seemed logical and well founded. Its analytics and the data on which the analysis was based were reliable. Nevertheless, within less than a year the supposedly moribund Iraqi tribes had rebounded and, in alliance with U.S. Marines and Iraqi security forces, had driven al-Qaeda out of the province. How did this happen?

For a partial explanation of why the unexpected reversal of coalition fortunes in al-Anbar province took so many military leaders and analysts by surprise, we must return to the oft-quoted but more often misunderstood work of the Prussian military philosopher Carl von Clausewitz. "*On War* is suffused with the understanding that every war is inherently a nonlinear phenomenon, the conduct of which changes its character in ways that cannot be analytically predicted," writes Ohio State professor emeritus Alan Beyerchen in a seminal article linking war to modern chaos theory published a decade and a half before the surge in Iraq. "Nonlinear systems . . . exhibit erratic behavior through disproportionately large or disproportionately small outputs, or they may involve 'synergistic' interactions in which the whole is not equal to the sum of the parts."[3] In other words, war is unpredictable because passion infuses human behavior and human interactions are erratic. If it were not so, the side with the biggest battalions would always win, and such is simply not the case.

Colonel Devlin and other military leaders were thinking linearly in an inherently nonlinear world. "The heart of the matter is that the [nonlinear] system's variables cannot be effectively isolated from each other or from their context," Beyerchen concludes. "Linearization is not possible, because dynamic interaction is one of the system's defining characteristics."[4] There were too many unknowns to gauge effectively the outcome of the ongoing conflict, other than to vaguely discern one possible trajectory out of many based on incomplete information— "a messy mix of order and unpredictability," in Beyerchen's words. "The work of Clausewitz indicates that knowing how the system functions at this moment does not guarantee that it will change only slightly in the next. Although it may remain stable, it might also suddenly (although perhaps subtly) pass a threshold into a thoroughly different regime of behavior. And the causes of such changes in a complex system can be imperceptibly small."[5] In the quest for certainty via metrics and statistical analysis, Multi-National Force–Iraq intelligence officers had overlooked the inherently nonlinear nature of war.

In fact, by the time Colonel Devlin wrote his assessment, the tide in al-Anbar province was already turning—however slowly and imperceptibly—against al-Qaeda and its minions. In seemingly conquering al-Anbar province, al-Qaeda overstepped its bounds, alienating the people whom it would govern and control. It was the people's unpredictable reactions to al-Qaeda's brutality—aided and abetted by the actions of some forward-thinking Army and Marine officers and ultimately by General Petraeus—that generated the Awakening and made possible the unexpected turnaround in the war in western Iraq.

U.S. Army and Marine officers had engaged Iraqi tribal leaders in al-Anbar province and elsewhere as early as 2004 and in a few cases even earlier, but these efforts to bring the tribes into alliance with the coalition and the Iraqi government were only sporadically successful due to political factors at play and the ongoing insurgent and terrorist violence to keep the tribes in check. The Sunni tribal sheiks in al-Anbar were angry due to the end of Sunni political control in Baghdad, the de-Ba'athification decree that eliminated jobs and sources of patronage, and the dissolution of the Iraqi army, in which Anbaris had served in prominent positions.[6] Sheiks hold leadership positions due to their ability to offer security and patronage to their tribes, and the U.S. invasion and its aftermath had compromised their ability in this regard. The resulting anger led some tribal sheiks to join the insurgency or to support al-Qaeda jihadists in their battle against the foreign occupiers of Iraq and what they considered to be their lackeys, an Iranian-sponsored regime in Baghdad. The alliance was a marriage of convenience, but a powerful one. Al-Qaeda offered leadership, organization, expertise, and funding, while the tribes provided manpower and shelter.

Despite the best efforts of U.S. Marines and U.S. Army soldiers, security in al-Anbar province went downhill steadily from 2003 to 2006. Lieutenant General John Allen, who, as a brigadier general, was the deputy commander of the II Marine Expeditionary Force (Forward), Multi-National Force–West from January 2007 to February 2008, put the matter bluntly: "[In] 2004, [security] was starting to get bad; 2005, it got worse; 2006, we killed about 1,700, almost 1,800 al-Qaeda, put another 4,500 of them in [Camp] Bucca [the coalition detention center in southern Iraq] and places like that, and the violence levels doubled."[7] Al-Qaeda declared the provincial capital of Ramadi to be the new capital of the Sunni caliphate that the group intended to establish to dominate the Middle East.

Due to the danger and violence, many leading sheiks and other prominent citizens left al-Anbar for Jordan, where U.S. intermediaries engaged them in discussions on the way ahead in Iraq. But in 2004 and 2005 the political conditions were not ripe for garnering the support of the tribes; the wounds of the invasion and subsequent disenfranchisement of the Sunni political class were still too raw, and Iraqi tribes needed time to sort themselves out after the fall of Saddam's regime. Al-Qaim in late 2005 was the first breakthrough with the Anbari tribes, but this foothold proved to be an isolated success. There were not enough U.S. or Iraqi forces in al-Anbar to protect the population against al-Qaeda's depredations or to secure sheiks who sought to reject al-Qaeda. In fact, the first ones to do so in al-Qaim were all subsequently killed. Additionally, American understanding of al-Anbar politics was shaky at best. "We were trying to engage with people, but we had a very immature understanding of Iraqi culture," stated Major Alfred B. Connable, a senior intelligence analyst. "We had a very immature understanding of the authority and the power of the tribes, the tribal leaders. We had a very poor understanding of the divisions within the tribes, the fact that tribes are not monolithic entities, that there are subentities within tribes, and we didn't really understand how the insurgency overlaid onto the tribes, and vice versa."[8] Increasingly, the tribal leaders who went to Jordan lost touch with what was happening in Iraq and proved unwilling to lead the fight against the jihadists. Younger tribal leaders who remained behind in Iraq gained power at the expense of those who had fled the country. Sheik Abdul Sattar Abu Risha al-Rishawi came from this group of younger sheiks who changed the course of the war in al-Anbar province.

Over the course of 2005 many Sunnis came to the conclusion that boycotting the electoral process had been a mistake. Increasing numbers decided that the ballot box was preferable to bullets in shaping the way forward; they realized that they had to have a seat at the table in the new Iraq. Sunni voter participation increased in the final two elections that year, supported by some nationalist groups that had been the cornerstone of the insurgency in its infancy. As a result, cracks formed in the façade of solidarity between these nationalist organizations and the jihadists, led by Abu Musab al-Zarqawi.[9] Al-Qaeda stepped up its campaign of targeted assassinations against tribal sheiks and other leaders who balked at supporting its campaign of terror. This murder and intimidation campaign was so successful that during the first half of 2006, al-Qaeda gained control of much of al-Anbar as the tribes moved to the sidelines and the security situation in the province fell apart. Al-Qaeda crushed resistance to its authority and imposed its morality on the Iraqis under its control.

As with parts of Baghdad, some cities in al-Anbar province became war zones. "By the middle of '06, Ramadi [the provincial capital] essentially looked like Stalingrad," Major Connable noted. "We were dropping shells in the middle of the city. . . . It was a disaster at that point."[10] Electricity, running water, and other services were scarce or nonexistent. Al-Qaeda controlled the hospital and most of the schools and mosques. With the exception of the government center and nearby buildings held by a company of Marines, al-Qaeda essentially controlled the moribund city.[11] The governor of al-Anbar province, Mamoun Sami Rashid al-Alwani, lacked authority among the populace and sat alone in the government compound in the center of Ramadi; the provincial council had decamped for the safer confines of Baghdad—which, given Baghdad's tenuous state of security in 2006, is saying a lot. Mamoun had survived more than thirty assassination attempts.[12] U.S. soldiers simply called downtown Ramadi "the heart of darkness."[13]

Al-Qaeda's ideology and its ruthlessness were its undoing. Jihadists imposed a strict and brutal interpretation of Shari'a law on a tribal culture that was largely secular. Smoking was banned, and anyone who was caught smoking had his or her fingers chopped off. Al-Qaeda operatives forced temporary marriages (presumably allowed under their version of Shari'a law) with local women to satisfy their desire for sex. Senior al-Qaeda leaders—most of them foreigners—demanded marriages with the sisters and daughters of tribal sheiks in order to cement their bonds to the tribes. The corpses of assassinated Iraqis were booby-trapped so that family members coming to collect them for burial would be killed and injured in the process. Headless corpses lay in the streets for days at a time, a sacrilegious act in a religion that demanded burial within twenty-four hours of death. Colonel Michael Walker, a civil affairs officer who served in al-Anbar province, stated that al-Qaeda operatives would "always have a torture chamber set up, and they always had their informants and executions going, and it was rule by terror. And then absolute rigid, extreme Islamic proselytization. . . . The Marines were offering security, governance, economy, and al-Qaeda's offering a trip back to the Dark Ages."[14]

Perhaps most egregious of all in the eyes of the Anbari sheiks, al-Qaeda cut into their smuggling routes from Syria and down the Euphrates corridor into central Iraq. The money garnered from smuggling was the lifeblood of the tribes. Without money, patronage networks collapsed. "Iraqi tribal sheiks are like the Sopranos," General Petraeus would say, noting that watching the HBO show of that name was good preparation for service in Anbar. "Every sheik has a trucking company, a construction company, and an import-export business." Al-Qaeda proved not just ruthless, but bad for business.

Sunni tribal sheiks attempted in late 2005 to form a united front, the "Al-Anbar People's Council," to fight both al-Qaeda and the American occupiers of al-Anbar. The effort quickly collapsed due to internal infighting, al-Qaeda's brutal campaign of targeted assassinations, and the group's failure to enlist the support of the coalition in fighting its most dangerous foe.[15] Al-Qaeda murdered more than three-quarters of the sheiks who made up the leadership of this stillborn tribal rebellion. "It was the night of the long knives," observed Colonel Sean MacFarland, commander of the 1st Brigade, 1st Armored Division. "Al-Qaeda just cleaned house."[16] Police recruiting collapsed in January 2006 after an al-Qaeda suicide bomber killed hundreds of recruits, along with the American officer in charge of organizing the police. The tribes were part of the equation, but they needed help to succeed.

Sheik Abdullah Jallal Mukhif al-Faraji, head of the Sunni Endowment for al-Anbar and regent sheik of the Abu Faraj tribe, put al-Qaeda's brutality in clear terms: "They did not know what resistance meant. They did not know what jihad meant. They did not know what humanity meant. And I speak in front of the camera, and I say it forcefully. They did not know what life meant."[17] Many Sunni Iraqis supported the resistance to the American occupation, but they hadn't signed up for al-Qaeda's extreme religious vision for Iraq's future. Al-Qaeda's brutality opened the door to much greater Sunni cooperation with American forces in Iraq. As the killings mounted, the people of al-Anbar looked for a way out of their seemingly hopeless situation. Dr. Thamer Ibrahim Tahir al-Assafi of the Muslim Ulema Council for al-Anbar and a member of the Ramadi City Council, summed up the situation succinctly: "Life became intolerable. So we started looking for salvation, no matter who it was."[18]

Salvation would come from an unlikely source. Sheik Abdul Sattar Abu Risha al-Rishawi, the thirty-five-year-old head sheik of a minor tribe located on the outskirts of Ramadi, decided to take action. Sattar, "a smoldering, swashbuckling enigma who to some Americans evoked a Hollywood fantasy of a charismatic Arab warrior-prince," could have starred in *Lawrence of Arabia*.[19] "Sattar was straight out of Hollywood central casting," recalled Lieutenant Colonel Tony Deane, commander of 1-35 Armor and one of the leaders who first interceded with the sheik. "He dressed impeccably, carried a chrome-plated Texas Sesquicentennial Colt .44, and had the charisma to fill the room. He was a natural leader."[20] After al-Qaeda killed his father and three of his brothers, he decided it was time to fight. One by one, he contacted fellow sheiks and invited them to join him in an alliance to rid al-Anbar of the jihadist presence.

On September 9, 2006, Sheik Sattar held a meeting at his compound with more than fifty other tribal sheiks in attendance to form the Sahwa al-Anbar (Awakening of Anbar). Five days later the sheiks issued a public communiqué with the following major points:

- To bring back the army to Anbar and to have tribal sons join the police and army;
- To declare war on al-Qaeda—described as "thugs and criminals";
- To bring back the respect that is due to tribal sheiks;
- To consider the American forces friendly, and to forbid attacks against them;
- To treat the Ba'athists humanely;
- To refuse cooperation or negotiation with al-Qaeda;
- To reopen the judiciary and bring criminals before the law;
- To enter the political system, engage in civil dialogue, and participate in elections;
- To contact the Iraqi central government in pursuit of reconciliation;
- To form an Anbar Salvation Council to take the place of the provincial council, which had fled the province.[21]

The Iraqi government and the Americans rejected the final request (eventually, the provincial council was expanded to include some of the tribal sheiks on the body), but the other points were in line with coalition goals for Iraq.

For the moment, Sattar's declaration was ignored outside the confines of Ramadi, but in retrospect there is no doubting the historic nature of the moment. The Awakening tied the tribes to the outcome of the battle for al-Anbar; the citizens of Ramadi now had skin in the game. Sattar was a media-savvy, larger-than-life personality who made clear his allegiance. "Abdul Sattar started stating openly what people were thinking (but did not dare to say publicly)," write Najim Abed al-Jabouri and Sterling Jensen (who served as an interpreter with the Ready First Combat Team in Ramadi): "that al Qaeda and Iran were the real occupiers in Iraq, not the Americans."[22] The Awakening was a political calculation by Sunni tribal sheiks that it was better to side with the Americans against al-Qaeda and the Shi'a government in Baghdad than to die a slow death in an unwinnable civil war. Sattar called out the terrorists and the Sunni fence-sitters alike—there was to be no more pretense of "honorable resistance" against U.S. forces, which he designated as "guests," to preclude the need to conduct jihad against them. The Awakening had arisen; the tribal war against al-Qaeda had begun.

Whether or not to deal with Sattar was a matter of some debate among American commanders and intelligence officers. Although the sheik had street credibility due to the killing of his father and three brothers by al-Qaeda, he was a small-time leader of a minor tribe that lacked *wasta* (influence) in the powerful Dulaimi tribal confederation. Other sheiks, jealous of Sattar's success and his connections with the Americans (which brought lucrative reconstruction contracts), branded him a small-time smuggler, thug, and criminal—which would not be surprising to most American leaders who knew Anbari sheiks well.[23] Nevertheless, a food fight of sorts erupted between the Marine Expeditionary Force headquarters in Fallujah and the U.S. Army headquarters in charge of Ramadi, the 1st Brigade, 1st Armored Division, commanded by Colonel Sean MacFarland. Some Marine staff officers objected to the alliance with Sattar and the Awakening, arguing that it would short-circuit the negotiations with more powerful tribal leaders in Jordan and undercut the official Iraqi provincial government. MacFarland brushed off these concerns and fully supported Sheik Sattar and the Awakening. "No matter how imperfect the tribal system appeared to us," MacFarland later wrote, "it was capable of providing social order and control through culturally appropriate means where governmental control was weak."[24] The tribal leaders in Jordan had not produced anything yet (and were unlikely to do so in the future), and the Iraqi provincial government was largely impotent. Since other leaders were accomplishing little, why not take a chance on Sattar?[25] Given that October 2006 brought the highest levels of violence ever in al-Anbar province, allowing the Awakening a shot seemed well worth the risk.

I had an intimate connection with the 1st Brigade, known as the Ready First Combat Team, having commanded it during its first deployment to Iraq in 2003–2004.[26] After our return to Germany, the brigade honed its training in counterinsurgency warfare. Although some soldiers rotated out, a solid core of leaders and soldiers who had experienced counterinsurgency duty and combat in Baghdad, Karbala, and Kufa remained to return to Iraq with the brigade in 2006. Their first stop was Tal Afar, where the Ready First Combat Team took over from the departing 3rd Armored Cavalry Regiment, commanded by Colonel H. R. McMaster. Colonel MacFarland and his leaders were able to experience firsthand the tactics, techniques, and procedures used by the cavalrymen to clear insurgents from Tal Afar's streets and then to hold the city against the inevitable counterattacks. By the time the brigade (minus one battalion, but with two marine battalions attached) moved to Ramadi in June 2006, it was a fully trained, combat-experienced unit that was the perfect instrument for the mission of clearing al-Qaeda out of the city. It also arrived in the city at the right time, when the people of Ramadi and the tribal sheiks had tired of al-Qaeda's brutality and were ready to take action against the jihadists.

Upon their arrival, MacFarland and his staff developed a plan to retake Ramadi. Rather than launch a massive assault on the city comparable to the second battle of Fallujah in November 2004, the planners focused on securing the city neighborhood by neighborhood, with small combat outposts and police stations as the anchors on which security would rest. This plan—a chapter from the playbook of the 3rd Armored Cavalry Regiment in Tal Afar—was in sharp contrast to the operations of previous units in Ramadi—or, for that matter, most U.S. forces in Iraq before the surge:

> Past coalition operations in Ramadi had originated from large FOBs on the outskirts of town, with most forces conducting "drive-by COIN" (or combat)— they exited the FOB, drove to an objective or patrolled, were attacked, exchanged fire, and returned to base. Because the physical geography and road network in Ramadi enabled the enemy to observe and predict coalition movements, nearly every movement into the center of the city was attacked multiple times by improvised explosive devices, RPGs, or small arms, often with deadly results. Moreover, the patrols played into the insurgents' information operations campaign: Al-Qaeda exploited any collateral damage by depicting coalition Soldiers as aloof occupiers and random dispensers of violence against the populace.[27]

A captured insurgent assessed the predicament of U.S. soldiers clearly when he told his interrogator, "You own that street for an hour out of the day. We own it for the other twenty-three. And everyone understands that."[28] At least that was true of the previous unit in Ramadi. Colonel MacFarland recalled, "If they caught a lot of contact in an area, they just stopped going there, especially in downtown Ramadi. So, there were big parts of the map, I kind of joked, that I said were labeled, 'Here be monsters.'"[29]

The tactics used by the Ready First Combat Team would change that equation, and they anticipated the directive that General Petraeus would issue on his first day in command—that to secure the people, coalition forces had to live with the people, rather than operate from large bases. The combat outposts—jointly staffed by U.S. and Iraqi forces—provided bases for dismounted patrolling, safe houses for special operations teams and civil-military affairs centers, and enduring surveillance platforms inside Ramadi. Their positioning restricted insurgent and terrorist movements and impinged on al-Qaeda's ability to control Ramadi's neighborhoods. Tactically a defensive measure, operationally the outposts were a means to go on the offensive and wrest the initiative from the enemy in the battle over control of the Iraqi people.

In July 2006 the Ready First Combat Team established more than a dozen combat outposts in Ramadi and then held them against enemy counterattacks. Al-

Qaeda operatives never seemed to miss an opportunity to impale themselves on these fortifications. A massive, citywide battle on July 24 enabled the Ready First Combat Team to pummel al-Qaeda with its superior firepower. The combat outposts restricted the ability of insurgents to move around the city, but by themselves were insufficient to clear the city of enemy forces.[30] For this task, a viable police force was needed—a lesson learned from the battle for Tal Afar.[31] Nevertheless, the outposts were one of the keys to turning around a war that was almost lost. Lieutenant Colonel Deane, whose battalion fought in Ramadi during the critical summer of 2006, states, "Building the combat outposts, creating the walled cities and getting into the community really set the conditions we needed in order to get the Iraqi populace to understand that we weren't leaving and that we were going to see this thing through. All that led the sheiks to get together and build a police force. Had the combat outposts not been built, we probably wouldn't have had a police force; the recruits would have melted away, like in the past."[32] The contention of some analysts that positioning U.S. soldiers among the Iraqi people made no difference in the ultimate outcome of the Iraq War is patently false.

One staff officer, Captain Travis Patriquin, created a stick figure PowerPoint show to explain in terms anyone could understand why police were the key to the security problem. Local police knew the people and the neighborhoods and therefore could tell insurgents and criminals from common folk. The great fear was that by empowering local police drafted from the tribes, U.S. forces would simply be creating tribal militias. Indeed, those accusations were made by some commentators after the Awakening began. Nevertheless, Patriquin's Power-Point briefing went viral and became famous for its simple, pragmatic approach to winning the war for al-Anbar province.[33] However, to make the plan work the brigade needed to find willing and capable partners among Ramadi's elites and to protect them once they decided to side with the coalition. Otherwise, there would be few recruits for the police force and even less intelligence forthcoming on al-Qaeda.[34]

The Awakening gave MacFarland the opening he was looking for. He used the deputy brigade commander, Lieutenant Colonel Jim Lechner, and Captain Patriquin as go-betweens between himself and the sheiks. For his part, Patriquin fit the role perfectly. I brought Travis onto the brigade staff when he arrived in Germany in 2004. His expertise in culture and languages made him the perfect choice to be the brigade civil-military affairs officer, a role he did not want but one in which he excelled. He had served as an enlisted soldier supporting Special Forces before his commissioning, so he was older and more mature than most of his peers. He spoke conversational Arabic, grew a thick mustache that impressed the Iraqis (and flagrantly violated Army regulations), and integrated himself into Iraqi tribal culture. Over countless cups of tea and hundreds of cigarettes, he worked magic with the tribal leaders.[35]

In the fall of 2006 Sheik Sattar and other tribal sheiks in the Awakening began offering up hundreds of their tribesmen to join the police force. The Americans responded by training, arming, and equipping them, and later, in the spring of 2007, at General Petraeus's direction, began paying their salaries until they could be brought onto the rolls of the Iraqi Ministry of the Interior. By mutual agreement, the Americans built a police substation in the Jazeera neighborhood of Ramadi to give the tribes added protection against al-Qaeda reprisals, and then for good measure parked an M1A1 tank outside Sattar's personal compound. Other police substations were soon constructed in the areas of those tribes contributing additional recruits to the police force. To appease staff officers in the Marine Expeditionary Force headquarters in Fallujah who objected to supporting the creation of what they viewed as de facto tribal militias, the brigade fudged the status of these new posts to make them appear as satellites of a downtown police station.[36]

The word about the police recruiting and the building of local substations soon spread, and other tribal leaders wanted in on the action. The Ready First Combat Team was inundated with recruits, who were sent to Baghdad or Jordan for training and then returned to work in their tribal areas or in downtown Ramadi. Hundreds of other tribesmen who did not qualify for the police force were outfitted as provincial auxiliaries or formed neighborhood watch organizations. The new police offered cultural savvy and local knowledge that opened the door to enormous amounts of intelligence on al-Qaeda and other insurgent groups. They also added additional staying power to the power of the Army and Marine combat outposts. The police were soon apprehending hundreds of al-Qaeda suspects and uncovering the organization's weapons caches. The tribes also formed small vigilante groups that sought out al-Qaeda operatives at night and killed them in a tit-for-tat struggle for supremacy in Ramadi.[37] The squeeze was on.

Al-Qaeda would not go quietly into the night. On August 21 a death squad killed Sheik Khaled A'rak Ehtami al-A'layawi'a of the Abu Ali Jassim tribe, which had provided its sons for the growing police force in Ramadi. The terrorists then dumped his body in a field, where it remained hidden for several days in violation of the Islamic mandate of burial within twenty-four hours of death. On the same day, a suicide bomber drove a dump truck full of explosives into the new police station in Jazeera.

Both incidents backfired on al-Qaeda. William Doyle, Travis Patriquin's biographer, writes of the attack, "In a stirring scene that reminded Colonel Sean MacFarland of the flag-raising at Iwo Jima in 1945—and signified for him 'a true turning point in the war'—the Iraqi police at the station refused to abandon their post, declined offers of evacuation from coalition forces, ran up a tattered Iraqi flag, and resumed patrols on the same day. 'They stood their ground,' recalls MacFarland, 'and proved they wouldn't be intimidated.'"[38] As for the desecration of Sheik Khaled's body, the incident only further enraged his fellow tribal leaders. In accordance with the ancient code of vendetta by which they operated, it was now war to the knife—and war to the death—between the tribesmen and the terrorists.

The day after the meeting at his house and the announcement of the Awakening, Sheik Sattar met with Mohammad Mahmoud Latif, the head of the 1920 Revolutionary Brigades, a major insurgent group, and convinced him to join the battle against al-Qaeda. His men and those of several other insurgent groups would cease attacking American and Iraqi forces. It was a huge turnaround in a war that had gone on for three years.[39]

As various areas around and within Ramadi were cleared of al-Qaeda operatives, the Ready First Combat Team sponsored civic action and humanitarian projects using millions of dollars from the Commander's Emergency Response Program. Contracts were let to remove rubble, restore trash collection, repair the electrical grid and water distribution system, fix schools, and refurbish medical clinics, among other essential services. Many of these contracts went to Sheik Sattar and his fellow Awakening members, which provided them a reward for supporting the coalition and an incentive for others to join in the tribal revolt.[40] The brigade also waged an extensive information operations campaign to persuade the citizens of Ramadi to support the tribal leaders in their war against al-Qaeda. In an article published in the spring of 2008, Colonel MacFarland and Captain Niel Smith explain why the presurge strategy of transition had failed, and why the surge was so crucial to success in Iraq: "Instead of telling [the tribal leaders] that we would leave soon and they must assume responsibility for their own security, we told them that we would stay as long as necessary to defeat the terrorists. That was the message they had been waiting to hear. As long as they perceived us as mere interlopers, they dared not throw in their lot with ours. When they began to think of us as reliable partners, their attitudes began to change."[41] Over the next few months, a number of other small tribes "flipped" their allegiance to support the coalition against their tormenters. By November 2006 the Awakening had become an undeniable force in the Ramadi area, though Ramadi itself remained in the grip of al-Qaeda. Beyond that, the development was taking on wider implications, an assessment transmitted by the senior State Department representative in al-Anbar to his superiors in Washington.[42]

The tribes were now in the fight, but recruiting for the Iraqi army still lagged. The Sunnis of al-Anbar distrusted the army units stationed in the province, composed as they were of Shi'a recruits. "Ramadi area inhabitants regarded them as agents of the Sadr militia or Badr Corps, with a covert agenda to kill off Sunni tribes and enable a Shi'ite takeover of Anbar," MacFarland and Smith contended.[43] The solution to this problem was to recruit more Sunnis into the army ranks, but young Sunni men resisted enlisting since they could then be sent elsewhere to serve away from home. MacFarland advocated a change, which was adopted, to give recruits from al-Anbar a "station of choice" option to enlist and then return to serve in battalions stationed near their homes.[44] It was another initiative that General Petraeus would support upon learning of it after his assumption of command in February.

∎

Al-Qaeda in Iraq clearly understood the importance of the Awakening, which threatened its base of power and leadership of the Iraqi insurgency. In response, on October 15 the group declared the formation of the Islamic State of Iraq under the leadership of Abu Omar al-Baghdadi. Al-Qaeda then went further and demanded sovereignty over all nationalist insurgent groups and Sunni tribes. This was a deal for which the Sunni insurgency had not signed up, and it deepened the fissures between nationalist insurgent organizations and al-Qaeda in Iraq.[45] The infighting between these groups and al-Qaeda would soon have national implications as surge forces arrived in Iraq in January, including augmentations to al-Anbar province in February.

By November 2006 most of the area north and west of Ramadi was cleared of al-Qaeda forces. The city and its eastern and southern reaches were still contested, with al-Qaeda using suicide car bombers to target newly established combat outposts and police stations in these areas. A key turning point occurred on November 25, when the leader of the Abu Soda tribe in the Sufiyah neighborhood of eastern Ramadi, Sheik Jassim Muhammad Saleh al-Suwadawi, decided to throw in his lot with the Awakening. Facing the loss of one of its most important support areas, al-Qaeda attacked the tribe with a fury born of desperation. Gunmen wantonly killed members of the tribe and then looted and burned their homes. Sheik Jassim and his tribesmen fought back valiantly, but they were outgunned and in danger of being overrun. Desperate, the sheik made an emergency call to Captain Patriquin on a satellite phone.[46]

Ready First Combat Team leaders huddled and made a quick decision to protect the tribe, even though it was not yet officially a part of the Awakening. They diverted troops of the 1st Battalion, 9th Infantry, to the area and called in air and artillery support. F-18 and armed Predator drone strikes, combined with artillery and M1A1 tank fire, killed dozens of al-Qaeda operatives. Al-Qaeda's attempt to intimidate the tribe had backfired; the quick reaction of the Ready First Combat Team had proved to the tribesmen that Americans could be relied upon to defend them in their hour of greatest need. Within two months, every tribe in eastern Ramadi had joined the Awakening. By February 2007 contacts with insurgents in the area had dropped 70 percent from their June 2006 levels.[47]

By the beginning of the surge in early 2007, U.S. forces in al-Anbar province had gained the allegiance of a number of tribes, but many still remained on the fence, and the area around Ramadi was still the only location in which appreciable change had taken place. Tribal leaders wanted more assurance of a long-term commitment to support them against al-Qaeda, and they were likewise uncertain about the willingness of the government in Baghdad to cut Iraqi Sunnis a fair share of the country's power and resources.[48] The surge, which brought tens of thousands of additional U.S. forces into Iraq, answered part of the psychological need for certainty regarding the U.S. commitment to win the war against al-Qaeda. Tying the Iraqi government closer to the tribal leaders was a more difficult issue, but one tackled head-on by General Petraeus starting in February and, after his arrival in March, by Ambassador Crocker as well.

After several months of vacillation, and with General Petraeus's strong encouragement, Marine commanders in Fallujah finally agreed to put their full support behind Sattar and the Awakening. Marine and U.S. Army leaders empowered the sheiks who chose to support them and by doing so, persuaded many others to flip their allegiance from the insurgency to the coalition. "We knew what we needed to do, so we empowered the sheikhs, we connected them to the civil leadership, and we supported them with indigenous Iraqi security forces," stated Brigadier General John Allen, who played a vital role in supporting the Awakening as the deputy commanding general of Multi-National Force–West during the first year of the surge. "And then we provided the security top cover through constant conventional and special operations throughout the width and breadth and depth of the province."[49] So far limited to the area around Ramadi, the Awakening would soon expand as more U.S. forces poured into Iraq and changed the psychology surrounding the conflict.

Regrettably, Captain Travis Patriquin would not live to see the outcome of the tribal rebellion that he had helped to precipitate. He was killed in a roadside bomb explosion on December 6, 2006, along with Marine Major Megan McClung and Specialist Vincent Pomante. The sheiks of Ramadi paid him a singular tribute by naming a police station in his honor.

After General Petraeus assumed command of Multi-National Force–Iraq on February 10, 2007, the first place outside Baghdad he visited was the headquarters of the Ready First Combat Team in Ramadi, just before it shipped out of Iraq and traveled back home to Germany. Petraeus was keenly aware that the coalition could not kill or capture its way to victory in Iraq; here was a unit that had succeeded in reconciling with Iraqi tribes to fight a common enemy. I badly wanted to go along to see my old unit, but General Petraeus wisely left me behind to monitor activities in the headquarters at Camp Victory. In Ramadi Colonel MacFarland briefed General Petraeus on the activities of the Ready First Combat team and the status of the Awakening. Petraeus had known of MacFarland's initiative; however, what he learned on this visit still astonished—and heartened—him. Here was an organization that was putting into practice the precepts of the counterinsurgency doctrine that he had just published. MacFarland handed Petraeus several of the battle drills that his brigade had perfected, such as quickly establishing combat outposts ("COP in a Box") and a wide-area loudspeaker system ("Voice of Ramadi") that could counter insurgent propaganda blared from the mosques and serve as a useful tool in the information operations battle.[50]

More important, Petraeus learned a great deal about the Awakening movement and the power of the tribal revolt against al-Qaeda in the Ramadi area. He developed a greater sense of what was possible if U.S. forces were willing to assume risk and embrace reconciliation—a key component of the "surge of ideas" that guided the employment of the surge of forces. In Ramadi, Iraqi Sunnis were supporting coalition operations against the insurgency not just with words but with deeds. Anbari tribesmen were shedding blood to rid the area of unwanted al-Qaeda terrorists. "It was a truly uplifting experience," General Petraeus recalled. "Ramadi validated that you could take fence-sitters and some insurgents out of the mix."[51] While the Marine command in al-Anbar thought the connections with Sheik Sattar were worth pursuing, they had put greater weight on the negotiations with the more prominent tribal sheiks in Amman. Petraeus reversed the priority, for one good reason: The sheiks in Amman "weren't on the ground and they weren't creating new facts on the ground the way Sheik Sattar and Sean McFarland were."[52] He made an immediate decision to throw the weight of Multi-National Force–Iraq behind the Awakening. It was a decision that would have immediate impact and enormous consequences for the future of the conflict.

Upon his return to Baghdad the following day, General Petraeus handed me a gift from Sean MacFarland—a Ready First Combat Team commander's coin. I wasn't able to link up with Sean until October, when he visited Baghdad in his new capacity as the Iraq desk officer on the Joint Staff in the Pentagon. I congratulated him on the Ready First Combat Team's accomplishments in Ramadi, and he graciously thanked me for turning over to him a well-trained brigade. Sean and his soldiers had accomplished a near-miracle in Ramadi, and he merited the well-deserved promotion to brigadier general that came soon thereafter.[53]

General Petraeus knew that something extraordinary was happening in al-Anbar province, and he was determined to take advantage of what the opportunities there offered to the wider war effort. If we were to ensure the Awakening was not smothered in the cradle, it was imperative to tie what was happening in Ramadi to the national government in Baghdad. After his trip, Petraeus encouraged Prime Minister Maliki to fly with him to Ramadi to visit Governor Mamoun, Sheik Sattar, and the leaders of the Awakening. Petraeus and Maliki made the trip together on March 13 in the first example of what Petraeus called "helicopter diplomacy." The hazardous condition of Iraq's roads prevented the Iraqi prime minister from traveling outside of Baghdad. To overcome this impediment, General Petraeus offered Maliki and his entourage transportation in U.S. helicopters. (Understanding that the leader of the Iraqi government should not have to rely on U.S. helicopters over the long term, Petraeus also ordered MNSTC-I to convert several Russian-made HIP helicopters into VIP transportation for the Iraqi government.)

The trip was a qualified success. Upon landing at Camp Blue Diamond, Maliki made his way into a palace to host a televised conference with Iraqi government and tribal leaders, while General Petraeus unobtrusively exited the other side of the aircraft and went the other direction to visit U.S. units and tour combat outposts and other facilities in Ramadi, where combat operations to clear the city were ongoing. Maliki's trip to al-Anbar was his first in several decades and showed the Anbaris that he was concerned about their affairs. Sheik Sattar demanded new provincial elections, declaring, "There are two enemies here: the Iraqi Islamic Party and the terrorists." The first group was a Sunni Islamist political party that was part of Maliki's government in Baghdad, but uniformly despised by the tribes.[54] Others asked for more government support in rebuilding infrastructure and providing essential services. The meeting was raucous and argumentative, but Maliki was attentive and listened civilly to the various demands. Though General Petraeus deliberately did not attend the meeting, he did have his longtime civilian translator and senior adviser, Sadi Othman, sit in as a member of the prime minister's delegation. General Petraeus was hopeful that the event would spark the creation of a more unified Sunni political identity, as well as convince Sunnis that Maliki's administration was a government for all Iraqis.

The task now was to nurture and expand the Awakening. Sattar was a sheik in a minor tribe that held little sway outside of the area around Ramadi. Eventually, the larger tribes would have to cast their lot with the Awakening for it to grow. Brigadier General Allen worked patiently with the tribal chieftains in Jordan and Syria, trying to persuade them to return home. His diplomacy paid dividends in early July 2007, when Sheik Mishan al-Jumaily, head of the powerful Jumaily tribe, returned to the Fallujah area. With his support, tribesmen volunteered to join a "provincial security force" to fight al-Qaeda and secure the outskirts of Fallujah. The Marines responded by training the force and providing reconstruction contracts to Sheik Mishan and others who allied themselves with the coalition. A strong Iraqi chief of police in Fallujah, Colonel Faisal Ismail al-Zobai, who as a former insurgent understood what it took to defeat the insurgency, also made a huge difference in the campaign to rid the city of al-Qaeda influence and intimidation.[55] Within a matter of weeks after Sheik Mishan's return, the number of security incidents in the Fallujah area dropped dramatically.[56] This development allowed the Marines to divide Fallujah into sectors, each of which they subsequently cleared and "gated" (using cement barriers and other obstacles coupled with an identification card system to monitor entry), and in which they then established Marine squads partnered with newly trained local police to provide local security.

Other leaders followed Sheik Mishan back to their tribal lands in al-Anbar province. Seeing their power slip away, the paramount sheiks of the Anbari tribes in Jordan and Syria filtered back into Iraq over the course of 2007.[57] The members of the Provincial Council returned to Ramadi from their self-imposed exile in Baghdad. The towns and cities of the Euphrates River Valley, once the hotbed of insurgent and terrorist activity, slowly returned to life.

Al-Qaeda made desperate attempts to destroy the Awakening, to no avail. The terrorists used chlorine bombs on a number of occasions in the winter and spring of 2007 to punish Anbaris for siding with the coalition, but these horrific attacks

failed to suppress the Awakening.[58] Suicide bombers attacked dozens of police stations, but the police remained at their posts and continued their operations to
round up al-Qaeda operatives. Al-Qaeda then planned a more kinetic strike on
Ramadi, but this attack also failed. On June 30 troops of the 1st Battalion, 77th
Armor Regiment, stumbled upon a meeting of upward of seventy armed insurgents who were preparing a strike on the city. In the ensuing all-night firefight,
U.S. soldiers killed nearly three dozen insurgents at the cost of two killed and
eleven wounded. The "Battle of Donkey Island" all but ended al-Qaeda's threat to
Ramadi.[59] Al-Qaeda fighters fled the province to sanctuaries elsewhere in Iraq.

Much of al-Anbar province had been reclaimed by the summer of 2007, although areas east and northeast of Fallujah would take longer. But to win the
larger war, MNF-I, along with Iraqi security forces and tribal allies, had to secure
Baghdad and its environs and destroy terrorist sanctuaries in Diyala, Salah ad-
Din, and Nineveh provinces. General Petraeus and Lieutenant General Odierno
had begun the process by moving U.S. forces off their large forward operating
bases and into the communities alongside Iraqi soldiers and police. General Petraeus now decided to extend the lessons of the battle for Ramadi—many of which
had already been codified in the new counterinsurgency field manual—to the rest
of Iraq. The "big idea" emerging from Ramadi was that stability would be achieved
by the bottom-up engagement of tribes and other Sunni groups as well as through
the pursuit of top-down reconciliation via the Iraqi government, albeit with a
heavy dose of fighting to clear areas of al-Qaeda and other irreconcilable elements.
Petraeus began the process of encouraging the expansion of the Awakening by
launching an information campaign to communicate the theme that al-Qaeda had
declared war on the Iraqi people.

The spread of the Awakening movement outside the borders of al-Anbar province
happened quickly, but in haphazard fashion. Initially, many Sunni tribal leaders
looked to Sheik Sattar as an intermediary between the tribes and the Americans.
Brigadier General John Allen, who helped the tribal movement flourish in 2007,
stated, "I would go see Sheikh Sattar, and he would have . . . a guesthouse full of
40 or 50 sheikhs. . . . These guys would be from Diyala Province, Salah-ad-Din
Province, Ninawa Province. They'd come from Baghdad, and all around the Sunni
Triangle, these Awakening movements were starting, almost like franchises."[60] But
as the battle for Ramadi demonstrated, the sheiks alone could not defeat al-Qaeda.
Despite Sattar's dedication to the cause, he needed help to cultivate the Awakening
on a broader scale.

Soon after General Petraeus's return from visiting the Ready First Combat Team
in Ramadi, senior coalition leaders convened at the Maude House, the Green Zone
residence of the senior British officer in Iraq. They decided to pursue reconciliation on a determined basis, and agreed to the formation of the Force Strategic Engagement Cell under the direction of Lieutenant General Graeme Lamb. Petraeus

gave U.S. commanders authorization and encouragement to partner with former insurgent groups and others willing to commit to the fight against al-Qaeda. There was not huge enthusiasm for this change in policy at first, as some officers resented having to deal with Iraqis who had American blood on their hands. But in meetings and visits with subordinate leaders, Petraeus drove the point home. Supporting reconciliation was not optional.[61]

In June, Prime Minister Maliki also appointed an Implementation and Follow-Up Committee for National Reconciliation (IFCNR), headed by Deputy National Security Adviser Dr. Safa Hussein, Brigadier General Adnan of the Office of the Commander in Chief, and Maliki's close confidant Dr. Bassima al-Jaidri, to pursue opportunities for outreach with insurgent and militia groups. General Petraeus directed British Foreign Office official Emma Sky, whom he'd known since her service in Kirkuk in 2003, to accompany Dr. Bassima on visits to the leaders of various groups around Baghdad, which picked up pace through the summer of 2007. The committee erected as many roadblocks as it opened doors, and U.S. commanders found working with the group frustrating and difficult. The sectarian outlook of the committee made compromise with Sunni groups tricky, but its formation was nevertheless a step in the right direction.

Initially, local deals were struck between U.S. commanders and Sunni groups that allowed for the formation of armed neighborhood watch organizations in Sunni areas. For example, in the Abu Ghraib region just west of Baghdad, the 2nd Battalion, 5th Cavalry Regiment, supported a force organized by the Zobai tribe (known as the Volunteers) whose activities substantially reduced violence in the area in the spring and summer of 2007.[62] In Baqubah in Diyala province, more than a thousand Sunnis had joined an organization known as the Baqubah Guardians.[63] U.S. commanders in Salah ad-Din, Babil, and Baghdad also sought out opportunities to engage local Sunni (and some Shi'a) tribes to gain their cooperation. However, it soon became apparent that these disparate arrangements needed to be centrally coordinated. Multi-National Corps–Iraq and Multi-National Division–Baghdad created reconciliation cells to seek out tribal leaders and recruit their tribesmen into armed neighborhood watch organizations, first labeled in Orwellian fashion as Concerned Local Citizens, and later, after U.S. commanders discovered through their cultural advisers that "concerned" translated into Arabic as "worried," by the more apt term *Abnaa al-Iraq*, "Sons of Iraq," or SOI.

One of the first conversions of Sunni insurgents in Baghdad occurred in Amiriyah, a district of twenty-five thousand Sunnis in the western part of the city that had been thoroughly infiltrated by al-Qaeda as terrorist operatives fled the Awakening movement in al-Anbar. In the spring of 2007, al-Qaeda designated Amiriyah the new capital of its caliphate in Mesopotamia. In May 2007 fourteen American soldiers died in the district, making it the most dangerous place in Iraq.[64] U.S. commanders established a policy that movement in the area could be carried out only in heavily armored tanks and infantry fighting vehicles; given that the enemy was using 750-pound deeply buried bombs, in some cases even these vehicles were insufficient to fend off enemy attacks.

Al-Qaeda brutality soon changed the attitude of the Sunni inhabitants. Terrorist operatives wantonly kidnapped or killed inhabitants, including young children and old men. Bodies were dumped in the garbage, some of them booby-trapped to prevent their retrieval and proper burial. Women without headscarves were disfigured with acid thrown on their faces. Finally, one insurgent leader, Saif Sa'ad Ahmed al-Ubaydi, also known as Abu Abed, had enough of the cruelty. Al-Qaeda operatives planted a roadside bomb in front of his house. When Abu Abed asked them to move the bomb to prevent his home from being targeted by coalition forces, they refused. Abu Abed decided it was time to declare war on al-Qaeda. His group, part of the "Islamic Army," started targeting al-Qaeda leaders for assassination.[65]

Abu Abed became the poster figure for the SOI movement. He was a former Iraqi intelligence major who joined the insurgency when Ambassador Jerry Bremer disbanded the Iraqi Army. Two of his brothers had been killed in the Iran-Iraq War, and two others had been abducted, tortured, and killed by Shi'a death squads during the height of the civil war in October 2006.[66] Although he and his insurgent group had decided to battle al-Qaeda, his relationship with the Americans in Amiriyah was uncertain. Then in late May al-Qaeda operatives kidnapped an elderly Christian man and dishonored his wife by pulling off her skirt. A local imam, Sheik Waleed al-Asawi, witnessed the event and encouraged local residents to resist the terrorists, who were acting outside the bounds of accepted Islamic morality. On May 30 Abu Abed and his men confronted the kidnappers and ended up in a two-day running gun battle, which al-Qaeda was on the verge of winning until Sheik Waleed called the local American unit for help.[67]

After consulting with Colonel J. B. Burton, the brigade commander in charge of northwest Baghdad, Lieutenant Colonel Dale Kuehl, commander of the 1st Battalion, 5th Cavalry Regiment ("Black Knights"), stationed in Amiriyah, decided to act. Kuehl sent two infantry platoons to support Abu Abed and his fighters, pinned down by al-Qaeda operatives near the Firdas mosque. Kuehl later led a convoy of Bradley fighting vehicles to make contact with Abu Abed. "My men thought I was nuts," Kuehl stated. "I went into a house, surrounded by former insurgents, thinking this could go either way. They [Abu Abed and his men] were ready to go on operations [against al-Qaeda] right away. It was surreal, fighters jumping on our vehicles."[68] Together Kuehl's forces and Abu Abed's men beat back al-Qaeda and took control of the streets.

Kuehl and his Iraqi counterpart from the 2nd Battalion, 1st Brigade, 6th Iraqi Army Division, supported the creation of a six hundred–strong force known as the *Forsan al-Rafidain* (Knights of the Two Rivers) under the control of Abu Abed. The formation of this group effectively provided the coalition with another battalion of light infantry in one of the crucial hotbeds of violence in Baghdad. To prevent fratricide and protect the civilian population from violence, the two commanders and Abu Abed agreed to control measures and a code of conduct that included limits on armament and procedures for handling detainees.[69] Abu Abed's men were also photographed, fingerprinted, and entered into a biometric database. The relationship turned out to be productive. Relations with the Sunni elite in Amiriyah created a new level of understanding for the U.S. military leaders in the area. "Abu Abed and the imams were also cutting deals within Amiriyah in order to gain more support," Kuehl noted. "As we got closer to the community we gained a greater understanding of the social mosaic we were dealing with which included influential imams, technocrats from the previous regime, former military officers, tribal sheiks, and businessmen."[70] Abu Abed and his men also knew who was affiliated with al-Qaeda, and together with the American and Iraqi soldiers, over the next several months they destroyed the terrorist infrastructure in Amiriyah.

A little more than a week later, while running on a Sunday morning at Camp Victory with Major Chip Daniels, the operations officer for the 1st Battalion, 5th Cavalry, General Petraeus heard about the incident in which the former insurgent fighters had fought with U.S. soldiers against al-Qaeda. This was a first for Baghdad, and therefore a critical turning point. Petraeus directed Daniels to take a message back to his commander—do not stop what you are doing, and don't let the U.S. chain of command or the Iraqi government interfere with your initiative.[71] The top cover encouraged Kuehl and other commanders to take risks that would have been frowned upon before the surge.

General Petraeus decided to meet with Abu Abed. We arranged a meeting through Dale Kuehl and drove to Amiriyah. After receiving a briefing on the area at a joint security station, General Petraeus decided to conduct a short dismounted patrol in the area. Abu Abed's men formed the outer security perimeter, while General Petraeus's personal security detachment formed the inner perimeter. I observed Abu Abed's men move through the streets of Amiriyah and was astonished by their tactical abilities. They were well equipped and well disciplined, and clearly had professional military training. *No wonder we had so much difficulty fighting these guys,* I thought to myself. The visit concluded without incident, but it made a deep impression on General Petraeus and the team.

What had happened in Amiriyah crystallized General Petraeus's thinking about the value of bottom-up reconciliation at the local level as a complement to top-down reconciliation legislation, which by mid-2007 looked to be going nowhere. He believed that Amiriyah was a promising example of local citizens helping to secure their own neighborhoods, an example he both supported and hoped to replicate elsewhere in Iraq, albeit with an eye toward the various local circumstances in different areas. Iraqis had tasted what al-Qaeda had to offer and largely rejected its extreme brand of Islam and excessively conservative social mores. An opportunity to engage the Sunni communities in their own defense was at hand, and in Petraeus's view coalition and Iraqi leaders needed to assume more risk in taking advantage of it. This support did not entail "arming the tribes," as some journalists presumed. In fact, most SOI personnel were already well armed. General Petraeus and General Odierno allowed U.S. commanders to arrange for ammunition resupply, but the more important function of U.S. support was to put structure behind SOI organizations, to provide rudimentary training, to pay salaries, and to link them closely to U.S. and Iraqi forces, as had already been done in al-Anbar province.

Another tough part of Baghdad was the northeast district of Adhamiya, an area for which the Ready First Combat Team was responsible back in 2003–2004 when I was in command.[72] By the summer of 2007 Adhamiya was firmly in the grip of the insurgency, the last remaining Sunni enclave east of the Tigris River. But even here, in one of the staunchest regions of Sunni rejectionism in Iraq, al-Qaeda's excesses would alienate the population. A defining moment came in early August 2007, when extremists murdered two nephews of a prominent Sunni leader, Sheik Wathiq al-Ubaidi. Wathiq was a former imam at the Abu Hanifa mosque, a famous Sunni religious center, and he had been involved in the insurgency as far back as the first year of the conflict.[73] When insurgents refused to allow Wathiq to bury his nephews in the Abu Hanifa cemetery, he denounced them as terrorists, gathered his clansmen, and stormed the mosque grounds, where a number of al-Qaeda operatives enjoyed sanctuary. The resulting melee led to the intervention of a local Iraqi army unit, which detained dozens of insurgents and seized an enormous cache of weapons and explosives on the mosque grounds and in the adjacent cemetery.[74]

Al-Qaeda quickly retaliated. A week later operatives bombed Wathiq's home, seriously wounding him and killing three of his relatives. Although Wathiq had not yet thrown in his lot with the coalition, U.S. leaders agreed to transport the badly injured sheik to Ibn Sina Hospital, the U.S. trauma facility located inside the Green Zone. Upon hearing the news, I was more than a bit bemused by the turn of events that would lead to my brigade's number one target being treated in a U.S. hospital for wounds received at the hands of al-Qaeda terrorists. Such was life (and death) during the surge. Although Adhamiya remained problematical for some time to come, a budding SOI movement slowly began to turn the district around.

Throughout the summer, General Petraeus pushed subordinate leaders to take advantage of the Sunni rejection of al-Qaeda to form local groups for self-defense where it made sense to do so. He also made extensive efforts to connect these local groups with the Iraqi government. In mid-August, Petraeus arranged meetings between SOI leaders in Amiriyah and Ghazalia and high-ranking American and Iraqi civilian officials. Ambassador Crocker and Deputy National Security Adviser for Iraq and Afghanistan Meghan O'Sullivan accompanied General Petraeus to

Ghazalia, while Deputy Prime Minister of Iraq Barham Saleh, Minister of Defense Abdul Qadir, and National Security Adviser Mowaffak al-Rubaie accompanied him on his visit to Amiriyah. Curious as to how Abu Abed and his men were doing, I went along on the visit to Amiriyah as well. The group met with Abu Abed at SOI headquarters and engaged in a lively discussion, which Sadi had difficulty translating in real time. The meeting was a turning point for the Maliki administration, which had serious concerns about cooperating with armed Sunni groups in Baghdad. Abu Abed was a fierce foe of al-Qaeda and hated the Jaish al-Mahdi, but he was not an enemy of the Shi'ites of Iraq. By putting a face on the Sons of Iraq, the meeting helped somewhat to assuage Iraqi government concerns about the newest members of the coalition arrayed against al-Qaeda.

The fact that these meetings took place at all was a hopeful sign that SOI groups, tired of al-Qaeda and Jaish al-Mahdi abuses on their communities, could be formalized as part of the solution to achieving "sustainable stability" in Iraq. Nevertheless, many Iraqi government officials remained wary of legitimizing these groups. General Petraeus felt it was vitally important that they do so, for the window of opportunity opened by the Anbar Awakening would not last forever. One of his tasks was to push the Iraqi government to take advantage of the opportunity offered by involving local citizens in the security of their neighborhoods. The visits to Amiriyah and Ghazalia were part of this process.

The most controversial part of the program came later. When it became apparent that large numbers of Iraqis were willing to assist the coalition in fighting al-Qaeda but had no jobs or resources to take care of their families, General Petraeus authorized the use of Commander's Emergency Relief Program funds to pay local groups for security services. The salary scale was fixed at $300 per person per month, which prevented al-Qaeda and the insurgency from easily outbidding the coalition for cheap Iraqi manpower. Contrary to what some commentators believe, the coalition did not merely "pay off" the insurgents to get them to switch sides. The various tribes and groups came over to the side of the coalition willingly in order to fight al-Qaeda, and only later did U.S. commanders decide to pay these Iraqis a living wage. Abu Abed and his fighters, for instance, signed their first security contract in late August, fully three months after they made common cause with Dale Kuehl and his battalion in their struggle against al-Qaeda in Amiriyah.[75] "Money was not the primary motivator for Abu Abed," Kuehl later remarked. "Instead, I believe he was driven by a desire to protect his family and bring stability to the Sunni areas. While he was very much against JAM, I would not label him as sectarian. Several of his closest aides were Shia. I would classify him as a nationalist if anything."[76] In fact, by the end of summer 2007 fewer than half of SOI personnel were under CERP contracts. During the course of the Sons of Iraq program, U.S. commanders signed 779 security contracts with local groups, paying as much as $30 million per month for these groups to assist in tamping down the insurgency and providing security and stability in Iraq.[77] For its manifest accomplishments in reducing violence in Iraq, the program was cheap at twice the price.

It is also not true, as some commentators have insinuated, that General Petraeus kept Washington in the dark regarding the SOI program. He did not ask for permission to begin the program, but he kept the secretary of defense updated both in person during Secretary Gates's visits to Iraq and via weekly written reports, which acknowledged the risks involved in creating the program (along with the efforts to tie the program closely to the Iraqi government to mitigate those risks).[78] And he updated President Bush during his and Ambassador Crocker's weekly video teleconferences, as well. At their peak, the SOI numbered more than 100,000 men—a significant addition to the force structure engaged in security duties in Iraq.[79] The melding of the formal organization of the U.S. military, "the strongest tribe" in the words of Bing West, and the informal patronage networks of the Iraqi tribes proved to be a powerful and winning combination.[80]

Coalition leaders were careful to ensure that the Sons of Iraq remained under positive control. SOI personnel were interviewed, photographed, fingerprinted, and entered into a biometric identity database.[81] SOI leaders reported to U.S. commanders and later, once the program was transferred to Iraqi control, to Iraqi military leaders. SOI personnel wore emblems to establish their role as security personnel—usually orange "road guard" vests or reflective belts supplied to them by American units. SOI personnel had to swear allegiance to the Iraqi government. Their ammunition resupply came through the Iraqi Ministry of Defense. And the golden rule applied—he who had the gold made the rules. SOI leaders understood who their paymaster was, and they acted accordingly.

The goal of many Sunnis who joined the SOI was to gain permanent employment as policemen. Maliki's government, concerned that the SOI were nothing more than an armed Sunni militia and therefore a potential regime threat, balked at incorporating them into the Iraqi security forces. The Iraqi administration eventually agreed to accept at least 20 percent of the SOI into the police, but threw up roadblocks whenever Multi-National Force–Iraq presented lists of names for vetting. The Force Strategic Engagement Cell, under Northern Ireland veteran Major General Paul Newton and Donald Blome, a senior aide to Ambassador Crocker, continued to press home to the Iraqi government the advantages of drawing the SOI into the system.[82] As General Petraeus and Ambassador Crocker clearly recognized, it would be difficult if not impossible to stamp out the Sunni insurgency without some sort of political reconciliation; bringing the SOI, many of whom were former insurgents, into allegiance with the government would hasten the war's end. To Shi'a Iraqis who had been persecuted for decades under Ba'athist rule, it was a tough sell. As Colonel Marty Stanton, the chief of engagement and reconciliation at MNC-I, stated, "The Sunnis recognize that they've lost, and they're coming to the table. The Shi'a don't recognize yet that they've won."[83]

Al-Qaeda recognized the enormous threat this development posed, and its operatives targeted SOI and Awakening leaders for elimination. On June 25 a suicide bomber detonated his explosive vest in the lobby of the Mansour Hotel in Baghdad, where a meeting of Awakening leaders was ongoing, killing a dozen people, including four sheiks affiliated with the Awakening.[84] A more strategically significant assassination was that of Sheik Sattar, the founder of the Awakening. He was killed by a roadside bomb in September 2007, just days after he fulfilled one of his dreams by meeting President George W. Bush, who had flown to Iraq to meet with Iraqi government leaders. Sattar's brother, Sheik Ahmad Abu Risha al-Rishawi, took over his position in the tribe and assumed leadership of the Awakening, which mourned Sattar's loss but continued unabated. Sheik Ahmad lacked his brother's swashbuckling aura, but he was an accomplished leader who provided a deft hand in transforming the Awakening into a political movement.[85] He had, in fact, apparently been the brains behind some of the earlier initiatives. The attacks had little impact on the Awakening.

Despite being targeted by al-Qaeda for assassination, being the enemy of its enemy did not exactly make SOI and Awakening leaders friends in the eyes of the Iraqi government. Harassment of SOI leaders took on many forms. Persecuted by both the Maliki administration and al-Qaeda, the SOI relied heavily on the coalition for protection and sustenance. Their survival after the U.S. withdrawal from Iraq was problematical.

Iraqi government officials did not have a problem with the Awakening in al-Anbar province. The police recruited from Anbari tribes were paid by the Iraqi Ministry of the Interior, and they secured areas in their tribal homelands, which were predominantly Sunni. The Maliki administration had more serious concerns about SOI groups in mixed sectarian areas of Iraq, where the battle between Shi'ites and Sunnis for local domination raged on. Indeed, Sunni groups in these areas had an agenda that often deviated widely from the quest for reconciliation with the government in Baghdad.[86] Many SOI personnel were former insurgents who had decided to pitch in their lot with the Americans to fight their al-Qaeda tormentors and keep the Iraqi government off their backs. The Iraqi government viewed them with a great deal of suspicion.

General Petraeus laid the issue out clearly to Secretary of Defense Gates in his report on June 2, 2007. "My sensing is that if we were to ask the Maliki Government if they support Sunni tribal engagement and reconciliation they would answer yes," Petraeus wrote. He continued:

In Sunni provinces like Anbar and Salah ad Din, they would likely mean yes. Closer to Baghdad they might say yes, but would act to slow roll any movement. In places like Diyala, they might say yes, but would be very unsure of how to proceed. The appetite of the Shi'a leadership for Sunni tribal engagement lessens significantly as the issue gets closer to Shi'a towns and neighbor-

hoods. Sustainable security necessitates first the building of a patchwork of localized political accommodations and security and then the stitching together
of these patches through true political reconciliation between the sects. We
are getting a glimpse of the difficulty of the latter in areas that really matter to
the Shi'a.[87]

In a nutshell Petraeus had spelled out the manifest difficulties of achieving national reconciliation, along with his strategy to reach that elusive goal from the
bottom up across Iraq.

General Petraeus argued that it was better to engage local groups than to fight
them. Co-option and power sharing would tie the SOI to the Iraqi government
and minimize the risk that supporting the SOI was doing nothing more than level-
ing the playing field for a resumption of the civil war at a future date. As had been
the case since the spring of 2003, General Petraeus believed that it was critical that
Sunnis be given incentives to support the new Iraq, or their sense of disenfranchisement would fuel the insurgency. But since American commanders paid the
SOI, the Iraqi government had limited control over their activities. Despite the
arguments of U.S. commanders that bringing former insurgents into the tent was
preferable to continuing to fight them, this dichotomy created a tension that remained unresolved until the program was transferred to Iraqi control in late 2008
and the Iraqi government came to terms with the SOI in its own—and predictably
Iraqi—way.[88]

Nevertheless, the Sons of Iraq program was instrumental to the success of
the surge. "The history of this reconciliation effort remains to be written but it
is one of courage," writes Lieutenant General Raymond Odierno. "Courage by
the Coalition to reconcile with former insurgents, courage by those insurgents to
cease fighting and seek to preserve Sunni rights through cooperation and political means, and courage by the mostly Shi'a elected leaders of Iraq to accept and
support these former enemies and fellow Iraqis. It was a calculated risk; the only
way this could have worked was to decentralize decisions to brigade, battalion
and company commanders. Senior commanders had to underwrite this risk and
provide the top cover for their junior commanders."[89] Both General Petraeus and
Lieutenant General Odierno underwrote the risk essential to allow subordinate
leaders to form and nurture SOI groups in their areas. By co-opting former insurgents to fight their enemies, senior coalition leaders paved the way forward in a
war deemed unwinnable by their critics.

To fast-forward just a bit, by November 2007 Amiriyah had become a different
place from the deadly battleground it had been the previous spring. "The results
of our efforts speak for themselves," Dale Kuehl opined on an Internet blog. "We
have not had a mortar or rocket attack within Amiriyah since July. Dead bodies
used to litter the streets, but we have not had a murder reported since August. The

last IED attack was on August 7th. Since that time, my battalion has suffered no casualties within Amiriyah, while 2/1/6 IA [Iraqi Army] has had only one wounded Soldier."[90] The improved security situation had enabled Kuehl's battalion to focus on improving essential services, such as trash pickup, sewage removal, and the provision of clean water to the community. The economy, while not yet vibrant, was improving. What factors accounted for this progress?

Kuehl remarked in an article in 2008 that many of the conditions required for the emergence of the Sons of Iraq in Amiriyah began to materialize before his unit arrived in Baghdad in November 2006 and included forces beyond his unit's control. But the surge was the key to nurturing these conditions to fruition. The rise of Sunni opposition to al-Qaeda "was not just about Amiriyah," Kuehl wrote. "It was tied to the greater forces acting themselves out throughout Baghdad itself and more specifically in northwest Baghdad. Factors in this decision included the commitment we had demonstrated to the protection of the population. The increasingly effective targeting we had been doing against al-Qaeda based upon our increased intelligence which included SOF operations. Another factor was the relationships we had continued to foster with the Sunni imams. The increase in combat power I had placed in Amiriyah which was enabled by the increase of forces in Mansour also played a role. . . . Now, with barriers and COPs to impede movement and additional forces to put pressure on AQI throughout Mansour, AQI really had nowhere to go. Bottom line the increase in the number of Soldiers in our area greatly enhanced our ability to defeat al-Qaeda."[91]

In an oral history interview conducted in 2009, the provincial reconstruction team leader for al-Anbar, James Soriano, listed four reasons for the restoration of coalition fortunes in that province. The first was the shift in Sunni opinion, which in 2006–2007 came to view al-Qaeda as an enemy while the United States was transformed into a friend and potential savior. The second was tribal engagement by U.S. commanders, which eventually persuaded the sheiks to side with the coalition. The third, which was closely tied to tribal engagement and was the most important factor, was police recruitment. The fourth was the increasing effectiveness of U.S. and Iraqi security force operations, including the impact of special operations forces that eliminated hundreds if not thousands of irreconcilables from the battlefield.[92] To this list Soriano also noted the impact of religious leaders on Iraqi Sunni sentiment: The role of the mosque is "something you don't even understand in public opinion. In '05, [imams] were calling for insurrection. By '06, they were calling for moderation. By '09, they were telling the people to get out and vote."[93]

When one looks at areas outside of al-Anbar, other factors—addressed in the following chapters—must be added to this list. But one factor was essential to all of them: the surge. Without the provision of U.S. reinforcements to Iraq, it is highly unlikely that the Awakening would have expanded beyond the borders of al-Anbar province, or that Iraqi Sunnis would have cast their lot with the American forces then occupying their country. The surge had an impact on the Iraqi psyche all out of proportion to its physical impact on the war. Thirty thousand additional American troops could not turn the tide in Iraq without other factors coming into play.

Sean MacFarland intuitively sensed the problem with U.S. strategy in Iraq in 2006. By emphasizing transition to Iraqi control and continually beating the drum about a forthcoming withdrawal of forces from Iraq, U.S. military and political leaders had basically sent the message that the Iraqis would soon be on their own. MacFarland later commented:

> Now, the sheiks had been pretty much benignly neglected by the 2-28th [ID] and the strategic communications message that they were giving to the sheiks was the same thing that all the Iraqis were being told by the Coalition forces at the time, which was, "Hey. Don't worry. The Coalition forces aren't going to stay here forever. We are not an occupying force. We are here today; but, we will be gone tomorrow." Well, that was exactly what was worrying them. I mean, they weren't going to talk to any Coalition folks if they knew that we were just a transient force, because al-Qaeda was not telling them that. Al-Qaeda was saying, "We are going to stay here forever and this is going to be the capital of our new caliphate." So, if you were an Iraqi and you had the Americans saying, "Hey. Don't worry. We are going to be gone soon," and the AQ guys saying, "You better worry because we are going to stay," who were you going to listen to? Are you going to throw in with the Americans who are going to be gone or mind your Ps and Qs so al-Qaeda doesn't come and saw your head off? So, we changed our strategic communications message to say, "Don't worry. We are not leaving. We are going to stand by you side by side and fight al-Qaeda until they are defeated." Then, as a visible demonstration of that, they saw our combat outposts, that first one going up there in the Jazeera area by "C" Lake up in the tribal area, that happened to coincide with a couple of tribes that were leaning toward the Coalition.[94]

By moving its units into the city and partnering with Sattar and other tribal sheiks, the Ready First Combat Team was able to change the mindset of the tribes around Ramadi. But its reach was limited. The spread of the Awakening—in effect, a decision by Iraqi Sunnis to engage with American forces in an attempt to arrest their declining fortunes—would require more substantial means of support. The surge, coupled with General Petraeus's decision to support the Awakening and other local movements that resulted in the creation of the Sons of Iraq, provided that crucial catalyst. Without the surge, the Awakening would have been much more limited in its scope and impact.

In war, the enemy gets a vote. In Iraq, al-Qaeda voted poorly. The jihadists initially gained momentum as they took advantage of U.S. mistakes to ingratiate themselves with Iraqi Sunnis. By early 2006 they had essentially gained control of much of al-Anbar province. Riding a wave of success, al-Qaeda leaders then allowed hubris to guide their decisions, with disastrous consequences. They ignored the nationalist ideology of their Iraqi compatriots. They instilled a severe version of Shari'a law inconsistent with Iraqi mores. They tortured and killed Iraqi citizens with no thought to humanitarian concerns. Their ignorance and brutality opened the way for the tribes to unite with American forces and thereby change the strategic calculus of the war.

"No matter their skills and good intentions, foreign troops cannot persuade the people of another nation to reject insurgents in their midst," writes military analyst and historian Bing West. "The people must convince themselves—and be willing to sacrifice for that conviction."[95] In Iraq in 2006 and 2007, enough Iraqis chose to reject al-Qaeda—and enough American commanders sided with them in their hour of greatest need—to have a decisive impact on the course of the war.

By the summer of 2007 the insurgent tide had crested. Whether it would reverse or not remained to be seen.

CHAPTER 6

Turning the Tide

The maximum use of force is in no way incompatible with
the simultaneous use of the intellect.
—Carl von Clausewitz

The first five months of the surge were a shaping period to set the conditions required to secure the Iraqi people, defeat al-Qaeda, and rein in or co-opt Sunni insurgent groups and Shi'a militias. Reinforcements deployed to Iraq, units left their forward operating bases to establish smaller joint security stations and combat outposts, U.S. and Iraqi forces cleared many of Baghdad's neighborhoods, the Awakening was nurtured, and special operations forces continued their relentless campaign to gut al-Qaeda. It was a bloody fight—in fact, the five months from February to June 2007 brought the most coalition deaths of any five-month period in the war—but one that was absolutely essential for the success of the decisive operations to come.[1] The tide turned in the summer of 2007, after Multi-National Corps–Iraq launched the "surge of offensive operations" that radically altered the trajectory of the Iraq War. While politicians in Washington bickered over whether and how to withdraw U.S. forces from the conflict, U.S. and Iraqi military personnel and police were creating the conditions for political dialogue. Their efforts significantly improved the situation in Iraq by the time of the congressional hearings in September 2007, which would determine the near-term fate of the U.S. war effort in Iraq.

The final month of shaping operations was particularly ugly. Early in the morning on May 12 a section of U.S. soldiers observing a roadside bomb hotspot south of Baghdad were ambushed, with four soldiers and an Iraqi interpreter killed and three soldiers taken prisoner. The capture of American soldiers in the Iraq War was a rare occurrence, and occasioned a maximum effort to retrieve them.[2] While in the end the three soldiers were killed by their al-Qaeda captors (who thoroughly ignored the dictates of the Geneva Convention regarding the treatment of prisoners while claiming its protection for its own detainees in coalition custody), the intensive search for them by the 10th Mountain Division disrupted enemy operations in the "triangle of death" south of Baghdad. Coalition deaths in May 2007 numbered 131 soldiers, the third-highest monthly total during the war.[3] "Some nights, if they followed a day with multiple casualties, horrific car bombings, or nasty political fights, you could see the energy flow out of [Petraeus]," I related a couple years later to Mark Bowden. "He didn't complain, but you could see it in his manner, his facial expressions, his body language, his receptiveness to conversation. He became quiet, reflective, but then he would buckle down and just keep working. He never expressed any doubt that we would succeed, in public or in private. But, as for me, I sometimes had my doubts."[4] General Petraeus was candid in his appraisal of the cost of these operations. "As I have cautioned previously, our forces are larger and taking a more active, offensive posture in areas in which the enemy has long had freedom of action, and this will likely result in elevated level of casualties for a couple of months until the tide can be turned," he wrote the secretary of defense. "The enemy has a vote and will resist us in areas he deems vital to his operations."[5]

One of the dead was 1st Lieutenant Andrew Bacevich, Jr., killed by a roadside bomb explosion in Salah ad-Din province. He was the son of retired U.S. Army Colonel Andrew Bacevich, a professor of international relations at Boston University and, coincidentally, my American history professor during my plebe year at West Point. General Petraeus and I were well acquainted with Dr. Bacevich's principled stand against the Iraq War. When I saw the condolence letter in the stack of pending correspondence, I brought it to General Petraeus's attention. He made a personal notation to express his heartfelt sympathy to the family. Every death was hard and a tragedy for the families involved; there was little we could do other than to honor the fallen and strive to ensure that their sacrifices were not in vain.

Part of the reason for the increased number of dead and wounded was that enemy weapons were becoming more sophisticated and lethal. Iran was supplying elements of the Jaish al-Mahdi with explosively formed penetrators, or EFPs, weapons that when detonated projected a semimolten slug of copper that could slice through even the thickest armor of the M1A1 tank.[6] These weapons were used in a minority of roadside bomb attacks but resulted in more casualties per detonation that any other improvised explosive device used against American soldiers in the war. Sunni insurgents, without access to the industrial capabilities of a nation-state, merely packed larger amounts of explosives into improvised explosive devices and vehicle bombs to create more damage. Some of these devices, buried in the ground, were deadly enough to flip sixty-eight-ton tanks upside down. On April 23 in one attack on a combat outpost in Baqubah in Diyala province, a pair of dump truck bombs exploded, collapsing part of the outpost and killing nine soldiers, even though the trucks hadn't been able to penetrate the immediate fortified perimeter around the outpost.[7] These truck bombs were huge; one similar device captured before its detonation carried six thousand pounds of explosives—more than the five thousand pounds of fertilizer used in the bombing of the Oklahoma City federal building in 1995.

On the brighter side, Prime Minister Maliki was increasingly willing to take the gloves off against Shi'a militias after the Sadrist ministers pulled out of his government in mid-April and Jaish al-Mahdi militia perpetrated violence in Diwaniyah and Nasiriyah in southern Iraq in May. Perhaps tired of the rockets being lobbed into the International Zone (the renamed Green Zone) from Sadr City, Maliki in mid-May authorized Multi-National Force–Iraq and Iraq forces to target those Jaish al-Mahdi operatives considered to be security threats. This was a critical development, since we had little hope of ending the civil war if we targeted only Sunni extremists.

Five months after President Bush announced the change in strategy and provided reinforcements to Iraq, the conditions were set for the initiation of decisive operations. The additional forces on the ground had generated considerable momentum in Baghdad and surrounding areas. Al-Anbar province had undergone an enormous transformation as tribal sheiks sided with U.S. forces against their al-Qaeda tormentors. U.S. and Iraqi forces were increasingly partnered in ever-increasing numbers of small joint security stations and combat outposts, which enabled greater contact with the population and significantly enhanced local security. Many of Baghdad's toughest neighborhoods had been cleared in deliberate fashion, with Colonel Steve Townsend's 3rd Stryker Brigade Combat Team, 2nd Infantry Division, augmenting "landowning" brigades in these operations.[8] The difference between the surge and what came before was that Multi-National Corps–Iraq and the Iraqi Baghdad Operations Command finally had enough forces to secure areas on a long-term basis. The focus for conventional forces in Baghdad was on clearing and holding areas such as Ghazalia, Adhamiya, and East and West Rashid where Sunni-Shi'a fault lines triggered sectarian violence, while special operations forces (which ramped up their operations tempo to the highest level yet in the war as the summer approached, augmented by increasing numbers of unmanned aerial vehicles) targeted al-Qaeda and Jaish al-Mahdi leaders in their strongholds in the Baghdad belts and Sadr City. U.S. and Iraqi forces positioned outside Baghdad were contesting al-Qaeda's presence in long-held sanctuaries. The final surge elements—a combat brigade, an additional aviation brigade, and a Marine Expeditionary Unit—arrived in Iraq in late May, setting the stage for the commencement of decisive operations in June.

■

As spring wore on a crisis was brewing at Camp Bucca, the expansive facility in southern Iraq where the coalition held the majority of its detainees. The camp was a powder keg waiting to explode. The problem was that it was designed as a minimum security installation, with detainees housed communally in tents in large enclosures and with free access to each other. As Multi-National Force–Iraq and special operations forces poured thousands of hardcore fighters into the facility, the extremists among them organized the prison population by intimidating the rank-and-file detainees into cooperating under their leadership. Al-Qaeda operatives tortured and occasionally murdered reluctant converts. During the spring of 2007 riots broke out in the camp. Detainees slung lethal "chai balls"—ingenious cement projectiles fused from tea, sand, and milk—at the guards with homemade slings. They torched their own tents in a display of violent noncooperation with their captors. In May 2007 there were more than ten thousand acts of violence inside U.S. detention centers in Iraq.[9] Yet in a near-fatal misreading of the rules of engagement, the guard force initially took no action to counter the increasingly lethal protests.[10]

The guard force at Camp Bucca was undermanned. To address the lack of military police support, General Petraeus diverted a field artillery battalion, under the command of Lieutenant Colonel Paul Yingling, from the third surge brigade to augment the guard force at the camp. Conspiracy theorists posited that Yingling was being sidelined due to his outspoken critique of American generalship in the Iraq War, but his publication record had nothing to do with the diversion of his battalion to guard duty.[11] In fact, Petraeus had requested Yingling by name, even though he was not originally part of the elements from his battalion to deploy for detention facility duties. In the counterinsurgency campaign in Iraq the least-used combat element was field artillery; therefore, it made sense to augment the military policemen at Camp Bucca with Yingling's troops rather than divert infantrymen to the task. In the late spring of 2007, one could also argue that the most decisive place on the battlefield was Camp Bucca, for reasons that will soon become clear.

Along with more guards, Camp Bucca required a makeover and more capacity. As Operation Fardh al-Qanoon (Enforcing the Law) progressed, thousands of detainees were sent south to an already overcrowded facility. Major General Jack Gardner, the commander of Task Force 134, a makeshift element assigned to oversee detention operations in Iraq, and his successor, Marine Major General Doug Stone, worked feverishly to upgrade and secure Camp Bucca. They devised a new arrangement whereby the most dangerous prisoners would be segregated from the bulk of the detainee population and housed in much more secure facilities (durable metal huts), with eight men to a building. Task Force 134 estimated that several thousand hardened prisoners—"irreconcilables"—would have to be removed from the general detainee population to ensure order at Camp Bucca and create conditions in which the other detainees could complete rehabilitation and basic skills training. Additional detention capacity was planned for Camp Taji (north of Baghdad) and in Ramadi in al-Anbar province, closer to where most of the detainees were captured. Local facilities would also ease transportation issues and make it more convenient for families to visit their relatives. Secretary of Defense Gates supported the expanded construction, which together with operational costs would require in the neighborhood of a quarter of a billion dollars.

Before these initiatives could mature, Camp Bucca exploded. On May 14 a riot by more than ten thousand prisoners nearly succeeded in breaching the wire. A concerned Doug Stone called me with the news, and I immediately connected him with General Petraeus. The situation was touch and go for several hours. We alerted a British mechanized immediate reaction force, based near Basra, to be prepared to head to Camp Bucca should that step become necessary. I posed to General Petraeus the question that was probably on everyone's mind, but had to be addressed openly: "At what point do we order the guards to open fire?" Thankfully, he never had to answer that question, though he did establish an open phone line with General Stone so that General Petraeus would be the one to make the call, if it had to be made. Heroic efforts by the guards, using nonlethal force and tear gas, augmented by every coalition soldier in the camp, contained the riot within the perimeter. The guards also took advantage of the event to move the most hardcore detainees into the higher security compounds that had just been completed.[12]

It was clear that the detention system had to be modified or another outburst was not just likely but inevitable. Major General Stone and the commander of Task Force Bucca, my good friend Colonel Jim Brown, oversaw numerous changes to the system that brought counterinsurgency "inside the wire." Until the surge, Multi-National Force–Iraq had treated detention as a warehousing problem. Provided detainees were kept secure and treated humanely, all was thought to be well. But all was not well. As jihadists gained control of the detainee population, they were able to radicalize a large number of them. "Detainees would be dropped into the detention system with a scant two statements saying they were bad and then when months later we were faced with total overcrowding and no evidence on why they should be there in the first place, they would be released," recalled Colonel Brown. "In the interim period they were exposed to the daily outrage of unjust detention and the 24/7 brain washing of the well established insurgent network in the camps. Complacency in the guard force shifted to fear as the insurgency in the camp moved from a mental battlefield to a kinetic one."[13] We were not just housing detainees; we were creating the next terrorist class. As one Special Operations commander put it, Camp Bucca had become "Terrorist University"; in fact, the recidivism rate was so high that General Petraeus had to stop detainee releases for several months in 2007. Changes had to be made.

General David Petraeus prepares to embark on his first combat patrol as commander of Multi-National Force–Iraq on February 11, 2007, a day after taking command. The level of devastation in Baghdad and the palpable fear among the people astonished us. There was clearly a lot of work ahead, and time was not on our side. Photo courtesy of Colonel Everett Spain

Emma Sky, political adviser to Lieutenant General Ray Odierno, walks alongside her boss. A committed pacifist and knowledgeable Arabist, Emma was a critical figure in furthering reconciliation among the warring factions in Iraq. U.S. Forces Iraq photo

Senator John McCain (R-AZ), left, and Senator Lindsay Graham (R-SC) accompany General David Petraeus on a market walk in Baghdad, April 20, 2007. With Senator Joe Lieberman (I-CT), McCain and Graham—the "Three Amigos"—were frequent visitors to Iraq and therefore had better firsthand knowledge of the progress of the surge than other political leaders. Multi-National Force–Iraq photo by Staff Sergeant Lorie Jewell

Defense Secretary Bob Gates, left, speaks with Iraqi Prime Minister Nouri al-Maliki in Baghdad, April 20, 2007. Sadi Othman, center, senior adviser to General David Petraeus, is translating the conversation in Arabic and English. Gates urged Iraqi officials to accelerate reconciliation among the country's various sects and factions, but progress toward justice and reconciliation in Iraq first required a significant reduction in ethnosectarian violence. Defense Department photo by Cherie A. Thurlby

United Kingdom Lieutenant General Graham Lamb, second from left, in conversation with *New York Times* reporter John Burns, Colonel Peter Mansoor, and another reporter. Lamb was instrumental in convincing General David Petraeus that reconciliation required negotiating with people who had coalition blood on their hands, a conversation that was the inspiration behind the creation of the MNF-I Force Strategic Engagement Cell. Author's photo

General David Petraeus briefs reporters in the Pentagon, April 26, 2007, on his view of the current military situation in Iraq during the first of his three trips back to Washington, D.C., to testify before Congress. Since the hearing in April 2007 was classified, it did not create a political firestorm as did his testimony in September 2007. Defense Department photo by R. D. Ward

Country music artist Toby Keith poses with, from left, Captain Johanna Mora, Captain Liz McNally, and Captain Kelly Howard before a USO concert at Camp Victory, Iraq, in May 2007. The three officers played significant roles on General Petraeus's staff as scheduler, speechwriter, and operations officer, respectively. Together with Colonel Peter Mansoor, Liz cowrote the draft of General Petraeus's September 2007 report to Congress. Photo courtesy of Major Kelly Howard

Lieutenant General Ray Odierno, commander of Multi-National Corps–Iraq, points out a location to Army Colonel John Charlton, center, commander of the 1st Brigade, 3rd Infantry Division, and Marine Corps Major General Walter Gaskin, commander of Multi-National Force–West, in downtown Ramadi, Iraq, June 25, 2007. Ramadi, birthplace of the tribal Awakening, had undergone an unbelievable transformation in the previous twelve months, a period that witnessed the evisceration of al-Qaeda in the city and the surrounding area. U.S. Army photo by Staff Sergeant Curt Cashour

Colonel Peter Mansoor, left, and counterinsurgency senior adviser David Kilcullen prepare to take Senator Joe Lieberman on an aerial tour of Baghdad, June 2007. Dave assisted Colonel H. R. McMaster, Ambassador David Pearce, and others in devising a new campaign plan for coalition forces in Iraq, as well as providing counterinsurgency advice to U.S. commanders and civilian personnel. Regrettably, Dave's tour was cut short after only four months in country. Author's photo

From left, Chief Warrant Officer Tom LeBrun, Colonel Bill Rapp, and Major Everett Spain pose for a photo. Bill played a significant role in the surge as the head of the Commander's Initiatives Group. Everett assisted General Petraeus as his aide-de-camp, while Tom protected General Petraeus as his personal security officer. Multi-National Force–Iraq photo by Staff Sergeant Lorie Jewell

General Petraeus's translator, Heather Wiersema, translates at a Crisis Action Cell meeting in October 2007. Chairing the meeting is Iraqi Prime Minister Nouri al-Maliki. In uniform at left is General Babikir Zebari, chief of staff of the Iraqi Joint Forces. Seated at the table on Maliki's right is Iraqi National Security Adviser Muwaffuk Rubaie. At right is Iraqi President Jalal Talibani. Heather had been raised in the Middle East since infancy and spoke fluent Arabic and English. Her insights into Arabic and Islamic culture and other matters were valuable contributions to our efforts during the surge. Multi-National Force–Iraq photo by Staff Sergeant Lorie Jewell

General David Petraeus and Colonel Peter Mansoor pose for a photo in the U.S. embassy annex office, October 2007. As General Petraeus's executive officer, Colonel Mansoor served as his gatekeeper and consigliere and provided strategic advice in the rare moments when the two were alone. Multi-National Force–Iraq photo by Staff Sergeant Lorie Jewell

Colonel Jim Brown shows General David Petraeus around Camp Bucca, the main U.S. detention facility in Iraq, November 2007. Marine Corps Major General Doug Stone and Jim were key figures in revamping U.S. detention efforts, transforming them from a disastrous situation in the spring of 2007 to a net plus for reconciliation in Iraq. Multi-National Force–Iraq photo by Staff Sergeant Lorie Jewell

Colonel Peter Mansoor and Colonel Jim Hickey enjoy a cigar atop the al-Faw palace in Camp Victory on Christmas Day 2007. Jim built the Counter–Improvised Explosive Device Operations Integration Center from the ground up upon his arrival in Iraq in late 2006, turning it into a major force in the effort to defeat the scourge of improvised explosive devices. Author's photo

Shortly after air assaulting into a farm field, U.S. Army Private First Class Kenneth Armbrister, assigned to Company A, 1-30th Infantry, scans for enemy activity during Operation Browning in Arab Jabour, Iraq, January 20, 2008. Note the participation of the Sons of Iraq (in Arabic headdress) in the operation. U.S. Army photo by Sergeant Luis Delgadillo

MNF-I Public Affairs Officer Colonel Steve Boylan prepares General David Petraeus for an interview, February 12, 2008. Steve was the crucial intermediary between General Petraeus and the media and ensured that the commander never went before the press unprepared. Multi-National Force–Iraq photo by Staff Sergeant Lorie Jewell

An MQ-1 Predator unmanned aerial vehicle takes off in support of Operation Iraqi Freedom, April 10, 2008, during the height of the fighting for Phase Line Gold in Sadr City. The Predator provided U.S. forces with extremely valuable armed reconnaissance, airborne surveillance, and target acquisition capabilities. Secretary of Defense Bob Gates supported General Petraeus's efforts to increase the number of unmanned aerial platforms for the wars in Iraq and Afghanistan. U.S. Air Force photo by Master Sergeant Rob Valenca

President George W. Bush, who championed the surge despite significant political headwinds, meets with General David Petraeus, commander of Multi-National Force–Iraq,
and U.S. Ambassador to Iraq Ryan C. Crocker, April 10, 2008, at the White House. White
House photo by Eric Draper

Ambassador Ryan Crocker discusses an issue with General David Petraeus in the U.S.
embassy annex in Baghdad, early May 2008. Colonel Peter Mansoor, executive officer
to General Petraeus, is at left; Sadi Othman, senior adviser to General Petraeus, is at
right; looking on with arms folded is Ali Khedery, who served as a crucial go-between
for Ambassador Crocker and various Iraqi political figures. Multi-National Force–Iraq
photo by Staff Sergeant Lorie Jewell

General David Petraeus presents Colonel Peter Mansoor with a hatchet as his going-away gift from the staff, May 2008. As the "Hatchet Man," Colonel Mansoor enforced discipline among the team and served as a catalyst to encourage the MNF-I staff to take action when needed. Multi-National Force–Iraq photo by Staff Sergeant Lorie Jewell

The "big idea" that changed the Multi-National Force–Iraq approach to detention operations was to look at detainees not as liabilities but as assets. Through late 2007, Major General Stone estimated that 160,000 Iraqis had been interned in coalition detention facilities.[14] Given the large family networks in Iraq, these detainees had a significant influence on a large part of Iraqi society upon release. How the coalition treated them in detention mattered a great deal. Under Major General Stone's leadership, Task Force 134 changed the priority of detention operations from warehousing prisoners to rehabilitating them with an eye toward their eventual reintegration into Iraqi society.

During the summer and fall of 2007, numerous changes to the detention system turned a potential nightmare into a net plus for the coalition. Several thousand hardcore prisoners were separated from the reconcilable population of detainees.[15] For the rest of the camp population, a number of rehabilitation programs were instituted on a strictly voluntary basis. Detainees were offered paid work in various trades, including a brick-making factory that produced bricks stamped with the Arabic phrase "Rebuilding the nation brick by brick." At morning roll call detainees would sing the Iraqi national anthem. An art studio allowed some of the more artistically talented detainees to create patriotic art in a variety of media. Literacy classes taught inmates to read to the third-grade level. Moderate imams were brought in to preach a more tolerant version of Islam. In addition, detainees were allowed family visits, although the remoteness of Camp Bucca inhibited many families from taking advantage of these opportunities. These measures empowered the moderate slice of the camp population and marginalized the extremists.

Most important, Major General Stone instituted a system that radically altered the method used to determine which detainees would be released. Until the spring of 2007 there were periodic mass releases of detainees based on a first-in, first-out arrangement that allowed many committed insurgents to return to the fight—a system derisively labeled "catch and release" by the troops. Detainees routinely complained about the uncertainty surrounding the length of their detention and their inability to argue their cases before a legal body, which created great uncertainty that often led to depression or a willingness to side with the more radical elements within the prison population. "Detaining a person too long can be as detrimental as releasing him too early because a detention facility can become a 'Jihad University' for detainees who are not already insurgents," wrote several officers involved in the detention system at Camp Bucca.[16] After the spring riots, Stone created panels of military officers to review detainee cases. Detainees were allowed to present their side of the story at these hearings, after which the boards would determine their suitability for release based not on guilt or innocence but on the board's assessment of the detainee's continued security risk and potential for reintegration into Iraqi society.[17] Boards took into account good behavior, which helped to tamp down violence in the detention camps. To test the system,

General Petraeus actually sat as a panel member for one board hearing during a visit to Camp Bucca (he voted for the release of the detainee). Detainees slated for release were grouped together and transported north to Baghdad, where they attended a formal reconciliation ceremony attended by members of the Iraqi government, tribal sheiks, coalition officials, and family members.

The new system produced extraordinary results. For those detainees who had undergone the rehabilitation program at Camp Bucca, the recidivism rate was less than 1 percent.[18] Violence within the detention system dropped dramatically as prisoners gained greater clarity on their path to release. During the height of the surge nearly twenty-seven thousand Iraqis were housed at any given time in coalition detention facilities. Instead of a strategic liability, Major General Stone viewed this population as twenty-seven thousand opportunities to enhance reconciliation within Iraqi society: He described the detainees as "moderate missiles" he would launch back into Iraqi society. The idea was not to win "hearts and minds" but to modify behavior to promote understanding and goodwill within Iraqi society. As with other aspects of the surge, this "big idea" led to a host of changes that significantly influenced the course of the war.

Mid-morning on June 13, terrorists blew up the minarets that had survived the February 2006 bombing of the al-Askari shrine in Samarra. Al-Qaeda hoped by this wanton violence to rekindle the fires of civil war and sectarian violence that had nearly torn Iraq apart a year earlier.[19] Prime Minister Maliki, along with Ambassador Crocker and General Petraeus, immediately recognized the seriousness of the event. They acted quickly and forcefully to forestall an outbreak of sectarian violence. Maliki imposed a strict curfew in Baghdad and Samarra to stifle those who might retaliate against Sunni mosques, while the coalition agreed to expedite the movement of a National Police brigade and the 4th Brigade, 4th Division, of the Iraq army to Samarra. Ambassador Crocker and General Petraeus immediately went to see the prime minister and urged senior Iraqi political and religious leaders to appear together at a press conference, in order to make public statements to reduce tensions and restore calm. In contrast to the reactions of Iraqi religious leaders in the aftermath of the bombing in February 2006, Grand Ayatollah Ali al-Sistani in Najaf, Islamic Supreme Council of Iraq leader Abdul Aziz al-Hakim, Muqtada al-Sadr, and others called for restraint, though Sadr characteristically blamed the coalition for the attack and called for peaceful demonstrations, which drew modest but largely peaceful crowds. Lieutenant General Odierno accompanied Prime Minster Maliki by helicopter to Samarra to examine the damage and review the security situation. Maliki publicly committed to rebuilding the shrine by signing an agreement with the United Nations Educational, Scientific, and Cultural Organization and a Turkish construction firm, which helped to tamp down emotions. Compared with the unrest after the attack in February 2006, the Iraqi people remained calm. Al-Qaeda had struck a blow, but it had failed to stoke the sectarian violence further.

Fortunately, the terrorist strike coincided with a long-planned coalition offensive that turned the momentum in the war against al-Qaeda and its adherents. The "surge of offensive operations" began on June 14 with the commencement of Operation Phantom Thunder, a Multi-National Corps–Iraq offensive that challenged insurgents in their long-held base areas in Baghdad and its environs. Like the Union offensives into the Confederacy in 1864, this was the coalition's first opportunity to put pressure on so many key locations at one time. Lieutenant General Odierno observed, "For the first time, MNC-I was orchestrating operations to place pressure on militants across the board [rather than] focusing operations in one area allowing insurgents to duck to other, quiet zones. Taking advantage [of] already planned division and brigade level operations, and building on the tactical focus on the population, its goal was to secure population centers, interdict accelerants, and deny the enemy his sanctuaries."[20]

One of the more difficult areas in Iraq in the summer of 2007 was Diyala province and its capital city of Baqubah. The mixed sectarian nature of the region, with multiple ethnosectarian fault lines, led to a heavily contested battle for supremacy among insurgents, Shi'a militias, Iraqi security forces, and coalition troops. After their expulsion from most of al-Anbar province, al-Qaeda terrorists also reinforced their presence in the area. Diyala meant a great deal as a staging location and safe haven to al-Qaeda; one must remember that the leader of AQI, Abu Musab al-Zarqawi, had been killed near Baqubah in June 2006. The organization's presence was undeniable, evidenced by the grisly discovery in late May of a terrorist prison south of Baqubah housing more than forty kidnap victims, many exhibiting signs of torture.[21] The surge enabled Lieutenant General Odierno to double the number of U.S. troops in Diyala over the course of the spring. One of the primary objectives of Operation Phantom Thunder was to clear Baqubah of its insurgent and terrorist presence.

Operation Arrowhead Ripper, which began on June 19 in Baqubah, was the Multi-National Corps–Iraq main effort. The 3rd Stryker Brigade Combat Team, 2nd Infantry Division, under the command of Colonel Steve Townsend deliberately cleared the city and its outskirts, which had been fortified by insurgents. As with the battle of Fallujah in November 2006, many senior insurgent and terrorist leaders fled the city in advance of the attack. The rank and file who remained were treated to a considerable amount of firepower from ground combat vehicles, attack helicopters, guided rockets, artillery, armed Predator drones, and fighter aircraft. In the first days of the offensive alone, soldiers uncovered (often with local Iraqi help) two dozen deeply buried roadside bombs and many dozens of other improvised explosive devices, a level of effort consistent with a typical obstacle belt in an insurgent sanctuary.[22] Insurgents had rigged several dozen houses to explode in an effort to kill American soldiers clearing them. Heavy fighting lasted for a week and sporadic combat continued through the summer, but the operation succeeded in routing the insurgency in Baqubah. U.S. and Iraqi forces killed the al-Qaeda emir in charge of the area, along with more than 100 insurgents, detained 424 suspected insurgents, uncovered 129 weapons caches, eliminated roughly 250 roadside bombs, and found and disabled 38 booby-trapped houses and 12 vehicle bombs.[23]

I recall Bill Rapp showing me the operations order for Arrowhead Ripper. To illustrate just how much things had changed since the beginning of the surge, under "Tasks to Subordinate Units," a standard part of a five-paragraph field order, one of the "units" listed was the 1920s Revolution Brigades, an insurgent organization that was repelled by al-Qaeda's brutality and chose to assist U.S. forces in defeating the terrorist threat to Baqubah.[24] A short time before they had been on the opposing side of the fight, and now they were being given a military task by U.S. commanders in a formal, written order. Bill and I shared an "I can't believe this is happening" moment and then went back to work.

Other operations complemented the main effort in Baqubah. After clearing Baqubah, U.S. and Iraqi units moved to secure Khalis and Khan Bani Sa'ad in Diyala province. To the southeast of Baghdad, Multi-National Division–Center cleared both sides of the Tigris River in the vicinity of Arab Jabour, Salman Pak, and Iskandariyah—all areas in the so-called triangle of death (which General Petraeus later renamed the "circle of life" after coalition operations significantly reduced the violence in the area). In Multi-National Force–West's zone, the Marine 6th Regimental Combat Team under Colonel Richard Simcock focused on the town of Karmah in eastern al-Anbar (long a sore spot ever since the days my brigade first cleared the town back in September 2003), while the 13th Marine Expeditionary Unit cleared the insurgent sanctuary and movement corridor northwest of Baghdad on the shores of Lake Tharthar.[25] The 1st Brigade, 1st Cavalry Division, under Colonel Paul Funk moved west from Taji to squeeze the insurgents in conjunction with the Marine operations. "At the tactical level, these fights were incredibly tough," Lieutenant General Odierno reflected. "The enemy protected areas with hundreds of IEDs, some equivalent to thousand pound bombs, and other booby traps, large and small."[26] Despite stiff resistance, U.S. offensive operations to clear the Baghdad belts were uniformly successful. And unlike in operations before the start of the surge, coalition forces would not clear and leave, they would clear and hold.

As part of Phantom Thunder, operations also continued in Baghdad with a focus on sectarian fault lines in Adhamiya, Rashid, and the area between Mansour and Kadhimiyah. Insurgent and terrorist leaders expelled by these operations were hard-pressed to find other sanctuaries in which to hide, since for the first time in the war the coalition and its Iraqi partners enjoyed sufficient forces to pressure the enemy across the breadth and depth of Iraq. Some al-Qaeda elements leaked north to Nineveh province, then held thinly in an economy-of-force effort that General Petraeus envisioned would be the objective of a future major operation.

Al-Qaeda was not the only target of coalition operations; special operations forces also targeted Shi'a militia leaders who were guilty of sectarian cleansing, attacks against coalition forces, and criminality. On June 30 special operators conducted a significant raid into Sadr City to capture a Jaish al-Mahdi special group operative with direct involvement in the movement and allocation of Iranian weapons and munitions. The teams picked up seventeen individuals at two raid sites, but during exfiltration were engaged by an in-depth series of ambushes, including roadside bombs, rocket-propelled grenades, and small arms fire. Return fire from the special operators and supporting aircraft killed twenty-six militia operatives, which piqued the interest of Iraqi Shi'a leaders.[27] General Petraeus had to remind the prime minister that there were no innocent civilians out on the street at 2 o'clock in the morning shooting RPGs and AK-47s at U.S. forces, and the full-motion video from a Predator drone that he was able to show the prime minister established the facts clearly. In return, Jaish al-Mahdi mortar and rocket teams pummeled the International Zone, in one case launching more than thirty mortar rounds in a short period from various firing points in Sadr City.[28] The death toll on all sides mounted, rattling Prime Minister Maliki and other Iraqi leaders. Perhaps feeling the pressure, Muqtada al-Sadr returned to Iran, after which his grip on the Jaish al-Mahdi, never certain, was loosened even further.

A month after the start of Arrowhead Ripper, in another of the local accommodations on which the success of the surge would depend, local leaders formalized a security organization known as the Baqubah Guardians.[29] This was followed by the creation of another organization of concerned local citizens in Khalis, an important development, since the town was a focal point of sectarian violence in Diyala. These initiatives paved the way for a broader reconciliation in the province. On August 19, more than one hundred tribal leaders met to form an Awakening movement and side with coalition and Iraqi security forces against both Sunni terrorists and Shi'a militias. As in al-Anbar, the growing Awakening movement in Diyala led to the creation of multiple Sons of Iraq organizations that thickened the police and provided local security in one of the most bitterly contested provinces in Iraq.[30]

The slow-moving nature of counterinsurgent operations does not make for great press. Only the passage of time shows their effects not just in ground gained and enemy killed, but in the establishment of security and the reduction of insurgent violence. Kimberly Kagan totals enemy casualties during Phantom Thunder at more than 1,100 dead and 6,700 detained, including 382 significant leaders—hardly the "hearts and minds" approach to counterinsurgency alleged by some critics of the surge.[31] Hit with a series of body blows, the insurgents recoiled and fought back with the weapons at their disposal. Roadside bombs, particularly those covered and concealed in deeply buried holes in roadways, took a toll on

U.S. soldiers. Indirect fire from rockets and mortars also continued to be problematic, with the most effective strike hitting a number of Blackhawk and Apache
helicopters at the army airbase in Taji. However, the disruption of insurgent sanctuaries in the Baghdad belts significantly reduced al-Qaeda's ability to build and
deploy its most potent weapons—vehicle bombs and individual suicide bombers.
In the annals of military history Phantom Thunder may not rise to the level of the
Normandy invasion, but it was an enormously important and successful operation
that in the summer of 2007 turned the tide of the war in Iraq.

A steady drumbeat of visitors, executive branch officials, and congressional delegations cycled through Iraq over the summer. The crush of VIPs was so heavy
that Secretary of Defense Gates quipped to General Petraeus at the start of one
briefing, "Between CODELS [congressional delegations], are you finding time to
prosecute the war?"[32] I found the most knowledgeable officials to be Senator John
McCain (R-AZ), Senator Joe Lieberman (I-CT), and Senator Lindsey Graham
(R-SC). They often traveled together (coming to be nicknamed the Three Amigos),
and their multiple trips to Iraq gave them a uniquely informed perspective among
elected U.S. officials. Senator Graham, a reserve Air Force colonel, remained behind on a few occasions to serve weeks of annual duty as a lawyer in the office
of Colonel Mark Martins, the outstanding MNF-I judge advocate general who
had been handpicked for the post by General Petraeus and had also been first in
his class at West Point in 1983 and a Rhodes scholar. I had the honor along with
counterinsurgency adviser Dave Kilcullen of escorting Senator Lieberman on a
helicopter tour of Baghdad in late May, after which we met for an hour to discuss
counterinsurgency theory and the progress of the surge.[33] Not far from anyone's
mind were the upcoming congressional hearings on the Iraq War, scheduled for
September. Away from the klieg lights and microphones, the politicians listened
politely as Ambassador Crocker and General Petraeus explained their views on
the progress of the surge and the future prospects for the war in Iraq. At this point
there was emerging evidence of a decline in ethnosectarian violence and a change
in the mindset of a large number of Sunnis, but the future was still murky and
political stances were solidified enough that the visits changed few minds.

President Bush realized that he had lost a great deal of credibility with the
American people, yet they needed to hear about the situation in Iraq from an authoritative source. Petraeus had the credibility that the president lacked; his voice
carried weight on all segments of the political spectrum. Nearly every day the
general conducted some sort of media event, which had the unfortunate side effect
of earning for him a reputation in some circles as a publicity hound. This accusation, at least as applied to the surge, was unfair. What critics did not understand
was that the president strongly encouraged Petraeus to appear before the media to
discuss the surge. In fact, during the first six months of 2007 the president invoked
General Petraeus's name in public at least 150 times.[34] Bush never told Petraeus

what to say, only to get his story out. As Operation Phantom Thunder kicked off, for instance, in one of their weekly meetings the president asked when General Petraeus would appear in the media to discuss the operation. Petraeus replied that the media plan involved Lieutenant General Odierno and his division commanders taking the lead. "With all due respect," President Bush responded, "the American people need to see you."[35] For someone as media savvy as General Petraeus, that was all the encouragement he needed. The calendar soon filled with a number of media events and engagements with reporters as General Petraeus fulfilled his designated role as the face of the surge. For his part, Secretary of Defense Gates was also supportive of increased media engagement, telling General Petraeus to be honest and not to worry about clearing statements with Washington.[36]

Since the beginning of the war the coalition had lost the battle of strategic communications to a more nimble insurgent media apparatus largely focused on the Internet. General Petraeus was determined to change the momentum in the information battle in our favor. He demanded that the Multi-National Force–Iraq public affairs apparatus become more agile to allow the command to be "first with the truth." This meant anticipating likely media events (such as coalition raids into Sadr City) before they happened and to prepare timely information releases to get ahead of enemy propaganda. Petraeus called this "the battle of the ticker"—the rolling information screen on the bottom of most major news channels. What he observed was that the side that was first with its narrative of events controlled the subsequent shape of the story. It was critical not to allow the insurgents to gain the momentum in this regard, because even if a piece of propaganda was disproven days or weeks later after a lengthy investigation, the reality was all too often buried in little-read or -watched news pieces that failed to have the same impact as the original story.

Early in the war U.S. commanders relied on the highly effective media embed program to communicate news to the world, but by 2007 there were fewer than a dozen reporters embedded in U.S. forces in Iraq at any given time.[37] Another method had to be found to beat the insurgency and al-Qaeda to the media punch. General Petraeus and Lieutenant General Odierno encouraged their subordinate commanders and the troops to seek out opportunities to engage with the media. The only stipulation was for leaders and soldiers to talk about what they knew, rather than to speculate on issues and events outside their purview. The Multi-National Force–Iraq strategic communications team, led by Major General Bill Caldwell, Major General Kevin Bergner, Rear Admiral Greg Smith, and Colonel Steve Boylan, worked tirelessly to communicate accurate information to the Iraqi people, the American public, and wider regional and worldwide audiences. Insurgent, militia, and al-Qaeda propaganda was promptly refuted, inaccurate news stories challenged, and accurate information presented in a timely and effective manner. Failure of the news media to meet the standard would lead to a démarche by Boylan or the deputy public affairs officer, Lieutenant Colonel

Joe Yoswa. For the first time in history, a U.S. military command used social networking tools as part of its communications strategy. Multi-National Force–Iraq
created a YouTube presence that for a time became one of the most watched parts
of the social networking scene.

The flip side of getting our story out to the public was to prevent the enemy
from doing the same. Abu Musab al-Zarqawi, the al-Qaeda terrorist leader in Iraq
killed in June 2006, once stated, "Our fight must have a face or every battle we
win will be lost in obscurity." He was right. Sunni insurgents and their supporters exploited all forms of media, especially the Internet, to pursue a massive and
far-reaching media campaign.[38] This media campaign had a significant effect on
the attitudes of the Sunni world and the Iraqi people toward what was happening
in Iraq. During the course of the surge, therefore, special operations forces and
Multi-National Corps–Iraq put a great deal of time and effort into targeting insurgent and terrorist media cells to reduce or eliminate their ability to spread propaganda. These special cells were designed to film and photograph attacks against
coalition and Iraqi security forces and post videos and photos on the Internet. The
cells would also engage in Internet chat with potential converts and conduct other
propaganda activities in cyberspace. Over the course of the surge U.S. and Iraqi
forces were able to shut down most of these media operations, which put a huge
dent in the enemy's ability to propagandize the Iraqi people. What little capability
remained was largely put on the defensive by coalition information operations,
which depicted al-Qaeda as the enemy of the Iraqi people and missed no opportunity to depict the terrorist organization's brutality in the darkest possible colors.

General Petraeus often commented that he was in a race against time, as measured by clocks in both Baghdad and Washington. His goal was to speed up the
Baghdad clock by improving security conditions to facilitate political progress and
reconciliation among competing sections and factions, while putting time back
on the Washington clock by demonstrating that victory (defined as "sustainable
stability") was possible within a reasonable period. This was a tall order, given the
common perception in the first half of 2007 that General Petraeus was leading a
hopeless effort in Iraq. Indeed, the steady drumbeat of negative commentary from
analysts and pundits seemed to us unduly harsh in light of the spread of the Awakening and the progress of Phantom Thunder in ripping the heart out of al-Qaeda
in Iraq. It often seemed as if perceptions in the United States lagged reality on the
ground in Iraq by several months.

General Petraeus decided to close the gap by inviting respected commentators to Iraq and showing them around. He tasked me with developing itineraries
for these small groups, which would be composed of authoritative figures from
all sides of the political spectrum, among them Max Boot from the Council on
Foreign Relations, Michèle Flournoy from the Center for New American Security,
Fred Kagan from the American Enterprise Institute and his wife Kim Kagan from

the Institute for the Study of War, Tony Cordesman from the Center for Strategic and International Studies, Tom Ricks from the *Washington Post,* Linda Robinson from *U.S. News and World Report,* author Bing West, and Ken Pollack and Michael O'Hanlon from the Brookings Institution. His guidance was simple: Show them everything they wanted to see along with those things we thought they needed to see, but don't spin anything. The pundits could write anything they wanted to during and after their trip, but at least they would be commenting from the vantage point of having seen firsthand on the ground in Iraq what was going on. The thinking was that these trips to Iraq would instill in the visitors a better understanding of the context in which our forces were operating, the ongoing tactical momentum of the surge, and how politically visible simplicities such as benchmarks did not comprehensively capture everything that was happening. In crafting itineraries I arranged for high-level briefings from senior coalition and Iraq officials, visits to combat outposts and joint security stations in Baghdad, and ventures farther afield in the provinces. I always entertained requests from our guests, as we endeavored to be as open and transparent as possible. For instance, one group wanted to visit Camp Bucca in southern Iraq to check out the detention system, a request we honored.

We did not expect that one of the most important op-ed pieces written during the course of the Iraq War would emanate from this program. Timing played a key role in this regard. During the month of July the Democrats in Congress put on a full-court press to force their Republican colleagues to agree to a timetable for withdrawal from Iraq. The pressure was having an effect. "There are, it seems, nearly as many Iraq proposals [to limit the involvement of American forces] circulating on Capitol Hill as there are senators who question the war," reported the *New York Times.*[39] Key Republican senators were defecting from the president's camp. In mid-July Senators John Warner of Virginia and Richard Lugar of Indiana unveiled a proposal that would have compelled the president to seek a new war resolution and to outline a strategy that would limit the involvement of U.S. forces in Iraq by the end of the year. Senator Majority Leader Harry Reid of Nevada minced no words about the goal of his party, stating, "The president and Senate Republicans need to understand that Democrats are absolutely committed to forcing the president to change the mission, bring our troops home responsibly and refocus our resources on Al Qaeda and the real threat that it poses."[40] Given their narrow majority in Congress, the Democrats could not force the issue without Republican support, which was why Warner and Lugar's proposal was so troubling to the administration. President Bush decried what he termed "the mad rush in Washington to the politically convenient."[41] The success of the surge was uncertain, but there was no doubt among those of us serving in Iraq that it would fail if Congress pulled its support within a matter of months. We needed more time on the Washington clock, which seemed to be approaching midnight.

The political pressure was building to a crescendo when on July 30 Ken Pollack and Michael O'Hanlon of the Brookings Institution, who had just returned from a trip to Iraq sponsored by MNF-I, cowrote an op-ed in the *New York Times* entitled "A War We Just Might Win."[42] Their first two paragraphs addressed the ongoing debate in Washington head-on:

> Viewed from Iraq, where we just spent eight days meeting with American and Iraqi military and civilian personnel, the political debate in Washington is surreal. The Bush administration has over four years lost essentially all credibility. Yet now the administration's critics, in part as a result, seem unaware of the significant changes taking place.
>
> Here is the most important thing Americans need to understand: We are finally getting somewhere in Iraq, at least in military terms. As two analysts who have harshly criticized the Bush administration's miserable handling of Iraq, we were surprised by the gains we saw and the potential to produce not necessarily "victory" but a sustainable stability that both we and the Iraqis could live with.[43]

The authors noted that on previous trips they had found U.S. soldiers "angry and frustrated—many sensed they had the wrong strategy, were using the wrong tactics and were risking their lives in pursuit of an approach that could not work."[44] On this visit, they noticed that "morale is high. The soldiers and marines told us they feel that they now have a superb commander in Gen. David Petraeus; they are confident in his strategy, they see real results, and they feel now they have the numbers needed to make a real difference."[45] Bingo.

Pollack and O'Hanlon noted that the focus had shifted to securing the Iraqi people in conjunction with Iraqi security forces, and that political and economic arrangements at the local level—tailored to the circumstances of local communities—had made a significant difference. Civilian deaths had been reduced by a third since the beginning of the surge. Supported by the work of Embedded Provincial Reconstruction Teams, local economies were regenerating as security improved. We had not sent Pollack and O'Hanlon on a cakewalk, either. They visited the scenes of some of the fiercest ethnosectarian violence in Iraq, including Ghazalia, Ramadi, Tal Afar, and Mosul. Indeed, they noted the bad along with the good. "All across the country, the dependability of Iraqi security forces over the long term remains a major question mark," they reported.[46] The National Police were "mostly a disaster."[47] Despite this caveat, Iraqi security forces had progressed, and the situation overall had improved a great deal since the authors' previous trip to Iraq, in late 2005. Sunni terrorists and Shi'a militias had both overplayed their hands, incurring the hatred of the Iraqi people. Areas cleared were now held; the "whack-a-mole" strategy was a thing of the past. Pollack and O'Hanlon were astonished by the transformation of the situation in Iraq; they had walked down the streets of Ramadi without body armor, an area where a year earlier they would have been killed outright in minutes. While the situation in Iraq remained grave and reconciliation among sects and factions remained uncertain, "there is enough good happening on the battlefields of Iraq today that Congress should plan on sustaining the effort at least into 2008."[48]

The publication in the notoriously anti-Bush "Paper of Record" by moderate intellectuals of their belief that the surge was having an effect and could lead to victory in Iraq was nothing less than an intellectual bombshell. The tenor of the debate in Washington immediately changed; politicians who had been tripping over one another trying to figure out how to force the Bush administration to withdraw from Iraq were now content to await the testimony of General Petraeus and Ambassador Crocker. The August congressional recess soon brought the threat of a legislated withdrawal from Iraq to an end, pending the outcome of the hearings scheduled for September.

Despite this stay of execution, a political crisis of the first order continued in Baghdad. Lack of political progress was worrisome, particularly on big pieces of legislation such as the hydrocarbon law, de-Ba'athification reform, and the provincial powers act. Plots by various actors within the Iraqi government kept politics on edge throughout the summer. After the second bombing of the al-Askari shrine in Samarra, the Office of the Martyr Sadr (OMS), the political party beholden to the fiery cleric Muqtada al-Sadr, threatened to pull out of the Council of Representatives in protest of poor security and the continued U.S. presence in Iraq. On June 11 a majority of lawmakers present in session voted to oust the Sunni speaker, Mahmoud Mashadani, for offensive behavior that included an assault on a colleague and other violent outbursts.[49] However, Mashadani refused to go quietly and rallied the major Sunni political bloc, Tawafuq, behind him. The Sunni bloc boycotted the Council of Representatives, demanding Mashadani's reinstatement, and in August pulled its five ministers out of Maliki's government to protest what they viewed as excessive dominance of the Shi'a and Kurdish parties.[50]

Without Tawafuq's presence, the parliament could not sustain a quorum, and legislation languished. In response, Prime Minister Maliki considered reforming his government without the participation of OMS and Tawafuq; however, while ousting the Sadrists was just fine with U.S. political leaders, alienating the major Sunni political bloc was not. The government needed to include all three of the major factions (Shi'a, Sunnis, and Kurds) in Iraq, or it would lack broad legitimacy. Passage of major pieces of reconciliation legislation would be meaningless if the Shi'ites and Kurds rammed them through without Sunni buy-in. "Is there anything [legislation] we can get?" the president lamented in one meeting with General Petraeus. "Any lay-ups? A free throw?" I thought of the "slam dunk" reference concerning intelligence on weapons of mass destruction in Iraq and cringed. General Petraeus wisely avoided the basketball analogy altogether, replying instead, "How about a Hail Mary?"[51]

In the midst of this turmoil, we did our best to remain sane during the long, hot summer. General Petraeus and the team met country singer Toby Keith one eve-

ning in June at the VIP villa at Camp Victory, after which I took some members of
the staff to his concert. Toby Keith's music, as usual, was thoroughly enjoyable. He
has been a stalwart supporter of American soldiers for many years, traveling often
to the war zones in Iraq and Afghanistan to entertain the troops. I had one of the
staff take a picture of Hanna Mora, Kelly Howard, Liz McNally, and me enjoying
the show; the photo was a hit with family and friends and is one of my favorites
from my second tour of duty in Iraq.

The team also thoroughly enjoyed the Fourth of July, Independence Day.
General Petraeus and Command Sergeant Major Marvin Hill held an enormous
reenlistment ceremony for nearly six hundred soldiers in the rotunda of the al-
Faw palace (MNF-I headquarters), followed by a citizenship ceremony for soldiers
who had completed the naturalization process. General Petraeus held a barbeque
afterward at his villa for members of his personal staff, his security detachment,
and his aviation detachment. My favorite activity during these festivities was hitting golf balls into the lake behind the villa with equipment donated by various
groups around the United States. There wasn't anything else quite as stress relieving in my book as smacking a golf ball with a hard-hit 5-iron into the lake border-
ing the al-Faw palace. It wasn't Pebble Beach, but it would do for the moment.

A few weeks later we celebrated with the Iraqis as their national soccer team
defeated Saudi Arabia 1–0 to bring home the first-place trophy in the Asian Cup
tournament. Spontaneous celebrations broke out across Iraq to celebrate the victory, earned by a team that had Shi'a, Sunni, and Kurdish players on the roster.
Iraqis waved their national flag, honked car horns, painted their faces in their
national colors, shot off fireworks (including liberal shooting of AK-47 rounds
into the sky), and celebrated well into the night.[52] Iraqis might disagree on their
politics, but they love their soccer. The celebrations were a sign to us that Iraqi
nationalism was still a potent force, despite the violence wracking the country.

As the congressional hearings approached and the pressure intensified, humor
often acted as the best stress reliever. On August 1, as the ministers of Tawafuq
walked out of Maliki's cabinet, President Bush began the weekly meeting by asking, "How are things out there, Ryan?" Ambassador Crocker's reply was classic.
"Words fail me, Mr. President, but I'll try."[53] The rest of us did our best to stifle our
laughter as the meeting soon got down to serious business. President Bush later
displayed his own wry sense of humor. Commenting that we needed to highlight
those civil institutions that were working, the president quipped, "I had no idea,
for instance, that the Iraqis passed sixty laws this year. Over here we've passed just
six; I've vetoed two, and the rest just name post offices after dead guys."[54]

As the summer wore on U.S. political leaders, Ambassador Crocker, and General
Petraeus pressured Iraqi leaders to make progress on "benchmark" legislation, the
important laws the passage of which would signal significant political progress.
The benchmarks were agreed upon by President Bush and Congress in May 2007

as part of the war funding bill, with an interim report due in mid-July and a more complete assessment in September.[55] I helped to edit the Initial Benchmark Assessment Report produced by the MNF-I and embassy staffs, and of course General Petraeus read every word and put his stamp on the final product. The description of the surge in the report spelled out plainly the purpose of the new way forward in Iraq:

> While our overarching strategy continues to emphasize a transition of responsibility to the Iraqi Government and its security forces, the New Way Forward recognized that, in response to the upsurge in sectarian violence in 2006, it was necessary for Coalition Forces to temporarily play a greater role, in conjunction with the Iraqi Security Forces, in securing the Iraqi population. This is not meant to replace Iraqi efforts to provide security, but to help provide the necessary time and space with which the Iraqi Government can continue to build its own capacity, can intensify efforts against the accelerants of the violence, especially al-Qaida in Iraq and some segments of the Jaysh al-Mahdi (JAM), and can meaningfully address the all-important issue of reconciliation among the various segments of Iraqi society. The strategy recognizes that the levels of violence seen in 2006 undermined efforts to achieve political reconciliation by fueling sectarian tensions, emboldening extremists, and discrediting the Coalition and Iraqi Government. Amid such violence, it became significantly harder for Iraqi leaders to make the difficult compromises necessary to foster reconciliation.[56]

The report noted that conditions had improved locally in a number of communities, but the full import of these changed conditions would not be apparent at the national level for some time to come. However, the deteriorating trajectory of 2006 had been reversed and the overall situation in Iraq had stabilized. We believed the achievement of political reconciliation, as evidenced by the passage of major pieces of legislation, was a lagging indicator of the success of the surge.[57]

The interim benchmark assessment was decidedly mixed. For those keeping score, progress in nine areas was rated entirely or partially "satisfactory" and in nine other areas was "unsatisfactory." Most of the security areas were progressing adequately: the Iraqi government had established supporting political, media, economic, and services committees in support of the Baghdad Security Plan; three trained and ready Iraqi brigades had deployed to support operations in Baghdad; the Iraqi government had enabled coalition and Iraqi security force operations throughout the breadth and depth of the country; surge operations had reduced sectarian violence; and U.S. and Iraqi forces had constructed and manned sixty-eight joint security stations and combat outposts in Baghdad. Additionally, the Iraqi government had made satisfactory progress toward completing a constitutional review, enacting and implementing legislation on procedures to form semi-autonomous regions, allocating funds to ministries and provinces (although the government lacked the organizational capacity to fully execute the budget), and protecting the rights of minority political parties in the Iraqi legislature.[58]

On the other hand, the really tough issues were sectarian and political, and in this regard the Iraqis had a long way to go. There was insufficient progress toward de-Ba'athification reform, legislation ensuring an equitable distribution of hydrocarbon resources, and the delineation of provincial powers and the establishment of a law governing provincial elections; political influence at a variety of levels undercut the ability of Iraqi commanders to target all extremists regardless of sectarian affiliation, particularly in the case of Shi'a militia leaders; Iraqi security forces operating on their own still evidenced sectarian behavior (although the ISF was much more evenhanded in the application of the law when partnered with coalition units); there had been inadequate progress in reducing Shi'a militia presence in a number of provinces and in the security services of a number of ministries; and Iraqi government officials continued in some cases to undermine Iraqi commanders by making false accusations against them, particularly in cases where prominent Shi'a leaders were targeted in military operations. Overall, Iraqi security units were still highly dependent on U.S. assistance and were in most cases a long way from operating independently, although their performance was good when partnered with U.S. units. Furthermore, since insurgent and militia groups had not yet decided to lay down their arms, conditions were not ripe for the provision of a general amnesty or for the disarmament and demobilization of militias.[59]

The failure of the Iraqi political system to produce results rankled American lawmakers of all stripes. Sunni intransigence and bad blood among the various Iraqi political factions blocked any feasible program of national reconciliation in the summer of 2007. President Bush, Ambassador Crocker, and General Petraeus could influence the Iraqi government only so far toward this elusive goal. U.S. congressmen and senators criticized the planned two-month recess for the Iraqi Council of Representatives, complaining that while U.S. troops were fighting and dying on the streets of Iraq, Iraqi lawmakers were doing little to achieve the elusive reconciliation that would signal an end to the conflict. In mid-July the Sunni Tawafuq and Shi'a Office of the Martyr Sadr blocs returned to the Council of Representatives and Iraqi lawmakers cut short their planned recess, but they argued (correctly) that since the various political parties had not come to consensus on the major pieces of legislation, there was little to work on. Major political deals in Iraq are cut privately in smoke-filled rooms, not openly in parliament.[60] It is not clear that the American political system is entirely different.

Baghdad and Washington were not the only two capitals with a huge stake in the outcome of the war; Tehran and Damascus were also deeply involved in the conflict. Syria played a key role as a transit conduit for suicide bombers and jihadists and as a center for insurgent organizers and financiers. In July, MNF-I estimated that 50 to 80 suicide bombers passed through Syria every month.[61] During the first half of 2007, nearly 280 suicide bombers killed themselves in terrorist acts in Iraq, accounting for roughly 5,500 casualties.[62] Since the vast majority of suicide bombers in Iraq were of foreign origin, gaining control of the Syrian border and halting the passage of jihadists through Damascus International Airport were important priorities. In an October raid near Sinjar in northwest Iraq, U.S. forces seized al-Qaeda records that enabled analysts at the Combating Terrorism Center at West Point to track the origins of suicide bombers entering Iraq from the outside. Of the 595 foreign nationals who entered Iraq as suicide bombers between August 2006 and August 2007, 41 percent were from Saudi Arabia, nearly 19 percent were from Libya, and assorted others were from Syria, Yemen, Algeria, Morocco, and Jordan. Of those jihadists whose occupations were known, 43 percent were university students, showing the strong al-Qaeda recruiting presence in Arab universities.[63]

In response to this challenge, General Petraeus and Lieutenant General Stan McChrystal jointly hosted a series of interagency video-teleconferences focusing on the facilitation of foreign terrorists into Iraq. The meetings included nearly two dozen representatives from the intelligence community, the Department of Defense, and other interagency organizations. These sessions increased organizational awareness, reaffirmed the need for interagency cooperation, and identified initiatives and mechanisms to enhance collaboration. The sessions dealt with terrorist movements, network finances, and challenges to coalition information operations.

Iran played a much more nefarious role, with the Qods force actively involved in recruiting, organizing, training, arming, equipping, funding, and in some cases directing special groups of the Jaish al-Mahdi. Explosively formed penetrators supplied by Iran were the most lethal munitions in Iraq and were responsible for hundreds of American deaths. The Iranian border was a sieve; commercial goods and illicit arms flowed relatively unimpeded despite the best efforts of Multi-National Corps–Iraq and Iraqi border guards to beef up security and implement a comprehensive inspection regime for cross-border traffic. In an attempt to shore up border security, Multi-National Corps–Iraq positioned an impressive infantry brigade provided by the nation of Georgia near Kut in Wasit province. The move had some effect, but even if the physical movement of illicit weapons could be disrupted, the Qods force had other means at its disposal to get what it wanted. Iran bankrolled a number of Iraqi political parties, buying influence and sympathetic ears in the halls of power in Baghdad.

Iran had three major goals in Iraq, each of which worked against U.S. efforts to stabilize the conflict. Iran's major goal was to create a weak and pliable Iraqi state on its western border, one allied with Iranian interests and a partner in its goal to extend Iranian hegemony across the heart of the Middle East. One method to accomplish this goal was to buy influence among Iraqi political elites; another was to pursue the "Hezbollahization" of the Shi'ites in Iraq through Jaish al-Mahdi surrogates. Iran's next–most important goal was to buy time for its nuclear program to build a viable weapon. With the United States focused on Iraq, Iran could continue enriching uranium unimpeded by the threat of U.S military action. The third goal was simply to bloody the U.S. military and thereby sap the will of the American people to support further military operations in the Middle East. Ironically, both the United States and Iran sought a stable Iraq, but on different terms. The result was continuing conflict and suffering, with the Iraqi people paying a stiff price.

In an attempt to reach a common understanding regarding Iraq, the United States and Iran agreed to talks between their ambassadors in Baghdad. Iran desired bilateral negotiations, while the United States demanded tripartite talks that included an Iraqi representative. Three rounds of talks took place in the spring and summer of 2007 in Prime Minister Maliki's offices in the International Zone in Baghdad, but they achieved little.[64] Ambassador Crocker presented the intelligence gathered on the nefarious Iranian activities in Iraq and then requested that Iran halt them.[65] The Iranian ambassador denied the allegations, but the Persians had been put on notice that the United States knew what they were doing in Iraq.

Given the disparate goals of the United States and Iran, it was just too hard to reach agreement on the way forward in Iraq, or anywhere else in the Middle East, for that matter. Another problem was that although Ambassador Ryan Crocker was an extraordinarily capable and empowered diplomat, his Iranian counterpart lacked authority to negotiate. The real power resided with Qassem Suleimani, the head of the Qods force in Tehran, a point made clear by a communication sent to General Petraeus in March 2008. In a message passed through a senior Iraqi leader, Suleimani wrote, "General Petraeus, you should know that I, Kassim Suleimani, control the policy for Iran with respect to Iraq, Lebanon, Gaza, and Afghanistan. And indeed, the ambassador in Baghdad is a Qods Force member. The individual who's going to replace him is a Qods Force member."[66] As General Petraeus noted wryly, such an arrangement makes traditional diplomacy difficult. The Iranians wanted to negotiate for the release of one of their most important operatives, Qais Khazali, still in U.S. custody. In so many words, they were told to pound sand.

There was one point of agreement between the United States and Iran, and that was the need to resolve the status of the Mujahedin-e Khalq, or MEK. The MEK is a leftist revolutionary organization founded in the 1960s, originally in opposition to the regime of Shah Mohammad Reza Pahlavi. The group took part in the 1979 Islamic revolution but soon fell out with the ruling clerics whose Islamic fundamentalism clashed with the MEK's Marxist philosophy. Driven from Iran, the MEK fled first to Paris, and then to Iraq, where it supported Saddam Hussein's war against Khomeini's regime. The State Department added the MEK to its list of foreign terrorist groups in 1997. After the U.S. invasion of Iraq in 2003, U.S. forces closed down the MEK's bases in the country and consolidated the remaining members of the group at Camp Ashraf, approximately sixty miles northeast of Baghdad in Diyala province. The thirty-three hundred–plus–member group existed under female leadership and had a cultlike devotion to its leader, Maryam Rajavi.

The disposition of the MEK was a tricky issue. Iraq wanted Camp Ashraf closed and the MEK dispersed. Iran offered to take the members back and to grant all but about fifty of them full amnesty, but few voluntarily accepted the offer. Unless the U.S. government allowed members of the group to enter the United States as refugees, few other nations were willing to do so. General Petraeus fittingly labeled the issue a "tar baby," the solution for which, as with everything in Iraq, would be neither easy nor quick.[67]

The creation of effective army and police forces was crucial if Iraq were to hold together over the long run. Building the Iraqi security forces was the job of the awkwardly named Multi-National Security Transition Command–Iraq (MNSTC-I), first led by General Petraeus in 2004–2005 and after that by Lieutenant General Martin Dempsey, followed in mid-2007 by Lieutenant General James Dubik. By the end of summer 2007, MNSTC-I had trained roughly 200,000 police and nearly 150,000 soldiers, along with additional small contingents of airmen, sailors, and special forces.[68] But raw numbers alone did not tell the tale of what was happening in this vital arena. Iraqi security forces were not just getting bigger; they were getting better as well. Six thousand advisers embedded in five hundred military and police advisory teams were themselves increasingly better trained and able to assist Iraqi units to address shortcomings in leadership, logistics, and training. Increased numbers of U.S. combat units available with the surge enabled more extensive partnering of U.S. and Iraq forces on the streets, which also served to improve Iraqi capacity by showing Iraqi troops what right looks like.

The crisis of 2006–2007 forced MNSTC-I to focus on the creation of combat units at the expense of institutional capacity, logistical means, and other structural building blocks of armed forces. The rapid increase in troop units led to a shortage of leaders, especially field grade and noncommissioned officers. General Petraeus encouraged Prime Minister Maliki to rehire military leaders sacked after the dissolution of the Iraqi Army in 2003, with proper vetting to ensure they had had no more than perfunctory ties with the Ba'ath Party, and with retraining as well. The Iraqi government agreed to the proposal, which helped somewhat to alleviate the leadership shortages.

A more important concern than the number of soldiers and police available was where their loyalties lay. Many soldiers and police maintained strong ties to their tribal and ethnosectarian or political affiliations, which made the loyalty of the security forces to the Iraqi government problematic. Some U.S. commanders ended up ordering the National Police to remain at their checkpoints for fear of alienating the local Sunni residents.[69] There was also clear sectarian bias in the appointment of senior military and police commanders, which translated to sectarian interference in military operations.[70]

Prime Minister Maliki would take action against sectarianism when General Petraeus presented convincing evidence; in the case of the highly sectarian National Police, the Iraqi government replaced the overall commander, both division commanders, all nine brigade commanders, and seventeen of twenty-seven battalion commanders—and some of the replacements were subsequently sacked as well.[71] MNSTC-I, in coordination with the Iraqi Ministry of the Interior, developed a "re-bluing" program—emphasizing human rights, rule of law, democratic policing, police ethics, and counterinsurgency tactics—to enhance the capabilities and professionalization of the National Police. The United Nations–funded, NATO-staffed Italian Carabinieri Mobile Training Team helped as part of this effort beginning in October 2007. Human rights abuses by some National Police and Iraqi security forces continued, but as a result of the re-bluing process and coalition scrutiny and mentoring, lessened considerably during the year.

Congress mandated an independent assessment of the readiness of the Iraqi security forces, their capabilities, and how support and training by U.S. forces contributed to their effectiveness. An independent commission chaired by retired Marine General James Jones, a former Supreme Allied Commander in Europe, traveled to Iraq for three weeks in July to gather information for the report, which was released less than a week before Ambassador Crocker's and General Petraeus's testimony to Congress on the progress of the surge. The Jones report rated the capabilities of the Iraqi security forces as uneven, but improving. The army and special forces received fairly high remarks, but other security forces came in for varying levels of harsher criticism. The report labeled the Ministry of the Interior "a ministry in name only" that was "widely regarded as being dysfunctional and sectarian."[72] The Iraqi police were "fragile," while the National Police force was "not viable in its current form" due to sectarianism and poor leadership.[73] The report recommended the disbandment of the force. The Department of Border Enforcement was "weak and ineffective."[74] Other shortcomings, such as the lack of institutional capacity and logistical shortfalls, were self-evident due to the priority put on the creation of combat forces to fight the counterinsurgency war.

Despite the negative aspects of the Jones report, there were encouraging signs as well. Iraqi security forces were bearing the brunt of attacks, incurring three times as many casualties as U.S. and coalition forces. Iraqi security forces also had some success in planning and executing security operations for major events, such as the Shi'a celebration of the life and martyrdom of the 7th Imam, Musa al-Kadhim, which featured a massive march of more than a million Shi'a worshipers across Baghdad to the Kadhimiyah shrine on August 9–10. During the observance of this event in 2005, nearly a thousand pilgrims were killed in a stampede caused by a panic over rumors of suicide bombers in the crowd.[75] Iraqi security forces took the lead on developing the security plan, which included curfews, vehicle bans, and multiple layers of checkpoints. In the event, the celebration went smoothly. Under the direction of Lieutenant General Abud and the Baghdad Operations Command, the Iraqi Army and police effectively executed the plan, controlled the crowd, and kept the public informed through the media. It was an impressive display of competence that showed just how far the security forces had come in the past three years.

Another positive development was the desire of the Iraqi government to purchase U.S. arms, ammunition, and equipment to outfit the Iraqi security forces. This decision would tie Iraq to a relationship with the United States for years to come and was therefore a welcome development. The problem was that the peacetime foreign military sales bureaucracy in the U.S. Department of Defense and the U.S. industrial base could not keep pace with the demand from Iraq for weapons, and was slow to move to a wartime footing. General Petraeus brought the issue to the attention of Secretary of Defense Gates, who intervened to speed up the process. With the training base in Iraq working at full capacity, the limiting factor for building new units now was equipment and leaders. We could make a positive impact on the first factor; the second was much more difficult and would take time to resolve completely.

In mid-August Multi-National Corps–Iraq began the next phase of the "surge of offensive operations." Operation Phantom Strike was the pursuit phase of the operations begun in mid-June during Operation Phantom Thunder. One of the problems with previous offensives was the ability of insurgents to relocate to other areas of Iraq, where they could regenerate their forces and wait out the coalition operations. The additional forces provided by the surge enabled Lieutenant General Odierno and his command to pressure insurgents across the breadth and depth of Iraq and deny them safe havens, thereby overcoming the "whack-a-mole" approach to operations all too prevalent earlier in the war. Odierno ensured that the tactical actions at battalion and brigade level were synchronized in such a manner as to contribute to the theater strategic objective.[76]

One of the areas targeted during Operation Phantom Strike was located northwest of Baghdad. After Colonel Jim Hickey and his team in the Counter IED Center plotted several years' worth of reporting on a map of Iraq, he noticed an intelligence "black hole" in the area between Taji and Lake Tharthar. Digging farther into the intelligence, Hickey discovered that maneuver units would not enter this area because hundreds of roadside bombs made driving deadly, while a robust air defense system made flying hazardous as well. In short, the insurgents had turned the area into a sanctuary, helped by the fact that it fell at the intersection of three division boundaries and therefore had been virtually ignored. Once U.S.

units began operations to clear the area in August, cache finds skyrocketed and car bombs dropped dramatically. By October, roadside bomb attacks along Route 1 between Baghdad and Samarra had dropped by 70 percent.[77]

Special operations forces also extended the reach of coalition operations and increased the pressure on al-Qaeda, Sunni insurgents, and Shi'a militia leaders. However, during the surge we learned that counterterrorism operations conducted by special operations forces were far more effective when combined with conventional operations in the same vicinity; indeed, counterterrorist operations were largely ineffective in their absence.[78] Conventional forces set the conditions in communities by making it difficult for terrorists, insurgents, and militia leaders to use the people as a base of support. Conventional forces living among the people developed the human intelligence necessary to prosecute targeted operations. Surge operations in Iraq in 2007 eliminated a large number of safe havens and forced insurgent, terrorist, and militia leaders to move and communicate more often. They could then be targeted and killed or captured more easily by special operations raids, with the improved security sustained by the presence in the areas of multiple small conventional force outposts.

Special operations forces were an important asset, but they were not the "war winner" that some advocates contend. All assets are necessary to put the squeeze on terrorist organizations. General Petraeus labeled the plan to defeat al-Qaeda the Anaconda Strategy, after the Civil War plan to blockade the Atlantic and Gulf coasts, cut the Confederacy in two along the Mississippi River, and squeeze the South through simultaneous offensives at multiple points along its borders. He had Bill Rapp and his team create a slide that summarized this strategy to defeat al-Qaeda, which became a staple of command briefings from the summer of 2007 onward. (The slide is reproduced in Appendix 3.)

To succeed, al-Qaeda in Iraq needed a command and control system and the ability to communicate with leaders and operatives outside the country. The organization required money, foreign fighters and locals willing to fight as insurgents and die as suicide bombers, safe havens inside Iraq, weapons, and an ideology that could appeal to the Sunnis in the population and entice them to support the terrorist cause. Multi-National Force–Iraq, supported by national assets, conducted a comprehensive campaign to deny these resources to the terrorist group. The Anaconda Strategy included kinetic operations to kill and capture terrorist operatives, reconciliation initiatives to reduce the base of support for al-Qaeda, counterinsurgency inside coalition detention facilities to turn insurgents into supporters of the legitimate government, nonkinetic programs to educate the population and restore government services to them, a comprehensive information campaign to influence the Iraqi people and inform the broader public, and diplomatic initiatives to reduce the flow of foreign fighters from other parts of the Arab-Islamic world.

Phantom Strike kept al-Qaeda off balance and denied the group the ability to influence the upcoming report on the surge to Congress. Targeted operations of up to battalion strength focused on the areas northeast of Baqubah in the Diyala River valley, south and east of Samarra in the Tigris River valley, northwest of Baghdad near Karmah and Lake Tharthar, and in selected areas south of Baghdad. The momentum of these operations took its toll on al-Qaeda, as the organization began to lose leaders faster than it could find qualified replacements. In Iraq, there would be no enemy surprise akin to the Tet Offensive during the Vietnam War.

Nevertheless, the terrorist movement was still dangerous. On August 14 terrorists detonated two truck bombs in a small Yezidi village near the Syrian border in northwestern Iraq; another truck bomb exploded nearby later that night. The result was more than five hundred killed and fifteen hundred wounded—the single-greatest casualty-producing attack of the Iraq War.[79] Al-Qaeda claimed that the bombings were justified by the "anti-Islamic" teachings of the Yezidi religion.[80] The attack against the defenseless Yezidi community, an ancient Kurdish-speaking group whose faith combines Islamic teachings with other ancient religions, highlighted both al-Qaeda's desperation and its still potent arsenal of suicide bombers. Our information operations in the aftermath of the attack showcased both al-Qaeda's disregard for human life and the humanitarian response by the Iraqi government and coalition forces.

With al-Qaeda increasingly on the ropes and a large number of Sunni insurgents joining the Sons of Iraq movement, Jaish al-Mahdi special groups became the main instigators of violence against U.S. forces in Baghdad as the summer wore on. In Shi'a communities with a strong Jaish al-Mahdi presence, counterinsurgency operations focused on protecting the people were less effective than in Sunni areas willing to commit to the war against al-Qaeda.[81] That does not mean the surge operations were ineffective in Shi'a areas. Indeed, due to the pressure put on the Jaish al-Mahdi, Sadr increasingly lost control of his movement, especially the special groups beholden to Iran. The detention of a number of Jaish al-Mahdi leaders put the organization in disarray. In an attempt to reach an accommodation with the coalition, Sadr's representatives reached out to Multi-National Force–Iraq leaders during the summer to broker a deal. This was an encouraging sign, since the Jaish al-Mahdi posed a long-term threat to Iraq as a Hezbollah-like entity, and dealing with the organization required both targeted strikes against its leadership and broad engagement to reconcile the rank and file to the legitimate government of Iraq.

The support of Prime Minister Maliki was the key to effective action against Jaish al-Mahdi leaders. Ever since the Sadrists had pulled out of the cabinet in the spring, Maliki had been intent on putting pressure on them wherever possible. A dustup in Nasariyah between Jaish al-Mahdi and government security forces (which were heavily infused with operatives from the rival Badr Organization) led

Maliki to urge General Petraeus to intervene with coalition assets; a special forces team with links to airpower quickly turned the tide of the battle. Relations between the Jaish al-Mahdi and its adversaries in the Islamic Supreme Council of Iraq (and its military wing, the Badr Organization) were at a boiling point in southern Iraq as the rival organizations battled for political control of the Shi'a heartland.[82] In June the governor of Diwaniya was nearly assassinated in a bomb attack that killed more than two dozen policemen outside his home. In separate attacks in August, Jaish al-Mahdi operatives killed provincial governors in Muthana and Qadisiyah provinces and their chiefs of police, using Iranian-supplied explosively formed penetrators.

Sadr and the Jaish al-Mahdi had overplayed their hand. As surge opera-tions improved security across Iraq, Shi'a communities once reliant on the Jaish al-Mahdi for protection were getting fed up with the heavy-handed actions and criminality of the organization. No longer the defenders of last resort (that role now being played by coalition and Iraqi security forces), the Jaish al-Mahdi came to be viewed by increasing numbers of Shi'a more as criminal gangs and thugs than as protectors. The hope was that the Shi'a communities would turn against the Jaish al-Mahdi as the Sunni communities had turned against al-Qaeda. In any case, although Multi-National Force–Iraq was not ready to take on the Jaish al-Mahdi in a full-scale battle in the summer of 2007, I mentioned to General Petraeus that the day when we would have to do so was not far off. My prediction would come to pass eight months later during the battle for Sadr City in the spring of 2008.

The battle for Shi'a supremacy in southern Iraq came to a head on August 27 during the celebration of mid-Sha'ban, which in Shi'a Islam marks the birth of Muhammad al-Mahdi, the last of twelve imams revered by Shi'ites, a ninth-century saint who would one day return to bring justice to the world. Hundreds of thousands of Shi'a worshipers flocked to the shrines of the Imam Husayn and the Imam Abbas in Karbala to celebrate the occasion. The shrines were not just religiously important; they were major sources of revenue for whichever group controlled them. During the festival, armed Jaish al-Mahdi operatives attempted to enter the shrines, instigating a gun battle with guards from the Badr Organiza-tion. The fighting soon spilled over onto the streets of Karbala, killing more than fifty bystanders and wounding around two hundred more.[83]

The fighting created a major crisis for Maliki's government. Ayatollah Ali al-Sistani canceled the religious celebration in Karbala and encouraged the worship-ers to return home—an equivalent action to the pope canceling Easter or Christ-mas Mass in St. Peter's Square at the Vatican. If Iraqi security forces could not restore control in Karbala, there was the very real possibility that Maliki's govern-ment would fall.

General Petraeus and I were at the house on the evening of August 27 when our cell phones started to ring as news of the fighting spread. On the other end were Islamic Supreme Council of Iraq interlocutors pleading for help. General

Petraeus authorized jets to fly over Karbala as a "show of force" at the request of the Iraqi authorities. Iraqi government officials soon requested the use of coalition helicopters to ferry Iraqi Army forces to Karbala. Accurate information was hard to come by, as the coalition lacked a presence in the city. My brigade had fought and defeated the Jaish al-Mahdi in Karbala in May 2004, so I knew the territory. The only place to land helicopters was in the open desert west of the city. The staff worked on the request, but the Iraqis grew impatient and decided instead to drive south from Baghdad in a large vehicular convoy—led personally by Prime Minister Maliki.

Early on the morning of August 28, Maliki entered Karbala at the head of a fifty-two-vehicle convoy, some sporting heavy 12.7mm DShK machine guns. More vehicles followed close behind. The townspeople cheered as the convoy rolled through the streets to the governor's compound. Maliki ordered the arrest of a number of Sadrist leaders, fired the commander in charge of Karbala operations (one of his cousins), and had an Iraqi Emergency Response Unit (equivalent to a U.S. SWAT team) raid twenty-five targets in the city. Maliki wore a pistol and brought a rifle with him; his leadership from the front was incentive enough for the troops to perform well in reining in the Jaish al-Mahdi.[84]

The Karbala episode had an enormous political and military impact. The Shi'a faithful were incensed that violence had marred the religious celebration of the birth of the Mahdi, and they put the blame squarely on Muqtada al-Sadr and the Jaish al-Mahdi in Karbala. In response to the outrage and realizing that he was in danger of being isolated politically, Sadr declared that his militia would stand down for six months "to restructure it in a way that would preserve its ideological principles."[85] The cease-fire applied even to operations against coalition forces.

The surge of offensive operations and the creation of the Sons of Iraq movement had severely weakened the insurgency and mauled al-Qaeda in Iraq, already reeling from the impact of the Awakening. Conventional and special operations forces had killed or captured thousands of terrorist and insurgent operatives. Now the Jaish al-Mahdi, the primary source of Shi'a violence against coalition forces, had agreed to stand down, at least temporarily. With the conditions set for an immediate, dramatic, and measurable decrease in violence in Iraq, the tide in the war had indeed turned, despite the immediate inability of Iraqi politicians to come to terms with one another.

General Petraeus was forthright about the progress made in both the military and the political arenas. In a report to the secretary of defense in mid-July, he wrote, "If our tactical momentum does translate into tangible progress on Iraqi's political front, we recognize that we still face the challenge of conveying to our lawmakers and the American public the sense that our efforts are on a viable path to produce stability in Iraq, protect our regional interests, and preserve our national strength—and all on an acceptable timeline."[86] In an open address to the troops seven weeks later, Petraeus wrote, "Many of us hoped this summer would be a time of tangible political progress at the national level as well. One of the justifications for the surge, after all, was that it would help create the space for Iraqi leaders to tackle the tough questions and agree on key pieces of 'national reconciliation' legislation. It has not worked out as we had hoped."[87] Nevertheless, it was now time to return to the United States and report on the state of the war to Congress. General Petraeus finished his letter to the troops with that thought in mind. "I will go before Congress conscious of the strain on our forces, the sacrifices that you and your families are making, the gains we have made in Iraq, the challenges that remain, and the importance of building on what we and our Iraqi counterparts have fought so hard to achieve," he concluded. Those hearings would determine whether the administration's strategy would be given more time to succeed, or whether Congress would impose a timetable for the withdrawal of U.S. forces from Iraq. The fate of the surge was in the balance.

CHAPTER 7

Testimony

I am neither an optimist nor a pessimist. I am a realist.
And Iraq is all hard, all the time.
—General David Petraeus

The testimony by Ambassador Ryan Crocker and General David Petraeus to Congress in September 2007 was the key political moment of the surge. Time was running out on the Washington clock as the American people tired of the seemingly unwinnable conflict in Iraq. Democrats, now the majority party in both houses of Congress, hoped to use the hearings as a springboard to mandate a withdrawal timeline for U.S. military forces and an end to American involvement in the war. Although the surge had succeeded in reducing the levels of violence in Iraq, most of the advances had come in the two and a half months before the hearings—not enough time for the American people or their elected representatives in Congress to grasp the shift in momentum (and mostly after the data cutoff date for the National Intelligence Estimate and General Accounting Office study on Iraq that were delivered to Congress shortly before Petraeus and Crocker testified). Iraqi political leaders were still deadlocked on the important issues that divided them, including control of oil revenues, provincial versus federal powers, and revision of the draconian de-Ba'athification decree of 2003. Congress was ready to assign Iraqi political leaders a failing grade. But Iraqi politicians were still talking, and political discourse in Baghdad continued. We didn't know whether they would succeed, but we did know that if the United States pulled its support, the Iraqi state would probably dissolve. As General Petraeus explained to Secretary of Defense Gates shortly after he took command, the surge had to be extended in time and space or it would fail. The consequences should Iraq collapse would be enormous. With continued support, there was still hope that the Iraqi people could come together to solve their differences through a political process, so those with the most votes and not the most guns would determine the future course of the country.

The September hearings would determine whether U.S. forces would receive more time to implement the counterinsurgency concepts ushered in by the surge and allow the other factors improving security in Iraq to run their course. Unless more time was put on the Washington clock, the surge would indeed fail and the war would be lost.

Before General Petraeus could render his report to Congress, he had to convince his own bosses that the surge was working. In the case of Admiral William "Fox" Fallon, the head of U.S. Central Command, this task was not easy. Fallon had been extremely skeptical that additional forces could change the trajectory in the Iraq War. He had repeatedly slow-rolled requests for more troops, requiring a full-scale effort by General Petraeus and his staff to overcome the obstacles to the provision of the resources necessary to fully implement a population-based counterinsurgency campaign.[1] In spring 2007 Fallon went a step further and appointed a two-man study team, led by Rear Admiral James "Sandy" Winnefeld (now the vice chairman of the Joint Chiefs of Staff) and Dr. Thomas Bowditch from the Center for Naval Analysis, to revisit the war strategy and propose how to reduce forces in Iraq. Regrettably, Fallon took this action without either consulting with General Petraeus or informing him of the true nature of the study team's mission, leading to strained relations between the two leaders when Petraeus learned what the two observers were doing.

Winnefeld and Bowditch were both capable individuals, but neither had spent any significant amount of time in Iraq. Neither did they have any background or experience in counterinsurgency warfare. They arrived in Baghdad without meeting with either General Petraeus or Lieutenant General Odierno to discuss the nature of their mission, then spent three weeks traveling around Iraq in relative obscurity, talking to military and civilian leaders. Charlie Miller in the Commander's Initiatives Group referred to Winnefeld as "the spy," a label that had the ring of truth behind it.[2] Winnefeld and Bowditch lacked impartiality about the surge; in the view of most officers who met with the team, they came to Iraq with preconceived notions as to why the surge was the wrong policy and searched for data to back up the need to change course.

At the end of his visit to Iraq, Rear Admiral Winnefeld briefed General Petraeus on the results of his trip. I sat in on the meeting to hear the admiral's assessment of the war effort—outside assessments were often useful in preventing "groupthink" in the headquarters. The admiral stunned us by announcing that he would recommend a significant reduction of U.S. forces in Iraq and a shift in focus to training Iraqi security forces. Special operations forces could continue the hunt for al-Qaeda and Jaish al-Mahdi special group leaders while Iraqi forces took over the mission of securing their homeland. The concept was a return to the policies of Multi-National Force–Iraq under General George Casey, which had failed once civil war broke out in 2006.

General Petraeus was incensed that someone with almost no time on the ground in Iraq would waltz into the country and in a period of just three weeks determine that the stated policy of the United States government in Iraq was wrong. He unloaded on Winnefeld, who took a tongue-lashing that was more properly directed at his boss (as indeed Petraeus later redirected it, when he confronted Admiral Fallon over the study during a visit to the CENTCOM Forward Headquarters in Qatar).[3] We felt the Winnefeld study team represented an egregious example of "magnet ball," named for the phenomenon of a first-grade soccer game, where everyone wants to focus on the ball rather than the wider field. President Bush had already determined the strategy in Iraq; it was Central Command's role to do its best to carry it out—to help Multi-National Force–Iraq, not to undermine the commander fighting the war. General Petraeus did not need another flag officer telling him how to run the war; he needed help with the wider regional dynamics that influenced the conflict in Iraq, such as the flow of suicide bombers from Arab states, the nefarious role of the Iranian regime, and the apportionment of air power and drones between the wars in Iraq and Afghanistan, all of which fell under the purview of U.S. Central Command, but which received little attention until General Petraeus started hosting interagency-wide video-teleconferences to achieve some focus on them.

Admiral Fallon wasn't listening. Instead, he told General Petraeus to prepare for a change of mission, the downgrading of population security to secondary concern in favor of transition. The return to a focus on transition was appropriate in the future, after the surge had time to fully take effect. But now was not the time to revert to that policy. General Petraeus respectfully voiced his disagreement with the approach, but in my view he had to use far too much intellectual energy and precious time discussing over the phone with Admiral Fallon issues that had already been decided in the White House. Their discussions were lengthy and serious; each leader believing his approach to the war was the best for the United States and for Iraq. The conversations were also unnecessary. If Admiral Fallon wanted to change course in Iraq, he should have voiced his concerns to the secretary of defense and the president rather than arguing the issue with the commander on the ground, who had already made clear his support for a population-based counterinsurgency campaign. Ultimately, Petraeus suggested that, with respect, perhaps the admiral should share his views with the president.[4] Little was heard after that.

General Petraeus also had to convince political and military leaders in Washington that they should sustain the surge well into the following year. One of the requirements in this regard was to ensure that they were receiving the best assessments possible of the situation in Iraq. The next National Intelligence Estimate on Iraq was due to be delivered in late August, and its conclusions would undoubtedly color congressional attitudes toward the upcoming hearings. The problem was that the intelligence professionals preparing the estimate in Washington, D.C., lacked the insights of their counterparts in Multi-National Force–Iraq. As with media reporting, the intelligence estimate lagged reality in Iraq by a number of weeks, mainly because the cutoff date for the data that went into it was two months before the report's issue date. Since most of the progress in reducing ethnosectarian violence in Iraq had come after the initiation of Operation Phantom Thunder in mid-June, the data lag was a significant issue.

To remedy this shortcoming, General Petraeus invited retired Major General John Landry, the National Intelligence Council coordinator for military issues, and several of his analysts to Iraq to discuss the soon-to-be-released report. Multi-National Force–Iraq staff officers showed them the latest data and discussed sources and methodology in an attempt to ensure the estimate reflected the facts on the ground. Landry and his team ultimately did incorporate some of what they learned into their report, which sounded a note of caution regarding the data used to compile the estimate. "Driven largely by the accelerating pace of tribal engagement and the increasing tempo of Coalition operations, developments in Iraq are unfolding more rapidly and with greater complexity today than when we completed our January NIE," the report stated.[5]

When released, the estimate more accurately reflected the progress that had been made in combating al-Qaeda and in reducing violence levels in Iraq, though it was still out of date by the time Petraeus and Crocker testified. It also threw cold water on Admiral Fallon's idea that a significant withdrawal of U.S. forces in the near term would help matters. Iraqi security forces were not ready to conduct major operations without coalition support. Furthermore, the authors concluded, "We assess that changing the mission of Coalition forces from a primarily counterinsurgency and stabilization role to a primary combat support role for Iraqi forces and counterterrorist operations to prevent AQI from establishing a safehaven would erode security gains achieved thus far."[6] Special operations raids could not substitute for conventional operations, since "Recent security improvements in Iraq, including success against AQI, have depended significantly on the close synchronization of conventional counterinsurgency and counterterrorism operations. A change of mission that interrupts that synchronization would place security improvements at risk."[7]

The report also accurately stated that political progress in Iraq had not matched progress in security.[8] Nevertheless, population security remained a crucial factor in creating the conditions for political reconciliation. "Coalition military operations focused on improving population security, both in and outside of Baghdad, will remain critical to the success of local and regional efforts until sectarian fears are diminished enough to enable the Shia-led Iraqi Government to fully support the efforts of local Sunni groups," the authors concluded.[9] The media focused on this aspect of the report. "The NIE is relentlessly bleak on the political side," Mary Louise Kelly reported on National Public Radio. "It casts serious doubts that Prime Minister Nouri al-Maliki can govern effectively. Bottom line: it judges that Iraq's government will become more precarious in the coming months."[10] The estimate was right on the mark in this regard in the near term, but as events in the spring of 2008 would show, political progress was possible in Iraq once the security situation was brought under control.

General Petraeus, Lieutenant General Odierno, and their staffs began planning in mid-July for the way ahead in Iraq—their recommendation to the secretary of defense and the president on whether and how to begin winding down the surge. Both commanders felt that it was premature to begin a wholesale withdrawal of the surge forces from Iraq, but that small adjustments could be made in the fall. For example, they recommended the withdrawal of the Marine Expeditionary Unit operating in al-Anbar province, which had been made much more secure by the Awakening, U.S. military operations, focused special mission unit operations, and growth in the capabilities of Iraqi forces. Petraeus and Odierno paid particular attention to the "battlefield geometry"—that is, the changing of unit boundaries and the stability of local relationships that would be affected by shifts in forces. Iraq was a geographic and cultural kaleidoscope, which made the planning incredibly complex. General Petraeus asked for as much time as possible before making his recommendation in order to better assess conditions on the ground, and Secretary Gates accommodated him by moving the decision briefing back to late August, the latest possible date, given the plan for Petraeus and Crocker begin their testimony on September 10.

Bill Rapp and the Commander's Initiatives Group began composing the congressional testimony for General Petraeus in late July. By mid-August they were ready with the first draft. I read the speech over and knew immediately it had been written by committee. Although the substance was technically solid, the writing lacked coherence, and transitions between sections were weak or missing. Bill asked me to pass it along to General Petraeus anyway to get his feedback. I placed the document in the general's inbox.

It wasn't long before General Petraeus asked me to step into his office. He had read perhaps a third of the document and was having difficulty following the flow of the argument. Bill and his team had done a magnificent job pulling together the vital metrics that would tell the story of security in Iraq, but the prose needed coherence. "Why don't you let Liz [McNally] and me take a crack at it?" I offered. General Petraeus readily agreed and allowed me to miss a number of meetings over the next two days to work on the testimony.

Liz and I sat down to work at my desk. Liz is an exceptionally bright person with a first-class intellect, a West Point graduate and Rhodes scholar. She had worked for General Petraeus two years earlier during his tenure as head of Multi-National Security Transition Command–Iraq and was now on his staff again, as his speechwriter. We both realized the problems with the testimony, but our approach to editing it could not have been more different. Liz likes to write quickly and put lots of prose on the screen before going back to edit it later. I prefer to agonize over every sentence and paragraph; an atypical, slower approach that nevertheless results in finished prose up front. We were the tortoise and the hare of the literary world.

Liz and I fought like brother and sister for two days while crafting the general's testimony into a more coherent product. When our task was done, we were both happy with the end result—a speech of approximately twenty-five minutes in length that summarized the results of the surge, the current security situation, and the way forward in Iraq. The document benefited from our eclectic approaches and the team effort required to produce it. The effort was intellectually satisfying and a lot of fun for me—a nice break from the routine grind of the office. When we were finished, I sent the testimony in to General Petraeus for his review. After a bit he called me into his office and with a smile said he was delighted with the rewrite. He wanted me to transfer the electronic file to his computer—he would "own the electrons" from this point forward. Liz's and my roles in crafting the testimony were over, at least for the time being. As it turned out, General Petraeus was either being kind to us or hadn't looked hard at the document. He did, indeed, take control of the electrons and unbeknownst to us significantly revised the speech, adding considerably to its length.

Not many days after we had finished drafting the testimony opening statement, disaster nearly struck the team. Shortly before 7 A.M. on August 22 a rocket launched by Shi'a militiamen from western Baghdad screamed into Camp Victory and hit the side of the house in which Captain Kelly Howard and Captain Johanna Mora lived. It was no doubt aimed at General Petraeus, who routinely left the adjacent villa around this time to head to the al-Faw palace for the morning battlefield update and assessment. The blast damaged the wall of the house and shattered the windows, which thankfully did not rain glass shards into the quarters, due to the protective plastic coating that had been applied to keep them semi-intact in case of an explosion. Kelly suffered minor ear damage, but thankfully there were no other injuries. Kelly and Hanna were shaken but otherwise fine, and each received the Combat Action Badge for being on the receiving end of enemy fire.

With the strategic options and testimony prepared, the next step was to brief the chain of command. General Petraeus had already shared the force-sizing options with General Peter Pace, the chairman of the Joint Chiefs of Staff, during one of his visits to Iraq, and of course had engaged in continual discussions with his immediate boss, Admiral Fallon at U.S. Central Command. The briefing to the Joint Chiefs of Staff on August 27 was the most difficult hurdle. The chiefs had required Petraeus to prepare assessments of three different options, none of which was in line with his thinking. Nonetheless, he and the staff dutifully drilled each option and provided an assessment regarding their feasibility of each. The chiefs were understandably concerned about the impact of continual and lengthy force rotations on the morale and health the force. They favored an earlier decision point to accelerate the drawdown from Iraq and felt that "conditions-based" criteria that Petraeus favored would give too much initiative to the Iraqi government, which could simply stall for time as U.S. soldiers and Marines fought, bled, and died on the streets of Iraq. The chiefs also pointed to broader regional and global interests and the need to reconstitute the strategic reserve in the United States. A reduction of forces would pressure the Iraqi government to act in its own best interests, they felt. This was the same mantra promoted by Multi-National Force–Iraq in 2006—not surprisingly, since General George Casey was now a member of the Joint Chiefs of Staff. He felt strongly that the Iraqi government would not act without being prodded to do so.

The real question was the exact nature of that prodding. General Petraeus felt strongly that creating a drawdown timeline would smack of a headlong American rush for the exits and lead Iraqis to begin planning for the day after the U.S. withdrawal rather than cooperating with U.S. forces in improving security in Iraq. "The quickest way to lose support is to give a sense that we're losing," Petraeus explained to the chiefs. Marine Corps Commandant General Conway responded bluntly, "What is it that is going to inspire the Iraqi government to get off its ass?" The benchmarks helped in this regard, General Petraeus replied. He maintained his view that a more rapid drawdown would be counterproductive. In the end, General Petraeus provided the assessments the chiefs had tasked him to produce. He told them the drill had been useful and the results would "inform" the recommendation he would make to the president in a few days. After Petraeus agreed to a minor modification in the MNF-I mission statement, the Joint Chiefs accepted the Multi-National Force–Iraq proposal, which Petraeus then presented to the president and the National Security Council without further alteration.[11]

Two days later I departed Iraq with Kelly Howard and Joe Yoswa to establish the offices for General Petraeus and his personal staff in the Pentagon in preparation for the congressional hearings. The spaces were cramped but functional; General Petraeus would for the most part work out of his quarters at Fort Myer, fitted with secure communications and Internet for just that purpose. The rest of the team, along with General Petraeus, followed us to Washington a few days later. On the day they departed Baghdad, another rocket slammed into the villa at Camp Victory, this one hitting General Petraeus's bedroom. The explosion damaged an air-conditioning unit but otherwise had little effect on the well-built structure. The enemy clearly had excellent targeting information, but fortunately was never able to cause serious injury or damage at the villa. Other soldiers on Camp Victory were not so fortunate; a number paid the ultimate price in these indirect fire attacks.

In preparation for the testimony to Congress and at General Petraeus's request, the Office of the Secretary of Defense convened a "murder board": a dress rehearsal in which civilian officials would put Ambassador Crocker and General Petraeus through the ringer before their date with the House and Senate Armed Services and Foreign Affairs Committees. General Petraeus led off the mock hearing with a recitation of his testimony, which I then learned he had personally rewritten, mushrooming it to forty-five minutes in length. It contained many excellent points—including the signature declaration that there had, indeed, been significant progress, but that it remained fragile and reversible—but it was clearly now too long. The episode reminded me of a remark by Blaise Pascal, the seventeenth-century French mathematician and philosopher, who once wrote, "I have made this letter longer than usual, only because I have not had the time to make it shorter." In taking control of the electrons, General Petraeus had continued to add important points to the testimony without cutting language to keep the speech at an acceptable length. I turned to General Petraeus and offered a suggestion, "Sir, let Liz and me see what we can do to cut it down." He agreed. Liz and I retreated into the basement offices of the Pentagon and booted up a computer.

Time was not on our side. It was late afternoon on Sunday, September 9. The hearings before the joint session of the House Armed Services and Foreign Affairs Committees were scheduled to begin at noon the following day. Clearly, my deliberate style of writing was not suitable in this situation, so Liz and I worked quickly to reshape the testimony. She wanted to use a scalpel; I preferred a meat cleaver. Entire paragraphs had to go to significantly reduce the length of the speech. Liz fought in vain to keep me from leaning too hard on the delete key, but within three hours we were able to cut the speech by more than a third, to twenty-seven minutes, barely longer than the version she and I had crafted back in Baghdad in mid-August. All the key points remained, but the fluff was gone. The language was shorter and crisper. We shipped the electrons off to General Petraeus at his quarters. He returned them with further edits, but the bulk of the language was still his, and we incorporated his final changes. By 8 o'clock that evening the testimony was in its final form. Liz e-mailed the text to the Joint Staff Printing Office for the preparation of copies that we would distribute to House members the next morning once General Petraeus had completed his opening statement.

Throughout this process, I received numerous requests for advance copies of the testimony from the National Security Council, the Office of the Secretary of Defense, various congressional offices, the Joint Chiefs of Staff, and U.S. Central Command. I politely stiff-armed them all and referred them directly to General Petraeus. General Petraeus knew that he would probably come under fire for the perception that he was a Bush administration mouthpiece; he was therefore careful to avoid any appearance of outside influence on his testimony. Indeed, in all the meetings with the president, not once did President Bush tell General Petraeus what to say to Congress. General Petraeus also no doubt wanted to avoid having others wordsmith his speech. In the end, he saved all of the various civilian and military offices from allegations that they had influenced his remarks. There were only five people who had a hand in crafting the testimony before it was delivered to Congress: General Petraeus, Colonel Bill Rapp, Lieutenant Colonel Charlie Miller, Captain Liz McNally, and me.

After a fitful night's sleep, I awoke the next morning to a bombshell. In a full-page ad in the *New York Times,* the antiwar group MoveOn.org attacked General Petraeus and accused him of "cooking the books" for the Bush administration. Under the title "General Petraeus or General Betray Us?" the ad read:

> General Petraeus is a military man constantly at war with the facts. In 2004, just before the election, he said there was "tangible progress" in Iraq and that "Iraqi leaders are stepping forward." And last week Petraeus, the architect of the escalation of troops in Iraq, said, "We say we have achieved progress, and we are obviously going to do everything we can to build on that progress."
>
> Every independent report on the ground situation in Iraq shows that the surge strategy has failed. Yet the General claims a reduction in violence. That's because, according to the New York Times, the Pentagon has adopted a bizarre formula for keeping tabs on violence. For example, deaths by car bombs don't count. The Washington Post reported that assassinations only count if you're shot in the back of the head—not the front. According to the Associated Press, there have been more civilian deaths and more American soldier deaths in the past three months than in any other summer we've been there. We'll hear of neighborhoods where violence has decreased. But we won't hear that those neighborhoods have been ethnically cleansed.
>
> Most importantly, General Petraeus will not admit what everyone knows: Iraq is mired in an unwinnable religious civil war. We may hear of a plan to withdraw a few thousand American troops. But we won't hear what Americans are desperate to hear: a timetable for withdrawing all our troops. General Petraeus has actually said American troops will need to stay in Iraq for as long as ten years.
>
> Today, before Congress and before the American people, General Petraeus is likely to become General Betray Us.[12]

The ad was a cynical, unfair attack on one of America's best battlefield commanders, and was factually inaccurate to boot. For starters, General Petraeus was not the architect of the surge, though he had certainly influenced it through conversations with Meghan O'Sullivan, General Pace, General (Ret.) Keane, and numerous others during the period leading up to President Bush's decision. Beyond that, and more significant, the authors had no idea of the reduction in the levels of violence during the summer of 2007, which was not surprising since American perceptions of the Iraq War often lagged reality in the conflict by several months. The more heinous charge was that General Petraeus had deliberately fudged facts at the bidding of the White House. This allegation was completely false. Ten days later, the *Washington Post* fact-checker would award the ad three Pinocchios for significant factual error and/or obvious contradictions.[13]

I folded up a copy of the newspaper as I headed out the door of my room. The general's personal security detail drove selected members of the team, who would sit behind General Petraeus at the hearings, over to his quarters at Fort Myer. General Petraeus was focused and clearly had on his "game face." Bill Rapp and I described the attack ad, and I asked the general whether he wanted to see it. He declined in no uncertain terms. (It turned out later that he had already seen it on the Internet.) His appointment was with the people's representatives in Congress, not with an unaccountable nongovernmental organization that simply had enough money to buy a full-page ad in one of the nation's leading newspapers.[14] Fair enough. General Petraeus then recounted a recent e-mail he received, which contained a copy of a poem entitled "If" by Rudyard Kipling:

If you can keep your head when all about you
    Are losing theirs and blaming it on you;
If you can trust yourself when all men doubt you,
    But make allowance for their doubting too;
If you can wait and not be tired by waiting,
    Or, being lied about, don't deal in lies,
Or, being hated, don't give way to hating,
    And yet don't look too good, nor talk too wise;

If you can dream—and not make dreams your master;
    If you can think—and not make thoughts your aim;
If you can meet with Triumph and Disaster
    And treat those two impostors just the same;
If you can bear to hear the truth you've spoken
    Twisted by knaves to make a trap for fools,
Or watch the things you gave your life to, broken,
    And stoop and build 'em up with worn-out tools;

If you can make one heap of all your winnings
    And risk it on one turn of pitch-and-toss,
And lose, and start again at your beginnings
    And never breathe a word about your loss;
If you can force your heart and nerve and sinew
    To serve your turn long after they are gone,
And so hold on when there is nothing in you
    Except the Will which says to them: "Hold on!"

If you can talk with crowds and keep your virtue,
    Or walk with Kings—nor lose the common touch;
If neither foes nor loving friends can hurt you,
    If all men count with you, but none too much;
If you can fill the unforgiving minute
    With sixty seconds' worth of distance run—
Yours is the Earth and everything that's in it,
    And—which is more—you'll be a Man, my son!

Kipling's poetry fit the situation perfectly. We put the attack ad behind us and piled into the cars waiting outside to make our way to Capitol Hill.

There were plenty of people in the nation's capital losing their heads that day. But throughout it all, General Petraeus and Ambassador Crocker remained calm and collected. Their ordeal began at 12:33 P.M. before a joint session of the House Armed Services Committee and the House Foreign Affairs Committee. As soon as the chairman of the House Armed Services Committee, Ike Skelton (D-MO), began to speak, demonstrators from the antiwar group Code Pink interrupted the proceedings. I had seen the demonstrators in the back of the room when we entered, and I ordered the staff not to turn around and look at them when they spoke up. With dozens of photographers poised in front of us in the hearing room, the last optic I wanted to see in the newspapers was a shot of General Petraeus's staff craning their necks to look at the demonstrators behind them. After a short outburst, Chairman Skelton ordered the demonstrators removed. Others interrupted the proceedings several times later in the hearing, with the same result. According to one report, among those removed was Cindy Sheehan, whose son had been killed while serving in Iraq and who had since become the face of the antiwar movement.[15]

Chairman Skelton began with a recitation of the problems of the U.S. involvement in Iraq since the beginning of the war. He doubted that the "technical progress" made during the surge would have a lasting strategic impact on the war, owing to the inability of Iraqi politicians to compromise with one another. "One of the great ironies of this hearing today is that General Petraeus, who sits here before us, is almost certainly the right man for the job in Iraq. But he's the right person three years too late and 250,000 troops short," Chairman Skelton stated.[16] The chairman of the House Foreign Affairs Committee, Tom Lantos (D-CA) picked up where Chairman Skelton left off. The surge had produced "technical successes" but had failed strategically, he said. The involvement of the United States in Iraq was wrecking U.S. military forces for no strategic benefit and depriving more pressing domestic needs of funds. The United States needed to rapidly withdraw its forces from Iraq to force the Iraqis to step up to their responsibilities. "Military progress without political progress is meaningless," Chairman Lantos intoned. "It is their country, and it is their turn. Prime Minister Maliki and the Iraqi politicians needed to know that the free ride is over and that American troops will not be party to their civil war. The situation in Iraq cries out for a dramatic change of course. We need to get out of Iraq, for that country's sake and for our own. It is time to go—and to go now."

As the Republican representatives began to speak, it became clear that the MoveOn.org ad had backfired terribly. Representative Duncan Hunter (R-CA), the ranking minority member of the House Armed Services Committee, rendered an impassioned defense of General Petraeus's integrity. He also stated his belief that to withdraw from Iraq before the Iraqi security forces were ready to assume responsibility for security of their country was a shortsighted policy. Representative Ileana Ros-Lehtinen (R-FL), the ranking minority member of the House Foreign Affairs Committee, continued the assault on MoveOn.org and others who accused General Petraeus "of presenting a report that is simply White House propaganda." She called on members of Congress "to publicly denounce the ad that says that you are cooking the books for the White House and to apologize to you, General Petraeus, for casting doubt upon your integrity." She also stated her belief that the United States should remain engaged in Iraq to fight Islamist extremists who would otherwise be emboldened by a precipitous withdrawal of U.S. military forces from that country.

With the opening statements concluded, Chairman Skelton stated, "General David Petraeus, the floor is yours." If the floor was his, the microphone certainly wasn't. As soon as General Petraeus began to speak, the sound system failed. After several minutes in which technicians scrambled to fix the problem, Chairman Skelton called for a short recess. During the break I told Major Everett Spain and Captain Liz McNally to hand out the written copies of General Petraeus's opening remarks, which ran to nine single-spaced typewritten pages. We thought we had printed sufficient copies of the testimony, but there were so many additional congressmen and -women and members of the media in the hearing room that we quickly ran out. In any event, the sound system was finally repaired and General Petraeus was invited once again to speak.

After the obligatory greeting, General Petraeus's testimony and accompanying charts laid to rest the claim that he had "cooked the books" for the White House. He noted that the testimony he was about to deliver was his own, with his assessment and recommendations submitted to members of his chain of command but not influenced by them. The remarks had "not been cleared by, nor shared with, anyone in the Pentagon, the White House, or Congress." He then rendered the essence of his assessment, that "the military objectives of the surge are, in large measure, being met. In recent months, in the face of tough enemies and the brutal summer heat of Iraq, Coalition and Iraqi Security Forces have achieved progress in the security arena. Though the improvements have been uneven across Iraq, the overall number of security incidents in Iraq has declined in 8 of the past 12 weeks, with the numbers of incidents in the last two weeks at the lowest levels seen since June 2006." There were several reasons for this progress, among them the losses sustained by al-Qaeda in Iraq, the disruption of Shi'a militia extremists, and coalition operations in Baghdad that had reduced the number of ethnosectarian deaths. Iraqi security forces were growing and shouldering more of the burdens and losses in combat, despite "continuing concerns about the sectarian tendencies of some elements in their ranks." The Awakening in al-Anbar province had taken root and spread to other locations. Given these manifest successes, General Petraeus believed the surge forces could be withdrawn by the following summer without jeopardizing gains made to date. Furthermore, he believed that although "the situation in Iraq remains complex, difficult, and sometimes downright frustrating, I also believe that it is possible to achieve our objectives in Iraq over time, though doing so will be neither quick nor easy."

General Petraeus then launched into a discussion of the nature of the conflict, the situation in Iraq before the surge, the current situation and trends, and the status of Iraqi security forces, and he concluded with his recommendations. The root cause of the conflict colored all else that happened in Iraq, he said. "The fundamental source of the conflict in Iraq is competition among ethnic and sectarian communities for power and resources," Petraeus stated. "This competition will take place, and its resolution is key to producing long-term stability in the new Iraq. The question is whether the competition takes place more—or less—violently. . . . Foreign and home-grown terrorists, insurgents, militia extremists, and criminals all push the ethno-sectarian competition toward violence. Malign actions by Syria and, especially, by Iran fuel that violence. Lack of adequate governmental capacity, lingering sectarian mistrust, and various forms of corruption add to Iraq's challenges." The fundamental question was how to channel the competition for power and resources into the nonviolent political realm.

General Petraeus then walked the representatives through the situation in Iraq. In the wake of the ethnosectarian violence instigated by the bombing of the al-Askari shrine in Samarra, security in Iraq had deteriorated badly. In December 2006, he noted, Ambassador Zalmay Khalilzad and General George Casey concluded that "the coalition was failing to achieve its objectives" and had requested additional forces to "protect the population and reduce sectarian violence, especially in Baghdad."[17] Since then U.S. and Iraqi forces had conducted counterinsurgency operations—living among the Iraqi people to improve security, especially in Baghdad. They had reduced al-Qaeda sanctuaries and disrupted the efforts of Iranian-supported militia extremists. The surge of offensive operations beginning in mid-June had expanded upon the gains achieved in the previous months in al-Anbar province and had cleared numerous enemy sanctuaries in Baghdad and its environs, as well as in Diyala province. With Multi-National Force–Iraq actively supporting reconciliation and the spread of the Sunni Awakening, many Iraqi tribes had joined the fight against al-Qaeda; moreover, the Iraqi security forces were improving in both quantity and quality, and provincial reconstruction teams had assisted in providing essential services to the Iraqi people.

The improvement in security was based on more than gut feel; the metrics gathered from both coalition and Iraqi sources were clear in this regard.[18] The data for these metrics had been gathered with "rigor and consistency," and indeed two U.S. intelligence agencies had determined that the data was "the most accurate and authoritative in Iraq." General Petraeus then displayed the first in a serious of charts that summarized the data concerning security and violence in Iraq. The number of security incidents had decreased significantly since mid-June and had returned to levels not seen since the spring of the previous year. Violent civilian deaths in Iraq had declined by more than 45 percent since the height of the sectarian violence in December and by nearly 70 percent in Baghdad; the number of those deaths judged to be from ethnosectarian violence had dropped by more than 55 percent in the same period countrywide and by 80 percent in Baghdad. The Iraqi capital was clearly being reclaimed from terrorist and militia violence and intimidation.

These Iraq-wide statistics were supported by other, more granular data. In the first eight months of 2007 coalition forces had uncovered 4,400 weapons and ammunition caches, nearly 1,700 more than were discovered the entire previous year. Roadside bomb attacks had decreased by a third since June. Car bombings and suicide attacks had declined from a high of 175 in March to 90 in August—still much too high, but a significant drop nonetheless. In al-Anbar province, attacks had declined from 1,350 in October 2006 to just over 200 in August 2007. Although trends in other Iraqi provinces were not as definitive, the overall trajectory of violence in Iraq was clearly downward.

Al-Qaeda in particular had taken it on the chin. U.S. and Iraqi conventional and special operations forces working in tandem had reduced terrorist sanctuaries, neutralized five major al-Qaeda media cells, and killed or captured more than one hundred key leaders and nearly twenty-five hundred operatives. The Islamist terror organization was not defeated, but it was disrupted. Operations had also targeted Shi'a militia extremists, the more lethal of whom were trained, armed, funded, equipped, and in some cases directed by the Iranian Revolutionary Guard Corps' Qods force.

The most significant development during the previous six months had been the blossoming of the Awakening and the emergence of the Sons of Iraq movement— both aggressively supported by Multi-National Force–Iraq—which had reclaimed al-Anbar province and harnessed the energy of Iraqi tribes and local citizens in a number of areas elsewhere in Iraq to join the fight against al-Qaeda. Some twenty thousand men had already been hired into the police force and more had volunteered for the army.

Despite some sectarian influence, inadequate logistics, the lack of institutional

infrastructure, and an insufficient number of leaders, Iraqi security forces continued to grow in both quantity and quality and to shoulder more of the burden in
securing Iraq. There were 140 army, national police, and special operations battalions in existence, with 95 able to engage in counterinsurgency operations with
limited coalition support. Iraqis were heavily involved in the fighting and were
suffering significant casualties in defense of their country. Total force strength
approached 450,000, with another 40,000 slated to enter the ranks by the end
of the year. Iraq was quickly becoming one of the major customers for foreign
military equipment sales in the United States, with roughly $3.4 million in sales
scheduled in 2007. Counterinsurgency operations being manpower intensive, the
growth in Iraqi security forces was a welcome development fully supported by
Multi-National Force–Iraq.

With his assessment completed, General Petraeus outlined the recommendations he had recently made to President Bush, Secretary Gates, Admiral Fallon,
and the Joint Chiefs of Staff. The concept was to continue securing the Iraqi people
while over time transferring security responsibilities to the Iraqi security forces,
first in partnership with U.S. and coalition forces and later with coalition forces in
support as advisers and backup. Iraqi security forces would continue to grow and
gradually over time assume more of the burden in the conflict. There would be no
"rush to failure," as transition would occur only when conditions permitted and
not based on an arbitrary timetable. The recommendations also highlighted the
importance of regional diplomacy to get Iraq's neighbors involved in an enduring
and positive relationship, along with the need to contest the extremist presence
in cyberspace. General Petraeus reiterated that "political progress will take place
only if sufficient security exists," and therefore population security and transition
would coexist as priorities for the foreseeable future. Handing off responsibilities
to the Iraqis too quickly would erode security gains made thus far and endanger
U.S. goals of stabilizing Iraq and creating a viable state in the longer term.

Based on the successes of the surge to date and projections for the future, General Petraeus stated his belief that the surge forces could be withdrawn from Iraq
by the following summer, beginning later in September with the Marine Expeditionary Unit currently operating near Lake Tharthar. Another brigade would
be withdrawn in mid-December. The other four surge brigades and two Marine
battalions would leave Iraq in the first seven months of 2008, on a schedule that
would evolve in accordance with conditions on the ground, with the presurge
force levels reached in July. Reductions beyond that point would be a matter for
future deliberation and debate, as events in Iraq were too volatile to forecast accurately beyond the summer of 2008. Multi-National Corps–Iraq would adjust
the "battlefield geometry" to ensure continuity as forces flowed out of country. The
strain on America's ground forces informed these decisions, but they did not drive
them. Organizing, training, and equipping America's armed forces were the jobs
of the Joint Chiefs of Staff, not the wartime commander in the field.

General Petraeus offered his belief that the United States could achieve its goals in Iraq, although doing so would require a long-term effort that would not be easy. However, a premature drawdown of forces would put at risk all the progress that had been made during the surge and could lead to the disintegration of the Iraqi state and its security forces, with the attendant negative consequences that such an outcome would entail. His recommendation was to continue counterinsurgency operations to protect the Iraqi people while targeting extremists, and transferring security responsibilities to Iraqi forces as conditions permitted.

General Petraeus closed with a word of thanks to the men and women in uniform who served in Iraq, America's "New Greatest Generation," as well as his appreciation to the congressional representatives for their assistance in ensuring that the forces under his command had the resources needed to succeed and for their role in taking care of the families at home. Congress had funded improved individual equipment, body armor, precision guided munitions, digital command and control systems, armed surveillance drones, counter–improvised explosive device systems, and mine-resistant vehicles that gave soldiers a much greater chance to survive enemy attacks. Funding for the Commander's Emergency Response Program provided commanders a critical tool in the counterinsurgency fight, while appropriations for detention operations enabled Multi-National Force–Iraq to prosecute counterinsurgency inside the wire.

Ambassador Crocker followed with his assessment of the political, economic, and diplomatic dynamics at play in Iraq. Although the task ahead was enormous, he said, he felt that the United States could achieve its objectives in Iraq—a secure, stable, democratic Iraq at peace with its neighbors. The trajectory in areas under his purview was upward, although he noted that "the slope of the line is not steep." Iraq had undergone a regime change, but that was not the end of the story. Iraq was experiencing a political revolution.[19]

Saddam Hussein had created a climate of fear in which no Iraqi citizen—even members of his own family—could feel safe. Kurds and Shi'ites had been persecuted and hundreds of thousands slaughtered to counter any potential opposition to the regime. When American forces deposed the dictator in April 2003, there was no Nelson Mandela waiting in the wings to assume power. "A new Iraq had to be built almost literally from scratch, and the builders in most cases were themselves reduced to their most basic identity, ethnic or sectarian," Ambassador Crocker stated. The social deconstruction fomented by Saddam Hussein's brutality led to the sectarian violence of 2006 and early 2007. Iraq was a traumatized society.

Iraqi politicians were grappling with fundamental questions, not just about the distribution of power and resources, but about the kind of state that would emerge from the ashes of Ba'athist Iraq. Iraqi politicians were sowing the seeds of national reconciliation in small ways, from the hiring of seventeen hundred Sunni policemen in Abu Ghraib to the outreach to members of the disbanded Iraqi army.

Oil revenues were being more or less equitably distributed even in the absence of comprehensive legislation. The issues confronting Iraqi leaders were immense, and they would take longer to resolve than anticipated, but Crocker felt that the Iraqis had the will to tackle the tough issues confronting them. Significantly, all Iraqi leaders (with the exception of Muqtada al-Sadr) had expressed a desire to develop a long-term relationship with the United States.

The political rejection of both al-Qaeda's philosophy and extremist Shi'a groups was a heartening development. The key now was to link progress at the provincial level with the Iraqi government in Baghdad. Although the Iraqi economy was underperforming, improvement in security was slowly energizing it. Budget execution by both the national and provincial governments was improving, stimulating business development and employment. The United States Agency for International Development, provincial reconstruction teams, U.S. embassy personnel, and the military via the Commander's Emergency Response Program were assisting the Iraqis in delivering essential services and in developing their economic potential.

There was some movement in regional and global diplomacy as well. After a hiatus of four years due to poor security conditions and the August 2003 bombing of the United Nations compound in Baghdad, the United Nations Assistance Mission in Iraq had once again opened its doors, with seventy-four countries pledging support for Iraqi economic reform. Iraq's neighbors had discussed various issues at a ministerial meeting in the spring, with further talks planned for later in the year. Commerce and political intercourse between Iraq and its neighbors were slowly unfolding. Regrettably, Iran and Syria continued to play unhelpful roles in abetting and fomenting violence in war-torn Iraq.

The surge had brought improvement to Iraq in 2007, Ambassador Crocker said, but enormous challenges remained. "Iraqis still struggle with fundamental questions about how to share power, accept their differences and overcome their past," he stated. But there was hope. "We have given the Iraqis the time and space to reflect on what sort of country they want. Most Iraqis genuinely accept Iraq as a multi-ethnic, multi-sectarian society—it is the balance of power that has yet to be sorted out." Iraqis would ultimately determine the outcome of this conflict, but the United States could shape a positive outcome with continued engagement and patience. Failure to do so would plunge Iraq into chaos that would include massive human suffering and regional chaos in which Iran and al-Qaeda would most likely be the winners. "Our current course is hard," he acknowledged. "The alternatives are far worse."

It was a virtuoso performance by two of the most capable public servants our nation has ever produced. The testimony explained a great deal, at least to those willing to listen to it with an open mind. The question period that followed showed that many had not, that most minds had been made up well in advance of the hearing. Chairman Skelton began with the key concern of most legislators—why should Congress expect there to be any progress on political reconciliation in Iraq in the next six months? Ambassador Crocker replied that everyone involved in the situation was frustrated, not least the Iraqi politicians themselves. The issues, which dealt with the fundamental nature of the Iraqi state, were incredibly complex and would take time to resolve. The benchmarks were not an end in themselves, but rather a means to national reconciliation. The surge had just hit its stride, and it would take some time before its impact would be felt in the political arena.

Chairman Lantos then asked Ambassador Crocker his opinion on whether a more substantial diplomatic outreach to Syria and Iran would be advisable. The ambassador replied that while Iran had been amenable to negotiations immediately after 9/11, his recent meetings with Iranian delegates had been extremely unproductive. Iran was not ready to engage seriously on the issues surrounding Iraqi security, particularly given the nefarious involvement of the Iranian regime in fomenting instability in Iraq. "The impression I came [away] with after a couple rounds [of diplomacy] is that the Iranians were interested simply in the appearance of discussions, of being seen to be at the table with the U.S. as an arbiter of Iraq's present and future, rather than actually doing serious business," Ambassador Crocker concluded. In a response to the next follow-up question, Ambassador Crocker stated his belief that just because Iraq's government now had a Shi'a majority did not mean that it would automatically gravitate to do Iran's bidding. The two nations had fought a bitter and bloody eight-year war in the 1980s. Iraqi Shi'ites were Arab, intensely nationalistic, and possessed of a different culture, language, and history than Persian Iran.

In a response to a question from Representative Ros-Lehtinen, General Petraeus added that Iraqi Sunnis had also displayed their nationalism, as they largely rejected al-Qaeda's indiscriminate violence and Taliban-like ideology. The key to security, in his view, was to empower local people to secure themselves and thereby reject the extremists in their midst. Stabilizing Iraq was essential to avoiding further humanitarian catastrophe, with as many as two million Iraqis already refugees outside the country and another two million internally displaced.

Representative Ros-Lehtinen then asked Ambassador Crocker to elaborate on the ramifications of a withdrawal from Iraq before conditions warranted such a course. "I sometimes think in this debate there is an implicit assumption that we can decide we don't want to be engaged in Iraq any longer or at least not in the way we have been and that, you know, the chapter comes to a close, the movie ends, and we all go on to other things," Ambassador Crocker replied. "Iraq will still be there. And the actors in Iraq will make calculations and take actions without us, as will the neighbors, as Iran is already indicating it's quite prepared to do. So I just think it's very important as we consider what our options are and where we're going in Iraq that we understand that this process will carry forward with or without us—and it's my assessment, at least, that going forward without us under current conditions would be extremely damaging for regional stability and for some of our own vital interests."

There were several hours of testimony to come, but the hearing continued along its predictable course—the Democrats questioning political progress in Iraq despite the limited "technical" successes of the surge, decrying the cost of the conflict, and questioning the wisdom of remaining involved in the middle of an ethnosectarian civil war with "no end in sight," while the Republicans focused on the likely consequences of a premature withdrawal from Iraq and continued to blast the MoveOn.org ad in the *New York Times.* Representative Dennis Kucinich (D-OH) stated harshly, "General Petraeus has been tasked with stalling Congress to keep the troops in the middle of a civil war. General Petraeus has failed to give Congress an independent assessment of the Iraq war. His statement sounds like the president's talking points."[20] Representative Chris Van Hollen (D-MD) added, "Our brave American service men and women are sacrificing daily for a policy that has no end in sight. A policy of more of the same is no strategic vision, strains our military to the breaking point, and enables Iraqi leaders to dither endlessly instead of reaching a political consensus over the future of their country."[21]

The only spark occurred when Representative Robert Wexler (D-FL) compared Petraeus to General William Westmoreland, whose testimony to Congress in April 1967 likewise touted progress in the midst of a difficult counterinsurgency war. "How many more men and women need to be killed in this fiasco in order to protect our so called credibility?" asked Wexler. General Petraeus fired back that no one was more concerned about the loss of American soldiers in Iraq than he was as the commander on the ground. As reported on a live blog of the hearings, "One reporter leaned over and whispered to his colleagues, 'We had to wait five-and-a-half hours for that?' It was [a] comment on the lack of fireworks at this hearing since Petraeus made his opening statement, as well as a compliment for how he and Crocker have neutralized Democrats today."[22] After six hours and twelve minutes of testimony and questions from thirty-five lawmakers, the hearings drew to a close.

It was nearly 7 P.M. in the nation's capital, but Ambassador Crocker and General Petraeus had not yet finished their day. We drove over to the studios of Fox News, where thankfully the network provided dinner before an hourlong show with anchor Brit Hume. During the show General Petraeus and Ambassador Crocker summarized their testimony and answered questions concerning the potential for reconciliation among the sects, Iranian involvement in the conflict, congressional benchmarks, Prime Minister Maliki's leadership, the capabilities of the Iraqi security forces, the fight against al-Qaeda in Iraq, the MoveOn.org ad, and the crafting of the testimony. Hume teed up topics but mostly provided a platform for Petraeus and Crocker to speak—perhaps disappointing for those who wanted to see journalistic fireworks, but an appropriate format after six hours of testimony before Congress. At 10 P.M. the day was finally over. We drove General Petraeus back to his home at Fort Myer, where his wife, Holly, was waiting for him. The rest of the team returned to our hotel and quickly went to bed. Testimony would begin anew in the morning on the sixth anniversary of the terrorist attacks of 9/11, this time in the Senate.

The Senate testimony was conducted in two sessions, with the Senate Foreign Relations Committee hearing in the morning followed by the Senate Armed Services Committee hearing in the afternoon. These hearings would have even more of a political overtone (if that was possible) than the House testimony, as there were no fewer than five presidential candidates serving on the two committees—Senator Joe Biden (D-DE), Senator Hillary Clinton (D-NY), Senator John McCain (R-AZ), Senator Christopher Dodd (D-CT), and Senator Barack Obama (D-IL). Senator Biden, the chairman of the Foreign Relations Committee, began the morning hearing with a moment of silence for the victims of 9/11. He then launched into his opening statement, questioning whether the surge had created the conditions for the resolution of political questions in Iraq. He was skeptical that Iraqis were any closer to the day when they would "stop killing each other and start governing together," or that giving the operations more time would significantly affect the outcome of the war.[23] Absent a political settlement among Shi'ites, Sunnis, and Kurds, he said, chaos would prevail in Iraq regardless of the tactical accomplishments of the troops on the ground.

The principal problem, in Senator Biden's view, was the fundamentally flawed strategy behind the surge—that

> we can achieve political progress in Iraq by building a strong national unity government in Baghdad that secures the trust of the Iraqi people.
>
> In my view, gentlemen, I don't think that's going to happen in the lifetime of any of us. There is no trust within that central government in Baghdad, no trust in the government by the people, and no capacity of that government to deliver security and services.
>
> And absent an occupation we cannot sustain or a return of a dictator we cannot want, Iraq, in my view, cannot be governed from the center at this point in history.

A better alternative, in Senator Biden's view, was to significantly reduce U.S. troop strength in Iraq and focus the remaining U.S. forces on training the Iraqi army, fighting al-Qaeda and securing the borders, and to create a federal, decentralized Iraq in which Shi'ites, Sunnis, and Kurds would each have their own region under the very loose control of a national government Baghdad.

I had heard this plan for the federalization of Iraq before, from Les Gelb, president emeritus of the Council on Foreign Relations. In my view, such a plan for Iraq would fail, as any movement toward a federalized Iraq of three ethnosectarian regions under the present circumstances would be a recipe for massive conflict among them and the eventual breakup of the Iraqi state.

Senator Richard Lugar (R-IN), the ranking minority member of the committee, posed the essential question underpinning the war in Iraq in his opening statement. "Benchmarks are an important starting point for debate, but they do not answer many questions, including the most fundamental question pertaining to Iraq," the senator remarked. "Namely, do Iraqis want to be Iraqis? By this, I mean are the Iraqi people, most of whom are now organized according to sectarian and tribal loyalties, willing to sacrifice their own pursuit of national or regional hegemony by granting their sectarian rivals political and economic power? Can a unified society be achieved despite the extreme sectarian fears and resentments incubated during the oppressive reign of Saddam and intensified during the recent period of sectarian bloodletting?" It was a fair question, and one to which only Iraqis could give the answer. While polling indicated that many Iraqis wanted to live in a united Iraq, they lacked the "political power and courage needed to stare down militia leaders, sectarian strongmen, [and] criminal gangs" that had co-opted violence for sectarian and personal ends. Regional actors could also foment instability in Iraq, while U.S. military participation was constrained in time by the unwillingness of the American people to remain engaged in the war indefinitely. The real question was not the immediate success of the surge but whether in the longer term Iraqis could achieve national reconciliation that would stabilize the political process and reinforce the social order. "In my judgment, some type of success in Iraq is possible," Senator Lugar concluded. "But as policy-makers, we should acknowledge that we are facing extraordinarily narrow margins for achieving our goals." The key was to leverage the additional troops and resources in Iraq to change the political equation in that country, as well as to engage in "bold and creative" regional diplomacy to enable Iraq's neighbors to be part of the solution to the conflict. I believe both Ambassador Crocker and General Petraeus would have agreed with those assertions.

Upon conclusion of the opening remarks by Senator Biden and Senator Lugar, both Ambassador Crocker and General Petraeus repeated their opening statements of the day before (again occasionally interrupted by protesters), after which questioning began. Senator Biden repeated his insistence that the time required to achieve the administration's current objectives in Iraq was beyond the tolerance of the American people to support, and therefore those objectives had to be changed to something more realistic—in his view the creation of a federal Iraq. Senator Lugar referenced an article in *Newsweek* by Babak Dehghanpisheh and John Barry entitled "Braniac Brigade" about the team General Petraeus had assembled, and about the shift in emphasis from top-down reconciliation to the creation of pockets of stability at the local level, with the eventual need to knit them together at the national level.[24] Ambassador Crocker commented that such developments were welcome, as Iraqis of all political and sectarian leanings were just coming to grips with what federalism meant and how they would apply the concept in the future. Senator Dodd cited polls in which Iraqis questioned the improvement of security since the surge began, decried the lack of political progress in Baghdad, and asked why General Petraeus felt that the current approach would make any difference. General Petraeus replied that even in the absence of legislation, Iraqis were making progress in various facets of reconciliation, such as the distribution of oil revenues, conditional immunity in places like Abu Ghraib, funding for local police in al-Anbar province, and so forth. Senator Chuck Hagel (R-NE) downplayed the significance of the surge and General Petraeus's statistics and pointed to a number of other reports that indicated little to no progress in Iraq. "Now, where is this going?" he continually asked. Without political reconciliation, his answer was an implied "nowhere." Ambassador Crocker reiterated the point that a reduction of ethnosectarian violence was a prerequisite to political progress, and it was only in the last three months that violence had dropped significantly. It was natural that political progress would lag improvements in security, since perceptions had to change, as well as reality. Al-Anbar province was an example where security improved, and a few months later political progress followed. General Petraeus pointed to the political shift among Sunni tribal sheiks, who were now opposing their former allies in al-Qaeda.

As the hearing progressed, many of the questions became repetitive, forcing Ambassador Crocker and General Petraeus to repeat previous answers. Senator John Kerry (D-MA) pointed to the historic nature of this testimony—the first time a serving U.S. military commander from a war zone had testified to Congress since General William Westmoreland's testimony in April 1967. He pointed to the lack of political progress, the absence of effective governance in southern Iraq, the sectarian cleansing that had changed the face of Baghdad, and the absence of achievement on the benchmarks that the Iraqi government had set for itself, and then asked why the Iraqis would be willing to reconcile by the following summer (the end of the surge) when they had made no progress to date? Ambassador Crocker reiterated that the recent reduction in violence would take time to manifest itself in the perception of Iraqi politicians. "It is not just a switch that you flip, that as the surge starts to make a real difference, at the beginning of the summer, then everyone is prepared to sit down and make historic compromises," Ambassador Crocker stated. "That is going to take time and effort. Will it succeed, how fast will it succeed, in what form will it succeed? I do not know." He spoke again about the importance of what was happening in al-Anbar province. General Petraeus talked about the importance of the Sons of Iraq and the efforts to tie them into the central government in Baghdad. He also spoke of the Iraqi solutions to Iraqi problems in southern Iraq, and how the absence of coalition forces in the southern provinces did not mean that we had just handed them over to the control of militias. The solutions that worked for Shi'a areas in southern Iraq, however, were not transferable to mixed sectarian areas such as Baghdad and Diyala provinces. (To be certain, militias were a problem in certain areas, such as Basra, which would lead Prime Minister Maliki to conduct a large security operation against them in March and April 2008—events covered in Chapter 9).

Other questioners were simply out to score political points. Senator Barbara Boxer (D-CA) spent her entire allotted time blasting the policy that took the United States to war in Iraq, attacking President Bush, and presenting her view that the major problem in Iraq was that the Iraqi people viewed U.S. troops as occupiers—without asking a single question until her time had expired. "I don't consider the surge a nuanced policy," the senator stated. "It's killing our soldiers at a great rate. . . . We are sending our troops where they're not wanted, with no end in sight, in the middle of a civil war, in the middle of the mother of all mistakes." It was not lost on the listeners in the hearing room that Boxer's own remarks were far from nuanced. Senator Obama likewise spoke for seven minutes on what he viewed as the serious policy and strategic mistakes made by the Bush administration in Iraq, then asked a hypothetical question as to what conditions would prompt a recommendation to withdraw U.S. forces from Iraq but gave General Petraeus no time to respond.

Senator Russ Feingold (D-WI) asked Ambassador Crocker and General Petraeus to prioritize Iraq within the broader war against al-Qaeda, and when they refused to do so—citing the fact that they were responsible for the war in Iraq and not the entire war on global terrorism—called their responses "a classic example of myopia." General Petraeus shot back, "With respect, Senator, what this is is an example of a commander focused on his area of responsibility. And that is my mission. It is to accomplish the military tasks that are associated with this policy, not to fight the overall global war." Senator Feingold then decried the loss of American lives in Iraq in 2007 and demanded to know when the losses would abate. "Senator, we are on the offensive," General Petraeus replied, "and when you go on the offensive, you have tough fighting. That was particularly true, again, during the period immediately after the start of the surge of offenses in mid-June and continued for a while. It appeared to have crested then and was coming down. And, again, we will have to see." Feingold's question completely ignored why the losses were occurring—more fighting meant more losses, at least until the population was secured and al-Qaeda sanctuaries and Shi'a militias were neutralized. If we wanted U.S. combat losses to drop to zero, we could just stay on our bases and let the sectarian fires rage.

The pontificating became so fierce that Senator John Sununu (R-NH) began his allotted time by stating, "I will take my question-and-answer time to ask questions, if it's all right with the committee and the witnesses." Senator Jim DeMint (R-SC) added, "I particularly appreciate both of you for enduring our hearings. As you have found, our hearings are more about listening to ourselves than listening to our witnesses. And I promise to continue that tradition myself."

Both Ambassador Crocker and General Petraeus testified that withdrawing

U.S. forces from Iraq before conditions were appropriate would probably harden Iraqi attitudes toward reconciliation and make the Iraqi people more likely to gird for a resumption of civil war. There were hopeful signs that the various sects and factions were beginning the process of reconciliation, even though political progress had not manifested itself in major pieces of legislation. Iran and Syria continued to play unhelpful roles, especially with the Qods force backing Shi'a militias inside Iraq. General Petraeus and Ambassador Crocker both deflected continual questions on a timeline for withdrawing all troops from Iraq. In fact, General Petraeus stated that doing so at this time would be a "disservice to our soldiers." Senator Jim Webb (D-VA) ended the hearing by expressing his belief that the continuation of the surge, which had already required the extension of combat tours in U.S. Army units to fifteen months, would be harmful to the health of the all-volunteer force. Throughout the proceedings, those who felt the surge either was not working or didn't matter in the grand scheme of things put forward no alternatives of their own.

It had been a long morning, and there was another hearing in front of us. We adjourned to a back room where the staff had arranged for a light lunch. General Petraeus hardly had time to eat, as a continual stream of senators came into the room for a private conference or a short greeting. Despite the strain of the day's events, he held up well. Everett Spain, "Aide Man," did his part by ensuring the general had a steady supply of ibuprofen at hand. We soon returned to the hearing room for testimony before the Senate Armed Services Committee.

The chairman of the committee, Senator Carl Levin (D-MI), opened the proceedings by thanking General Petraeus and Ambassador Crocker, as well as the men and women they led, for their service in Iraq. He then blasted the Iraqi politicians who were unable to reconcile with one another for the good of their country. "The Iraqi politicians dawdle while our casualties and our expenditures keep climbing," he stated.[25] The president had overpromised and underdelivered on Iraq; "the American people's patience with Iraq's political leaders has run out." Senator Levin then stated his belief that the administration should begin withdrawing troops from Iraq to force Iraqi leaders to step up to their responsibilities and embrace the recommendations in the Iraq Study Group report. Senator McCain countered that establishing a timetable for withdrawal of U.S. forces in Iraq was tantamount to setting a date "for American surrender in Iraq." His position on the Iraq War and the surge was clear. "I believe we cannot choose to lose in Iraq," Senator McCain stated. "And I will do everything in my power to see that our commanders in Iraq have the time and support they request to win this war." A legislated withdrawal date would lead to certain failure, the enormous consequences of which the United States would have to live with for years to come. A premature U.S. withdrawal from Iraq would be a perceived victory for the jihadists, and it would embolden Iran and lead in due course to the creation of a terrorist sanctuary in the heart of the Middle East.

After General Petraeus gave a slightly shortened version of his opening state-ment (Ambassador Crocker waived his opening remarks), the questioning began. Senator Levin queried why more Iraqi army units were not taking the lead in se-curity operations, even with limited coalition assistance, but his rapid-fire style of asking questions did not allow General Petraeus to give a complete answer. Sena-tor McCain asked General Petraeus whether he felt that Iraq was now the central front in the war on terror. General Petraeus replied that indeed it was, based on conversations with the director of the Central Intelligence Agency and Lieutenant General Stan McChrystal, head of the Joint Special Operations Command, which was operating not just in Iraq but also in Afghanistan and the rest of the world against al-Qaeda. Both believed that Iraq was al-Qaeda's central front. Senator Mc-Cain then asked Ambassador Crocker his views on a "soft partition" of Iraq. The ambassador replied that Iraqi politicians were discussing what federalism meant for their country, but that federalism was not partition. "Partition, in my view, is not a viable outcome for the situation in Iraq," he testified. "Baghdad, in spite of all of the violence it has seen and all of the population displacements, remains a very mixed city, Sunnis and Shi'a together. Any notion that that city of over 5 million people can be neatly divided up or painlessly cleansed of a huge number of people is just incorrect." Why not allow sectarian cleansing to continue, as some peo-ple have suggested, Senator McCain queried? Ambassador Crocker replied that the human cost of the sectarian violence was already too high. "To simply say this is a good thing would be I think in both practical and moral terms roughly equivalent to some of the ethnic cleansing we saw in the Balkans," he stated. Sena-tor McCain then asked what General Petraeus was doing to curb the sectarian abuses of the Iraqi National Police. General Petraeus replied that the Iraqi minister of the interior had already replaced the overall commander, both division com-manders, all nine brigade commanders, and seventeen of twenty-seven battalion commanders. Additionally, National Police units were being rotated out of the line for a monthlong retraining course, which helped in some cases to moderate their behavior. Furthermore, Prime Minister Maliki realized that militias had to be dissolved over time. Senator McCain then asked whether the success in al-Anbar province could be replicated in other areas of Iraq, to which General Pe-traeus responded that indeed it could, if not exactly in the same form. Senator Mc-Cain's questioning led to a lighter moment when he asked Ambassador Crocker to assess his level of confidence that Prime Minister Maliki's administration would "begin to do the things that we've been asking them to do for a long time?"

"My level of confidence is under control," the ambassador replied, to peals of laughter from the gallery.

Senator Ted Kennedy (D-MA) was not amused. He continued the Democrats' line of questioning as to whether the surge would have any impact on the ability of the Iraqi elites to reconcile. General Petraeus replied that although the big pieces of benchmark legislation had not passed, there were signs of reconciliation—the sharing of oil revenue in provincial budgets and conditional immunity via the Iraqi national reconciliation committee were just two examples.

A simple query of General Petraeus near the end of Senator John Warner's (R-VA) questioning nearly derailed the hearing: "Are you able to say at this time if we continue what you have laid before the Congress here as a strategy, do you feel that that is making America safer?" General Petraeus misunderstood the intent of the question and for the only time in two days of hearings, fumbled the response. "Sir, I don't know, actually," he replied. "I have not sat down and sorted it out in my own mind. What I have focused on and been riveted on is how to accomplish the mission of the Multi-National Force–Iraq. I have not stepped back to look at—and you've heard, with other committees, in fact, you know, what is the impact on—I've certainly taken into account the impact on the military. The strain on our ground forces, in particular, has very much been a factor in my recommendations. But I have tried to focus on doing what I think a commander is supposed to do, which is to determine the best recommendations to achieve the objectives of the policy from which his mission is derived. And that is what I have sought to do, sir."

"Uh oh," I thought. General Petraeus was no doubt getting tired, but when asked whether he felt the Iraq War was making the United States safer, he hadn't given a definitive answer. That spelled trouble. Sure enough, Colonel Steve Boylan, the public affairs officer, soon handed me a note that the news tickers were afire with statements to the effect that General Petraeus was unsure whether the war in Iraq was making America safer. For the first time in two days of hearings, I did something I had hoped not to do. I wrote a note concerning the impact of the answer in the news media and handed it to General Petraeus while the hearing was still in session. He read it without emotion. (He later noted that he knew immediately that he'd flubbed the answer to Warner's question and was already thinking about how he could clarify his answer in subsequent responses.)

Questioning by Senator Robert Byrd (D-WV) continued the Democrats' assault on the achievements of the surge and the inability of the Iraqi government to pass benchmark legislation. Senator James Inhofe (R-OK) jabbed back at Senators Kennedy and Byrd, telling them that if they took the time to go to Iraq, they would probably come away with different ideas as to the future of that country. He then returned to the issue of the credibility of General Petraeus's testimony. "Who put it together?" the senator asked. General Petraeus replied, "Senator, I've got a brain trust of bright guys. They wrote two drafts of it. And I took control of the electrons last week or two weeks ago and basically rewrote it and wrote that myself. Obviously, I shared it back and forth with them, but what I delivered here today was very much, by and large, my testimony. And it certainly had not been cleared with nor even shared with anyone." I looked down the line at the team; they were focused but clearly beaming with pride at the compliment.

Later in Senator Inhofe's questioning, General Petraeus used an opportunity to amend the record on whether the Iraq War made America safer. "And to come back to that, if I could, I mean, let me be very clear," General Petraeus stated. "I believe that if we can achieve our objectives in Iraq, that is obviously a very good thing for the United States and would make us safer. The converse, I think, is also true, depending on how it turned out."

Senator Joe Lieberman (I-CT) was next in the queue. He was nominally an independent, but only because he had lost the Democratic Party primary in the previous election and had to run as an independent to get reelected. He caucused with the Democrats, but was affiliated with Senator McCain's stance on the Iraq War and was intimately familiar with conditions in the country, having taken several trips to see the war firsthand. Senator Lieberman summarized the two days of testimony succinctly. "It strikes me, as I've watched your testimony over the last few days, that you left the real war in Iraq and came over onto the battlefield of the political war here in Washington about Iraq. And I would say, on this battlefield you have gained considerable ground over the last two days. And I say so because too often on this battleground, the forces are divided according to partisan loyalties, and there's a lot of hype and spin. You have given testimony that is thoroughly nonpartisan, nonpolitical and realistic. It's quite obvious that just today, this afternoon, that all the answers you have given have not been answers that the administration would have wanted you to give."

Senator Lieberman then asked General Petraeus about the conditions for the withdrawal of additional forces from Iraq. General Petraeus stated that the withdrawal of the surge forces was based on the most realistic estimate of security conditions in Iraq going forward, but that the pace could be adjusted either way as security improved or conditions deteriorated. He rejected any switch to a counterterrorism mission as insufficient to provide the level of security needed to create the environment necessary for political progress in Iraq. Senator Lieberman then threw cold water on calls for a "diplomatic surge," asking Ambassador Crocker whether in his meetings with the Iranian ambassador the other side had shown any inclination to moderate its behavior. Ambassador Crocker replied that it had not.

Senator Jeff Session (R-AL) asked a question that allowed General Petraeus to discuss at length the techniques of counterinsurgency warfare that Multi-National Force–Iraq was applying on the ground to differentiate the operations during the surge from those that had preceded it. "We are trying to employ the forces in very appropriate ways," General Petraeus concluded. "And the truth is, in some cases they're doing what you might identify as counterterrorism, really, targeted raids. In other cases, it really is classical counterinsurgency. In some cases, it's almost peace enforcement, in others, it's nation-building." The flexibility in operations was appropriate for the kaleidoscope of conditions in Iraq, which defied the simplistic notions prevalent in too many circles regarding how victory there could be achieved.

The chasm in the level of knowledge between the senators and the witnesses was exemplified by an exchange between Senator Jack Reed (D-RI) and Ambassador Crocker. Senator Reed asked, "Ambassador Crocker, to date, the nation-building effort in Iraq has faltered dramatically. And it seems the emerging strategy is one based on tribalism. Do you think that is a long-term and appropriate approach to stabilizing the country?" Ambassador Crocker's reply displayed both the depth of his knowledge and the complexity of Iraq:

> Again, Senator, it's hard to do nation-building or reconciliation in the face of widespread sectarian violence, which has been the situation over the last 18 months. And, as you've seen from General Petraeus' charts, it's really just been in the last few months that we've seen a significant reduction in that. I think that nation-building, reconciliation in Iraq is going to take a lot of forms.
>
> In certain areas, the tribal dimension is key. If you're dealing with Anbar, you're dealing in tribal terms. And what is interesting and somewhat encouraging to me there are those tribal elements that have emerged [that] have shown a considerable interest in linking up with the central government in Baghdad. About 10 days ago, the leader of the Anbar awakening, Sheik Abdel Sittar, came to Baghdad. I spent some time with him. His main purpose, though, was to meet with the prime minister and kind of establish a relationship and see what might develop out of that.
>
> In other parts of the country, it is going to be a somewhat different story. Diyala, for example, the Baqouba area, you have tribal elements. But, given the inter-mixture of Sunni, Shi'a and Kurds, unlike Anbar, which is all Sunni, you've also got a very complex sectarian element. So the dynamic is going to work differently in Diyala.
>
> Similarly in the south, there is a tribal dimension there. It has a different form and shape than the tribal dimension in the predominantly Sunni areas. But there, too, we're seeing some signs of a desire on the part of southern Shi'a tribes to connect with us, to connect with their own central government in the face of violent extremism practiced by elements of Jaish al-Mahdi.
>
> In Baghdad, the tribal dimension is less dominant—although, in many areas still present. But we're also seeing, as General Petraeus has pointed out, in some Sunni Baghdad districts the same kind of backlash against Al Qaida, the same desire to step up and cooperate with our forces, and then to go the next step for these neighborhood watches to link up with their own central government and come under the authority of the Ministry of Interior.
>
> So, again, it is very complex and it is going to vary from place to place. The tribes are part of it. Different areas of the country are going to have different dynamics.

Senator Reed's time was up, so that was the end of the discussion.

Senator Susan Collins (R-ME) asked General Petraeus and Ambassador Crocker to project forward a year ahead what their recommendation would be absent improvement in the political and military situation. Neither would offer a specific recommendation, other than to say he would assess the situation when the time came and make his recommendations appropriately. In the meantime, Ambassador Crocker put it best, "The cumulative trajectory of political, economic and diplomatic developments in Iraq is upward, although the slope of that line is not steep." It was not the answer many wanted to hear, but it was a realistic assessment of the situation in Iraq. Ambassador Crocker also outlined the regional diplomatic initiatives that were under way to engage Iraq's neighbors in such areas as border security, refugees, and energy.

The committee then recessed for a Senate vote, which gave General Petraeus and Ambassador Crocker a few moments to use the facilities, take a sip of water, and collect their thoughts. I discussed with General Petraeus the impact of his answer to Senator Warner about whether the Iraq War made America safer, and we talked through the issues. He had been thinking in terms of homeland security rather than the broader national security objectives at stake in the Middle East. It had been a long two days and it was unrealistic to expect General Petraeus to remain on top of his game during the entire ordeal. He would seek an opportunity to correct the record when the hearings resumed.

The opportunity arose during Senator Lindsey Graham's (R-SC) questioning. The senator added a bit of levity to the hearings by beginning with the statement, "I'm not so sure two days of this is Geneva Convention compliant, but we'll keep going." He then asked General Petraeus whether the loss of blood and treasure in Iraq was worth it. General Petraeus swung hard at the pitch. "Well, the national interests that we have in Iraq are substantial. An Iraq that is stable and secure, that is not an Al Qaida sanctuary, is not in the grip of Iranian-supported Shi'a militia, that is not a bigger humanitarian disaster, that is connected to the global economy, all of these are very important national interests." Senator Graham then proceeded to discuss with Ambassador Crocker and General Petraeus the implications of a failed state in Iraq, which were considerable. General Petraeus laid out the consequences: "Again, it could include Al Qaida regaining lost ground and its freedom of maneuver. It would certainly be a very, very heightened ethno-sectarian level of violence. These alliances of convenience with outside forces would certainly flow from that; a humanitarian disaster of enormous proportions, for which we would share responsibility; and possibly some dislocation in the global economy, depending on what happens, obviously, with the flow of oil."

Senator Ben Nelson (D-NE) had a productive exchange with Ambassador Crocker and General Petraeus about what reconciliation would look like in the absence of passage of big pieces of legislation, and what a long-term force presence in Iraq would require and what it could accomplish. Ambassador Crocker discussed what effective governance would entail. "One thing we had seen is a lot of frustration among Iraqis and even within the Iraqi government over where this heavy focus on sectarian and ethnic balance in the cabinet has taken the country, in terms of effective governance," Ambassador Crocker stated. "So if it has brought them to the level of frustration where the key leaders are prepared to say good governance is more important than strict sectarian and ethnic balance, then that I would consider progress." General Petraeus discussed a recent staff study that examined what a long-term force might look like. He concluded, "The challenge, obviously, is getting there from here, trying to do it as expeditiously as we can, but, again, without rushing to failure along the way."

As occurred with all three hearings, the questioning became fairly repetitive as the hearing progressed. Senator Evan Bayh (D-IN) returned to the question of whether the Iraq War made America safer, giving General Petraeus another opportunity to revise and expand the record. "Candidly, I have been so focused on Iraq that drawing all the way out was something that for a moment there was a bit of a surprise," General Petraeus responded. "But I think that we have very, very clear and very serious national interests in Iraq. Trying to achieve those interests— achieving those interests has very serious implications for our safety and for our security."

"I judged by your response to Senator Graham that you'd given that a little additional thought."

"Immediately after, actually." I suppressed the urge to smile at the general's response.

"That happens to all of us, including those of us on this side of the table as well," Senator Bayh charitably added.

Others were less charitable. Senator Clinton, a candidate for the Democratic Party nomination for president, was particularly harsh. "I want to thank both of you, General Petraeus, Ambassador Crocker, for your long and distinguished service to our nation," she began. "Nobody believes that your jobs or the jobs of the thousands of American forces and civilian personnel in Iraq are anything but incredibly difficult. But today you are testifying about the current status of our policy in Iraq and the prospects of that policy. It is a policy that you have been ordered to implement by the president. And you have been made the de facto spokesmen for what many of us believe to be a failed policy. Despite what I view as your rather extraordinary efforts in your testimony both yesterday and today, I think that the reports that you provide to us really require the willing suspension of disbelief." It was a below-the-belt sound bite guaranteed to make the evening news. The accusation was particularly unfair given the scrupulous attention General Petraeus had applied to ensuring the metrics used in his testimony were as accurate as possible. General Petraeus had been careful to cultivate his relationship with Senator Clinton in the past and he had always thought highly of her; though he would not say so publicly or to the staff, I know the comments wounded him deeply.[26]

Senator Clinton proceeded to attack the administration's policy in Iraq, with dozens of camera people and reporters grouped on the floor in front of her table recording every word and expression. It was a campaign performance. "I give you tremendous credit for presenting as positive a view of a rather grim reality," Senator Clinton remarked near the end of her time. "And I believe that you, and certainly the very capable people working with both of you, were dealt a very hard hand. And it's a hand that is unlikely to improve, in my view." In my view she should have started her remarks with that comment and left matters there. We might have disagreed with the statement, but at least it had the virtue of presenting honest disagreement without impugning General Petraeus's character.

The hearing thankfully ended on a more upbeat note. Senator John Thune (R-SD) stated, "You've been exposed to a political dimension of the debate that occurs here in Washington, in the last few days that—on a level that's regrettable. But notwithstanding that, I think the majority of Americans and a lot of us up here want to see you succeed." Senator Mark Pryor (D-AR) had the room rolling with laughter when he added, "I'd like to start, if I could, with a question for both of you. And that is, after two days on Capitol Hill, are you two ready to get back to Baghdad?" Senator Mel Martinez (R-FL) gave General Petraeus an opening to discuss his concept of how to enable Iraqi security forces to take over responsibilities for securing their country without setting them up for failure: first U.S. and coalition forces would take the lead, then they would partner with Iraqi security forces in their areas, and finally they would move into tactical overwatch of Iraqi forces. The process would be flexible and based on conditions as they evolved. Senator Claire McCaskill (D-MO) discussed the use of private contractors in Iraq and the system in place to ensure their accountability. She concluded by stating, "Well, I think privatization is the future. I just think we need to work harder at getting it right. . . . So I appreciate that, but I do think we have got a long way to go, in terms of the accountability piece on the privatization issue." Regrettably, we had a longer way to go than even the senator realized.

After ten hours of testimony in two sessions, the hearings ended at 7 P.M. The congressional testimony, in the words of journalist Mark Bowden, had not been "the loyal soldier reporting back from the front to a grateful nation; this was an inquisition."[27] General Petraeus and Ambassador Crocker would spend the next few days with the media, hosting a joint news conference the next day at the National Press Club. When asked by Charlie Sennott of the Boston Globe to comment on the MoveOn.org ad, Petraeus responded, "Needless to say—I mean, to state the obvious—I disagree with the message of those who are exercising the 1st Amendment right that generations of soldiers have sought to preserve for Americans. Some of it was just flat completely wrong, and the rest is at least more than arguable."[28] They also appeared on PBS *NewsHour*, as well as conducting nearly two dozen other media events. They would spend a few days with their families before heading back to Baghdad. As for me, I flew home to Fort Leavenworth, Kansas, for two weeks of midtour leave before heading back to the fray.

The hearings had highlighted divisions over the conduct of the war and the wisdom of American involvement in it, but they had not persuaded the American people or their elected representatives in Congress to pull the plug on the effort in Iraq. If Congress wanted to change the administration's policy, it would have to use the power of the purse and cut off funding for the war. At that point, the senators and representatives would own the consequences—a step, given the tentative progress of the surge, they were not yet willing to take. The pressure for a mandated timeline for withdrawal from Iraq eased. As we walked out of the hearing room, I remarked to General Petraeus, "Sir, you just bought us six more months." Cynics might have claimed that this was just another meaningless extension during which nothing significant would happen to change the outcome of the war. They could not have been more wrong.

CHAPTER 8

Power Politics

Our current course is hard. The alternatives are far worse.
—Ambassador Ryan Crocker

Nine months into the surge Multi-National Force–Iraq and Iraqi security forces had made substantial progress in improving security conditions in Iraq, but every political and military leader involved in the conflict understood that without political progress, any success would be short-lived. Ambassador Crocker and General Petraeus returned from Washington with a clear goal to prod Iraqi political leaders into making the concessions and compromises necessary to end the civil war and place the conflict over power and resources into the political arena. There was only so much they could do in this regard, but the attempt had to be made. In the end, the Iraqis themselves had to decide whether or not to end hostilities and substitute political dialogue for violent conflict. When the war of bombs and bullets became a war of words waged in legitimate political channels, then the conflict would be on its way, however slowly, to resolution.

The improvement in security during the surge was substantial. Between February and December 2007, security incidents in Iraq declined from more than fourteen hundred to fewer than six hundred per week.[1] Violent civilian deaths had declined over the same period from more than three thousand per week to around seven hundred per week.[2] High-profile attacks, such as car bombs and suicide bombs, were reduced from roughly one hundred per week in January to forty per week in December.[3] Iraq was still a very dangerous place, but the trend was in the right direction.[4]

Improved security was also reflected in the drop in coalition casualties, from 86 killed in January to a high of 131 killed in May, and then a steady reduction to 25 killed in December—the second-lowest monthly death toll in the war to date.[5] More coalition service members died in 2007 than in any other year of the war, with 961 fatalities recorded. But the death toll was heavily concentrated in the first six months of the surge, with killed in action declining sharply in the second half of the year. Iraqi security force casualties showed a similar decline, from 1,151 in the first half of 2007 to 679 in the second half of the year.[6] Every fatality was a tragedy for the families involved, but the reduction in friendly casualties provided welcome relief from the darker days of the war, when the fate of coalition military operations hung in the balance.

U.S. military personnel were also the beneficiaries of improved equipment as the surge progressed. The days of making excuses—"You go to war with the army you have, not the army you might want or wish to have"—were over.[7] In the fall of 2007, new mine-resistant, ambush-protected (MRAP) vehicles began pouring into Iraq. These vehicles, built with significant armor protection and V-shaped hulls to deflect roadside bomb blasts up and away from the crew compartment, were a significant improvement over the flat-bottomed, up-armored Humvee. The MRAP was to the Iraq War what the P-51 Mustang fighter was to World War II—a rapidly fielded weapon developed to solve a pressing tactical and technical challenge on the battlefield. General Petraeus had pushed hard for them, and Secretary of Defense Gates drove the project to completion much more rapidly than had been expected. Meanwhile, General Petraeus came up with an idea (subsequently approved by Secretary of Defense Gates and Prime Minister Maliki) to transfer some eighty-five hundred M114 up-armored Humvees to the Iraqi Security Forces as U.S. forces received new MRAP vehicles.[8] The Iraqi government would purchase the Humvees, which would be refurbished by Army Materiel Command to fully mission-capable condition, for a nominal fee. It was a win-win proposition.

In addition to the MRAP vehicles, General Petraeus continually pushed for more armed reconnaissance assets. When the United States invaded Iraq in 2003, unmanned aerial vehicles were a scarce commodity. Now we sought to darken the skies with their ubiquitous presence. Armed Predator drones were the coin of the realm, but there were simply not enough of them to go around. Secretary of Defense Gates was, once again, particularly helpful in shaking up the services and the defense bureaucracy to force them to focus on these critical assets—perhaps not as glamorous as F-22 fighters and the Army's (subsequently canceled) Future Combat System, but just as vital to victory (indeed, more so) in the wars we were fighting in Iraq and Afghanistan. In the final four months of 2007 alone, the number of Predator drones plying the skies twenty-four hours a day above Iraq doubled from twelve to twenty-four platforms, providing a key new capability in the counterinsurgency fight.

By this point in the war Multi-National Force–Iraq had also significantly ramped up its information operations capabilities. Gone were the days when insurgent propaganda outmaneuvered the land of Madison Avenue and Hollywood. Multi-National Force–Iraq contracted with a very competent civilian firm to produce public service announcements encouraging the Iraqi people to support the Iraqi army and police, shun participation in militias, and reject extremism. We saturated Iraqi television, radio, and print media, as well as the Internet, with these targeted messages, which subsequent polling indicated were responsible for a significant lessening of Iraqi support for extremism and sectarian violence.[9] General Petraeus viewed and approved every one of these media campaigns, and was gratified that the advances made in information operations were finally beginning to rival those already made in signals interception and intelligence capabilities.

There were also numerous but less obvious manifestations of improved security. During the Eid al-Fitr celebrations that marked the end of Ramadan, thousands of Iraqi families jammed Baghdad's amusement parks, which were now open for business. Kids played soccer in refurbished fields across the city. In many areas of the city (albeit mostly the Shi'a neighborhoods), trash heaps disappeared as waste-disposal services resumed. There was also a surreal moment in early November when we saw, while flying over Baghdad, six two-man sculls rowing on the Tigris River. *Sometimes you just can't make this stuff up,* I thought. (When General Petraeus related by phone to an official in the United States that he'd just seen six sculls on the Tigris, he was asked, "What happened to the bodies?")

The fate of private security contractors in Iraq in 2007 was less happy. On September 16, 2007, Blackwater security contractors guarding a State Department convoy in Baghdad fired on Iraqis halted in a traffic jam in Nisour Square, killing seventeen Iraqis and wounding eighteen others.[10] U.S. military reports corroborated Iraqi government allegations that the Blackwater guards opened fire without provocation and used deadly force without adequate justification, killing numerous innocent Iraqi citizens in the process.[11] Despite several investigations that faulted the Blackwater guards for improper use of force, the Iraqi government could not bring the contractors to trial since a Coalition Provisional Authority decree granting them immunity from local prosecution was still in effect. Iraqi public opinion was incensed by the incident. Prime Minister Maliki called for an official apology and compensation for the victims, and demanded that the guards be held accountable for their actions. The incident led the prime minster to revoke Blackwater's license to operate in Iraq and later resulted in the withdrawal of immunity for all private contractors serving in the country.

The Nisour Square incident highlighted the danger of relying on private security contractors to perform military functions in a combat zone. In Iraq private security contractors lacked access to robust quick-reaction forces and fire support that could respond when a convoy or unit was threatened. The fate of the four security contractors who mistakenly drove their vehicle into Fallujah in March

2004, leading to their deaths and eventually to a full-scale U.S. assault on the city in retaliation for the desecration of their bodies, should have provided a warning that reliance on civilian contractors to fulfill a military function in war was wrong-headed. But the Nisour Square incident pointed to a larger problem—the lack of accountability for the actions of private security contractors in combat zones.

Private security contractors are paid to guard people and material and to ensure that they arrive at their destinations safely. Yet the actions of some private contractors in the performance of these functions—from running civilian vehicles off the road and other reckless behavior to shooting civilians without adequate justification—was detrimental to the overall success of the war effort. General Petraeus likened their behavior at times to that of Mr. Toad in the children's book *The Wind in the Willows,* driving his car at high speed and honking his horn while forcing other motorists off the road. Soldiers and Marines occasionally made these same poor judgments, but since they wore the uniform of the United States of America, they were held accountable for their actions under the Uniform Code of Military Justice. Although the contractors in this incident were indicted on criminal charges back in the United States, they were not held accountable. Regrettably, more than two years after the incident Judge Ricardo M. Urbina of Federal District Court in Washington dismissed the charges against the Blackwater contractors, citing violation of the defendants' constitutional rights in the government's handling of the case.[12] As the Blackwater incident showed, private security contractors lacked the same degree of accountability as U.S. military personnel in the performance of their duties. The increased use of private security contractors in Iraq and Afghanistan, in my view, was a serious mistake. If the United States needed more security personnel in these war zones, then it should have increased the size of its military forces, despite the cost, rather than relying on mercenaries to fill the need.

Other attempts to bring accountability and justice to Iraq were more promising. Colonel Mark Martins, the outstanding Multi-National Force–Iraq staff judge advocate, and a fifty-five-person team staffed with Justice Department and military personnel worked with Iraqi authorities to create a "Rule of Law" complex in central Baghdad. The $50 million complex combined courts, jails, and a police academy in a secure area. Iraqi investigators, judges, and their families lived in this "Legal Green Zone" free from harassment and threats, which were commonplace in other areas of Iraq. Nevertheless, justice was not always served. In a closely watched trial of the Shi'a deputy health minister and his chief of security, both accused of ordering the murders of Sunnis in Baghdad's hospitals, the presiding judge dismissed charges despite compelling evidence of their guilt.[13] Shi'a extremists had intimidated witnesses, leading many to question the efficacy of the justice system.[14] Blast barriers could not protect the Rule of Law complex against the sectarian agendas of officials in the Iraqi Ministry of the Interior, which continued to influence some trials, but it was better than the haphazard legal system that sputtered on in other areas of the country.[15] Similar complexes were planned for Tikrit,

Mosul, and Ramadi to expand the concept regionally across Iraq, and they began to be established in 2008.

To enhance the conditions for reconciliation, Multi-National Force–Iraq and the U.S. embassy put forth substantial efforts to increase Iraqi civil capacity, restore or improve essential services, and improve economic conditions in Iraq. Each week staff officers would brief General Petraeus on progress or lack thereof in improving electricity and oil production, job creation, agricultural concerns such as the spraying of date palm trees with insecticide, and the like. General Petraeus possessed a wide grasp of economics, and he prodded his staff, the embassy, and the Iraqi government on issues ranging from a single-point mooring system to increase the outflow of oil from the Gulf, to the provision of diesel fuel from Kuwait to improve electricity generation in Baghdad, to the clearance of wrecks from the Shatt al-Arab to increase the capacity of that waterway for commercial shipping. His interest and reach on these issues seemed limitless.

The top-down approach to reconstruction used by the Coalition Provisional Authority had largely failed to address the critical needs of the Iraqi people; for this, a bottom-up approach to building civil capacity was needed as well. The State Department established the first of ten provincial reconstruction teams in November 2005 to help develop and coordinate governance, economic aid, infrastructure improvement, rule of law, and public diplomacy. The new approach emphasized the improvement of village, district, and provincial governance while tailoring reconstruction to local conditions. The provincial reconstruction teams were an improvement over the centralization of reconstruction aid in the Green Zone, but even then the teams remained too detached from the Iraqi people to fully administer to their needs.

One of the key developments during the surge was the creation of ten additional teams, known as embedded provincial reconstruction teams, which worked with brigade combat teams in their areas to provide much-needed civil capacity and expertise. Before the surge, brigade combat team commanders had to rely on uniformed civil affairs personnel, engineers, and ad hoc staff elements to plan and administer reconstruction measures such as the Commander's Emergency Response Program (through which U.S. forces spent $915 million in fiscal year 2007 alone).[16] The civilian and military personnel in embedded reconstruction teams filled this need and gave brigade commanders a powerful tool for waging the softer side of counterinsurgency war. The heads of embedded provincial reconstruction teams worked closely with brigade commanders as coequals and provided them with much-needed staff expertise in nonsecurity lines of operation. In return, brigades provided the personnel in embedded provincial reconstruction teams with security and transportation, as well as a much better feel for their areas of operation. "As powerful as the PRTs [provincial reconstruction teams] were independently, they became even more effective when teamed with the BCTs [brigade combat teams], as [they] gave our State Department experts access to the local communities for the first time and the freedom to move throughout the battlespace," recalled Lieutenant General Ray Odierno. "The close coordination brought on by embedding created conditions for efficient synchronized interagency effort at the tactical level and was a key to helping the Government of Iraq fill the 'gap' between popular expectations and Government of Iraq capabilities."[17] Despite these successes, the nagging lack of manpower (by December 2007 only 234 of 323 positions had been filled, which prompted the State Department to send a plea to the various war colleges for volunteers) limited the capacity of the provincial reconstruction teams in Iraq.[18]

The provincial reconstruction teams also helped to improve the capabilities of the Iraqi government. The 2008 Iraqi national budget provided $3.47 billion in capital funds to provincial governments, a 38 percent increase over the previous year.[19] Effective budget execution was a major priority for provincial reconstruction teams. Improvement in the provision of services would promote economic development, which in turn would help to dry up the pool of unemployed manpower on which the insurgents and militias relied to fill their ranks.

Jobs were the key metric in economic development at this point. Employed Iraqis were much less likely to participate in criminal, militia, or insurgent activities than were unemployed young men. One source of jobs was in the antiquated state-owned industries, which represented the worst of Soviet-style socialism. They were shuttered in 2003, throwing tens of thousands of Iraqis out of work and stoking resentment against the U.S. occupation. Former Silicon Valley executive Paul Brinkley, deputy undersecretary of defense for business transformation, was the Bush administration point person for reenergizing these industries, but the way ahead was difficult. The industries for the most part were uncompetitive, and therefore unattractive to commercial investors. Those state-owned industries that functioned, such as the ceramics factory in Ramadi, the pharmaceutical factory in Mosul, and the clothing factory in Najaf, used antiquated technology and functioned mainly as a source of jobs rather than as competitive businesses. But jobs were important in reducing violence, so the United States supported the state-owned industries, which eventually provided jobs for a quarter of a million Iraqis.[20]

Personnel from the State Department and the U.S. Agency for International Development also worked with military civil affairs teams and others to improve economic development at the local level. Congress assisted by providing hundreds of millions of dollars to the Commander's Emergency Response Program and other development funds for use in Iraq. Microgrant and economic development programs lent more than $60 million to twenty-six thousand Iraqi businesses in 2007.[21] Altogether, U.S. forces spent $991 million on roughly eighty-six hundred projects under the Commander's Emergency Response Program in 2007.[22] Not all projects panned out, but those that did helped to energize the Iraqi economy and put Iraqis to work. "CERP transformed money into a weapon system as essential as any other at the commander's disposal," Lieutenant General Odierno concluded.[23]

The reopening of the al-Qaim port of entry on the Iraqi-Syrian border on November 15 also gave Iraqi trade a boost. The port had been closed for security reasons for more than two years, and its reopening (following a security makeover) boded well for the future of al-Anbar province. The projected increased economic interaction between Syria and Iraq could help solidify the security progress achieved in al-Anbar and energize the economy of the Euphrates River valley.

By the end of 2007 Iraq was enjoying roughly 6 percent growth in its gross domestic product, electricity production had eclipsed prewar levels (although demand had grown by several orders of magnitude), oil production was improving, and budget execution was going well enough that Iraqi lawmakers had discovered the wonders of the supplemental appropriation.

Improvements in security, the economy, and rule of law were important, but they all supported the truly critical arena in which the war would be decided—politics. The tactical momentum of the surge had not been matched by political momentum at the national level. Prime Minister Nouri al-Maliki oversaw a government that was dysfunctional at best and highly sectarian at worst. Maliki himself may not have been overtly sectarian or beholden to Iran (although the jury was still out in this regard), but he was certainly surrounded by people who were. He was mostly interested in consolidating his power.

Provided he worked through constitutional means, his actions did not cross any red lines. But despite the legality of his actions, Maliki was failing as a strategic leader. He was not leading the effort to improve essential services, he continually objected to the Sons of Iraq initiatives that were helping to rid Iraq of al-Qaeda, and he constantly complained in public about coalition operations (usually those against Shi'a targets), forcing Multi-National Force–Iraq to confront accusations of wrongdoing. He was particularly suspicious of the Sons of Iraq, calling them a "hidden army" and expressing fear that they would come back to haunt the Iraqi government in the future. General Petraeus and Lieutenant General Odierno pointed out that they were hardly hidden; indeed, the biometric identity information we had gathered on the Sons of Iraq and the fact that Multi-National Force–Iraq (and ultimately the Iraqi government) was their paymaster made them easier to control, not more dangerous.

On top of all of this, Maliki was overconfident regarding the success of the surge—which led President Bush to quip in one meeting that he could lend Maliki a "Mission Accomplished" banner.[24] Everyone got the point: this was no time to declare victory. Furthermore, General Petraeus and other U.S. leaders had to continually remind Iraqi political leaders that the violence and intimidation generated by Shi'a extremists was just as threatening to their ability to govern as was the threat posed by al-Qaeda and Sunni insurgents. Too often these admonitions fell on deaf ears, regardless of the evidence. Jaish al-Mahdi special groups continued to attack and kill American soldiers, in some cases using dangerous new techniques. In one attack in November on four U.S. combat outposts, Shi'a militants launched, from rails on trucks at close range, 107mm rocket motors attached to cylinders filled with bulk explosive and ball bearings. Over the course of the twenty-five-minute attack, thirty-one projectiles resulted in twelve wounded American soldiers, seven vehicles destroyed and another seventeen damaged, and multiple buildings damaged. The innovative technique smacked of Iranian involvement.

Maliki's relationships with other members of the nominal national unity government, especially Sunni Vice President Tariq al-Hashemi, were notoriously stormy. Both politicians felt emboldened by the improved security situation in Iraq and the successful testimony of General Petraeus and Ambassador Crocker to Congress. Neither knew how to work together effectively in a coalition government. The prime minister lacked vision, while Hashemi was trying to lay claim to the Sons of Iraq movement—the last thing the Iraqi government wanted to see happen. Neither of these politicians could set aside personal differences to work for the betterment of the nation, an animosity that would eventually lead Maliki to level criminal charges against Hashemi upon the departure of U.S. forces from Iraq at the end of 2011.

The Iraqi government was weak and divided. Indeed, it was not a true unity government but rather an accommodation to differing sectarian, ethnic, and political interests. We were asking a lot of it, especially in the immediate aftermath of the worst sectarian violence the nation had ever seen. The Interim Benchmark report explained the dysfunction of the Iraqi government in clear terms:

> Effective steps toward national reconciliation will require national leadership from all communities and expression of a common national political will, or "vision," that has so far been lacking. The consensus nature of Iraqi politics, and the checks and balances built into the Iraqi governance structure, inhibit Prime Minister Nuri al-Maliki's ability to govern effectively—and would pose obstacles to any prime minister. These inhibitors slow progress on high-priority legislative benchmarks, although they are designed to create a decision-making process through which all major communities have a voice and a stake. The increasing concern among Iraqi political leaders that the United States may not have a long-term commitment to Iraq has also served in recent months to reinforce hedging behaviors and made the hardest political bargains even more difficult to close.[25]

Put in American terms, de-Ba'athification reform was as politically difficult as asking the U.S. Congress to pass comprehensive civil rights legislation during the height of Reconstruction in the 1870s. Reforming provincial powers was like forcing the resolution of federal versus states' rights in the United States in 1860. Passage of hydrocarbon legislation could be compared to arguments over entitlement reform in the United States. On top of all of this, we were asking the Iraqis to tackle all of these issues within a period of a few months as violence continued to wrack the country and divide the electorate.

If political progress was to occur, Maliki needed support—despite his weaknesses as a politician. There were few other choices. Deputy Prime Minster Barham Saleh was the most competent technocrat in the government, but since he was Kurdish, he would never be acceptable as prime minister. Vice President Adel Abdel Mahdi, the candidate favored by the Islamic Supreme Council of Iraq, was a skilled politician, but getting the votes to install him as prime minster would be difficult. Engineering a vote of no-confidence in the Council of Representatives was a lot easier than finding the votes to install a successor. By default, we had no choice but to support Maliki.

One of the problems with Iraqi politics was the "closed list" system used to elect candidates to office. In a closed-list system, voters cast ballots for a party and allow party leaders to determine who will fill the seats. This system, used in Iraq in the elections of 2005, led to sectarian and party divisions and a lack of individual accountability to the people. Ambassador Crocker made it clear to the president that any future elections should be held under an "open list" system, in which voters elected individuals by name for their offices. In the meantime, we had to deal with the politicians who were in power, regardless of their idiosyncrasies or weaknesses. Saddam had had many of the competent Iraqi leaders executed; there was no George Washington waiting in the wings to lead the nation to a better future. We had to deal with the situation as it was, not as we wished it to be.

At the time, General Petraeus's relationship with Prime Minister Maliki was businesslike, at times contentious, but in the end productive. (Over time a degree of affection would develop between the two, after Petraeus bailed out Maliki's offensive to Basra—a development covered in the next chapter.) General Petraeus and Ambassador Crocker would jointly meet with Maliki in private once a week, with Sadi Othman acting as translator (even for Ambassador Crocker, who spoke excellent Arabic). General Petraeus would use these meetings both to inform the prime minister and to make requests of him. Occasionally the conversations would get heated, with General Petraeus displaying (usually deliberately) "the full range of emotions" to get his points across, but they always remained civil.[26] These intermittent arguments should not be seen as a sign of a poor relationship; on the contrary, even close allies—such as the United States and Great Britain in World War II—often engage in heated discourse over important strategic issues. Furthermore, history suggests that the more intense the arguments, the better the outcomes. Dialogue forces leaders to expose the assumptions behind their thinking and prevents the outbreak of groupthink.

Notwithstanding continued gridlock at the national level, there was progress being made in reconciliation at the local level. Sunni sheiks in al-Anbar

were reaching out to Shi'a sheiks in Karbala on issues of mutual interest. In mid-
October several key leaders of the Islamic Supreme Council of Iraq, led by heir apparent Amar al-Hakim, met with more than a hundred Awakening members, led
by Sheik Ahmed Abu Risha (the very capable and politically astute brother of the
recently slain Sheik Sattar Abu Risha). They expressed their support for one another and established a committee to address and formalize the issue of displaced
Iraqis. In southwest Baghdad around fifty community leaders of both sects came
together to sign a reconciliation accord under the auspices of Dr. Safa Hussein
and Dr. Bassima al-Jaidre of the Iraqi Implementation and Follow-up Committee on National Reconciliation. Prime Minister Maliki, Vice President Adel Abd
al-Mehdi, Sheik Ahmed, and other dignitaries attended formal ceremonies during
which detainees no longer considered security risks were released.

Nevertheless, despite these manifest local successes, resistance and concerns
had stalled progress at the top. "Good morning, Mr. Sunshine," President Bush
opened one meeting with Ambassador Crocker around this time. Ambassador
Crocker was quick on the uptake. "That being the case, Mr. President, I thought
today I'd start with the good news," he replied. "But don't worry, it won't take
long."[27]

As so often happened in Iraq, events on the battlefield interjected themselves into
the political discourse. On October 21, 2007, a special operations raid into Sadr
City to capture an Iranian-backed Jaish al-Mahdi special group leader turned into
a lethal confrontation in which more than forty militiamen were killed, along
with some regrettable civilian casualties. The blowback was substantial, as Jaish
al-Mahdi propaganda painted U.S. forces as trigger happy and inconsiderate of
civilian lives, gaining strategic leverage from a tactical event. The incident sparked
a full-scale political crisis in Baghdad, as members of the Council of Representatives took to the floor to rail against U.S. lack of regard for Iraqi sovereignty. Prime
Minster Maliki publicly denounced the U.S. actions before an investigation could
reveal the truth of the matter, straining relations for a period of time.[28] This outcome was unfortunate; with al-Qaeda on the ropes, the long-term threat to Iraqi
sovereignty was in the Shi'a militias backed by Iran. Maliki balked at confronting
them head-on.

The immediate casualty of the Sadr City raid was progress on the long-term
security agreement currently under negotiation between U.S. and Iraqi statesmen.
President Bush badly wanted an agreement on long-term security arrangements,
as well as its counterpart dealing with economic, educational, and cultural issues,
the strategic framework agreement. He rightly felt it was crucial for Iraqis to understand that the United States would be engaged in their country over the long
haul to prevent hedging behavior predicated on the fear that U.S. forces would
soon leave. A long-term security agreement between the United States and Iraq
would also provide a legal basis for U.S. operations in the country and allow the

United Nations Security Council resolution authorizing multinational force operations in Iraq to lapse. National Security Council staffers Megan O'Sullivan and Brett McGurk worked on the long-term security agreement through the summer and fall of 2007 and made some headway with Iraqi politicians, but the furor over the raid into Sadr City temporarily stymied these negotiations.

Since the long-term security agreement now had no chance of coming to fruition before the end of the year, it was imperative that the Iraqi government request an extension of United Nations Security Council Resolution (UNSCR) 1546 to enable multinational force operations in Iraq to continue into 2008. The UNSCR gave Multi-National Force–Iraq legal authority to act against threats to international peace and security under Chapter VII of the United Nations' charter. The Iraqi government viewed it as an infringement on its sovereignty, but there were no other choices at this point. Given the chaos that would result without an UNSCR extension, we believed it was in the Iraqi government's own interest to request one, and indeed Prime Minster Maliki promised President Bush a "swift, clean, and simple" UNSCR extension.[29] Nevertheless, inking the deal was far harder than it should have been.

General Petraeus chose me to represent Multi-National Force–Iraq on the negotiating team, which included Ambassador David Satterfield, Ambassador Marcie Ries, British Ambassador Christopher Prentice, and Sadi Othman. The Iraqi government was represented by Dawa Party diehards: National Security Adviser Mowaffak al-Rubaie; Sami al-Askari, a member of the Council of Representatives; and two senior political advisers to Prime Minister Maliki, Sadiq al-Rikabi and Dr. Tariq Abdullah. The negotiations concerned the language of the letter that Iraq would submit to the United Nations Security Council requesting an extension of the UNSCR. They were anything but "swift, clean, and simple." For several nights the parties discussed the terms of an UNSCR extension, the coalition negotiators requesting a simple letter asking for a one-year extension of the mandate, while the Iraqi negotiating team brought up continual references to sovereignty issues and demanded wording that would have severely constricted coalition authority to operate in Iraq.[30] After an exchange of letters between Maliki and Bush and line-by-line editing of the renewal letter itself, we eventually settled on compromise language that resulted in the passage of UNSCR 1790, the final United Nations Security Council resolution concerning the Iraq War.[31] It extended the U.N. mandate in Iraq to December 31, 2008, after which U.S. and coalition forces would have to operate under yet to be negotiated status-of-forces agreements. Given the pain we had gone through in negotiating the UNSCR extension, we fully expected future negotiations concerning a status-of-forces agreement to be exceedingly difficult. One thing was certain: We would demand a more representative negotiating team on the Iraqi side, rather than crossing pens again with Dawa Party hard-liners.

The negotiations were a fascinating experience for me in the world of diplomacy, but they were about as enjoyable as a root canal, and I was happy to get back to my day job when they were over. General Petraeus wrote me a nice note on December 7 at the conclusion of the negotiations: "Pete, well done, again, on the UNSCR. Lots of feedback about how much you helped. Thanks. [General Petraeus's wife] Holly says to present you the Patience of Job award! Great work (and great updates that were full of insight and shared). Thx."

As if we didn't have enough problems in Iraq, in October the Kurdistan Workers' Party, or PKK, a terrorist organization dedicated to the creation of an independent Kurdistan and greater cultural and political rights for the Kurds in Turkey, executed several high-visibility attacks against Turkish forces in southeastern Turkey. Since PKK bases existed across the border in the Iraqi Kurdish region, Turkish cross-border retaliation with artillery fire, air strikes, and eventually ground operations created a series of international incidents. The Turkish reaction was precisely as the PKK intended; the party had banked on Turkish military operations creating support for the PKK among ethnic Kurds in Turkey and Iraq. Turkey wanted Iraq to act against the PKK base camps on its territory, but Iraqi military forces lacked the capabilities to do so, and in any case, the bases were in the mountainous Kurdish region. If any military force was able to act it was the Kurdish Peshmerga, but the likelihood of Kurdish leaders ordering the Peshmerga to combat the PKK was zero to none. General Petraeus made it clear to his superiors that the United States should not get involved (other than to share intelligence with Turkey), since we did not want to be seen killing ethnic Kurds on Iraqi soil. Any kinetic action by Multi-National Force–Iraq would take assets away from the war against al-Qaeda and Shi'a extremists and create another enemy, for little to no gain.

In the midst of this crisis the U.S. Congress was less than helpful. After a 27–21 vote in the House Foreign Affairs Committee, on October 11 U.S. House Speaker Nancy Pelosi (D-CA) proposed bringing to a vote House Resolution 106, reaffirming U.S. condemnation of the purported genocide of 1.5 million Armenians by Turkish forces in 1915.[32] Regardless of the reasons behind the resolution (mostly to do with domestic politics and the Armenian constituencies in the districts of the House members who drafted it), passing it would have been akin to poking Turkish leaders in the eye with a sharp stick. A number of American political and military leaders successfully pressured the speaker to delay the vote, which for the moment salvaged U.S.-Turkish relations. The episode reminded me of why the framers of the Constitution put the executive branch in charge of foreign affairs and gave the power of advice and consent regarding foreign treaties to the Senate rather than the House.

The Turkish crisis came to a head on the weekend of October 20–21 when PKK guerrillas killed a dozen Turkish soldiers, wounded sixteen, and kidnapped eight others. Emotions in Turkey ran high as flag-draped coffins of the slain soldiers were shown on television.[33] Turkey threatened to invade northern Iraq to retrieve its soldiers; Kurdish leader Massoud Barzani stated that the Peshmerga would defend the Kurdish region against any outside invading force. Neither Iraq nor Turkey wanted or could afford prolonged hostilities; the value of cross-border trade and the export of Iraqi oil through the northern pipeline into Turkey were too important to both nations.

In view of the sensitivity of the issue, General Petraeus decided to get involved personally to get the captured Turkish soldiers freed. Drawing on the relationship he had built with Kurdish Regional Government President Massoud Barzani during his two previous tours in Iraq, he asked Barzani for assistance. He said he was going to fly to Irbil airport in the Kurdish region on November 3, and he would sit there with the Iraqi minister of defense until the soldiers were delivered to him. He noted that he looked forward to Barzani's personal intervention to free the soldiers and would be grateful for his assistance. Petraeus and Minister Adbul Qader flew north and sat at the airport for a couple of hours, with Petraeus relaying growing frustration. He passed the message that he was, in his words, "getting exercised." Under that pressure, reason prevailed. An hour or so later, the eight Turkish soldiers were delivered to General Petraeus and the Iraqi minister of defense after being freed by the PKK in a deal brokered by Barzani. Petraeus and Abdul Qader flew the freed captives to the three-star head of Turkish Special Operations Forces at a Turkish camp in the mountains of northern Iraq. The Turkish officer greeted the released soldiers coldly, perhaps considering their surrender dishonorable.[34]

During subsequent meetings with Kurdish Regional Government President Massoud Barzani and Prime Minister Nechervan Barzani, General Petraeus underscored the seriousness of the situation and recommended actions to choke off PKK support, such as manning checkpoints to cut PKK supply routes, controlling movement into and out of the Mahkmoor U.N. Refugee Camp southwest of Irbil that contained a significant PKK support base of around ten thousand Turkish Kurd refugees, conducting checks at Irbil and Sulaymaniyah airports to prevent PKK movement through them, directing efforts to stop the flow of financial assistance to the PKK, and releasing a statement calling for diplomatic engagement to resolve the crisis and rejecting the PKK's use of violence to achieve its objectives.[35] Winter weather soon suspended PKK actions, but we fully understood that Turkish-Kurdish tensions would continue well into the future until and unless the Turkish government dealt with the root causes of the Kurdish insurgency in the country. A couple of weeks later General Petraeus visited Ankara to meet with Turkish Vice Chief of Defense Ergin Saygun, who made a return visit to meet with General Petraeus in Baghdad in January. They discussed Turkish objectives, the impact of cross-border operations, and the need for the Turkish government to engage the Iraqi Kurdish Regional Government on the issue of the PKK. Turkey needed a counterinsurgency solution to the PKK, not the continuation of a failing counterterrorist program. The advice fell on deaf ears in the Turkish government, which continued to publicly trumpet every cross-border attack it conducted against the PKK, including a sizable ground incursion in mid-February 2008 in knee-deep snow and subfreezing temperatures that ran into stiff PKK resistance in the difficult, mountainous terrain of northern Iraq.[36]

Turkey was not the only regional neighbor on the mind of Ambassador Crocker and General Petraeus. Both of them traveled extensively in the fall of 2007 to neighboring countries and the Gulf States to persuade them to support the new Iraq. General Petraeus visited the United Arab Emirates, Bahrain (for the U.S. Central Command coalition conference), Saudi Arabia, Kuwait, and Jordan. He understood the importance of solidifying relations in the region for the Iraqis and felt that Prime Minister Maliki needed to work harder to overcome the lack of confidence in him among the Arab states. Both Ambassador Crocker and General Petraeus sensed positive momentum building; they pressured Arab governments to reestablish embassies in Baghdad and build bridges to the Iraqi Shi'ites despite their mistrust of the Maliki regime.

Crocker and Petraeus also worked with Lieutenant General Doug Lute, the assistant to the president and deputy national security adviser for Iraq and Afghanistan (also known as the "War Czar"), to energize the interagency to reduce foreign fighter flow to Iraq by working with source countries in the region. A series of meetings cohosted by General Petraeus and Lieutenant General Stan McChrystal brought together representatives from more than a dozen agencies worldwide, including the National Security Council, Department of State, Office of the Secretary of Defense, the Joint Staff, the National Security Agency, the Central Intelligence Agency, the Defense Intelligence Agency, the National Geospatial-Intelligence Agency, and five combatant commands. The group reviewed the progress being made in reducing al-Qaeda in Iraq, the importance of quickly passing actionable intelligence to those entities best situated to act on it, the need to use cyberspace authorities against jihadi networks, means of interrupting terrorist financing, the capabilities and limitations of information operations, and the criticality of reducing foreign fighter transit through Syria.[37] In this regard, General Petraeus offered to visit Damascus (to which he'd been invited by Syrian President Bashar al-Assad) to discuss al-Qaeda and foreign fighter network issues, a suggestion that the president vetoed.[38]

General Petraeus generally travelled in the region with a small staff—Colonel Bill Rapp, Sadi, Major Everett Spain, and his protective detail. During these travels I was left in the headquarters at Camp Victory to mind the store and act as a conduit of information. During one of General Petraeus's trips in early winter I was nearly killed in a rocket attack. I was out running around the base late one afternoon when the indirect fire alarm sounded. I was on a bridge spanning a canal at the time, with nowhere to hide. I sprinted to reach a bunker, but as I picked up the pace, a rocket screamed directly overhead, landing in the water scarcely a hundred feet from me. Fortunately the water absorbed most of the explosion, and

I emerged from the incident unharmed. After the "all clear" sounded, I finished my run. *Just another day at the office,* I quipped to myself.

In early November, General Petraeus was called back to Washington to chair the Army's brigadier general promotion board, an important assignment for the future of the force (and one that was generally viewed as unprecedented—bringing a battlefield commander back for a promotion board). I knew of this detail, but had withdrawn my name from consideration for promotion after accepting an offer from the Ohio State University to fill the General Raymond E. Mason Jr. Chair of Military History. My assignment as executive officer to General Petraeus would be the last of my twenty-six-year Army career. My future would consist of teaching, researching, and writing military history, engaging the media and various public audiences regarding national security issues, and training graduate students. The position at my graduate school alma mater satisfied a lifelong passion to study and research military history, and was a great way to segue into a fulfilling, relevant second career. I will always be grateful to the Army for the education, training, and experiences it provided, but I decided it was time to depart the service on my terms and move on.

While General Petraeus was in Washington, Bill Rapp, Sadi, and I made the rounds as his emissaries to engage various Iraqi leaders on the key issues of the day. We ate for our country in lunches and dinners with General Babakir Zebari, the Kurdish chairman of the Iraqi Joint Chiefs of Staff; former Iraqi Prime Minister Ibrahim al-Ja'afari; Tawafuq leader Adnan al-Dulaimi; Finance Minister Bayan Jabr; and Speaker of the Council of Representatives Mahmoud Mashadani. Bill and I noted that General Babakir had the best chow (his lamb kabobs fresh off the grill could not be beat) and Bayan Jabr the best recreation room (where Bill and I played a few games of pool while waiting on the minister to appear), but perhaps the most important interaction was with Speaker Mashadani, who took an interest in my Arabic background. We discussed the importance of various pieces of legislation while enjoying the usual feast at his home. Mashadani would turn out to be the key figure in untangling the political bottlenecks in the Council of Representatives, a role few observers expected him to perform after he had nearly been kicked out of his job the previous summer.

The arrival in Iraq of the new United Nations representative, Staffan de Mistura, helped on the diplomacy front. De Mistura had spent time in Baghdad in the 1980s and appeared serious about tackling Article 140 issues surrounding the status of Kirkuk and the return of refugees to Iraq. Article 140 of the Iraqi Constitution mandated the completion of a census in Kirkuk, followed by a referendum to determine the status of the area (and its potential incorporation into the Kurdish federal region) not later than the end of 2007. Before the accession of Saddam Hussein to power, the area was heavily Kurdish and to a lesser extent, Turkoman. During the 1970s and 1980s Saddam displaced many Kurdish and Turkoman families and replaced them with Arabs to solidify the loyalty of the oil-rich area to Baghdad. Since the beginning of the Iraq War in 2003, the Kurds had been working hard to reverse this ethnic cleansing, which brought them into conflict with the Sunni Arabs on the ground who now considered Kirkuk home. Resolving Article 140 issues, with contentious boundary determinations for the extent of the Kurdish region, was going to be extraordinarily complicated and emotional. Whether this capable diplomat could make any headway on this issue remained to be seen, but his energy and the renewed sense of purpose he brought to the United Nations Mission in Iraq were welcome additions to the diplomatic scene.

As winter approached, the political crisis in Baghdad heated up. It was clear that Prime Minster Maliki lacked a political strategy to get legislation passed, and his visceral dislike of Vice President Tariq al-Hashemi stymied attempts at reconciliation between the Sunni Tawafuq political faction and the Shi'a bloc. By late fall the Justice and Accountability Law (de-Ba'athification reform) had been introduced in the Council of Representatives, but opposition to the law remained among some Shi'a and Kurdish lawmakers. The latest draft of oil legislation continued to be mired in Kurd-Arab politics. Maliki was intent on issuing an amnesty decree, but the specifics at this point were vague. Shi'a factions were split on the devolution of power to the provinces, with the Islamic Supreme Council and Fadillah (a Shi'a party centered on Basra) in favor of expanded provincial powers, and Dawa (Maliki's party) and the Sadrists opposed. There were two bright spots. One was the passage of the Unified Pension Law, which reformed the civil and military pension systems to make them more financially sustainable. It also provided pensions for service regardless of Ba'ath Party affiliation, which would help to tamp down the severe disgruntlement sparked by the enactment of the draconian de-Ba'athification decree by the Coalition Provisional Authority in May 2003. Another highlight was the budget; with oil prices at record highs, the budget grew from $41 billion in 2007 to more than $48 billion for 2008. The fiscal accommodations to various groups made the passage of the budget in the Council of Representatives more certain; they also brought with them the specter of corruption in a country notorious for its lack of budget transparency.

In what would become its modus operandi, in early December the Maliki administration had the Iraqi Army place Adnan al-Dulaimi, the leader of the Sunni coalition Tawafuq, under house arrest after allegations that his personal security detail was engaged in terrorist and criminal activities. Dulaimi denied the accusations, causing the Sunni alliance to boycott the Council of Representatives. After a few days Dulaimi was allowed to move into a hotel in the International Zone, but the political situation remained tense.

Time was at a premium. The Council of Representatives had difficulties gaining a quorum on any given day, since the average attendance was usually just over half of the 275 representatives. The Tawafuq walkout would make gaining a quorum even more difficult. On top of this problem, a large number of representatives planned to depart in mid-December for a three-week government-sponsored hajj to Mecca. Lack of a quorum meant that the parliament could continue with readings of draft laws but could not vote on them. By law the Council of Representatives could not adjourn until it passed an annual budget, so Speaker Mashadani extended the legislative session into the new year. The extra time would prove crucial to political progress in Iraq, as General Petraeus and Ambassador Crocker worked with Iraqi lawmakers to tee up other pieces of legislation before the parliament adjourned. Secretary of Defense Gates pressed Prime Minister Maliki to move on legislation while he still had time. Recounting his visit with the prime minister during a trip in December, Gates stated, "I told Maliki there is no longer a Baghdad clock or a Washington clock, there is only a George Bush clock. You need to move and get things done while your best friend is still in the White House."[39]

The lack of political progress led some Iraqi leaders to test the waters regarding the formation of a new government. In dinners with General Petraeus, leaders of the Islamic Supreme Council of Iraq and Kurdish parties expressed enormous concern and deep frustration with the inability of Prime Minster Maliki and those around him to take advantage of improved security to move Iraq forward politically.[40] His ineffective leadership and isolated decision making was alienating the other parties in the government, the discord marked by an emerging coalition between the Kurdish parties and the Sunni Iraqi Islamic Party (led by Maliki's nemesis, Vice President Tariq al-Hashemi) and the provision of letters to Maliki demanding the he broaden his governing style.[41] The sharks were circling.

Throughout the month of December, Baghdad was rife with rumors of a change in government, which led Prime Minister Maliki—already suspicious and inclined by nature to see conspiracies everywhere—to become even more paranoid, insular, and estranged from just about every group in the government with the exception of his own Dawa Party.[42] The prime minister's inner circle—the same folks who had made the renewal of the UNSCR so difficult—stoked his fears. The pressure and stress resulted in Maliki seeking medical care in London, but after a week of treatment he returned to his offices in Baghdad. General Petraeus stressed to the president that we needed a "clear-eyed assessment" of the way ahead. The fact was that our legislative strategy was doing more to move issues forward than any efforts by the prime minister and his sectarian advisers.

In the midst of this turmoil, we paused just a bit to celebrate Christmas. Secretary Gates expressed his greetings to General Petraeus at the end of a meeting just before the holiday. "Merry Christmas and Happy New Year," the secretary stated. "What you and your forces have done in 2007 has defied expectations."[43] My family had done its part, sending me decorations for my desk and room and a variety of small wrapped gifts to open. Included in the decorations were small figurines of Santa and Clarice from the cartoon "Rudolph the Red Nosed Reindeer," which belted out "Jingle, Jingle, Jingle," and "There's Always Tomorrow" at the push of

a button. I placed Santa and Clarice on my desk in the al-Faw palace and had
them sing every morning when I arrived in the office, much to the staff's delight.
The Tongan soldiers who guarded the headquarters did their part to lift holiday
spirits, performing a wonderful concert of Christmas music made more special by
their deep, melodic voices. General Petraeus threw a nice Christmas party in the
villa for his personal staff and security detachment. The general appeared in good
holiday cheer, complete with four silver stars on his Santa hat, and took photos in
front of the Christmas tree with the troops. On Christmas Day he traveled in a
Marine V-22 Osprey to visit bases in the far west of Anbar and at the northeastern
end of the Diyala River valley in the same day. I stayed in Baghdad and enjoyed a
nice dinner at Camp Victory with my good friend Colonel Jim Hickey. Jim and I
capped off the event by retiring to the roof of the al-Faw palace to smoke a Monte
Cristo and drink a near beer. Then it was back to work.

The New Year began inauspiciously. General Petraeus, knowing I was a diehard
Ohio State fan, allowed me to miss the morning battlefield update to watch the
Buckeyes play against the Louisiana State University Tigers in the 2008 NCAA
football national championship. Needless to say, given the game's outcome, I
should have gone to the meeting instead. Then, eleven days into 2008 and for
the first time in anyone's memory, it snowed in Baghdad. "Everyone who offered
to reenlist when hell freezes over, now's your chance," I wrote in jest to the staff.
General Petraeus celebrated the event by going out for his usual Friday morning
run. He and the team returned happy and caked in mud.

Multi-National Corps–Iraq began the year by launching an offensive to continue the pursuit of al-Qaeda in the Diyala River valley, Mosul, and areas south
of Baghdad. The operation was also intended to stem corruption emanating from
insurgent and criminal networks associated with the Bayji oil refinery, a source of
revenue for al-Qaeda and other nefarious actors in Iraq. The operation stemmed
in part from an intelligence briefing given by Colonel Jim Hickey to Lieutenant
General Odierno on December 5, 2007, during which Hickey noted that al-Qaeda
in Iraq was wounded, but not yet finished; that it was establishing support zones
in the vicinity of Mosul; that it was living off money generated via corruption and
intimidation in Bayji and Kirkuk; and that it was trying to protect its lines of communication to Syria and Iran. Odierno turned to Colonel Mike Murray, the corps
operations officer, and had his staff prepare orders for what would become Operation Phantom Phoenix.[44] The operation resulted in tough fighting in Diyala province, Mosul, and elsewhere, which eliminated a number of insurgent sanctuaries
in northern Iraq. Efforts to improve governance and essential services at the local
level also continued, aided by improved security in many areas of the country.
Operation Phantom Phoenix continued the string of coalition military successes
in Iraq, with violence lowered by the end of February to levels not seen since the
spring of 2005.[45] The security trends were clearly moving in the right direction.

The main theater of action, however, had shifted to the Iraqi Council of Representatives, where Speaker Mashadani and Deputy Speaker Khalid al-Attiyah were both energized and working hard at getting legislation passed. The Accountability and Justice Law (de-Ba'athification reform) survived unscathed through the amendment process, and the parliament, in a unanimous vote, approved the bill on January 12. Various versions of a provincial powers law were under debate, but compromise seemed possible on this vital piece of legislation since both Sunni and Shi'a political leaders exhibited a growing interest in provincial elections. The sticking point was the ability of the prime minister to fire governors and the ability of governors to take control of federal security forces in an emergency. As usual, Maliki favored centralization of power in his office, while others favored a decentralized solution. Nevertheless, whether due to the threat of a no-confidence vote, his recent medical treatment, or other factors, Maliki seemed more willing to compromise and to meet regularly with a newly formed Executive Council, composed of President Jalal Talibani, Prime Minister Nouri al-Maliki, Vice President Tariq al-Hashemi, and Vice President Adel Abd al-Mehdi.[46] It remained to be seen whether this attempt at power sharing would work, especially because of the poor relations between Maliki and Hashemi. Even on this score, things seemed to be looking up. Maliki and Hashemi temporarily found some common ground in supporting the Sunni commander in Mosul, Lieutenant General Riyadh Jalal Tawfiq, against both al-Qaeda terrorism and Kurdish attempts to move the Green Line south into Nineveh province.

The budget was also a contentious issue. Shi'a parties objected to the traditional Kurdish demand for 17 percent of total Iraqi revenue plus funding for the Kurdish Peshmerga, the military forces of the Kurdish Regional Government. In previous years, the Kurdish Regional Government had been allocated 17 percent of the federal budget, but the Dawa, Iraqiyah, and Sadrist parties now argued that the Kurds made up only 13 percent of the Iraqi population. What the region really needed was a census, but such a step was political dynamite, as it would fix the population of the Kirkuk area, something the Kurds were trying to avoid as they created "facts on the ground" with the reintroduction of Kurdish families into the region.

Speaker Mashadani had transformed himself into a political dynamo. He operated with passion, pressing for the compromises needed to keep legislation flowing through the Council of Representatives. After the Accountability and Justice legislation passed, he tackled a symbolic—but contentious—issue by introducing legislation to redesign the Iraq flag, considered a symbol of Ba'athist Iraq. The new design removed from the flag the three stars that represented the Ba'athist trinity of unity, freedom, and socialism and replaced the phrase "Allahu Akbar" (God is greatest) in Saddam's handwriting with the same phrase drawn in a style of calligraphy native to Iraq. After the bill's passage, Prime Minster Maliki personally raised the new flag over the Council of Ministers building in Baghdad, while the

Kurdish regional parliament came back from winter recess to the raise the new Iraqi flag over the region for the first time since 2003. However, in a sign that sectarianism was not dead, most Sunnis opposed the flag's redesign, particularly the removal of the three stars from its design.[47]

Mashadani was just warming up. After walkouts by various parties on Tuesday, February 12, the speaker threatened to dissolve the Council of Representatives. He came back the next day with the kind of compromise that only a skilled politician could engineer, and one that gave all the major factions some form of political victory. The Council of Representatives passed the 2008 budget, an amnesty law, and a provincial powers act in a "grand bargain." Resurrecting himself after being nearly jettisoned the previous summer, Mashadani fashioned a compromise that brought various factions together to approve the package deal. An ecstatic General Petraeus reported to the secretary of defense, "The past week has been among the more heartening since I returned to Iraq a year ago."[48]

The Kurds retained a 17 percent share of Iraqi revenues, while conceding that future percentages would be decided through a census. The Kurdish demand for central government funding for the Peshmerga was deferred for later resolution. The Sunni parties got an amnesty law—a key demand of the Tawafuq alliance to return to full participation in the government. The Shi'a United Iraqi Alliance overcame its internal disputes to back a provincial powers act that balanced the power of the national and provincial governments. The act required the passage of an elections law within ninety days and the holding of provincial elections no later than 1 October. Having passed the budget, the Council of Representatives recessed until mid-March. Two days later, on the one-year anniversary of the start of Fardh al-Qanoon, Lieutenant General Ray Odierno and III Corps headed home to Fort Hood, Texas, turning over the reins of Multi-National Corps–Iraq to Lieutenant General Lloyd Austin and the XVIII Airborne Corps. The grand bargain, which had been made possible in part by their service and sacrifice, was a fitting way for Odierno and his troops to commemorate the end of their time in Iraq.

The grand bargain was the type of political breakthrough the surge—by improving security conditions in Iraq and reducing ethnosectarian violence—was meant to facilitate. Improved security had reenergized Iraqi political life. Significantly, Iraqi politicians were finally brokering deals across ethnic and sectarian lines. The progress was welcome, but we were well aware that other issues, such as hydrocarbon legislation and the Article 140 status of Kirkuk, remained problematical. Nevertheless, progress was progress. At the Campaign Assessment Synchronization Board on the Saturday following the grand bargain, Ambassador Crocker and General Petraeus could glimpse "the first real indication that that the goals of the joint campaign plan set for the summer of 2008 might actually be attained."[49]

As the surge progressed, General Petraeus and Ambassador Crocker came up with a culturally acceptable way to nudge reconciliation forward. Noting that in Iraq

much business was conducted over lavish meals, they decided to invite Iraqi dignitaries to lunch or dinner at the embassy, beginning with an Iftar meal (the breaking of the fast during Ramadan) for the members of the Iraqi Implementation and
Follow-up Committee for National Reconciliation. The committee's work, headed
by Dr. Safa Hussein and Dr. Bassima al-Jaidre, was a tangible measure of the Iraqi
government's willingness to engage seriously in the hard work of reconciliation,
though not surprisingly the committee seemed to put more effort into reconciliation with Jaish al-Mahdi operatives than with Sunni leaders. General Petraeus
came away impressed with both Dr. Safa and Dr. Bassima. Dr. Bassima had been a
leading figure in the sectarian Office of the Commander in Chief, or OCINC, but
was now playing a more constructive role. Despite her sectarian leanings, she was
an impressive and capable figure in what was otherwise a mostly mediocre sea of
talent in the Iraqi government.

After a couple of these dinners, Sadi and Heather broke some bad news to
General Petraeus—the Iraqis hated our chow. The dining facility staff did the best
they could, but what we really needed was an Iraqi caterer who could prepare
traditional Arab fare—lamb, rice, kabobs, flat bread, tabouleh, hummus, baklava,
and the like. General Petraeus put the staff on the hunt for the right caterer, and
Sadi soon found one who could produce excellent Arabic food, much of it baked
and grilled right on the spot. From this point forward, we would book the Blackhawk Conference Center in the International Zone and arrange for catered Arabic
meals. One of the first of these dinners, complete with an Arabic band right out
of *One Thousand and One Nights,* was in honor of Speaker Mashadani, Deputy
Speaker Khalid al-Attiyah, and Deputy Speaker Arif Tayfur in recognition of their
hard work in advancing legislation through the Council of Representatives. We
ditched the band after this event, but booked the conference center on a weekly
basis thereafter. General Petraeus had us arrange lunches or dinners with Iraqi
groups that shared similar interests and functions, such as oil and electricity, reconciliation, legislation, and security. I gladly conceded the cultural point: The
meals were a much more enjoyable way to conduct business than routine meetings around a table.

Sadi was a key adviser throughout General Petraeus's time in Iraq, but he
played an especially critical role during this period of political ferment. As General Petraeus's alter ego, he was constantly on the phones with Iraqi interlocutors
at all hours of the day and night. He would convey messages from General Petraeus and relay messages to him in return. The Iraqis trusted Sadi, trust that went
a long way in enhancing General Petraeus's relations with his Iraqi counterparts.
Sadi's desk in the embassy annex was adjacent to mine, and we would frequently
engage in spirited conversation on a variety of issues. He and I also shared a passion for red grapes (no doubt the result of our shared Palestinian ancestry), and we
would share a stash that I always kept handy for a healthy snack.

Since nothing in Iraq came easily, Vice President Adel Abd al-Mehdi vetoed the Provincial Powers Act over provisions that gave the prime minister and Coun-cil of Representatives a role in dismissing provincial governors and that estab-lished administrative restrictions on gubernatorial authority, providing yet one more political hurdle in the already cumbersome legislative process. The silver lining on this particular cloud was that his objections to the law had nothing to do with Sunni-Shi'a relations but rather with the Islamic Supreme Council of Iraq's desire to control the nine regions in southern Iraq with a more or less free hand. After several weeks of negotiations, on March 19 the Presidency Council withdrew its objections to the Provincial Powers Act. Vice President Abd al-Mehdi based the withdrawal of his veto on an agreement that the Council of Representatives would amend the law before provincial elections were held. The act required the passage of an elections law by May 14 and provincial elections no later than October 1, a tight timeline that ultimately was pushed back by four months.

As politics in Iraq continued apace, National Security Council representative Brett McGurk and Ambassador Robert Loftus led the U.S. effort to negotiate a strategic framework agreement and a status-of-forces agreement with the Iraqi government. The strategic framework agreement would expand upon the Declara-tion of Principles signed by Prime Minister Maliki and President Bush in Novem-ber 2007 and govern U.S.-Iraqi relations over the long term. The status-of-forces agreement would replace the U.N. Security Council Resolution 1790 governing the status of U.S. forces in Iraq. President Bush wanted a fairly rapid resolution of the negotiations to prevent them from getting caught up in U.S. presidential election politics. The Iraqis naturally wanted the agreements to address their con-cerns over sovereignty issues and were particularly sensitive to the need to have the Council of Representatives ratify any agreements to give Maliki political top cover. The most difficult issues in the negotiations related to jurisdiction over ci-vilian contractors, coalition authority to hold detainees, and Iraqi control over coalition combat operations. At least the Iraqi negotiating team did not consist of the prime minister's inner circle of advisers. The negotiations would prove to be protracted and difficult, but in the end both governments agreed that a continuing relationship was far preferable to none at all.

General Petraeus also focused during this period on how the surge would end. The improvement in security conditions on the ground facilitated the withdrawal of the surge brigades, albeit slowly and with an eye toward the operational geometry of the battlefield. Multi-National Force–Iraq planners posited a number of options to draw down the surge brigades by midsummer. The larger question was whether to continue reductions after that point and if so, how fast. President Bush and Secretary of Defense Gates agreed with the withdrawal of the surge forces by the end of the July, and furthermore accepted the concept of a forty-five-day period of consolidation and evaluation at that point to gauge the pace of further withdrawals based on conditions in Iraq. General Petraeus would return to Washington in early April to present the plan to Congress.

General Petraeus's future was also up in the air. He would, at some point in the near future, step down as commander of Multi-National Force–Iraq. The end of the surge seemed to many the logical point at which to change commanders. Given a choice, General Petraeus would have preferred to be nominated as the supreme Allied commander in Europe, a position his father-in-law, General William Knowlton, had once aspired to fill. Petraeus's wife, Holly, had been partly raised in Europe and spoke fluent French, so the position was a good fit for her as well. The president and secretary of defense seemed supportive of the move, especially after a private conversation that Petraeus had with President Bush in Kuwait.[50]

Momentum seemed to be moving in this direction when fate intervened. In early March, *Esquire* published a profile of Admiral William "Fox" Fallon that indicated that the admiral disagreed with Bush administration policy regarding Iran and was challenging the president over political matters.[51] The resulting media firestorm ended with Fallon's resignation, a regrettable end to his forty years of distinguished service to the nation. Ironically, by this time Fallon and Petraeus saw eye to eye on the way ahead in Iraq and had forged a cooperative relationship, quite an evolution from the first seven months of the surge. The surge was now ending, and the question was not whether but how fast to withdraw troops from Iraq. That was a debate more along Fallon's line of thinking.

Fallon's resignation elevated Lieutenant General Marty Dempsey, the deputy commander of Central Command, into temporary leadership of the organization. But Dempsey had not logged enough experience at the three-star level to take over a combatant command on a permanent basis. President Bush and Secretary Gates, looking over the universe of general and flag officers in the U.S. military, settled on the logical choice to assume the position. After relinquishing command of Multi-National Force–Iraq, General Petraeus would take over U.S. Central Command. After the announcement of his nomination, Lieutenant General Lloyd Austin congratulated General Petraeus at the next morning update. General Petraeus replied with muted humor, "Well, it was going to be wine and cheese in Brussels, but instead it's beer and Cheetos in Tampa." The room erupted in laughter. (Ultimately, Petraeus would come to regard command of U.S. Central Command as the best position in the military.)

As winter in Iraq drew to a close, we could look back with some satisfaction on the political progress made since the testimony to Congress the previous September. While Iraq political leaders had not yet reached the nirvana of national reconciliation, they were talking to one another in meaningful ways. The surge, which had done so much to reduce violence in Iraq, had now entered its second year. New leaders and units were rotating into Iraq, bringing with them fresh energy and optimism concerning the way forward. Multi-National Force–Iraq was looking forward to what we believed would be the next phase of the campaign, focused on the reduction of al-Qaeda concentrations in Mosul and northwestern Iraq. General Petraeus and his planners were crafting plans to end the surge and reduce the U.S. force presence in Iraq even further by the end of the year. His personal staff was preparing for another round of congressional testimony. Then, in the midst of this activity, the nonlinear nature of war once again threw off our calculations regarding the way ahead, as Prime Minister Nouri al-Maliki asserted his prerogative as commander in chief of the Iraq armed forces to order a massive operation in Basra, the oil capital of southern Iraq. What ensued was a series of events that were in many respects among the most decisive of the surge. Just as the unforeseen Awakening had led Sunni tribal sheiks to fight al-Qaeda, Maliki was about to go to the mat against his coreligionists, the Shi'a Jaish al-Mahdi. The impact of his decision would shake up not only the military situation in Iraq but the political equation as well.

CHAPTER 9

Charge of the Knights

War is not a linear phenomenon; it's a calculus, not arithmetic.
—General David Petraeus

Three major developments changed the face of the Iraq War in 2007 and 2008. The surge and the Awakening are relatively well known, and covered elsewhere. The final event, Prime Minister Nouri al-Maliki's military actions in the spring of 2008 to clear the Jaish al-Mahdi out of Basra, Sadr City, and Amarah, is unknown to most Western observers. But the "Charge of the Knights" (*Saulat al-Farsan*), as the Iraqi government labeled the operation, arguably was at least as important as the Awakening, for it changed the political calculations of many Iraqi leaders and made politics the operative forum for the division of power and resources in Iraq going forward. Just as the Awakening pitted Sunni tribesmen against Sunni militants, the Charge of the Knights pitted a largely Shi'a Iraqi military under the command of a Shi'a prime minister against largely Iranian-supported Shi'a militiamen. These developments convinced the Iraqi political elite that religion, while a strong influence in Iraqi society, was not necessarily the dominant force in determining Iraq's political future. Once the elite cleared this conceptual hurdle, politics based on mutual interests rather than sect and ethnicity became possible.

It is doubtful that Maliki made this calculation beforehand. Rather, his decision seemed impulsive. He probably believed the operation would be quick and decisive, much like his foray to Karbala the previous August after the gun battle near the Hussein shrine. But Karbala was not a Jaish al-Mahdi stronghold; the brigade I commanded during the first year of the war, the Ready First Combat Team, had largely cleared Karbala of its Sadr-backed militia presence in the spring of 2004.[1] Basra, Sadr City, and Amarah were different altogether. By confronting the Jaish al-Mahdi and other militias in Basra, Maliki was taking on powerful Shi'a political and economic interests. His actions also put Iran on the horns of a dilemma. The ayatollahs in Tehran could support their proxy irregular military force in Iraq, or they could back the legitimate government in Baghdad. Qods force leaders tried to walk this tightrope at various points by arranging a cease-fire among the combatants, one that Maliki accepted and then largely ignored. He staked his political future on this bold action, but his ultimate victory, albeit earned only when coalition forces came to the rescue of the Iraqi Army, cleared the way for a provisional resolution of the civil war that had plagued Iraq since the spring of 2006.

Positioned deep in Shi'a-dominated southern Iraq, Basra was not supposed to be so difficult. Since it had never been a Ba'athist stronghold, coalition military leaders believed the city would escape the type of violence that plagued Baghdad, Mosul, Baqubah, Ramadi, and other cities in Sunni-dominated or mixed-sectarian areas of Iraq. Early in the war British troops patrolled the city with a light touch, forgoing helmets and body armor and generally leaving the city government for Iraqis to sort out. This "berets in Basra" approach worked—for a while. But Basra's status as the major export terminus for Iraqi oil and its proximity to Iraq's only port inevitably led to conflict over who would control it. Basra's importance was summed up in a comment made by Muqtada al-Sadr to a couple of his lieutenants from the city who came to see him. "I smell gasoline," he sniffed.[2] If the Sunnis did not contest control of the city, the Shi'ites were more than capable of fighting among themselves for it.

    Coalition military leaders had assigned responsibility for Basra and its environs to forces from the United Kingdom. The British division that invaded Iraq in 2003 took the city after some relatively brief but stiff fighting, and for several years garrisoned it without incident. The calm was deceiving. While U.S. forces surged into Iraqi streets in 2007 to turn around a losing war effort, British forces were moving in the other direction, consolidating onto a single large forward operating base at Basra airfield. The deployment out of Basra to the airfield was consistent with the presurge Multi-National Force–Iraq strategy of repositioning the military away from cities and into larger bases on their periphery. For the British, the withdrawal from Basra was also politically convenient in that it limited their exposure to casualties. As with the U.S. consolidation on larger forward operating bases on the periphery of Baghdad, however, the British move was bound to fail. British forces could not "overwatch" what was happening inside Basra without being stationed with Iraqi forces in the city. Furthermore, when the U.S. strategy changed with the implementation of the surge to getting off the big bases and living with the people we were seeking to secure, the British failed to adjust their approach.

This left British forces in the awkward position of being stuck at Basra airfield with very limited intelligence and no real role except defending themselves. It was a losing proposition.

Why this occurred requires some explanation.

The relevant experiences of the British Army after the end of the Cold War centered on peacekeeping and counterterrorism operations. Moreover, the memories of much of the British officer corps that had served in Northern Ireland in the two decades leading up to the Iraq War focused on the recent counterterrorism struggle against the Irish Republican Army, as opposed to the more difficult operations earlier in the conflict. Despite the rich British historical experience in colonial and irregular wars, lack of formal institutional education and training in counterinsurgency warfare led all too many British officers to reach inappropriate conclusions regarding the way ahead in Basra. Faulty institutional memory exacerbated the effects of inadequate professional military education grounded in the study of history.[3]

The peacekeeping model used by British forces in Basra worked as long as the underlying social and political conditions in the city remained stable. Uninformed pundits held up the British Army as the model for other coalition forces in Iraq, as if its imperial legacy gave it an inborn advantage in counterinsurgency operations. In late 2005 British Brigadier Nigel Aylwin-Foster published a scathing critique of U.S. operations in Iraq in *Military Review,* one of the premier U.S. Army service journals.[4] His criticisms, which were valid for the period he observed, stemmed from his service in Iraq in 2004, when the U.S. Army and Marine Corps had not yet undergone their doctrinal renaissance regarding counterinsurgency warfare. Yet while American armed forces slowly adapted, the British Army remained locked in a mindset that treated southern Iraq as if it were Northern Ireland in the final years of that endeavor. Cultural sensitivity and proper conduct were no substitute for a clear-eyed political and military assessment of the situation and understanding of political differences among the Shi'ites.

British Colonel Richard Iron, who spent a great deal of time in Basra, agrees that coalition leaders made several mistakes in their approach to garrisoning the city. He writes, "One of the biggest mistakes we made was our policy towards the police, where we thought that recruiting the militias into the police force would encourage all parties 'into the tent,' whereas the reality was that it handed over control of large parts of the police to JAM [Jaish al-Mahdi, Sadr's militia], whom we armed and trained," he stated. "In hindsight it was naive; if we were going to do this we should have built in much stronger controls to ensure their primary loyalty to the state."[5] If various Shi'a groups did not contest the British for control over Basra early in the war, it was due only to their temporary weakness and the subsequent British policy of incorporating them into the security forces, not because British soldiers had won over the population with their exemplary conduct.

By 2006, the Jaish al-Mahdi and other Shi'a political entities such as Fadillah and the Islamic Supreme Council for Iraq and its Badr Organization were ready to contest for superiority in Basra. Security deteriorated noticeably as British forces lost their grip on the city. Helmets and body armor reappeared on British troopers as the militias targeted British forces. Responding to increased violence with Operation Sinbad, British forces attempted to clear militiamen from the streets of Basra through a series of cordon-and-search operations. These operations suffered, however, from the same deficiencies as the contemporaneous "Together Forward" operations in Baghdad—areas cleared could not be held without keeping sufficient troops positioned among the people. Neither the Maliki administration nor General George Casey and Multi-National Force–Iraq were willing to support more robust operations in southern Iraq at the time. Iraqi military and police forces in southern Iraq were too few and too poorly trained to take on the responsibility for securing Basra. Rushing the transition from British to Iraqi control also caused a loss of situational awareness. Predictably, the "clear and leave" operations did not achieve enduring security gains, as the Iraqi security forces to which the British quickly transferred control of cleared areas proved unable to keep them clear. As a result, Operation Sinbad was an exercise in futility, and Sadrist militiamen soon regained control of their safe havens in Basra. The alternative to renewing the fight, in the minds of British political and military leaders, was to cut a deal.

In fact, the British were not the only ones looking to talk with Shi'a militia leaders. The real question was whether to negotiate from a position of strength, or to make the best deal possible while playing a bad hand. The surge in U.S. and Iraqi forces, their efforts to protect the Iraqi people while eliminating terrorist and insurgent safe havens and sanctuaries, and the Awakening and Sons of Iraq movements gave coalition leaders the leverage they needed to engage forcefully with Shi'a militia leaders. The Jaish al-Mahdi was increasingly fragmented, with a variety of groups claiming the mantle of Sadr while pursuing intentions ranging from benign to nefarious. While Sadrist leaders viewed their movement as a nationalist party with wide grassroots support, Iranian-backed splinter groups continued to routinely target and kill American and British soldiers. Under British leadership, the MNF-I Force Strategic Engagement Cell reached out to those reconcilable Sadrists willing to abide by the cease-fire, while coalition and Iraqi special operations forces targeted the Shi'a "Special Groups" beholden to Iran. Impeding Iranian influence and destroying the Special Groups without provoking a populist backlash that could reunify the Jaish al-Mahdi, not to mention keeping the Iraqi government mollified, required a nuanced approach. General Petraeus made it clear that while targeted raids were essential, we could not kill our way out of the "JAM problem." Nor did we have to. Muqtada al-Sadr himself was increasingly moving his organization toward a more nonviolent agenda. The increasing rejection of extremism among the Iraqi people made possible by the surge and the splintering of the Jaish al-Mahdi presented opportunities for the way ahead.

But the British wanted to move quickly to extricate their forces from Basra.

They persuaded General Petraeus to support the targeted release of a number of Jaish al-Mahdi detainees in exchange for promises of goodwill from the Sadrists. In truth, as Petraeus recognized, there was really no option, given the prevailing sentiment in London. He had earlier persuaded Prime Minister Tony Blair to keep larger numbers of British soldiers in Iraq than had been planned, but the pressure to draw down had developed a level of momentum that he could slow but not halt.[6]

In the end, the promises the British negotiated with the Shi'a groups were a smoke screen. Before the British withdrew their forces from Basra Palace to the airport at the outskirts of the city in August 2007, Shi'a militia groups ramped up their attacks on the palace in an effort to claim credit for forcing the British out of Basra. The situation then calmed for several months as Sadrist detainees were released in small batches. After the last of the Jaish al-Mahdi detainees were released in early January, British forces came under virtual siege at the airport as militiamen fired a steady stream of rockets and mortars at them, an eventuality that General Petraeus had foreseen before the handover.

The three weak Iraqi Army battalions left behind in Basra (eventually increased to nine battalions over the next six months) were unable to hold the city, while Basra's police force was thoroughly penetrated by the militias.[7] Despite the lack of security, the coalition handed Basra province over to Iraqi control on December 16 (although it had ceded de facto control when British forces left Basra Palace several months earlier). The Jaish al-Mahdi assumed control of large sections of Basra, inflicting on its residents a severe brand of Shari'a law that forced women to wear the *jihab* on pain of death, closed barber shops and music stores, and generally made life miserable for city residents. The situation proved yet again that without control or protection of the population, counterinsurgency efforts would fail and the Iraqi people would suffer. For his part, Muqtada al-Sadr took credit for forcing the British out of Iraq.[8]

By withdrawing their forces from Basra and consolidating them on a single base at the city outskirts, British political and military leaders had abdicated responsibility for the city's security. Shi'a militia leaders had contested control of the city and outlasted the British will to continue the fight. In the ensuing competition among Shi'a groups for power in Basra, the Jaish al-Mahdi came out on top. It was now in control of Basra's streets and by extension the economic wherewithal that came with control over Iraq's imports and its oil exports.[9] As General Petraeus remarked, by the end of 2007 Basra came to resemble a fifteenth-century Italian city-state. If the British were content with this situation, Prime Minister Nouri al-Maliki certainly was not, but his immediate political struggles left him powerless at the moment to do anything about it.

Before we departed for the United States for the September 2007 congressional hearings, I suggested to General Petraeus that at some point soon Multi-National Force–Iraq needed to shift its main effort from destroying the local branch of al-

Qaeda (a goal I believed we were well on our way to accomplishing) to combating Shi'a militias that presented the longer-term political and economic threat to Iraq. It was clear that this idea was in line with General Petraeus's own thinking, as he had noted during the summer that bottom-up reconciliation among the Sunnis could leave Shi'a extremists as the largest security threat in Iraq. But as he noted, we could take on only so many fights at one time, and we needed to consolidate our significant gains against the Sunni extremists before embarking on a major offensive against the Shia militias, even though many of the U.S. units had made considerable headway against them. Although hard to read at times, Prime Minister Maliki seemed to agree. In a meeting in early November he stated that his next priority in the campaign would be to clean up Basra.

Coalition military leaders were, however, still focused on the destruction of al-Qaeda in Iraq, looking to the north, to Mosul. Al-Qaeda fighters had gravitated in that direction ever since their defeat in al-Anbar and Baghdad provinces. As 2007 wore on, Mosul gained the unenviable reputation as the most violent city in Iraq. The situation in Nineveh province was tricky, with Kurdish aspirations of moving the Green Line south conflicting with al-Qaeda desires to create a sanctuary among the disaffected Sunni Arab inhabitants of the province. As long as the main effort remained in Baghdad, the commanders in Nineveh made do with a single U.S. brigade and some fairly decent Iraqi Army and police forces. Due to Sunni Arab angst at Kurdish aspirations in the area, the region had yet to see a serious Awakening movement. This state of affairs gave al-Qaeda an inroad into the population, a reality that made most coalition political and military leaders agree that the final battle against al-Qaeda would occur in Mosul.

Lieutenant General Odierno and Multi-National Corps–Iraq launched Operation Phantom Phoenix in January 2008 in part to target al-Qaeda operatives in northern Iraq and eradicate terrorist safe havens in Diyala and Nineveh provinces. The operation succeeded in pressuring al-Qaeda and putting its destruction within reach. In early February, Prime Minister Maliki flew to Mosul for a meeting with the local crisis action committee, which included the provincial governor, the provincial director of police, and the commander of the Nineveh Operations Command. Maliki appointed an excellent Sunni general from Mosul, Lieutenant General Riyadh Jalal Tawfiq, to take over operations in Nineveh. Maliki's forceful intervention was welcome news to the Sunni Arabs who resented Kurdish control over the local government. Maliki also complemented Multi-National Force–Iraq's efforts with some skillful moves with the tribes in many areas north of Baghdad. In our view, the main effort in the campaign was clearly shifting to the north.

Events conspired to prove otherwise. On January 22, 2008, during the Shi'a celebration of Ashura, Jaish al-Mahdi militants attempted to kidnap the Iraqi national security adviser, Dr. Mowaffak al-Rubaie, at a mosque in the Shulah neighborhood of Baghdad. At last Maliki's eyes were opened concerning the intimidation that was occurring outside the well-protected International Zone. The incident turned Rubaie and Maliki against the Jaish al-Mahdi and particularly against its heavily armed Special Groups. After the incident, the two Iraqi leaders went on the warpath against the Iranian-backed militants of the Jaish al-Mahdi Special Groups.

Sadr attempted to calm matters by announcing that he would extend for another six months the cease-fire he had imposed on Jaish al-Mahdi forces the previous August after Maliki had confronted Sadr's forces in Karbala. In fact, Sadr's movement appeared divided and confused. Some elements focused on social services and civic outreach, some competed for political power, while others (some supported by Iran) continued anticoalition violence or engaged in mafia-like criminal activity. The unstable situation carried great risks, but also opportunities for coalition and Iraqi government interlocutors to reach out to Sadrist leaders in an effort to moderate their behavior and encourage constructive political participation among them and their followers.

In late January, Ambassador Crocker stopped in Basra on his way back to the United States. As he reported to President Bush, while in Basra he had a sobering conversation with Iraqi Army General Mohan al-Firayji, Chief of Police Major General Jalil Khalaf, and various tribal sheiks who complained about the deeply entrenched militias and criminal organizations, Iranian penetration of southern Iraq, and insufficient and outgunned Iraqi security forces to counter these threats. The Iraqis sought a surge in Basra similar to that which had cleared Baghdad. General Mohan did not think there would be substantial fighting in Basra, since the city and its oil-rich region represented the "goose that lays the golden eggs" for the Shi'ites in Iraq. The key dynamic was competition among the Sadrists, Badr, and Fadillah for control over oil exports. The president told Ambassador Crocker and General Petraeus to devise a strategy for Basra.

Maliki was one step ahead of Bush. His political flank once again shored up by the grand political compromise of February 2008, Maliki pressed General Mohan for action in Basra. On February 19 Mohan admitted he needed help to rein in the Jaish al-Mahdi and asked his coalition military adviser, British Colonel Richard Iron, to help devise a plan. Iron worked with the British-led Multi-National Division–Southeast and developed a scheme similar to the one used by British forces in Belfast in the 1970s and 1980s. Iraqi forces would be increased numerically and improved qualitatively, and they would deploy over time in a number of company and battalion bases scattered in militia strongholds. Iraqi soldiers and police would staff a large number of fixed vehicle checkpoints throughout the city. The leaders would seek to arm Iraqi forces in Basra with heavier weapons, including tanks. Iraqi security forces would also do more to prevent smuggling of arms from across the Iranian border. After shaping operations lasting several months, Iraqi Army forces would directly confront the Jaish al-Mahdi in the late summer.[10] It was a decent plan, provided the resources and time were available to implement it.

Colonel Iron knew that time was at a premium and the Iraqi Army in Basra would need significant help if the plan was to work, so he jumped several layers of the chain of command and wrote me directly to see whether he could get a concept of the draft plan into the commanding general's office. I forwarded the note to General Petraeus, and he immediately acted on it. He had me arrange a working dinner for Wednesday, March 5, at the Blackhawk Conference Center with General Mohan and Colonel Iron, along with all of the relevant Iraqi and coalition civil and military leaders who had a stake in the plan, including Mowaffak al-Rubaie, the Iraqi national security adviser, the ministers of interior and defense, and the coalition commanders of Multi-National Corps–Iraq and Multi-National Division–Southeast.

Over a feast of lamb kabobs, rice, and other Arabic dishes, the group debated the merits of Mohan's plan. The Iraqis were cool to the idea, claiming that the problem was Mohan's leadership rather than the Jaish al-Mahdi. Multi-National Force–Iraq staffers were likewise lukewarm to the plan, which they viewed as a sequel to the pending surge in Mosul, not as an operation to be conducted simultaneously. General Mohan stressed that the plan was not entirely kinetic, as he realized that his forces were insufficient to combat the militias in Basra. While his forces were being strengthened, he would also focus on the resolution of conflicts between rival political factions and Basra's tribes. General Petraeus, not willing to wait as long as the plan proposed, directed the development of a hybrid plan. He and Rubaie formed a joint Iraqi-coalition committee, cochaired by Lieutenant General James Dubik of Multi-National Security Transition Command–Iraq and General Faruq al-Araji of the Office of the Commander in Chief, to determine what could reasonably be done in a more expeditious fashion with the available resources that could be spared for the effort in the south. A follow-on meeting was planned for just over two weeks later.

As the group assembled again on Friday, March 21, Sadi Othman hit me with a bombshell. The prime minister's office had called and relayed that Prime Minister Maliki wanted to see Ambassador Crocker and General Petraeus the next morning to discuss Basra. The meeting that night went well, but the planning was for naught. Meanwhile, General Petraeus received information that Maliki had issued orders to various Iraqi units to deploy to Basra within forty-eight hours. That information was confirmed when Crocker and Petraeus met Maliki on Saturday morning and the prime minister informed them that he had ordered several Iraqi Army battalions to deploy to Basra. The prime minister had been spooked by unconfirmed reports of militia forces raping women in Basra and carrying out other violent actions, and he was determined to extend Iraqi governmental control throughout Iraq, including the Jaish al-Mahdi strongholds in Basra, Sadr City, and Amarah. Furthermore, he would fly to Basra immediately to personally oversee Iraqi Army operations, accompanied by the ministers of defense and the interior. "Prime Minister Maliki informed us that he intends to go personally to Basra on

Monday, with his AK-47, to meet with local leaders to resolve the situation," General Petraeus informed Secretary of Defense Gates.[11]

The action was similar to Maliki's intervention in Karbala the previous August, which had been a fairly easy win for the prime minister. Maliki no doubt viewed Basra in the same light; the problem in his view was criminality, not insurgency. However, the situation in Basra was much more challenging than the prime minister knew. The prime minister's decision could only be characterized as impulsive: The stage was set for a military and political crisis of the first order. Regardless, when Maliki asked General Petraeus whether he would support the Iraqi operation, Petraeus responded that of course he would, in every way possible, but that he needed for the prime minister to buy a few days. That would allow Lieutenant General Lloyd Austin to reposition various U.S. assets to the south to augment Iraqi and British forces. Maliki pledged to do so, stating that he understood the importance of "setting conditions" before committing Iraqi forces, and that he would conduct several days of political discussions with tribal, government, and security force leaders in Basra before he gave the order to Iraqi forces to enter the city and attack.

Maliki was acting on poor intelligence, and he proved unable or unwilling to stall for the several days that General Petraeus needed for U.S. forces to reposition to support the operation. In the end, Colonel Iron summed up the issue well when he wrote, "None of the pre-conditions that Mohan thought necessary for success was in place."[12] Basra was not the easy target Maliki's advisers painted it out to be. In fact, the prime minister was marching into a hornet's nest. By personally leading the operation, he was staking his political reputation on its results. The move nearly backfired, and indeed, for a short period the hastily planned operation seemed on the verge of failure as the Jaish al-Mahdi fought Iraqi Army forces to a standstill in the urban jungle of Basra's streets. One newly formed brigade of the Iraqi Army's 14th Division stationed in Basra largely dissolved rather than fight, with upward of twelve hundred soldiers deserting the ranks.[13] The 14th Division lacked coalition advisers and therefore links to resources such as intelligence and airpower. The British Army in Iraq had made the decision several years earlier not to embed advisers in Iraqi Army units, a decision that now backfired.[14] Other units, including Iraqi special operations forces, emergency response units, special weapons and tactics units, Iraqi Army reconnaissance elements, and several battalions from al-Anbar province, performed better, despite a critical shortage of supplies and an initial lack of linkage to coalition air power.

Iraqi forces suffered most from a lack of logistical support and firepower. The reason for the former shortcoming was inherent in the manner in which the Iraqi security forces had been created. Due to the crisis caused by the developing insurgency, Multi-National Security Transition Command–Iraq focused first on creating combat units at the expense of logistical infrastructure, with logistical support initially provided by the coalition. The lack of a coherent supply organization was evident in the Basra operation: Iraqi logistical planning amounted to little more than handing sacks of cash to commanders and telling them to buy what they needed on the local economy. However, when military operations began in Basra, the local markets closed and economic activity all but ceased, placing Iraqi forces in a severe bind. And the challenges were compounded when, rather than Maliki's buying a few days' time through discussions with the tribes, as he had pledged, the battle was joined immediately: Iraqi forces found themselves in a fight immediately upon arriving at the outskirts of Basra. Prime Minster Maliki, holed up in Basra Palace and under fire from Jaish al-Mahdi rocket and mortar teams that killed the head of his security detail, was in desperate straits.

General Petraeus, despite being somewhat concerned about the prospects of success when the Iraqi attack began prematurely, was determined to support the Iraqi operation to the full extent of Multi-National Force–Iraq capabilities. He understood that failure in Basra would probably lead to the fall of Maliki's government, with all the turmoil and disruption that would result from such an outcome. He made it clear that Multi-National Force–Iraq was totally committed to helping Maliki and Iraqi forces succeed.

To bolster Iraqi forces in Basra, we first needed a better picture of what was happening on the ground. General Petraeus sent Rear Admiral Edward Winters, a former SEAL team commander, to Basra to serve as his personal liaison to Maliki. Lieutenant General Lloyd Austin, the new Multi-National Corps–Iraq commander, deployed his deputy commander, Marine Major General George Flynn, and the Corps' forward command post to Basra to bolster the British-commanded Multi-National Division–Southeast, help coordinate efforts to support the Iraqi forces there, and provide the communications links to the U.S. assets being rapidly deployed to the south. Multi-National Force–Iraq logistician Steve Anderson assisted the Iraqi military with ramping up the flow of supplies to the forces in Basra, much of which the Iraqis flew south in Iraqi Air Force C-130 cargo planes. Petraeus also ordered U.S. Special Forces teams and a U.S. airborne infantry company to Basra, where it was broken down into smaller elements to help enable Iraqi forces and provide them access to coalition fire support. He then piled on firepower assets, including U.S. Air Force fighters, AC-130 gunships, Apache attack helicopters, and armed Predator drones to overwhelm the militia forces in Basra. For his part, Maliki ordered the experienced 1st Division headquarters and an additional brigade from al-Anbar province (accompanied by its U.S. Marine military advisers) to join the fight down south.[15] After a problematic start to the operation, the tide of battle began to turn. But it had been a close-run affair.

In the end, the British also came through. The acting British commander in southern Iraq, Brigadier Julian Free, realized that the British Army needed to do more to support Iraqi forces in the fight from the British base. With his boss out of the country on leave, he directed the deployment of British advisory teams to link up with the 14th Iraqi Army Division. Significantly, Brigadier Free took this action without asking for political approval; rather, as General Petraeus noted approvingly many times after the battle, Free only informed London of his actions; he did not wait for permission to proceed.[16] That made him Petraeus's kind of guy. Meanwhile, the Iraqi commander in Basra, General Mohan, supported the move after seeing the salutary effect of U.S. Marine advisers on Iraqi Army performance in the fighting and their welcome reception by the city's residents. British forces quickly returned to Basra, supporting the Iraqi units they had trained but until now had not accompanied into combat.[17]

Augmented with coalition advisers, intelligence, and firepower, the Iraqi Army dominated the brave but poorly trained militia fighters. Colonel Richard Iron recorded the outcome of the tactical fight on April 2:

> We found it easy to identify them with drones, and then destroy them one by one with Hellfire missiles. For example, in the al-Latif area of northern Basra, the militia attempted to block the northward movement of the National Police brigade by establishing road blocks and fighting positions around Qarmat Ali Bridge on the main north-south route into Basra. We quickly identified their headquarters and resupply centre in al-Latif school, and that they used a taxi to carry ammunition to their various defensive positions. We simply followed the taxi on the drone camera until we had identified all the positions, and then destroyed them with missiles.
>
> By the end of the day, it was obvious to all who had won. The Iraqi Security Forces had captured all their objectives and the main routes were clear. Although Jaysh al-Mahdi still occupied their strongholds in the urban ghettoes, the initiative had swung dramatically to the Government forces.[18]

After that day, the Jaish al-Mahdi never again contested control of Basra. Sadr's militia was on its heels. For the citizens of Basra, Charge of the Knights brought a palpable sense of relief from the draconian misrule of Shi'a Islamic hard-liners.

The fighting in Basra put Iran on the horns of a dilemma. If the Iranians supported the Jaish al-Mahdi, an organization they hoped to turn into a Hezbollah-like surrogate in Iraq, then they would incur the wrath of the duly elected Iraqi government. On the other hand, if the Iranians backed Maliki's actions against the Jaish al-Mahdi, then they could lose a valuable ally in Iraq. Under some pressure from Iranian interlocutors, Muqtada al-Sadr attempted to squirm out of this predicament by announcing yet another cease-fire.[19] Prime Minister Maliki welcomed the development, but he was far too shrewd to allow the Jaish al-Mahdi to escape the moment of reckoning only to resurface strengthened later. Maliki pocketed the accord, but when the cease-fire expired eleven days later, he ordered his troops to continue to clear the city. With significant backing from U.S. and British forces, during the month of April the Iraqi Army gained control of Basra's neighborhoods and ejected the Jaish al-Mahdi from the city. Maliki extended this victory by swiftly ordering his forces to secure the port of Um Qasr and the oil complex at Zubayr, facilities that had been significant sources of revenue for rogue Shi'a militias, and by reaching out to the tribes of southern Iraq with that trademark Iraqi diplomatic instrument—suitcases full of cash. The prime minster also announced an emergency infusion in Basra of $100 million in aid, which would be used to restore essential services and energize economic activity. The extent of Iranian involvement in Iraq became clear as Iraqi forces uncovered massive caches of Iranian-supplied arms and munitions in the area.[20]

The Jaish al-Mahdi was not about to go down without a fight. On the ropes in Basra, the militia retaliated against coalition and Iraqi government facilities in Baghdad. Attacks in Baghdad jumped nearly fivefold during the first week of operations in Basra. The Jaish al-Mahdi was clearly looking for a fight, as close engagements with better-armed U.S. forces increased eightfold.[21] During the first week of operations in Basra, Jaish al-Mahdi militiamen overran half of the Iraqi police checkpoints in and on the perimeter of Sadr City.[22] Rockets launched from points in Sadr City rained down on the International Zone. One rocket hit the U.S. embassy annex just eighty feet from General Petraeus's office, cascading stone fragments to the ground and knocking out the electricity to the building. The civilians in the building grew nervous and jumpy; those of us who had been under fire before, much less so. With nothing more productive to do while waiting for the restoration of power to the facility, the office staff took impromptu (and very restful) naps at our desks.

After Prime Minister Maliki requested coalition assistance in battling the rocket teams and defeating criminal militia forces, General Petraeus spoke to him about the need to clear Sadr City, and the restrictions Maliki had imposed on coalition operations there the previous fall were lifted. The fight then began in earnest. Multiple unmanned aerial vehicles and attack helicopters, with close air support overhead, prowled the skies over Sadr City, hunting enemy rocket–and-mortar teams. Sadr City, essentially off-limits to coalition military personnel (except for targeted raids) after the operation in October 2007 that killed several dozen militiamen and civilians, now became the scene of intense combat.

Air power alone could not stop the rocket and mortar attacks. The militiamen who launched these munitions had become expert in emplacing their weapons and firing off a volley of rockets or mortars within a matter of minutes, often before drones or aircraft could respond. To stop the attacks, ground forces would have to seize control of the launch sites, most of them southwest of al-Quds Street, or Route Gold as it was marked on U.S. military maps. This mission fell to Colonel John Hort, commander of the 3rd Brigade Combat Team, 4th Infantry Division. John and I had worked together in the mid-1990s as majors in the 11th Armored Cavalry Regiment at the National Training Center in Fort Irwin, California. I remembered him as a hardworking and competent officer. His training and expertise were about to be tested as never before—and he and his brigade came through.

The ground combat operations evolved in two phases. From March 26 until mid-April, infantrymen from the 1st Squadron, 2nd Stryker Cavalry Regiment, and Iraqi forces seized the urban terrain southwest of Route Gold while a combined-arms battalion of the 68th Armored Regiment and Iraqi forces worked to control areas west and north of Sadr City.[23] Jaish al-Mahdi militiamen defended their turf, and although they were nowhere near as well trained or equipped as the U.S. soldiers whom they faced, within a week they had destroyed six Stryker combat vehicles with rocket-propelled grenades.[24] Colonel Hort and his division commander, Major General Jeffrey Hammond, decided to reinforce the Strykers with M1A1 Abrams tanks and M2A2 Bradley infantry fighting vehicles. The tanks, which could withstand the punch from rocket-propelled grenades that the Stryker combat vehicles could not, provided the overmatch that U.S. troops needed to remain in the area.

Nevertheless, militia fighters could still use the warren of streets and alleyways to infiltrate southwest of Route Gold and ambush American and Iraqi forces. To secure the area against enemy attacks, American and Iraqi leaders decided to erect a two-and-a-half-mile-long cement barrier along Route Gold. Operation Gold Wall took nearly a month to complete, but it decided the outcome of the battle for Sadr City. From mid-April to mid-May, U.S. engineers installed nearly three thousand large cement "Alaska" barriers along Route Gold.[25] The Jaish al-Mahdi fought back ferociously, as militia leaders understood that completion of the wall would limit their ability to get to the areas from which they could most accurately hit the International Zone with mortars and rockets; this would in turn reduce their influence on political developments in Iraq. In an interview with Lesley Stahl on the CBS program *60 Minutes,* Colonel Hort stated that "the building of the T-wall became a magnet for every bad guy in Sadr City. . . . It was literally concrete barrier by concrete barrier. We just wasn't [*sic*] goin' out there puttin' up some barriers. I mean, it was a fight every inch of the way."[26] Militia fighters planted 300 roadside bombs, of which 120 exploded against U.S. armored vehicles.[27] On particularly bad days only eight slabs of concrete went up.

But this was exactly the kind of fight the U.S. military could win in a walkover. Navy SEAL sniper teams augmented Hort's troops. U.S. Air Force fighter jets and armed Predator drones, along with U.S. Army Apache attack helicopters, provided close air support. U.S. soldiers countered militia snipers with more than eight hundred rounds of tank fire and more than twelve thousand rounds of 25mm Bushmaster chain gunfire—putting the lie to contention that the surge was nothing more than a futile exercise in winning hearts and minds and nation building. A variety of high-tech instruments were employed to overwhelm the enemy, but the key was improved intelligence that flowed to the units and leaders directly in the fight.[28] Colonel Hort and his brigade had access to vastly more reconnaissance assets than entire divisions had at the start of the war in 2003. Shadow unmanned aerial vehicles and other intelligence, surveillance, and reconnaissance assets identified and tracked militia fighters, while armed Predator drones and Apache attack helicopters rained Hellfire missiles down from sky to earth to destroy them. By mid-May, the Jaish al-Mahdi was a spent force, its rank and file decimated and its leaders either dead, in hiding, or in self-imposed exile in Iran.

On May 12 Sadr threw in the towel and declared another cease-fire, the fifth one he had announced since the first Jaish al-Mahdi uprising in April 2004. Once again, Prime Minister Maliki was not about to allow Sadr's militia to regenerate in safe havens as it had done so many times before. His toughness in the face of adversity astonished his friends and enemies alike.

The failure of the British forces in securing Basra from 2003 to 2008 was not due to any lack of courage or competence on the part of British soldiers, who had both qualities in abundance. Rather, the failure was strategic and operational, a shortcoming of political and military leadership at the highest levels. In an article in *British Army Review* in 2009, I wrote an epitaph to the British operations in southern Iraq:

> As the British people lost the will to fight at home, British forces were hampered by political constraints thrust upon them by an unsympathetic government, which insisted on running operations from Whitehall rather than nesting them into the Multi-National Force–Iraq campaign. Instead, British commanders attempted to cut deals with local Shi'ite leaders to maintain the peace in southern Iraq, an accommodation that was doomed to failure since the British negotiated from a position of weakness—a fact well known to the Shi'ite leadership. The failure to adopt an alternative approach, one that relied on the conduct of operations based on protecting the Iraqi people, led to a defeat that thankfully was not permanent.[29]

British leaders failed to understand the political dynamics at play in southern Iraq, and were increasingly reluctant to risk blood and treasure to conduct an effective counterinsurgency campaign as the British people turned against the war. The results of this dynamic were political constraints that reduced British forces to unrealistic force levels given the goals of the campaign, then shackled them to rules of engagement that prohibited British troops from conducting the kinds of operations, such as embedded advisory duty, needed to get a grip on the Jaish al-Mahdi in Basra.

Colonel Richard Iron likewise analyzed the outcome of the campaign in Basra and came to similar conclusions regarding what went wrong. By 2007 the British had concluded—incorrectly—that coalition forces were the reason for militia violence in Basra. Since nine out of every ten attacks in the city were against British forces, the reasoning went, if British forces just pulled out of Basra, then everything would be fine. The logic, based on the notion that the war centered on coalition forces, was flawed. If British leaders had viewed the conflict through the Iraqi lens, Colonel Iron notes, they would have seen that "90 per cent of attacks were against us because we were the only ones contesting control of the city on behalf of the [Iraqi] Government. Once we left, we ceded not just British control, but the Government of Iraq's control too, whom we were supposed to be supporting. By looking at the problem through the single lens of the reaction to the invader, we lost sight of what we were really supposed to be doing: helping the legally constituted, democratically elected, Government of Iraq establish its legitimate authority in Basra."[30]

The second flawed assumption was that the main problem in Basra was criminality, not insurgency: that Basra was more like Palermo than Beirut. What British analysts missed was the connection between organized crime and Shi'a militia organizations like the Jaish al-Mahdi. Crimes such as smuggling bankrolled the insurgents' operations and should not have been viewed, as British analysts who had cut their teeth in Northern Ireland viewed them, as "decent honest crime."[31] And then there was the Iranian connection. As Colonel Iron relates, "When we started questioning captured Jaysh al-Mahdi insurgents during Charge of the Knights, one of the recurring themes was their training in Iran. Many of their trainers were Lebanese Hezbollah, returning experts to train new insurgents under the aegis of the Revolutionary Guards. So not only was it not Palermo, it really *was* like Beirut."[32]

The third conceptual failure was the misreading of the depth of malign Iranian influence in southern Iraq. "Although our intelligence throughout stressed the anti-Iranian credentials of Moqtada al-Sadr and his Jaysh al-Mahdi," Colonel Iron writes, "the reality was that they were heavily dependent on Iran. It is inconceivable that Moqtada could run his organisation from Iran, train his insurgents in Iranian-run training camps, or provide them with Iranian-supplied weapons, without explicit support from Iranian Revolutionary Guards."[33] Iran wanted to keep Iraq pliant and weak. The Jaish al-Mahdi was one of the tools used by Iran to accomplish this goal.

The final failure was in believing that the Iraqi military needed to be cut loose from coalition support to force it to learn how to get by on its own. Instead of teaching Iraqi forces how to cope, the failure to support them in their efforts to secure Basra resulted in militia dominance over poorly supplied and inadequately trained forces. The Iraqis, for instance, needed fortification material (known as Hesco bastions) to complete their outposts inside Basra. General Mohan asked Colonel Iron for help, but British commanders refused to release any matériel from their stockpiles. The Iraqis needed to learn how to acquire what they needed through their own system, the thinking went. "I knew we had 24 km of Hesco in our engineer resources yard, but I couldn't get the British to release any," Colonel Iron laments. "The British answer was if we helped them now they'd never learn. Meanwhile, nearly every night Iraqi soldiers were being killed and injured guarding half-completed forts as Jaysh al-Mahdi tried to destroy them, fully understanding what these forts meant: if they were completed, the Iraqi Army would be able to wrest back control of the city from the militia. Not helping the Iraqi Army in their hour of need is not one of our proudest moments."[34]

To be fair, British political and military leaders finally realized their mistakes during Charge of the Knights and reversed the policies that had kept British forces from adequately supporting Iraqi forces in Basra. Brigadier Free's order to send advisory teams into the city ranked as a particularly courageous action. Regrettably, the realization came much too late that the key to victory in Basra was not to hand over the battle to insufficiently armed and trained Iraqi forces but to support them with British advisory teams, technical capabilities, logistics, and firepower. "Our model of forcing Iraqi self-reliance by not helping was completely wrong," Colonel Iron concludes. "We should have [instead] focused on winning the war."[35]

Whatever the military merits of tackling the Jaish al-Mahdi in Basra before finishing the fight against al-Qaeda in Mosul, Prime Minister Maliki had acted decisively in an area of vital concern to his government and the Iraqi state. "In some sense, Maliki is doing what we have sought to empower him to do: use Iraqi forces to respond to an Iraqi security problem in a province that has been transitioned to Provincial Iraqi Control," General Petraeus wrote to Secretary of Defense Gates.[36] Not surprisingly, Maliki had a much better handle on the internal politics of Iraq than we did. He had proven that a Shi'a Iraqi prime minister could tackle the challenges presented by rogue Shi'a militias, at least if he had robust coalition support. Moreover, after a week of vacillation and political intrigue at the start of the Basra operation, the Presidency Council came out publicly in support of Maliki and called for a reorganized unity government under his leadership. General Petraeus relayed the news to Secretary of Defense Gates in his weekly report:

> Faced with a choice between Maliki and the Sadrists, the major parties unanimously chose to back Maliki, and expressed their new unity in the Political Committee on National Security pronouncement on April 5 that said that no Iraqi party with a militia would be allowed to participate in elections. Faced with unprecedented opposition, the Sadrist members of parliament began to realize their isolation. In contrast to the vulnerability perceived by the Sadrists, the Prime Minister and the major parties now enjoy a sense of relative union and strength. Convinced that popular opinion is with them, they are taking steps and making statements against the Sadrists that would have been unthinkable a few months ago.[37]

Maliki had succeeded in changing the political dynamics in Baghdad, isolating the Sadrists, and harnessing increased support for his government.

Of course, Iraqi and coalition operations were not designed to destroy the entire structure of the Jaish al-Mahdi, only those portions of it that were beholden to the Iranian Qods force or could not be reconciled with a nonviolent political solution to Iraqi governance. General Petraeus made this clear in a report to Secretary of Defense Gates at the height of the fighting in Sadr City:

> Our basic approach remains constant—partner with the Iraqis to bring as many reconcilable members of the Sadr movement into the political process as possible. To this end, we will continue our own engagement, taking care not to get too far out in front of the Iraqi government. We will also press for progress in Iraqi humanitarian assistance and reconstruction in recent conflict areas. Open warfare between the Iraqi government and the entire Sadrist movement is still not in anyone's best interest.[38]

In the labyrinth of Iraqi politics, Petraeus recognized, yesterday's enemies could become tomorrow's allies. (That later turned out to be the case between Maliki and Sadr, who joined forces after the 2010 elections to dominate the Iraqi government.)

While the crisis in Basra played out, Ambassador Crocker, General Petraeus, and their staffs traveled to Washington, D.C., for another round of congressional testimony on April 8–9. Although the testimony occurred amid the backdrop of the presidential primary season, the atmosphere was somewhat less intense than the previous September. The surge was clearly coming to an end in the near future, and negotiations were ongoing regarding coalition troop presence in Iraq after the United Nations Security Council Resolution expired at the end of the year. The question now was the pace of the drawdown, not whether to begin one.

Senator Carl Levin (D-MI), chairman of the Senate Armed Services Committee, opened the hearings. He used the recent fighting in Basra to bash the Bush administration's policy in Iraq, claiming that the fighting raised questions about the success of the surge and showed that civil conflict in Iraq was growing. He contended that the administration's policy allowed Iraqi leaders to avoid making the tough decisions necessary to achieve reconciliation and bring the civil conflict to an end. A pause in troop withdrawals in July would send the wrong message to Iraqi leaders. Furthermore, American taxpayers were being asked to bankroll reconstruction operations that the Iraqis were quite capable of paying for themselves, a point aggravated by gas prices that were approaching four dollars per gallon for the first time in history. Prime Minister Maliki's "incompetence and excessively sectarian leadership" jeopardized the little progress on reconciliation that had been made to date. "Last week, this incompetence was dramatized in the military operation in Basra," Senator Levin continued. "Far from being the defining moment that President Bush described, it was a haphazardly planned operation, carried out apparently without meaningful consultation with the U.S. military or even key Iraqi leaders, while Maliki made unrealistic claims, promises and threats."[39] The senator was correct on every point except the main one. Against all odds, the Basra operation proved to be a defining moment in the Iraq War. It was just too early to evaluate it as such.

Senator John McCain (R-AZ), the ranking minority member and a presidential candidate, highlighted the progress the surge had made in pulling Iraq back from the brink. Indeed, he had staked his campaign on support for the surge. "But today it is possible to talk with real hope and optimism about the future of Iraq and the outcome of our efforts there," the senator intoned. "For while the job of bringing security to Iraq is not finished, as the recent fighting in Basra and elsewhere vividly demonstrated, we're no longer staring into the abyss of defeat and we can now look ahead to the genuine prospect of success." Americans needed to reject calls for a "reckless and irresponsible" withdrawal of U.S. forces from Iraq, he said, making a clear jab at the Democratic presidential candidates who were competing with one another to tell primary voters how quickly they would withdraw U.S. forces from Iraq if elected president.

It was then General Petraeus's turn at the microphone. As we had the previous September, the staff and I sat directly behind General Petraeus to take in the proceedings with front-row seats. It was another heady moment for those of us who had been so intimately involved in crafting the congressional testimony in the weeks before the hearings. In his opening statement, General Petraeus remarked on the improvement being made in reducing ethnosectarian violence in Iraq, but he noted that while the progress was significant, it was uneven, fragile, and reversible. Four major factors accounted for the progress, he said: the surge of U.S. and Iraqi forces since January 2007, the employment of those forces in a concerted counterinsurgency campaign to protect the Iraqi people, the Sunni Awakening and the concomitant creation of the Sons of Iraq, and Muqtada al-Sadr's cease-fire order of August 2007 (only recently broken and then renewed). One wild card in Iraq's future was the extent of Iranian involvement, recently highlighted by the fighting in Basra. "Though a Sadr stand-down order resolved the situation to a degree, the flare-up also highlighted the destructive role Iran has played in funding, training, arming, and directing the so-called Special Groups and generated renewed concern about Iran in the minds of many Iraqi leaders. Unchecked, the Special Groups pose the greatest long-term threat to the viability of a democratic Iraq," Petraeus remarked. He also noted that while Syria had taken some steps to reduce the flow of foreign fighters through its territory, it had not done enough to shut down the network that supported al-Qaeda in Iraq. Despite these headwinds and the lack of Iraqi government capacity, the competition for power and resources in Iraq was increasingly channeled into political dialogue rather than armed confrontation.

A series of slides then displayed graphically the situation in Iraq and the progress made in stemming ethnosectarian violence since the beginning of the surge. Security incidents had dropped to early-2005 levels, and civilian deaths had dropped to the levels that existed before the bombing of the al-Askari shrine in February 2006. Violence in Baghdad had decreased dramatically, especially in mixed-sectarian areas (which, despite the claims of pundits, still existed). Incidents of car bombings and suicide attacks were still too high but had been cut in half since the beginning of the surge. The growth of the Sons of Iraq, with more than ninety-one thousand Iraqi citizens (Shi'a as well as Sunni) under contract, showed that Iraqi tribes and communities were stepping forward to protect their areas despite death threats from al-Qaeda terrorists. Local intelligence provided by the Sons of Iraq and ordinary citizens had allowed U.S. and Iraq forces to quadruple the number of arms and ammunition caches discovered since the beginning of the surge. Al-Qaeda was losing ground in Iraq, and although the organization still had some strength in the Mosul area, it had lost its sanctuaries in al-Anbar province and elsewhere in Iraq.[40]

General Petraeus also highlighted the growth of Iraqi security forces and their qualitative improvement. Half of Iraq's eighteen provinces were now under Iraqi control. Iraqi security forces now numbered more than 540,000 servicemen and women, with more than one hundred Iraqi combat battalions now capable of taking the lead in operations. In the past sixteen months Iraqi forces had grown by 133,000 soldiers and police, which meant that the Iraqi surge dwarfed that of U.S. forces. Iraqi Army and police casualties were triple those of coalition forces, so Iraqis were clearly fighting and dying for their country. The fighting in Basra had, indeed, exposed weaknesses in some units, but others fought well and gained confidence as a result. Nevertheless, the lack of logistical wherewithal, force enablers, staff development, and command and control would require more attention in the months and years ahead.

One of the more important slides General Petraeus presented was entitled "Anaconda Strategy vs. AQI." This slide summed up his thoughts on how to defeat the al-Qaeda terrorist franchise in Iraq through relentless pressure in multiple areas. He had designed it to rebut the arguments of those who said that special operations and counterterrorist forces alone could achieve our objectives in Iraq; rather, Petraeus explained, a comprehensive civil-military approach was required—one in which special operations forces contributed important capabilities, but one that also required the engagement of all elements of military and civilian power. As the slide depicted, to survive, an extremist or insurgent organization needed access to money, foreign fighters, and weapons, and it also required a command and control system to propagate senior leader guidance and ideology. Popular support was a plus, but more important were safe havens in which terrorists cells could operate with impunity. Countering al-Qaeda necessitated a broad, interagency approach to strategy and not just kinetic counterterrorist operations, as many members of Congress believed. Conventional forces, coalition and Iraqi, were needed to clear and hold areas controlled by the insurgents. A robust training and equipping effort was required to help develop Iraqi security forces. Interagency assets were needed to work with source and transit countries to reduce foreign fighter flow, conduct strategic communications (public diplomacy) and information operations, and monitor the Internet for terrorist Web sites and communications. U.S. diplomats and military leaders were essential in the effort to encourage tribal awakenings and political reconciliation in conflict areas. Fusion of intelligence from a variety of sources was the key to effective kinetic operations, which required both special and conventional forces working together to achieve maximum effect. Nonkinetic "nation building" assistance was necessary in fostering the creation of jobs, essential services, and education, and in the conduct of religious engagement. Finally, counterinsurgency "inside the wire"—inside detention facilities—was required to create rehabilitation centers that would turn reconcilables into supporters of legitimate government bodies.[41]

General Petraeus also focused on nefarious Iranian involvement in Iraq, specifically, on Iranian support for the Special Groups of the Jaish al-Mahdi. Regarding the Special Groups, he stated:

> These elements are funded, trained, armed, and directed by Iran's Qods Force, with help from Lebanese Hezbollah. It was these groups that launched Iranian rockets and mortar rounds at Iraq's seat of government two weeks ago, causing loss of innocent life and fear in the capital, and requiring Iraqi and Coalition actions in response. Iraqi and Coalition leaders have repeatedly noted their desire that Iran live up to promises made by President Ahmedinajad and other senior Iranian leaders to stop their support for the Special Groups. However, nefarious activities by the Qods Force have continued, and Iraqi leaders now clearly recognize the threat they pose to Iraq. We should all watch Iranian actions closely in the weeks and months ahead, as they will show the kind of relationship Iran wishes to have with its neighbor and the character of future Iranian involvement in Iraq.

Given past Iranian behavior, we were not sanguine about the chances of Iran acting in a responsible manner toward its Iraqi neighbors, but the diplomatic door still needed to be left ajar, if only slightly.

General Petraeus concluded his testimony with various recommendations. He encouraged Congress to pass additional funding for the Commander's Emergency Relief Program, or CERP, needed to pay salaries for the Sons of Iraq. Given the improvements in security brought about by these organizations, the salaries paid to keep them in business were more than repaid by the vehicles and personnel saved from destruction through their services. General Petraeus relayed his recommendations to Secretary of Defense Gates and President Bush that the drawdown of the surge brigades continue until complete in July, followed by a forty-five-day pause to assess the situation and determine whether additional withdrawals were warranted. This recommendation gave the commander in Iraq maximum flexibility to protect the gains made by the surge, rather than withdrawing forces on a more politically convenient, fixed timetable. "With this approach," General Petraeus concluded, "the security achievements of 2007 and early 2008 can form a foundation for the gradual establishment of sustainable security in Iraq. This is not only important to the 27 million citizens of Iraq; it is also vitally important to those in the Gulf region, to the citizens of the United States, and to the global community. It clearly is in our national interest to help Iraq prevent the resurgence of Al Qaeda in the heart of the Arab world, to help Iraq resist Iranian encroachment on its sovereignty, to avoid renewed ethno-sectarian violence that could spill over Iraq's borders and make the existing refugee crisis even worse, and to enable Iraq to expand its role in the regional and global economies."

Ambassador Crocker was next. He reaffirmed his belief that political, economic, and diplomatic progress, albeit slow and uneven, was being made in Iraq. Continuing U.S. commitment was necessary to ensure that progress would continue into the future. He noted the passage of a number of key laws in recent months—a pension law, de-Ba'athification reform, amnesty legislation, a national budget, redesign of the Iraqi flag, and a provincial powers law—that advanced the cause of reconciliation. Provincial elections would occur in the fall (these were later delayed until January 31, 2009). The Iraqi Council of Representatives, while not a perfect institution, was debating complex issues and producing compromise legislation. The Iraqi people were increasingly rejecting extremism, and while Iraqi politics still had a sectarian bent, they were becoming more fluid. "The security improvements of the past months have diminished the atmosphere of suspicion and allowed for acts of humanity that transcend sectarian identities," the ambassador noted. He also countered accusations that the fighting in Basra showed that the surge had failed, noting that Maliki's actions showed instead that a Shi'a-majority government could tackle militias regardless of sectarian affiliation, that Iraqi security forces could take the lead in conducting operations (albeit with substantial coalition support), and most important, that the Basra operation had shaken up Iraqi politics by isolating the Sadrists. In short, by making possible the return of political activity and government based on issues rather than sectarian affiliation, the surge was working as intended.

Crocker also alluded to the next step in the U.S.-Iraqi relationship: the drafting of a status-of-forces agreement and strategic framework agreement that would govern relations after the expiration of the United Nations Security Council Resolution at the end of the year. The Bush administration would conclude these agreements to ensure the next president entered office "with a stable foundation upon which to base policy decisions."

Despite the progress made, Crocker acknowledged the challenges that remained. The Iraqi government remained politically unbalanced and prone to corruption. Boundary disputes over Kirkuk threatened to stoke Kurd-Arab tensions. Millions of refugees and internally displaced persons had to be resettled. The rights of women and minorities had to be protected. Hydrocarbon and oil rev-

enue–sharing legislation was still required to govern Iraq's all-important oil industry. Electrical production was not up to the increased demand of Iraqi consumers
(although unsaid was that until the Iraqi government forced people to pay for electricity rather than distributing it free of charge, demand would always exceed supply). The agricultural sector needed structural improvements. Although there had
been some improvement in the economy and the provision of essential services,
more needed to be done in these areas. Nevertheless, inflation had been tamed, the
dinar remained strong, oil exports were expanding, and the Iraqi budget for reconstruction was growing. The U.S. network of twenty-five provincial reconstruction teams and ministerial advisers was assisting with capacity development, budget execution, and improved governance, using primarily Iraqi resources rather
than U.S. taxpayer dollars. Although Arab governments were lagging in sending
ambassadors to Baghdad, and tensions remained along the northern border with
Turkey, various diplomatic initiatives were assisting Iraq with debt relief, refugees,
and Article 140 (status of Kirkuk) issues. Iran was playing a particularly unhelpful role in Iraq, supporting the training of "criminal militia elements" that were a
destabilizing factor.

"Iraq has the potential to develop into a stable, secure, multiethnic, multi-sectarian democracy under the rule of law," Crocker stated. "Whether it realizes that
potential is ultimately up to the Iraqi people. Our support, however, will continue
to be critical." The alternative, to cast Iraq adrift, would result in the rejuvenation of al-Qaeda in Iraq, the strengthening of the Iranian role in Iraqi affairs, the
growth of Sh'ia militias, increased suffering of the Iraqi people, and the possibility
of a regional struggle that would enmesh the heart of the Middle East in sectarian
conflict. "Mr. Chairman, as monumental as the events of the last five years have
been in Iraq, Iraqis, Americans and the world ultimately will judge us far more on
the basis of what will happen than what has happened," Crocker concluded. "In
the end, how we leave and what we leave behind will be more important than how
we came." This perceptive statement was more prescient than any of us could have
imagined at that moment.

It was the turn of the senators to ask questions. The Democrats focused on the
withdrawal timeline, the lack of political reconciliation in Iraq, the administration's seemingly open-ended commitment there, the strain of continued deployments on U.S. Army and Marine forces, the monetary cost of the war to U.S. taxpayers, the perceived failure of the Basra operation, and the diversion of resources
from the war against al-Qaeda in Afghanistan and Pakistan, while the Republicans focused on the gains made to date by the surge and the risks in withdrawing
American forces too quickly and allowing Iraq to collapse into a failed state. The
continued hammering on the perceived failure of the Basra operation, an operation that turned out to be a huge strategic success, showed once again why the
framers of the Constitution gave executive authority over the armed forces and

foreign affairs to the president and the executive branch of government, and not to Congress.

The pattern of questioning was similar for the Senate Armed Services and Foreign Relations Committees on April 8 and the House Armed Services and Foreign Relations Committees the following day. Various demonstrators against the war, like the chorus in a Greek tragedy, added their voices to the proceedings but did not disrupt them for long.

True to form, the presidential candidates did more speechifying than questioning. Everyone knew that no change in American policy in Iraq would occur until the next year, after the presidential election determined who would lead the United States for the next four years, as well as the composition of the incoming Congress.

As if to cement in my mind the progress made by U.S. and Iraqi forces during the surge, on Monday, April 21, General Petraeus visited Karmah in Anbar province, the scene of a major operation by the Ready First Combat Team, which I commanded, back in September 2003. The town in the intervening period had turned into a significant al-Qaeda safe haven, but it was now sufficiently secure that General Petraeus could walk down the main street with his small protective detail. The market had revived and the town leaders were unanimous in their condemnation of the terrorist group that had oppressed them for many years.

As gratifying as this development was, my time with General Petraeus was drawing to a close. After fifteen months in Iraq, I would redeploy in early May to begin my transition out of the U.S. Army and into a life in academia at the Ohio State University. In fact, beginning late in 2007 there was a wholesale turnover in General Petraeus's staff. I fretted that we would not be able to find replacements for the exceptional team we had gathered the previous year, but I need not have worried. The incoming team was every bit as talented as the outgoing team. Colonel Mike Bell, a fellow West Point History Department alumnus with a Ph.D. from the University of Maryland, replaced Bill Rapp as head of the Commander's Initiatives Group. Janel Voth, a hard-driving military policewoman, replaced Captain Hanna Mora as the scheduler. Haley Dennison, a West Point graduate who had recently lost her husband in combat, replaced Captain Kelly Howard as the operations officer. The new speechwriter was Erica Borggren, the top graduate in her West Point class and like Liz McNally, a Rhodes scholar. After reviewing a number of outstanding officers, General Petraeus chose as my replacement Colonel Bjarne "Mike" Iverson, a Middle East foreign area officer who had lived in the Middle East for thirteen years, had served several combat tours in Iraq, and was fluent in conversational Arabic. Unlike our transition with the outgoing team at the beginning of the surge, we brought these officers in for a full thirty-day overlap, with complete transparency. The transition was as seamless as we could make it.

On May 8, 2008, I left Iraq for good. Having said good-bye to General Petraeus the night before, I sent him a farewell e-mail. I wrote, "Sir, as I head out the door, I leave you not with Rudyard Kipling, but with Bobby Knight:

When my time on Earth is gone
and my activities here are passed
I want them to bury me upside down
so my critics can kiss my ass.

Don't listen to the naysayers who say that Iraq is a lost cause. Like Grant, keep whittling away—remember it's not just about what the enemy can do to us, but also about what we can do to the enemy!" The general's reply was brief and on the mark: "Lick 'em tomorrow!" My farewell present from the staff was a hatchet engraved "Hatchet Man."

In the evening I boarded a plane for the first of a series of flights home. As if I needed any reminders that I was no longer working for one of the most powerful military officers in the nation, my travel home took three days and at the end of it all, my duffel bag ended up in Fort Benning, Georgia, while I returned to my family in Fort Leavenworth, Kansas. My journey with General David Petraeus had come to an end.

The surge continued until mid-July 2008. As Prime Minster Maliki successfully wielded his power and leveraged coalition assistance to force the Jaish al-Mahdi to comply with his orders to cease its attacks, the increasingly effective Iraqi Army moved to secure militia safe havens in Sadr City and Maysan province. In the second week of May, Maliki unleashed U.S. and British special operations forces to conduct raids into Sadr City and Maysan province to kill or capture Special Groups leaders, which put great pressure on the Jaish al-Mahdi to back down.[42] Shaken militia leaders abandoned their followers to flee to Iran.[43] In an operation planned by Lieutenant General Abud and the Baghdad Operations Command, on May 20 the Iraqi Army's 44th Brigade, augmented by other elements, moved across Route Gold and occupied the remainder of Sadr City, unchallenged by the militia fighters. Jaish al-Mahdi fighters, increasingly leaderless and perhaps over-whelmed by continued raids and aerial attacks, and now confronting not just U.S. forces but their own countrymen, abided by Sadr's cease-fire declaration. For the first time since the fall of Baghdad in April 2003, the Iraqi government was in charge of all areas in the capital city.

The last major Jaish al-Mahdi urban stronghold to fall was the city of Amarah, the capital of Maysan province in southern Iraq. The city's proximity to Iran made it especially critical in stemming malign Iranian influence in Iraq. "Over the longer term, the success of Coalition and Iraqi efforts to secure southern Iraq from criminal gangs, illegal militias, and Iranian-supported SGs [Special Groups] will depend on stopping the flow of lethal aid from Iran," wrote General Petraeus to

Secretary of Defense Gates on June 9. "Most senior SG leaders have now fled to Iran, and reporting indicates that the Iranians are working to enhance their training and effectiveness."[44] Iraqi Army forces entered Amarah unopposed on June 19, ending their conventional military operations against the Jaish al-Mahdi. The atmospherics were encouraging that the Iraqi forces would hold the city. On the Yugoslav Bridge in downtown Amarah, a militia fighter had scrawled, "We'll be back." Below it, an Iraqi soldier replied, "We'll be waiting for you."[45]

The security situation in southern Iraq and Baghdad had now stabilized, while operations in Nineveh province continued apace. In July, Iraqi military forces began major clearing operations in Diyala province, with excellent results. Iraqi and U.S. special operations forces continued their raids against al-Qaeda operatives, which kept the terrorist group on its heels. The situation was conducive to the end of the surge operations that had done so much to improve security in Iraq. As the surge concluded, General Petraeus published updated counterinsurgency guidance, which was meant to capture the lessons of the past eighteen months of fighting.[46]

By mid-July the final surge brigade withdrew from Iraq. The situation by this time had improved dramatically. The number of security incidents in Iraq in July 2008 (roughly 250 per week) mirrored the number of incidents in early 2004, after the defeat of the first insurgent Ramadan offensive and the capture of Saddam Hussein made political progress possible.[47] U.S. political and military leaders had failed to capitalize on the earlier window of opportunity, which ended with the April 2004 uprisings. It remained to be seen whether Iraqi and U.S. leaders would do any better this time around, but the early indications were promising. On a positive note, the Sunni Tawafuq coalition returned its ministers to the government, ending a boycott that had stymied political progress in recent months. Ambassador Crocker and General Petraeus deemed the near-term objectives of the campaign plan met and mandated the beginning of a change in emphasis from protecting the population to assisting Iraqi security forces and civil institutions in maintaining an acceptable level of security with reduced coalition involvement.[48]

With the military situation well in hand, the spotlight moved to political negotiations over the strategic framework and status-of-forces agreements. The negotiations were volatile, with both Muqtada al-Sadr and Iran using them to fan the flames of Iraqi nationalism in an effort to force U.S. withdrawal from Iraq.[49] Prime Minister Maliki's shifting position on the negotiations reflected the domestic and foreign pressure he was under.[50] The prime minister did not want the stigma of agreeing to a continued presence of foreign forces on Iraqi soil to be his alone, so he demanded that the Council of Representatives ratify any agreement. He played hardball in the negotiations, overestimating the capabilities of Iraqi security forces and perhaps fearful as well of Iranian pressure.[51] But in the end he was unwilling to allow U.S. forces to depart at the end of 2008, as they would have done absent an agreement.

On November 17, 2008, Ambassador Crocker and Iraqi Foreign Minister Hoshyar Zebari signed the strategic framework and status-of-forces agreements, the latter formally entitled the "Agreement between the United States of America and Republic of Iraq on the Withdrawal of United States Forces from Iraq and the Organization of Their Activities during Their Temporary Presence in Iraq." The political message to the Iraqi people was clear enough—Iraq had exercised its sovereignty, and if Iraqi leaders wished, the tenure of U.S. forces on Iraqi soil was finite. Civilian contractors not under U.S. military control would now fall under Iraqi jurisdiction, and U.S. military and civilian personnel would come under Iraqi jurisdiction when committing "grave premeditated felonies" while off-duty and outside agreed-upon facilities and areas (conditions that made Iraqi jurisdiction extremely unlikely). U.S. combat forces would withdraw from Iraqi cities and villages by the end of June 2009, while all U.S. forces would withdraw from Iraq by the end of 2011.[52] The withdrawal date, three years into the future, presumably would provide enough time to negotiate a longer-term agreement for a continued presence of U.S. forces in Iraq to assist with such matters as counterterrorism, intelligence, logistics, and training. Sadly, this failed to happen.

In my last appearance in uniform before retiring, CBS reporter Lara Logan questioned me about the impact of the events in Basra during the Charge of the Knights. During the interview, which appeared on the CBS program *60 Minutes* on Sunday, February 22, 2009, I ventured that historians would look back and see the events of the spring of 2008 as a turning point in the Iraq War, the point at which the Iraqi government began to own the conflict.[53] Before this operation, General Petraeus and other senior Iraqi and U.S. military leaders believed the way ahead involved a major operation in Mosul in northern Iraq to continue the destruction of al-Qaeda, complemented in Basra by a methodical counterinsurgency campaign to clear the city in much the same manner that U.S. forces had cleared Ramadi in 2006 and 2007. But proving the Prussian military philosopher Carl von Clausewitz's contention that war is an extension of policy, Prime Minister Nouri al-Maliki changed the military equation by ordering Iraqi forces south to Basra to confront the Jaish al-Mahdi militants who had taken over large parts of the city. U.S. military leaders, focused on crushing al-Qaeda, only belatedly realized that the prime minister's political calculations were different from those that up to then had driven the military campaign in Iraq.

As General Petraeus realized, war is not a linear phenomenon. Instead of trying to talk the prime minister out of the hastily planned operation, Petraeus immediately decided to support it with all of the assets at his disposal. Consequently, what appeared in its first few days to be a potential disaster instead turned into one of the greatest victories in the Iraq War, the point at which Iraqi political leaders began to believe that a government led by a Shi'a prime minister could indeed serve the best interests of the nation as a whole. Whatever the merits of that political calculation, it was the perception at the time that counted. As the surge ended and the Bush administration left office, the Iraqi people looked forward with renewed confidence to the complete exercise of their sovereignty and the next set of elections that would, they hoped, usher in a government more fully representative of their interests.

CHAPTER 10

The Surge in Retrospect

Let us learn our lessons. Never, never, never believe any war will be smooth and easy, or that anyone who embarks on the strange voyage can measure the tides and hurricanes he will encounter. The Statesman who yields to war fever must realize that once the signal is given, he is no longer the master of policy but the slave of unforeseeable and uncontrollable events. Antiquated War Offices, weak, incompetent or arrogant commanders, untrustworthy allies, hostile neutrals, malignant Fortune, ugly surprises, awful miscalculations—all take their seats at the Council Board on the morrow of a declaration of war.
—Winston Churchill

War is a contest of wills. In late 2006, after nearly four years of drift in U.S. strategy, President George W. Bush decided to stake his administration's legacy on the outcome of the war in Iraq. His determination to succeed in a conflict of choice gave renewed purpose and authority to the surge. Had the president wavered, the U.S. effort in Iraq would have ended in ignominious defeat, one largely of our own making. In the moment of crisis, President Bush grasped the levers of power and decisively exercised the powers of his office to change course in a difficult and frustrating conflict. He did so while battling against strong political headwinds, both at home and overseas. In January 2007 the ultimate outcome of the war was uncertain at best. Most onlookers gave the surge a small chance of success, if any at all.

Yet against all odds, the surge succeeded. In truth, two surges succeeded: the surge of ideas—the new concept for the employment of forces; and the surge of forces—the reinforcements that enabled the implementation of the new strategy quickly enough for General Petraeus to report significant progress to Congress in September 2007 (without which the policy would have collapsed). By the end of the surge in July 2008, violence in Iraq had been reduced by more than 90 percent—to levels that existed in early 2004, after the defeat of the first insurgent Ramadan offensive and the capture of Saddam Hussein had taken the wind out of the sails of the early insurgency. Al-Qaeda in Iraq had been reduced considerably, marking the first significant setback for the legions of Osama bin Laden outside South Asia, one made even more significant by the fact that much of the credit lay with Sunni tribesmen, supported and empowered by the U.S.-led coalition, who had simply had enough of the terrorist brutality and rejected outright the Islamist political program. The surge reduced violence in Iraq to a level conducive to the resumption of political discourse, which was its goal. Indeed, by the summer of 2008 when the surge ended, Iraqi politics had finally become unstuck from the gridlock of the previous half-decade of conflict. When Iraqis of all sects, ethnicities, and political persuasions decided that the way ahead lay through debate in political bodies and the ballot box, then politics once again became the operative mechanism through which disputes over power and resources could be adjudicated. That the subsequent history of Iraq has not turned out to be as peaceful nor as politically productive as one would have hoped has had more to do with how U.S. policy makers and their Iraqi counterparts fumbled the political endgame than with the concept or military outcome of the surge itself.[1]

The conflict in Iraq was a war of choice begun badly for vague strategic reasons and then nearly lost. Indeed, some commentators contend that early U.S. strategic failures doomed any counterinsurgency campaign from the start.[2] The war was, in many respects, a bloody trial for the Iraqi people, more than 116,000 of whom died in the ensuing hostilities.[3] But just because a war begins badly does not mean it has to end in tragedy. As counterinsurgency expert David Kilcullen once noted, "Just because you invade a place stupidly doesn't mean you have to leave it stupidly."[4] Ambassador Ryan Crocker agreed. "Disengagement can have greater consequences than intervention," he observed.[5]

What is clear is that by the end of 2006, Iraq was coming apart along ethnosectarian fault lines. Its dissolution would have jeopardized the stability of the entire Middle East, an area of much greater strategic concern to the United States and the West than Afghanistan. Al-Qaeda in Iraq would have gained a safe haven from which to inject its deadly brand of terror into neighboring states. Iran would have gained a position of semihegemony in the Middle East. The risk premium built into every barrel of oil shipped out of the Gulf would have risen by an order of magnitude.

Defeat in war has severe consequences. Critics of the surge failed to present a compelling argument that alternatives to the surge, including accelerating transition of security tasks to Iraqi forces, as General Casey recommended, or launching a diplomatic initiative, as the Iraq Study Group proposed, would have led to a better strategic outcome. Those pundits who advocated an early withdrawal from Iraq instead of a surge or another approach owed the American people a plan to protect U.S. interests and manage the consequences. Such a plan was never provided. It is likely that a premature departure would have led to a full-blown civil war in Iraq that would have embroiled the broader Middle East in a wider conflict, one in which the United States probably would have had to engage. An appropriate historical analogy is the withdrawal of U.S. forces from the Korean peninsula in 1949, followed by their reintroduction the next year under desperate circumstances to prevent the collapse of South Korea.

In short, wringing our hands about the flawed decision to invade Iraq was an interesting academic exercise and a convenient political foil, but it had zero utility in the real world of policy formulation in late 2006. Surging U.S. forces to Iraq in an attempt to reverse the declining fortunes of the coalition and its Iraqi partners was the right decision, even if it was merely the best of a lot of bad options. The successful outcome of the surge offered Iraqi elites the chance to secure a peaceful future for themselves and their posterity, and represented a significant strategic defeat for al-Qaeda that tarnished its brand worldwide.

The surge was the right strategy at the right time. Indeed, it would not have worked earlier in the war, at least not after the disastrous political mistakes of May 2003 that spawned the insurgency: de-Ba'athification without reconciliation and disbanding of the Iraqi Army without announcing what would happen to those rendered unemployed by that action. More troops, properly employed, might have been able to keep a lid on the violence, but they would not have been able to change the mindset of those Iraqis who refused to accept the new political order in the country. Until Sunni Arabs in Iraq came to terms with a power structure that included Shi'ites and Kurds—indeed, with Shi'ites holding most of the key positions—the war would continue. For Iraq to stabilize, Sunnis had to participate and cooperate in the way ahead. Until they understood they would lose a full-blown civil war, that recognition would not be forthcoming. In this sense a case can be made for General Casey's strategy in 2004 and 2005. The problem was the failure to understand the implications of increased ethnosectarian violence in the wake of the bombing of the al-Askari shrine in February 2006, which propelled Iraq into civil war and led to a terrifying increase in violence.

The disastrous events that ensued, however, had an important positive result—they convinced many Iraqi Sunni Arabs that it would be better to throw in their lot with U.S. forces and take their chances in the political arena than continue down a road that would clearly lead to defeat by Shi'a militias and brutality at the hands of al-Qaeda and other Sunni extremists. Al-Qaeda in Iraq became its own worst enemy; without its excesses, the surge might not have worked. As it was, Iraq's

Sunni Arabs came to reject al-Qaeda's message as the group's barbaric extremism became clear. Al-Qaeda reached its zenith in the summer of 2006, until its brutal control over the Iraqi people led some of them to courageously rebel against their coreligionists. In 2007, as the surge progressed and enabled Iraq's Sunnis to take a wider stand against their tormenters, the people increasingly rejected al-Qaeda, its ideology, and its violent methods—even when doing so came at the risk of their own lives.

Shortly before he died in a terrorist bombing, Sheik Abdul Sattar Abu Risha al-Rishawi was asked by author Bing West why the tribes hadn't awakened earlier. "You Americans couldn't convince us [to fight al-Qaeda]," the sheik replied. "We Sunnis had to convince ourselves."[6] Whether that assessment is accurate or not (as there were cases of successful reconciliation in Mosul in 2003 and in Tal Afar in 2006), what is clear is that the Awakening alone could not have turned the tide of the Iraq War, as some observers argue. The Awakening became decisive only after General Petraeus decided to back it with the full resources of Multi-National Force–Iraq, aided by the new surge strategy and the additional forces that flowed into Iraq in the first five months of 2007. At that point U.S. forces adjusted their role from being enablers of the Shi'ites in an intracommunal civil war to one of protecting all Iraqis against those who wished them harmed. This shift in priorities and mindset had an enormous impact on the course of the war.

A few critics have claimed that the surge in Iraq was not a change of strategy but merely a tactical shift that did little to address the fundamental strategic errors occasioned by the decision to go to war in the first place.[7] They are wrong. If strategy is the application of ways and means to achieve a desired goal, then the surge was indeed a dramatic shift in the strategic course of the Iraq War. The surge provided additional means in terms of troop reinforcements, coupled with a major change in operational methods (ways) to emphasize the protection of the population as the most important security task in order to achieve the goal of stabilizing Iraq and empowering political actors to compromise. The midterm ends were modified as well, from the overambitious goal of attempting to create a fully functioning multiparty democracy in the heart of the Middle East to ensuring "sustainable stability" so that Iraqis could form a representative government. In time, the hope was that that government would enjoy a greater degree of legitimacy than the monarchy and dictatorships that had ruled the country since the dissolution of the Ottoman Empire at the end of World War I.

The surge strategy was also much more comprehensive than the "pop-centric COIN" label that its detractors have used to denigrate it as a mere tactical adaptation to a losing war effort. General Petraeus likened the surge strategy to a modern-day Anaconda Strategy, an all-encompassing, multifaceted effort to squeeze the lifeblood out of al-Qaeda and other extremist organizations (see Appendix 3 for a graphic representation of this strategy).[8] To be sure, protecting the population by stationing of U.S. and Iraqi soldiers among them was a central component of this strategy—arguably *the* central component. But the surge was much more than that. Conventional forces cleared enemy sanctuaries and then held the ground once cleared. Special operations forces ramped up their targeting of terrorist, insurgent, and militia extremists in operations made more effective by the synergy gained through increased melding of conventional and special operations—all greatly aided by improved intelligence, surveillance, and reconnaissance operations, enhanced by the creation of intelligence fusion centers[9] and a massive in-theater intelligence database.

But kinetic operations alone could not end the civil war in Iraq. Indeed, had the surge occurred much earlier than it did, it is unlikely that it would have had nearly the impact that it did in 2007, after the Iraqi people had stared into the abyss and realized that they did not want to end up in it. To a great extent, of course, the Iraqi people were agents of their own destiny; nonetheless, they needed help to create a more hopeful future. Their most significant contribution, the tribal rebellion against al-Qaeda in Iraq, became a central element of the new strategy. The important point to remember in this regard is that the surge—of ideas as well as of forces—was instrumental in helping to spread the Awakening, not just in Ramadi, but elsewhere in al-Anbar province and then across Iraq. Without the deliberate decision by General Petraeus to support the Awakening with all the tools at his disposal, especially additional forces, the tribal rebellion would probably have remained localized, as had previous such initiatives. The surge was thus a catalyst that accelerated, and in many cases made possible, the growth of various awakenings across Iraq.[10] Put another way, the Awakening, from which followed the creation of the Sons of Iraq, was of critical importance in turning around the situation in Iraq in 2007 and 2008. But without the surge and the decision to support the spread of the Awakening, it would not have contributed to the reduction in violence beyond the narrow confines of Ramadi.

Beyond the kinetic realm, however, the surge also featured diplomatic and nation-building aspects that helped to separate the reconcilables from the irreconcilables—and to turn some of the latter into the former. Additionally, reconstruction activities, jobs programs, the provision of essential services, and civic outreach helped to restore a sense of community in many neighborhoods while providing the Iraqi people the hope for a better life ahead. Religious engagement programs encouraged imams to promote a more moderate version of Islam, one that dissuaded young men from joining terrorist movements that employed such barbaric tactics as suicide bombs and car bombs which indiscriminately killed all in their path—most of the victims being Iraqi Muslims. Ambassador Crocker, General Petraeus, and others worked with leaders of other Arab countries in an effort to choke off the supply of young men heading to Iraq to practice jihad. Many, if not most, of these idealistic young men ended up losing their lives as they were used by al-Qaeda as suicide bombers or cannon fodder. Despite the criticism that nation-building tasks amounted to little more than a campaign to win "hearts and minds," these activities undeniably had an impact on the mindset of the Iraqi people, who, as the surge progressed, increasingly rejected violence as the solution to their problems and developed a stake in the success of the new Iraq.

MNF-I ramped up the information war as the surge progressed. No longer were we content to allow the enemy to set the news agenda through false and misleading accusations. General Petraeus demanded that his commanders and strategic communications personnel be "first with the truth," to force the enemy to react to our accurate version of events and not vice versa. The information campaign had important results as well. As the surge progressed, Shi'a Iraqis came to view portions of the Jaish al-Mahdi as little more than protection rackets. Through the information war, we hung around Muqtada al-Sadr's neck the assassination of governors and police chiefs in southern Iraq, as well as the unconscionable violence in Karbala in August 2007. These broadsides had their effect, as Sadr declared a unilateral, six-month cease-fire that ended only with the Charge of the Knights operation in March 2008.

The surge also entailed a wholesale recasting of detainee operations. "Counterinsurgency operations inside the wire" separated the worst of the extremists from the other prisoners; the former were now held in secure facilities, while the latter were offered voluntary educational courses and job training. All detainees were allowed to present their cases before review panels, which ended up releasing thousands back to their communities—not willy-nilly, but after reconciliation and reintegration measures diminished their enthusiasm for further conflict. The result was that over the course of 2007, violence at Camp Bucca declined dramatically, and the recidivism rate of those released who had undergone reconciliation training approached zero.

The Iraqis surged along with us. The building of the Iraqi Army and police forces was another critical component of the surge, as it had been to the strategy of the coalition since the publication of the first campaign plan in 2004. By the end of the surge in July 2008, Iraqi security forces were ready to take on more security responsibilities—partly because their forces were now more numerous and more capable, but also because the surge had succeeded in reducing the threat to manageable proportions. Without the surge, Iraqi forces would have continued to splinter along ethnic and sectarian lines, as Iraq dissolved into competing domains. Thanks to the efforts and sacrifices of all those who served in Iraq in 2007 and 2008, that dire future was averted.

Nevertheless, too much is often made of T. E. Lawrence's famous dictum, "Do not try to do too much with your own hands. Better the Arabs do it tolerably than that you do it perfectly. It is their war, and you are to help them, not to win it for them."[11] To begin with, we should recall the context of his remarks. Lawrence was advising Arab guerrillas (essentially insurgents) in a very specific set of circumstances during World War I. Indeed, Lawrence recognized the peculiar nature of his mission and situation in the second part of the admonition, which is almost never mentioned, "Actually, also, under the very odd conditions of Arabia, your practical work will not be as good as, perhaps, you think it is."[12] One wonders whether Lawrence's advice would have been different had he been advising the Turkish army instead of Arab irregulars. In the case of the Iraq War, allowing the fledgling Iraqi security forces to continue to operate without adequate support would have been a recipe for failure. The tribes could not have defeated al-Qaeda by themselves; they needed help, which thankfully was forthcoming in al-Qaim, Ramadi, Fallujah, and elsewhere. Likewise, the Iraqi Army could not win in Baghdad or Basra without significant assistance from U.S. and British forces. The key in all of these cases was that increasingly the initiative to fight came from Iraqi, not U.S., leaders, which gave Iraqis eventual ownership of the outcome.

Colonel Sean MacFarland came away from Iraq with the belief that indigenous forces are the key to winning in counterinsurgency warfare.[13] He is right. Yet nearly everything the Coalition Provisional Authority and the U.S. military command did early in the war went against this principle. Ambassador Jerry Bremer disbanded the Iraqi Army, the one indigenous force that might have been useful in helping to secure postwar Iraq. He all but ignored the tribes during his tenure as head of the Coalition Provisional Authority. Most U.S. military commanders were likewise slow to embrace the possibilities in this arena. General Petraeus, on the other hand, was quick to capitalize on the Awakening and to determine how to fund the Sons of Iraq, and did his best to tie them firmly to the government of Iraq. Regrettably, the departure of U.S. forces from Iraq in 2011 left some of those tribesmen who supported the fight against al-Qaeda on precarious ground, shunned (albeit in most cases still funded) by their own government and targeted for retaliation by the terrorists. "Anybody who watched our experience in Vietnam kind of has to really swallow hard when we say, 'Don't worry. We are not going to leave you behind,'" MacFarland noted prophetically in an oral history conducted in 2008.[14]

A number of factors coalesced to alter the trajectory of the war in 2007 and 2008. President Bush went "all in" during the surge, changing the psychology and political calculus of Iraqi elites, while increasing the levels of U.S. resources committed to the war effort. The tribal rebellion, the beginning of which predated the surge, took off and expanded beyond the borders of al-Anbar province, aided by command support and additional forces. U.S. and Iraqi forces, now increasingly based in smaller outposts and acting according to a coherent set of counterinsurgency principles, partnered to take control of the streets of Baghdad and a number of other key localities. As the surge progressed, U.S. reinforcements and the growth in Iraqi security forces finally gave coalition commanders enough troops to protect the population and deny the enemy sanctuaries. Special operations forces ramped up their missions to kill or capture terrorist, insurgent, and militia operatives. A large number of Iraqi Sunnis decided to throw their lot in with U.S. forces, leading to the creation of the Sons of Iraq movement that suppressed insurgent violence in many parts of the country. Some (albeit by no means all) neighborhoods underwent sectarian cleansing, which reduced violence among the remaining residents—but not on the boundaries of those areas, at least not until U.S. and Iraqi forces moved in and built gated communities to separate the warring factions. The excesses of the Jaish al-Mahdi led to the discrediting of the major Shi'a militia and Muqtada al-Sadr's declaration of a unilateral cease-fire, which reduced militia violence. Nouri al-Maliki's growth as the prime minister of Iraq (and his impulsiveness) finally led him to confront Shi'a militias with Iraqi security forces in Basra and elsewhere. Together, these actions changed the outlook of Iraq's political elites. Finally, after a half-decade of war, Iraqis were growing increasingly weary of the struggle and recognized the imperative to engage increasingly in politics.

However, none of these factors alone was sufficient to reverse the declining fortunes of Iraq. To accomplish this goal, the surge was essential. The surge strategy acted as a catalyst that brought together all of the factors that impinged on the situation in Iraq and enabled them to develop and mature. As former U.S. Ambassador to Iraq Ryan Crocker later wrote, "Iraqis certainly deserve credit for this transformation; but it would not have happened without intensive, sustained U.S. engagement, particularly by those in the military who carried the surge forward. The hardest months of my life came in the first half of 2007, as our casualties mounted with no guarantee that the strategy would work. But it did, and the people of both nations owe a tremendous debt to those who fought to secure the Iraqi population, one hard block at a time."[15]

Scholarly studies are validating this assertion.[16] In a recent peer-reviewed article, Stephen Biddle, Jeffrey Friedman, and Jacob Shapiro examine the impact of the surge on the war's outcome, using both quantitative and qualitative measures to determine how much the new strategy was responsible for declining violence in Iraq. They conclude that the surge of forces was a necessary but insufficient cause for declining violence, and that the synergy between the Awakening and the surge was responsible for the progress made in defeating the insurgency beginning in 2007.[17] Absent the surge, the authors argue, "sectarian violence would likely have continued for a long time to come—the pattern and distribution of the bloodshed offers little reason to believe that it had burned itself out by mid-2007."[18] These conclusions track with the narrative analysis of the surge presented in earlier chapters.

The publication of the new counterinsurgency doctrine before the surge also played a role in the war's outcome. A great deal of adaptation occurred in U.S. forces before the surge, but not in a coherent fashion; brigade and battalion commanders largely danced to their own tunes. In 2007, echoing the tenets of the newly published field manual, General Petraeus and Lieutenant General Odierno forced a coherent operational construct to take hold, and thereby cemented into place standard counterinsurgency principles across the force. Protection of the population became not just one of many competing priorities, but *the* priority for

U.S. forces in Iraq. Writing of surge operations in Diyala province in 2007, historian Kimberly Kagan observes:

> These operations were successful because they were designed from beginning to end with the goal of establishing stable security in the region, not of transitioning to Iraqi control.[19] As operations progressed, commanders were attuned to opportunities not only to advance current clearing operations but also to lay the preconditions for long-term stability in the area. The kinetic operations themselves were designed and conducted with that ultimate goal in mind—separating the insurgents from the population, defending those members of the population willing to oppose the insurgents, and protecting the population against retaliation and efforts to re-infiltrate.[20]

This change in emphasis came at just the right time, and it made a huge impact on local security throughout those areas of Iraq in which U.S. forces operated. U.S. troops, widely seen, in Bing West's words, as "the strongest tribe," served as the honest broker that kept disparate groups working toward a common objective of local security. Such bottom-up reconciliation made progress possible even while Iraqi national elites remained at loggerheads in the Green Zone.

Some contend that the surge was unnecessary because sectarian violence and cleansing had already separated the warring factions in Iraq by early 2007. This notion is refuted by the evidence.[21] In Baghdad in particular, sectarian violence had by no means ended by the beginning of the surge. Iraq's capital was still roughly a third Sunni. That made Baghdad, as General Petraeus noted, both Iraq's largest Shi'a and its largest Sunni city.[22] Many of its neighborhoods were still composed of mixed sects and ethnicities, as censuses taken by U.S. troops during the surge confirmed. Relying on ethnic and sectarian cleansing to end the war would have resulted in an even greater bloodbath than the horrors that were visited upon Baghdad and other mixed areas during the war. Moreover, there is no way to tell when or where that cleansing would have ended, nor how long the fighting would have lasted along the boundaries between the enclaves of various groups.

One of the accusations leveled at the surge was it was merely an attempt to win the "hearts and minds" of the Iraqi people. Nothing could be further from the truth. In practice, protecting the population meant controlling people and the areas in which they lived, while reducing insurgent and militia forces and hunting down irreconcilables. In 2007 more American soldiers were killed in action than during any other year of the war.[23] They died in offensive operations and while securing the Iraqi people against al-Qaeda, insurgent groups, and Shi'a militias. Furthermore, U.S. conventional and special operations forces killed more than seventy-four hundred insurgents and terrorists in 2007, an increase of roughly 50 percent over the number killed the previous year under the old, and supposedly more kinetic, strategy.[24] The Iraqi people in large measure applauded the improvement of security, but their attitude toward the American presence in Iraq was to a certain extent irrelevant. The purpose of the surge was to make the Iraqi people safer from insurgent and militia violence and intimidation, and thus make possible political progress on the difficult issues affecting Iraqi society.

The highest rate of casualties in the Iraq war occurred from January to June 2007, which puts the lie to the contention that the surge was merely a "hearts and minds" campaign. "Winning hearts and minds is a misleading slogan," journalist Jim Michaels writes. "This [kind of war] is not about convincing people that democracy or capitalism is superior to other systems. It is about an alignment of interests. Tribes in Iraq changed sides only when they were convinced that America was a reliable partner, that the United States would not leave and that it would ultimately prevail."[25] In the end, U.S. and Iraqi forces partnered together—and with Iraq's tribes—to prevail in a tough fight.

There are those who believe that the same outcome could have been achieved had the United States adopted a so-called counterterrorism approach to the war in Iraq. Kill or capture enough enemy leaders, the reasoning goes, and the insurgency would have simply fallen apart. Such simplistic notions are belied by the record. Al-Qaeda in Iraq and other networked terrorist groups, it turns out, were much more robust than once believed. A decapitation strategy simply would not have resulted in the organization's collapse. Rather, successful operations against networked terrorist and insurgent groups required a combination of special operations and conventional forces. Conventional forces were needed to clear and hold areas, develop intelligence, and disrupt transit routes and staging areas, which forced terrorist and insurgent operatives to move and communicate, thus making them vulnerable to targeting by special operations forces. In his end-of-the-year report in 2007 to Secretary of Defense Gates, General Petraeus remarked:

> By living among the population we reinforced the Awakening Movements already underway and further empowered local communities that decided to reject extremism. We came to more clearly recognize that sheiks and tribes have important roles to play as key organizing structures in Iraq's culture of honor. By enmeshing them in our counterinsurgency effort to secure the population, we tapped into the power of the people at the grass roots level, a factor that should resonate with us given our own heritage and culture. We also sharpened our understanding of the relationship between high-end counterterrorist operations and COIN operations, essentially reaching the conclusion that you can't do one without the other. If the sanctuaries in which CT targets live and work are not reduced by securing the population, then nightly raids conducted by our top end units will have no lasting effect on the disposition of the population or the ability of the terrorist network to thrive.[26]

With both conventional and special operations forces working together during the surge, Multi-National Corps–Iraq and the Joint Special Operations Command were able to gut al-Qaeda in Iraq, but only after months of fighting and the killing or capturing of more than twenty-five thousand insurgent and terrorist operatives, of which perhaps one-fifth were hardcore irreconcilables. Only then did al-Qaeda's network degrade to the point where we could envision victory against the organization in Iraq.

That al-Qaeda in Iraq was allowed off the ropes to a degree in subsequent years was due to our inability to remain sufficiently engaged in Iraq and to lingering shortcomings of Iraqi security operations, not to the failure of the surge as a strategic concept. President Bush used to emphasize that Iraq needed to look like South Korea, where U.S. forces remain in place more than a half-century after the armistice that ended the fighting, and not like Vietnam, where the withdrawal of U.S. forces led to defeat within two years of their departure. Unfortunately, the lack of an American bipartisan consensus on the stationing of U.S. forces in Iraq and the nationalistic impulses of Iraqi politicians led to the withdrawal of U.S. forces in 2011 after the Obama administration failed to negotiate a new status-of-forces agreement. After the administration demanded that the Council of Representatives approve any new agreement, the Iraqi government balked at providing U.S. troops immunity from prosecution in Iraqi courts, a precondition for the continued presence of American forces in the country. The result has been a slow downward spiral in security (exacerbated by a civil war in Syria) and a halt in any movement toward national reconciliation. But we should not interpret the failure of the Obama administration's Iraq policy as a failure of the surge strategy, which provided a window for success that other policies could not.

The experience of the surge highlights the importance of individual agency in war. The Iraq War would have turned out significantly differently had Sheik Abdul Sattar Abu Risha al-Rishawi not offered to ally his tribe with Colonel Sean MacFarland and the Ready First Combat Team, or had leaders other than George W. Bush and Nouri al-Maliki been in charge in Washington and Baghdad. The relationship between Bush and Maliki was an important factor in making the surge work. Ambassador Ryan Crocker, General Dave Petraeus, and Lieutenant General Ray Odierno also played key roles, displaying a degree of competence and teamwork that is all too rare in war. Of all these actors, President Bush was the most important. He proved that even a lame duck president could force his chosen strategy on a reluctant national security apparatus, and he eventually found the military leaders he needed who could implement it. "Lincoln discovered Generals Grant and Sherman," wrote President Bush later. "Roosevelt had Eisenhower and Bradley. I found David Petraeus and Ray Odierno."[27]

The surge was certainly a long shot, as those of us who helped to develop and execute it noted at the time.[28] Some observers would later contend that we got lucky in Iraq during the surge, since it had been planned with only a vague knowledge of the impact of the Awakening on future events. General Petraeus acknowledges this reality, but he had returned to Iraq in 2007 knowing that reconciliation had to be part of the strategy. Thus his response to those who contend that the spread of the Awakening was serendipity is to note that it resulted from his decision to support what had begun outside Ramadi and to recall, in the words of the Roman philosopher Seneca, that "luck is what happens when preparation meets opportunity." The surge worked in large part because we were intellectually and operationally ready to capitalize on the enemy's mistakes and on the opportunities—unanticipated as well as anticipated—presented to us.

The surge in Iraq also confirms that war is, as historian Alan Beyerchen has noted, a nonlinear phenomenon. Indeed, some of the variables that went into the success of the surge were unknowable at the beginning. Who would have guessed that a minor, third-tier sheik from Ramadi would prove to be the most important figure in turning Iraqi tribes against al-Qaeda? The cautionary note here is not to divorce counterinsurgency doctrine from its historical context or political foundations. "It seems clear that in *On War* Clausewitz also senses that any prescriptive theory entails linearization, which is why he holds a dim view of such theory in the real world in which war actually occurs," Beyerchen notes. "Thus theory must be based on a broader sense of order rooted in historical experience, leading to descriptive guidelines. Theorists must not be seduced into formulating analytically deductive, prescriptive sets of doctrines that offer poor hope and worse guidance."[29] Principles such as "protect the people" and "money is ammunition" are useful as guides to judgment, but by themselves they provide no more than "a mirage shimmering above the distinct abstractions of implicitly idealized, isolated systems; the denseness of Clausewitz's forest of caveats and qualifications more faithfully represents the conditions and contexts we actually encounter."[30] The Iraq War was a complex, nonlinear system summed up well by General Petraeus when he stated, "Iraq is all hard—all the time."

Because the surge succeeded, the competition for power and resources in Iraq moved into the political realm, underpinned by the new distribution of power in Baghdad. Consolidation of the gains made during the surge, however, required a long-term commitment by the United States to stability in Iraq and a deft handling of the diplomacy and politics required to moderate the sectarian instincts of many in the Iraqi government. This commitment regrettably has not been forthcoming.[31] For reasons of national pride, the historical legacy of colonialism, and public opposition to the continued presence of foreign forces on Iraqi soil, the Iraqi Council of Representatives would not approve a status-of-forces agreement that conferred immunity on U.S. military personnel. "This is now the hard reality of Iraq's constitutional system: a system assertive of its sovereignty, responsive to public opinion, and impervious to direct U.S. pressure," states Brett McGurk, who worked with the U.S. embassy in Baghdad in an effort to ink a new agreement.[32] On the other hand, the new administration in Washington saw the withdrawal of U.S. forces from Iraq as the fulfillment of a campaign promise to its domestic base, so it acquiesced in the withdrawal of U.S. forces from Iraq at the end of 2011 without protest.[33] When the last U.S. troops departed at the end of 2011, the United States lost much of its leverage with the Iraqi government, and Iraq lost the one force in the country that for nine years had tried to keep a lid on sectarian bloodletting.

It was no coincidence that shortly after the last U.S. forces departed the country, sectarianism once again publicly reared its ugly head. Iraqi Prime Minister Nouri al-Maliki went after his political enemies, indicting Vice President Tariq al-Hashemi on allegations of running a death squad.[34] There were plenty of Iraqi politicians of both sects with blood on their hands; the fact that Maliki went after a Sunni politician rather than a Shi'a political leader with connections to the Jaish al-Mahdi Special Groups was not lost on Iraqi elites. Over time, the result of that action and subsequent ones by Prime Minister Maliki has been the gradual revival of al-Qaeda in Iraq, a group once nearly destroyed but now given a second lease on life by the intransigence of Iraq's government and America's consequent inability to remain engaged over the long haul.

Despite subsequent challenges, the enormous progress during the surge was worth the cost in blood and treasure. Although Iraq could still implode at some point, it would do so under far different strategic conditions than those that prevailed in 2006. Iraq is blessed with abundant natural resources, a talented and educated population, and a modern communications infrastructure. Thanks to the efforts of the United States and its coalition partners, Iraqi security forces have shown increasing capability to deal with extremists, provided the political will exists to take action against them. If Iraqi elites can work out their political differences, and provided the Iraqi government does not devolve once again into a dictatorship (admittedly, two huge caveats), the future of the country will be a bright one. "The Shia are afraid of the past—that a Sunni dictatorship will reassert itself," writes Ambassador Crocker. "The Sunnis are afraid of the future—an Iraq in which they are no longer ascendant. And the Kurds, with their history of suffering, are afraid of both the past and the future."[35] Despite these misgivings, given the demonstrated ability of Iraqis to muddle through difficult times, the future may still work out for them in the end if the United States remains engaged to encourage the adoption of an inclusive representative government. Although Iraq seems at the moment to be headed toward dictatorship, the tides of history wash in strange directions. The effects of the Arab spring and other currents in the Arab world will undoubtedly influence Iraq as well. It is thus unlikely that we will know the true outcome of the U.S. military adventure in Iraq for decades to come.

Despite the manifest success of the surge in Iraq, one should be careful not to extrapolate from it a template for certain success in counterinsurgency warfare. The situation in Iraq in 2007 and 2008 was unique to that time and place in history. And even though the surge succeeded in lowering violence and providing a path to victory, the United States badly mishandled its aftermath. Emma Sky, who was in Iraq to witness both the surge and what transpired afterward, warns:

> The United States should also learn that without an overarching political strategy, even the most successful counterinsurgency tactics cannot deliver sustainable change or irreversible momentum. It should learn how the development industry creates perverse incentives in attempts to "nation build," how there is no mythical cadre of civilians who can be parachuted into developing countries to "fix" them, how interactions with elites can unintentionally encourage kleptocracy and how security assistance can facilitate a return to authoritarianism if not combined with reform of the security sector. Critically, America could learn that money can't buy love, that relationships are key, that strategic patience is needed, that allies should not be ignored and that a regional approach is needed as well as a bilateral one.[36]

Current and future administrations would be wise to heed her words of warning.

Indeed, lessons extrapolated from the surge in Iraq, when applied to other places in other times, will probably produce different results as determined by the unique political, military, historical, geographic, and cultural factors at play in each case. The current struggle to turn Pashtun tribes in Afghanistan against the Taliban is a case in point. The surge there has succeeded in largely reclaiming the contested provinces of Helmand and Kandahar, but given the sanctuaries in Pakistan enjoyed by the insurgents, the surge in Afghanistan has not turned the tide of war irrevocably against the Taliban.[37] Further research is required to determine whether the reason for diminished success in Afghanistan is the establishment of a departure date for surge forces simultaneously with the announcement of the surge there, the failure of Pashtun tribes to turn against the Taliban, the provision of insufficient forces to conduct a fully resourced counterinsurgency campaign, the ineptitude and lack of legitimacy of the Afghan government, the presence of external insurgent sanctuaries across the international border in Pakistan, or, most likely, a combination of all of these factors.

Despite the difficulty of fighting counterinsurgency wars, the U.S. military should not forget the lessons of the past decade, as it largely did after the end of the conflict in Vietnam.[38] U.S. forces have fought counterinsurgency wars throughout the history of the nation, and they will probably do so again at some point in the future. In relating the lessons he learned during fifteen months of combat duty in Baghdad during the surge, Lieutenant Colonel Jim Crider states, "Pragmatism guides the path to victory for a counterinsurgent force. While there is no specific set of steps that will lead us to assured victory in asymmetric conflicts, counterinsurgents need local people to serve as allies in the battle against insurgents. To achieve this requires a deep understanding of the cause of the insurgency as well as the culture in which it is happening. The counterinsurgent must create opportunities and supply motivation in order to gain the allegiance of the people. This occurs in the form of personal engagement with and protection of the population. Equally important is the promise of greater economic opportunity and a political process that allows residents to address grievances peacefully."[39] Other analysts and military leaders as well are beginning to grasp the lessons of the wars in Iraq and Afghanistan.[40] What U.S. military leaders should not do is wring their hands and complain that fighting insurgencies is just too hard, for, as history shows, insurgents lose more often than they win.[41] The U.S. military and government agencies should take the time to analyze and digest the implications of these conflicts, for, as the ancient Greek historian Thucydides reminds us, "Human nature being what it is, [past events] will, at some time or other and in much the same ways, be repeated in the future."[42]

The wars of 9/11 began with an attack by al-Qaeda on the U.S. homeland, which resulted in retaliation against the terrorist base in Afghanistan and two years later led the Bush administration to launch a preventative war against Iraq. By the late spring of 2003, the United States appeared triumphant in both conflicts, but underneath the veneer of victory there were innumerable challenges, not the least of which were deep-seated problems rooted in the U.S. military doctrine of the post–Cold War era.

Simply put, the pursuit of defense transformation based on fighting mirror-imaged enemies got in the way of fighting the wars we had to fight. In the 1990s, various military officers and defense analysts posited a coming revolution in military affairs based on information dominance coupled with precision guided munitions. Concepts such as network-centric warfare envisioned near-perfect intelligence from manned and unmanned sensors, satellites, and other intelligence, surveillance, and reconnaissance assets. Accurate and timely information would lead to battlespace dominance, precision attacks on targets from extended ranges, and the execution of rapid, decisive operations that would quickly and precisely collapse an enemy armed force or regime at its center of gravity. Defense Secretary Donald Rumsfeld viewed Afghanistan and Iraq as laboratories in which to validate this concept.

But advanced sensors and precision-guided munitions are tactical and operational capabilities—they are not a strategy. Those leaders who staked the outcome of the Afghanistan and Iraq wars on rapid, decisive operations misread the nature of war—and not just the nature of war in the post–Cold War era but the nature of war in any era. Despite the high-tech capabilities of the U.S. armed forces, uncertainty and the interplay of friction and chance on military operations will remain integral to war for the indefinite future.

The Bush administration would have done well to study more history before engaging in such wars of choice. War has always been an uncertain undertaking, and even the most skillful diplomats and power brokers have worked hard to steer clear of it. Even Otto von Bismarck, the "Iron Chancellor" who united Germany through a series of wars with neighboring states in the late nineteenth century, was no fan of conflict. As historian Marcus Jones notes, "For Bismarck, the sledge-hammer of the military was a poor substitute for the scalpel of diplomacy, and wars represented the least attractive strategic instrument in most cases: difficult to contain, uncertain in their outcome, and given to slippage in their aims and justifications. Wars frequently destroyed more than they created, and Bismarck preferred throughout his career to exhaust almost every other option before re-sorting to the armed conflict."[43] Just because the U.S. armed forces are the most capable in the world does not mean they should be the first choice for policy mak-ers looking for solutions to difficult problems.

There is a larger point here. The emphasis on technology over an understand-ing of the realities of war and conflict reflect the ahistoricism not only of too much of the U.S. military officer corps but of the American educational system as well. Our mistakes in Iraq and Afghanistan were the result of a pervasive failure to under-stand the historical framework within which insurgencies take place, to appreciate the cultural and political factors of other nations and people, and to encourage the learning of foreign languages. In other words, in Afghanistan and Iraq we managed to repeat many of the mistakes that we made in Vietnam, because America's political and military leaders managed to forget nearly every lesson of that conflict.

In the end, one must agree with David Kilcullen's conclusion: "The Surge worked: but in the final analysis, it was an effort to save ourselves from the more desperate consequences of a situation we should never have gotten ourselves into."[44] President Bush would have been better served if the intense probing and debates surrounding the surge strategy in 2006 had occurred instead during the run-up to the invasion of Iraq in 2003. Strategic consensus should be the result of vigorous debate, which serves to sharpen the assumptions upon which various courses of action rest, test their viability, and lay out what could go wrong. Such debate did not occur until far too late in the war. Only after President Bush de-cided to overrule the advice of his commander on the ground—and most of those in the Pentagon and the White House as well—did he find the way to a sound strategy that could achieve some measure of victory. The history of the surge ar-gues for more civilian involvement in the development of strategy, not less.

The Prussian war philosopher Carl von Clausewitz noted nearly two centuries ago that war is subject to emotion and chance as well as to reason. In relying on a best-case analysis and the vaunted tactical and technological capabilities of the U.S. armed forces to win a quick and tidy war, U.S. policy makers put the nation in jeopardy of a major strategic defeat in the Middle East. As the Duke of Wel-lington once claimed of the Battle of Waterloo, the surge was a "near-run thing." It salvaged a war almost lost, but only by the slimmest of margins. American lead-ers should learn from this experience that when the iron dice roll, unpredictable things can and will happen. If this realization prevents an even greater strategic tragedy in the future, then perhaps the lessons learned at such enormous cost dur-ing the nine years of conflict in Iraq will not have been in vain.

Report to Congress on the Situation in Iraq

General David H. Petraeus
Commander, Multi-National Force–Iraq
September 10–11, 2007

Mr. Chairmen, Ranking Members, Members of the Committees, thank you for the opportunity to provide my assessment of the security situation in Iraq and to discuss the recommendations I recently provided to my chain of command for the way forward.

At the outset, I would like to note that this is my testimony. Although I have briefed my assessment and recommendations to my chain of command, I wrote this testimony myself. It has not been cleared by, nor shared with, anyone in the Pentagon, the White House, or Congress.

As a bottom line up front, the military objectives of the surge are, in large measure, being met. In recent months, in the face of tough enemies and the brutal summer heat of Iraq, Coalition and Iraqi Security Forces have achieved progress in the security arena. Though the improvements have been uneven across Iraq, the overall number of security incidents in Iraq has declined in 8 of the past 12 weeks, with the numbers of incidents in the last two weeks at the lowest levels seen since June 2006.

One reason for the decline in incidents is that Coalition and Iraqi forces have dealt significant blows to Al Qaeda–Iraq. Though Al Qaeda and its affiliates in Iraq remain dangerous, we have taken away a number of their sanctuaries and gained the initiative in many areas.

We have also disrupted Shi'a militia extremists, capturing the head and numerous other leaders of the Iranian-supported Special Groups, along with a senior Lebanese Hezbollah operative supporting Iran's activities in Iraq.

Coalition and Iraqi operations have helped reduce ethno-sectarian violence, as well, bringing down the number of ethno-sectarian deaths substantially in Baghdad and across Iraq since the height of the sectarian violence last December. The number of overall civilian deaths has also declined during this period, although the numbers in each area are still at troubling levels.

Iraqi Security Forces have also continued to grow and to shoulder more of the load, albeit slowly and amid continuing concerns about the sectarian tendencies of some elements in their ranks. In general, however, Iraqi elements have been standing and fighting and sustaining tough losses, and they have taken the lead in operations in many areas.

Additionally, in what may be the most significant development of the past 8 months, the tribal rejection of Al Qaeda that started in Anbar Province and helped produce such significant change there has now spread to a number of other locations as well.

Based on all this and on the further progress we believe we can achieve over the next few months, I believe that we will be able to reduce our forces to the pre-surge level of brigade combat teams by next summer without jeopardizing the security gains that we have fought so hard to achieve.

Beyond that, while noting that the situation in Iraq remains complex, difficult, and sometimes downright frustrating, I also believe that it is possible to achieve our objectives in Iraq over time, though doing so will be neither quick nor easy.

Having provided that summary, I would like to review the nature of the conflict in Iraq, recall the situation before the surge, describe the current situation, and explain the recommendations I have provided to my chain of command for the way ahead in Iraq.

The Nature of the Conflict

The fundamental source of the conflict in Iraq is competition among ethnic and sectarian communities for power and resources. This competition will take place, and its resolution is key to producing long-term stability in the new Iraq. The question is whether the competition takes place more—or less—violently. This chart shows the security challenges in Iraq.[1] Foreign and home-grown terrorists, insurgents, militia extremists, and criminals all push the ethno-sectarian competition toward violence. Malign actions by Syria and, especially, by Iran fuel that violence. Lack of adequate governmental capacity, lingering sectarian mistrust, and various forms of corruption add to Iraq's challenges.

The Situation in December 2006 and the Surge

In our recent efforts to look to the future, we found it useful to revisit the past. In December 2006, during the height of the ethno-sectarian violence that escalated in the wake of the bombing of the Golden Dome Mosque in Samarra, the leaders in Iraq at that time—General George Casey and Ambassador Zalmay Khalilzad—concluded that the coalition was failing to achieve its objectives. Their review underscored the need to protect the population and reduce sectarian violence, especially in Baghdad. As a result, General Casey requested additional forces to enable the Coalition to accomplish these tasks, and those forces began to flow in January.

In the ensuing months, our forces and our Iraqi counterparts have focused on improving security, especially in Baghdad and the areas around it, wresting sanctuaries from Al Qaeda control, and disrupting the efforts of the Iranian-supported militia extremists. We have employed counterinsurgency practices that underscore the importance of units living among the people they are securing, and accordingly, our forces have established dozens of joint security stations and patrol bases manned by Coalition and Iraqi forces in Baghdad and in other areas across Iraq.

In mid-June, with all the surge brigades in place, we launched a series of offensive operations focused on: expanding the gains achieved in the preceding months in Anbar Province; clearing Baqubah, several key Baghdad neighborhoods, the remaining sanctuaries in Anbar Province, and important areas in the so-called "belts" around Baghdad; and pursuing Al Qaeda in the Diyala River Valley and several other areas.

Throughout this period, as well, we engaged in dialogue with insurgent groups and tribes, and this led to additional elements standing up to oppose Al Qaeda and other extremists. We also continued to emphasize the development of the Iraqi Security Forces and we employed non-kinetic means to exploit the opportunities provided by the conduct of our kinetic operations—aided in this effort by the arrival of additional Provincial Reconstruction Teams.

Current Situation and Trends

The progress our forces have achieved with our Iraqi counterparts has, as I noted at the outset, been substantial. While there have been setbacks as well as successes and tough losses along the way, overall, our tactical commanders and I see improvements in the security environment. We do not, however, just rely on gut feel or personal observations; we also conduct considerable data collection and analysis to gauge progress and determine trends. We do this by gathering and refining data from coalition and Iraqi operations centers, using a methodology that has been in place for well over a year and that has benefited over the past seven months from the increased presence of our forces living among the Iraqi people. We endeavor to ensure our analysis of that data is conducted with rigor and consistency, as our ability to achieve a nuanced understanding of the security environment is dependent on collecting and analyzing data in a consistent way over time. Two US intelligence agencies recently reviewed our methodology, and they concluded that the data we produce is the most accurate and authoritative in Iraq.

As I mentioned up front, and as the chart before you reflects, the level of security incidents has decreased significantly since the start of the surge of offensive operations in mid-June, declining in 8 of the past 12 weeks, with the level of incidents in the past two weeks the lowest since June 2006 and with the number of attacks this past week the lowest since April 2006.

Civilian deaths of all categories, less natural causes, have also declined considerably, by over 45% Iraq-wide since the height of the sectarian violence in December. This is shown by the top line on this chart, and the decline by some 70% in Baghdad is shown by the bottom line. Periodic mass casualty attacks by Al Qaeda have tragically added to the numbers outside Baghdad, in particular. Even without the sensational attacks, however, the level of civilian deaths is clearly still too high and continues to be of serious concern.

As the next chart shows, the number of ethno-sectarian deaths, an important subset of the overall civilian casualty figures, has also declined significantly since the height of the sectarian violence in December. Iraq-wide, as shown by the top line on this chart, the number of ethno-sectarian deaths has come down by over 55%, and it would have come down much further were it not for the casualties inflicted by barbaric Al Qaeda bombings attempting to reignite sectarian violence. In Baghdad, as the bottom line shows, the number of ethno-sectarian deaths has come down by some 80% since December. This chart also displays the density of sectarian incidents in various Baghdad neighborhoods and it both reflects the progress made in reducing ethno-sectarian violence in the Iraqi capital and identifies the areas that remain the most challenging.

As we have gone on the offensive in former Al Qaeda and insurgent sanctuaries, and as locals have increasingly supported our efforts, we have found a substantially increased number of arms, ammunition, and explosives caches. As this chart shows, we have, so far this year, already found and cleared over 4,400 caches, nearly 1,700 more than we discovered in all of last year. This may be a factor in the reduction in the number of overall improvised explosive device attacks in recent months, which as this chart shows, has declined sharply, by about one-third, since June.

The change in the security situation in Anbar Province has, of course, been particularly dramatic. As this chart shows, monthly attack levels in Anbar have declined from some 1,350 in October 2006 to a bit over 200 in August of this year. This dramatic decrease reflects the significance of the local rejection of Al Qaeda and the newfound willingness of local Anbaris to volunteer to serve in the Iraqi Army and Iraqi Police Service. As I noted earlier, we are seeing similar actions in other locations, as well.

To be sure, trends have not been uniformly positive across Iraq, as is shown by this chart depicting violence levels in several key Iraqi provinces. The trend in Ninevah Province, for example, has been much more up and down, until a recent decline, and the same is true in Sala ad Din Province, though recent trends there and in Baghdad have been in the right direction. In any event, the overall trajectory in Iraq—a steady decline of incidents in the past three months—is still quite significant.

The number of car bombings and suicide attacks has also declined in each of the past 5 months, from a high of some 175 in March, as this chart shows, to about 90 this past month. While this trend in recent months has been heartening, the number of high profile attacks is still too high, and we continue to work hard to destroy the networks that carry out these barbaric attacks.

Our operations have, in fact, produced substantial progress against Al Qaeda and its affiliates in Iraq. As this chart shows, in the past 8 months, we have considerably reduced the areas in which Al Qaeda enjoyed sanctuary. We have also neutralized 5 media cells, detained the senior Iraqi leader of Al Qaeda–Iraq, and killed or captured nearly 100 other key leaders and some 2,500 rank-and-file fighters. Al Qaeda is certainly not defeated; however, it is off balance and we are pursuing its leaders and operators aggressively. Of note, as the recent National Intelligence Estimate on Iraq explained, these gains against Al Qaeda are a result of the synergy of actions by: conventional forces to deny the terrorists sanctuary; intelligence, surveillance, and reconnaissance assets to find the enemy; and special operations elements to conduct targeted raids. A combination of these assets is necessary to prevent the creation of a terrorist safe haven in Iraq.

In the past six months we have also targeted Shi'a militia extremists, capturing a number of senior leaders and fighters, as well as the deputy commander of Lebanese Hezbollah Department 2800, the organization created to support the training, arming, funding, and, in some cases, direction of the militia extremists by the Iranian Republican Guard Corps' Qods Force. These elements have assassinated and kidnapped Iraqi governmental leaders, killed and wounded our soldiers with advanced explosive devices provided by Iran, and indiscriminately rocketed civilians in the International Zone and elsewhere. It is increasingly apparent to both Coalition and Iraqi leaders that Iran, through the use of the Qods Force, seeks to turn the Iraqi Special Groups into a Hezbollah-like force to serve its interests and fight a proxy war against the Iraqi state and coalition forces in Iraq.

The most significant development in the past six months likely has been the increasing emergence of tribes and local citizens rejecting Al Qaeda and other extremists. This has, of course, been most visible in Anbar Province. A year ago the province was assessed as "lost" politically. Today, it is a model of what happens when local leaders and citizens decide to oppose Al Qaeda and reject its Taliban-like ideology. While Anbar is unique and the model it provides cannot be replicated everywhere in Iraq, it does demonstrate the dramatic change in security that is possible with the support and participation of local citizens. As this chart shows, other tribes have been inspired by the actions of those in Anbar and have volunteered to fight extremists as well. We have, in coordination with the Iraqi government's National Reconciliation Committee, been engaging these tribes and groups of local citizens who want to oppose extremists and to contribute to local security. Some 20,000 such individuals are already being hired for the Iraqi Police, thousands of others are being assimilated into the Iraqi Army, and thousands more are vying for a spot in Iraq's Security Forces.

Iraqi Security Forces

As I noted earlier, Iraqi Security Forces have continued to grow, to develop their capabilities, and to shoulder more of the burden of providing security for their country. Despite concerns about sectarian influence, inadequate logistics and supporting institutions, and an insufficient number of qualified commissioned and non-commissioned officers, Iraqi units are engaged around the country.

As this chart shows, there are now nearly 140 Iraqi Army, National Police, and Special Operations Forces Battalions in the fight, with about 95 of those capable of taking the lead in operations, albeit with some coalition support. Beyond that, all of Iraq's battalions have been heavily involved in combat operations that often result in the loss of leaders, soldiers, and equipment. These losses are among the shortcomings identified by operational readiness assessments, but we should not take from these assessments the impression that Iraqi forces are not in the fight and contributing. Indeed, despite their shortages, many Iraqi units across Iraq now operate with minimal coalition assistance.

As counterinsurgency operations require substantial numbers of boots on the ground, we are helping the Iraqis expand the size of their security forces. Currently, there are some 445,000 individuals on the payrolls of Iraq's Interior and Defense Ministries. Based on recent decisions by Prime Minister Maliki, the number of Iraq's security forces will grow further by the end of this year, possibly by as much as 40,000. Given the security challenges Iraq faces, we support this decision, and we will work with the two security ministries as they continue their efforts to expand their basic training capacity, leader development programs, logistical structures and elements, and various other institutional capabilities to support the substantial growth in Iraqi forces.

Significantly, in 2007, Iraq will, as in 2006, spend more on its security forces than it will receive in security assistance from the United States. In fact, Iraq is becoming one of the United States' larger foreign military sales customers, committing some $1.6 billion to FMS already, with the possibility of up to $1.8 billion more being committed before the end of this year. And I appreciate the attention that some members of Congress have recently given to speeding up the FMS process for Iraq.

To summarize, the security situation in Iraq is improving, and Iraqis elements are slowly taking on more of the responsibility for protecting their citizens. Innumerable challenges lie ahead; however, Coalition and Iraqi Security Forces have made progress toward achieving sustainable security. As a result, the United States will be in a position to reduce its forces in Iraq in the months ahead.

Recommendations

Two weeks ago I provided recommendations for the way ahead in Iraq to the members of my chain of command and the Joint Chiefs of Staff. The essence of the approach I recommended is captured in its title: "Security While Transitioning: From Leading to Partnering to Overwatch." This approach seeks to build on the security improvements our troopers and our Iraqi counterparts have fought so hard to achieve in recent months. It reflects recognition of the importance of securing the population and the imperative of transitioning responsibilities to Iraqi institutions and Iraqi forces as quickly as possible, but without rushing to failure. It includes substantial support for the continuing development of Iraqi Security Forces. It also stresses the need to continue the counterinsurgency strategy that we have been employing, but with Iraqis gradually shouldering more of the load. And it highlights the importance of regional and global diplomatic approaches. Finally, in recognition of the fact that this war is not only being fought on the ground in Iraq but also in cyberspace, it also notes the need to contest the enemy's growing use of that important medium to spread extremism.

The recommendations I provided were informed by operational and strategic considerations. The operational considerations include recognition that:

- military aspects of the surge have achieved progress and generated momentum;
- Iraqi Security Forces have continued to grow and have slowly been shouldering more of the security burden in Iraq;
- a mission focus on either population security or transition alone will not be adequate to achieve our objectives;
- success against Al Qaeda–Iraq and Iranian-supported militia extremists requires conventional forces as well as special operations forces; and
- the security and local political situations will enable us to draw down the surge forces.

My recommendations also took into account a number of strategic considerations:

- political progress will take place only if sufficient security exists;
- long-term US ground force viability will benefit from force reductions as the surge runs its course;
- regional, global, and cyberspace initiatives are critical to success; and
- Iraqi leaders understandably want to assume greater sovereignty in their country, although, as they recently announced, they do desire continued presence of coalition forces in Iraq in 2008 under a new UN Security Council Resolution and, following that, they want to negotiate a long term security agreement with the United States and other nations.

Based on these considerations, and having worked the battlefield geometry with Lieutenant General Ray Odierno to ensure that we retain and build on the gains for which our troopers have fought, I have recommended a drawdown of the surge forces from Iraq. In fact, later this month, the Marine Expeditionary Unit deployed as part of the surge will depart Iraq. Beyond that, if my recommendations are approved, that unit's departure will be followed by the withdrawal of a brigade combat team without replacement in mid-December and the further redeployment without replacement of four other brigade combat teams and the two surge Marine battalions in the first 7 months of 2008, until we reach the pre-surge level of 15 brigade combat teams by mid-July 2008.

I would also like to discuss the period beyond next summer. Force reductions will continue beyond the pre-surge levels of brigade combat teams that we will reach by mid-July 2008; however, in my professional judgment, it would be premature to make recommendations on the pace of such reductions at this time. In fact, our experience in Iraq has repeatedly shown that projecting too far into the future is not just difficult, it can be misleading and even hazardous. The events of the past six months underscore that point. When I testified in January, for example, no one would have dared to forecast that Anbar Province would have been transformed the way it has in the past 6 months. Nor would anyone have predicted that volunteers in one-time Al Qaeda strongholds like Ghazaliyah in western Baghdad or in Adamiya in eastern Baghdad would seek to join the fight against Al Qaeda. Nor would we have anticipated that a Shia-led government would accept significant numbers of Sunni volunteers into the ranks of the local police force in Abu Ghraib. Beyond that, on a less encouraging note, none of us earlier this year appreciated the extent of Iranian involvement in Iraq, something about which we and Iraq's leaders all now have greater concern.

In view of this, I do not believe it is reasonable to have an adequate appreciation for the pace of further reductions and mission adjustments beyond the summer of 2008 until about mid-March of next year. We will, no later than that time, consider factors similar to those on which I based the current recommendations, having by then, of course, a better feel for the security situation, the improvements in the capabilities of our Iraqi counterparts, and the enemy situation. I will then, as I did in developing the recommendations I have explained here today, also take into consideration the demands on our Nation's ground forces, although I believe that that consideration should once again inform, not drive, the recommendations I make.

This chart captures the recommendations I have described, showing the recommended reduction of brigade combat teams as the surge runs its course and illustrating the concept of our units adjusting their missions and transitioning responsibilities to Iraqis, as the situation and Iraqi capabilities permit. It also reflects the no-later-than date for recommendations on force adjustments beyond next summer and provides a possible approach we have considered for the future force structure and mission set in Iraq.

One may argue that the best way to speed the process in Iraq is to change the MNF-I mission from one that emphasizes population security, counter-terrorism, and transition, to one that is strictly focused on transition and counter-terrorism. Making that change now would, in our view, be premature. We have learned before that there is a real danger in handing over tasks to the Iraqi Security Forces before their capacity and local conditions warrant. In fact, the drafters of the recently released National Intelligence Estimate on Iraq recognized this danger when they wrote, and I quote, "We assess that changing the mission of Coalition forces from a primarily counterinsurgency and stabilization role to a primary combat support role for Iraqi forces and counterterrorist operations to prevent AQI from establishing a safe haven would erode security gains achieved thus far."

In describing the recommendations I have made, I should note again that, like Ambassador Crocker, I believe Iraq's problems will require a long-term effort. There are no easy answers or quick solutions. And though we both believe this effort can succeed, it will take time. Our assessments underscore, in fact, the importance of recognizing that a premature drawdown of our forces would likely have devastating consequences.

That assessment is supported by the findings of a 16 August Defense Intelligence Agency report on the implications of a rapid withdrawal of US forces from Iraq. Summarizing it in an unclassified fashion, it concludes that a rapid withdrawal would result in the further release of the strong centrifugal forces in Iraq and produce a number of dangerous results, including a high risk of disintegration of the Iraqi Security Forces; rapid deterioration of local security initiatives; Al Qaeda–Iraq regaining lost ground and freedom of maneuver; a marked increase in violence and further ethno-sectarian displacement and refugee flows; alliances of convenience by Iraqi groups with internal and external forces to gain advantages over their rivals; and exacerbation of already challenging regional dynamics, especially with respect to Iran.

Lieutenant General Odierno and I share this assessment and believe that the best way to secure our national interests and avoid an unfavorable outcome in Iraq is to continue to focus our operations on securing the Iraqi people while targeting terrorist groups and militia extremists and, as quickly as conditions are met, transitioning security tasks to Iraqi elements.

Closing Comments

Before closing, I want to thank you and your colleagues for your support of our men and women in uniform in Iraq. The Soldiers, Sailors, Airmen, Marines, and Coast Guardsmen with whom I'm honored to serve are the best equipped and, very likely, the most professional force in our nation's history. Impressively, despite all that has been asked of them in recent years, they continue to raise their right hands and volunteer to stay in uniform. With three weeks to go in this fiscal year, in fact, the Army elements in Iraq, for example, have achieved well over 130% of the reenlistment goals in the initial term and careerist categories and nearly 115% in the mid-career category. All of us appreciate what you have done to ensure that these great troopers have had what they've needed to accomplish their mission, just as we appreciate what you have done to take care of their families, as they, too, have made significant sacrifices in recent years.

The advances you have underwritten in weapons systems and individual equipment; in munitions; in command, control, and communications systems; in intelligence, surveillance, and reconnaissance capabilities; in vehicles and counter-IED systems and programs; and in manned and unmanned aircraft have proven invaluable in Iraq. The capabilities that you have funded most recently—especially the vehicles that will provide greater protection against improvised explosive devices—are also of enormous importance. Additionally, your funding of the Commander's Emergency Response Program has given our leaders a critical tool with which to prosecute the counterinsurgency campaign. Finally, we appreciate as well your funding of our new detention programs and rule of law initiatives in Iraq.

In closing, it remains an enormous privilege to soldier again in Iraq with America's new "Greatest Generation." Our country's men and women in uniform have done a magnificent job in the most complex and challenging environment imaginable. All Americans should be very proud of their sons and daughters serving in Iraq today.

Thank you very much.

Multi-National Force–Iraq Commander's Counterinsurgency Guidance

Headquarters Multi-National Force–Iraq
Baghdad, Iraq
APO AE 09342-1400
15 July 2008

- **Secure and serve the population.** The Iraqi people are the decisive "terrain." Together with our Iraqi partners, work to provide the people security, to give them respect, to gain their support, and to facilitate establishment of local governance, restoration of basic services, and revival of local economies.
- **Live among the people.** You can't commute to this fight. Position Joint Security Stations, Combat Outposts, and Patrol Bases in the neighborhoods we intend to secure. Living among the people is essential to securing them and defeating the insurgents.
- **Hold areas that have been secured.** Once we clear an area, we must retain it. Develop the plan for holding an area before starting to clear it. The people need to know that we and our Iraqi partners will not abandon them. When reducing forces, gradually thin our presence rather than handing off or withdrawing completely. Ensure situational awareness even after transfer of responsibility to Iraqi forces.
- **Pursue the enemy relentlessly.** Identify and pursue Al Qaeda–Iraq and other extremist elements tenaciously. Do not let them retain support areas or sanctuaries. Force the enemy to respond to us. Deny the enemy the ability to plan and conduct deliberate operations.
- **Employ all assets to isolate and defeat the terrorists and insurgents.** Counter-terrorist forces alone cannot defeat Al Qaeda and the other extremists. Success requires a comprehensive approach that employs all forces and all means at our disposal—non-kinetic as well as kinetic. Employ Coalition and Iraqi con-

ventional and special operations forces, Sons of Iraq, and all other available non-military multipliers in accordance with the attached "Anaconda Strategy."

- **Generate unity of effort.** Coordinate operations and initiatives with our embassy and interagency partners, our Iraqi counterparts, local governmental leaders, and non-governmental organizations to ensure all are working to achieve a common purpose.
- **Promote reconciliation.** We cannot kill our way out of this endeavor. We and our Iraqi partners must identify and separate the "irreconcilables" from the "reconcilables" through thorough intelligence work, population control measures, information operations, kinetic operations, and political initiatives. We must strive to make the reconcilables part of the solution, even as we identify, pursue, and kill, capture, or drive out the irreconcilables.
- **Defeat the network, not just the attack.** Focus to the "left" of the explosion. Employ intelligence assets to identify the network behind an attack, and go after its leaders, explosives experts, financiers, suppliers, and operators.
- **Foster Iraqi legitimacy.** Encourage Iraqi leadership and initiative; recognize that their success is our success. Partner in all that we do and support local involvement in security, governance, economic revival, and provision of basic services. Find the right balance between Coalition Forces leading and the Iraqis exercising their leadership and initiative, and encourage the latter. Legitimacy of Iraqi actions in the eyes of the Iraqi people is essential to overall success.
- **Punch above your weight class.** Strive to be "bigger than you actually are." Partner in operations with Iraqi units and police, and employ "Sons of Iraq," contractors, and local Iraqis to perform routine tasks in and around Forward Operating Bases, Patrol Bases, and Joint Security Stations, thereby freeing up our troopers to focus on tasks "outside the wire."
- **Employ money as a weapon system.** Money can be "ammunition" as the security situation improves. Use a targeting board process to ensure the greatest effect for each "round" expended and to ensure that each engagement using money contributes to the achievement of the unit's overall objectives. Ensure contracting activities support the security effort, employing locals wherever possible. Employ a "matching fund" concept when feasible in order to ensure Iraqi involvement and commitment.
- **Fight for intelligence.** A nuanced understanding of the situation is everything. Analyze the intelligence that is gathered, share it, and fight for more. Every patrol should have tasks designed to augment understanding of the area of operations and the enemy. Operate on a "need to share" rather than a "need to know" basis. Disseminate intelligence as soon as possible to all who can benefit from it.
- **Walk.** Move mounted, work dismounted. Stop by, don't drive by. Patrol on foot and engage the population. Situational awareness can only be gained by interacting with the people face-to-face, not separated by ballistic glass.

- **Understand the neighborhood.** Map the human terrain and study it in detail. Understand the local culture and history. Learn about the tribes, formal and informal leaders, governmental structures, religious elements, and local security forces. Understand how local systems and structures—including governance, provision of basic services, maintenance of infrastructure, and economic elements— are supposed to function and how they really function.
- **Build relationships.** Relationships are a critical component of counterinsurgency operations. Together with our Iraqi counterparts, strive to establish productive links with local leaders, tribal sheikhs, governmental officials, religious leaders, and interagency partners.
- **Look for Sustainable Solutions.** Build mechanisms by which the Iraqi Security Forces, Iraqi community leaders, and local Iraqis under the control of governmental institutions can continue to secure local areas and sustain governance and economic gains in their communities as the Coalition Force presence is reduced. Figure out the Iraqi systems and help Iraqis make them work.
- **Maintain continuity and tempo through transitions.** Start to build the information you'll provide to your successors on the day you take over. Allow those who will follow you to "virtually look over your shoulder" while they're still at home station by giving them access to your daily updates and other items on SIPRNET. Deploy planners and intel analysts ahead of time. Encourage extra time on the ground during transition periods, and strive to maintain operational tempo and local relationships to avoid giving the enemy respite.
- **Manage expectations.** Be cautious and measured in announcing progress. Note what has been accomplished, but also acknowledge what still needs to be done. Avoid premature declarations of success. Ensure our troopers and our partners are aware of our assessments and recognize that any counterinsurgency operation has innumerable challenges, that enemies get a vote, and that progress is likely to be slow.
- **Be first with the truth.** Get accurate information of significant activities to the chain of command, to Iraqi leaders, and to the press as soon as is possible. Beat the insurgents, extremists, and criminals to the headlines, and pre-empt rumors. Integrity is critical to this fight. Don't put lipstick on pigs. Acknowledge setbacks and failures, and then state what we've learned and how we'll respond. Hold the press (and ourselves) accountable for accuracy, characterization, and context. Avoid spin and let facts speak for themselves. Challenge enemy disinformation. Turn our enemies' bankrupt messages, extremist ideologies, oppressive practices, and indiscriminate violence against them.
- **Fight the information war relentlessly.** Realize that we are in a struggle for legitimacy that will be won or lost in the perception of the Iraqi people. Every action taken by the enemy and our forces has implications in the public arena. Develop and sustain a narrative that works and continually drive the themes home through all forms of media.

- **Live our values.** Do not hesitate to kill or capture the enemy, but stay true to the values we hold dear. Living our values distinguishes us from our enemies. There is no tougher endeavor than the one in which we are engaged. It is often brutal, physically demanding, and frustrating. All of us experience moments of anger, but we can neither give in to dark impulses nor tolerate unacceptable actions by others.
- **Exercise initiative.** In the absence of guidance or orders, determine what they should be and execute aggressively. Higher level leaders will provide a broad vision and paint "white lines on the road," but it will be up to those at tactical levels to turn "big ideas" into specific actions.
- **Empower subordinates.** Resource to enable decentralized action. Push assets and authorities down to those who most need them and can actually use them. Flatten reporting chains. Identify the level to which you would naturally plan and resource, and go one further—generally looking three levels down, vice the two levels down that is traditional in major combat operations.
- **Prepare for and exploit opportunities.** "Luck is what happens when preparation meets opportunity" (Seneca the Younger). Develop concepts (such as that of "reconcilables" and "irreconcilables") in anticipation of possible opportunities, and be prepared to take risk as necessary to take advantage of them.
- **Learn and adapt.** Continually assess the situation and adjust tactics, policies, and programs as required. Share good ideas. Avoid mental or physical complacency. Never forget that what works in an area today may not work there tomorrow, and that what works in one area may not work in another. Strive to ensure that our units are learning organizations. In counterinsurgency, the side that learns and adapts the fastest gains important advantages.

David H. Petraeus
General, United States Army
Commanding

APPENDIX 3

Anaconda Strategy versus al-Qaeda in Iraq

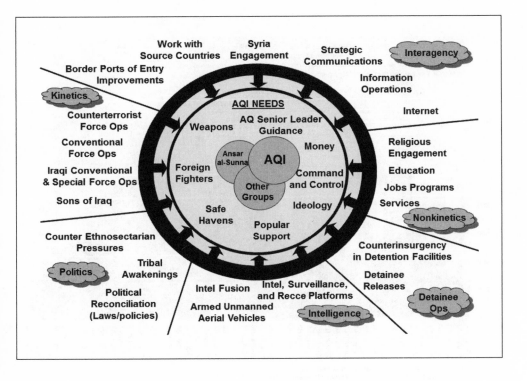

APPENDIX 4

Security Incidents in Iraq

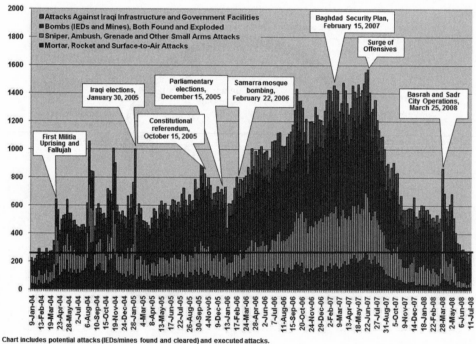

Chart includes potential attacks (IEDs/mines found and cleared) and executed attacks.
Sources: SIGACTS (CF reports) as of July 12, 2008; weekly beginning January 3, 2004.

Notes

Foreword

1. I also testified to members of Congress in closed hearings in April 2007. For those hearings, the deputy secretaries of state and defense, as well as the vice chairman of the Joint Chiefs of Staff, accompanied me, but I ended up answering well over 90 percent of the questions, even those that were in the arena of State, the Agency for International Development, and other civilian agencies, as I often had more detail on the programs than they did. Upon returning to Iraq, I proposed to Ambassador Crocker and our respective superiors in Washington that the hearings in September should involve just the ambassador and me, even if each of us would as a result have to participate in hearings with committees other than those to which we normally would have testified. As a result, we testified before both the foreign relations and armed services committees of the House of Representatives and the Senate.

2. General Ray Odierno succeeded me in September 2008 as commander, Multi-National Force–Iraq and is now chief of staff of the U.S. Army. I often described "General O" as the "operational architect" of the surge.

3. General Lloyd Austin succeeded General Odierno in September 2010 as commander, U.S. Forces–Iraq and remained in that role until the withdrawal of U.S. forces from the country at the end of 2011. He is now vice chief of staff of the U.S. Army and has been selected as the next commander of U.S. Central Command.

4. The various components of the comprehensive approach are captured in the "Counterinsurgency Guidance" memorandum and the "Anaconda Strategy" slide that are included as Appendixes 2 and 3.

5. William Doyle provides a superb account of the establishment of the Ramadi Awakening and the remarkable captain who played a key role in it in his book *A Soldier's Dream: Captain Travis Patriquin and the Awakening of Iraq* (New York: NAL Caliber, 2011). Tragically, Captain Patriquin was killed by an improvised explosive device in December 2006 and did not live to see the extraordinary effects of the Awakening movement that he and Colonel MacFarland had helped to cultivate. Sadly as well, Sheik Sattar al-Rishawi, their key Iraqi partner, was killed by a roadside bomb in September 2007, the target of an assassination planned by al-Qaeda operatives as revenge for his role in the Awakening.

6. General McChrystal would later command the NATO International Security Assistance

Force in Afghanistan before retiring in the summer of 2010. Admiral McRaven took command of the U.S. Special Operations Command in the summer of 2011.

7. We preferred to capture insurgent and militia leaders, as their interrogation inevitably generated intelligence that led to improvements in our understanding of the enemy networks and generated actionable intelligence for follow-on targeted operations. I might add that all of our detainee operations were conducted in accordance with the U.S. Army field manual on "Human Intelligence Collector Operations" that was published in 2006, the same year we published the field manual on counterinsurgency.

8. I commanded the 101st Airborne Division in Iraq from the initial operations in late March 2003 until February 2004. I returned with a team from the 101st on short notice for a couple of weeks in late April and early May 2004 to assess the performance of the Iraqi Security Forces during the so-called April uprising, and then returned in early June to establish the Multi-National Security Transition Command–Iraq, departing in September 2005 (and then conducting a five-day assessment of the train–and–equip effort in Afghanistan for Secretary of Defense Rumsfeld on the way home).

9. General Martin Dempsey is now the chairman, Joint Chiefs of Staff. Lieutenant General Jim Dubik retired in September 2008 after completion of nearly thirteen months as the commander of the train-and-equip effort.

10. Now–Brigadier General Martins is currently the chief prosecutor in the Office of Military Commissions, which oversees the military tribunals of the detainees in Guantánamo. I was privileged to have this brilliant officer—first in his class at West Point, a Rhodes scholar, and a Harvard Law graduate—as a member of my staff in four different assignments over the years.

11. Human terrain teams were small cells of a half-dozen or so contractors educated and trained in such academic specialties as cultural anthropology and political science.

12. The count of attacks reflects adjustments and additions made months and, in some cases, years later, as we continually refined the databases on enemy attacks and a host of other actions that we tracked.

13. The final surge brigade returned to the United States without backfill in July 2008, some sixteen months after the first surge elements arrived in Iraq.

14. I recognize clearly that there are many continuing challenges in Iraq. Elements of al-Qaeda show their residual capability with periodic attacks, militia members are still present, and major unresolved political disputes preclude progress in a host of areas. To date (March 2013), however, despite numerous internal disputes, Iraqi leaders have managed to avoid a relapse to the terrible violence of 2006 and 2007, and various important sectors (especially oil production) have shown significant improvement.

15. At one point in the fall of 2007, I had my initiatives group chief, Colonel Bill Rapp, and our other metrics experts spend two days with key press representatives in an on-the-record conference, walking through the metrics we used to measure progress, what they meant to us, and how they were determined. My intention was to be fully transparent in this regard, as all of us understood the importance of these metrics and the need for them to be as accurate as possible.

16. This description was first used by Tom Brokaw, author of *The Greatest Generation,* after he spent time with our troopers during a visit with the 101st Airborne Division in northern Iraq in the summer of 2003. After seeing all that our soldiers were engaged in, he turned to me before leaving and shouted over the roar of a helicopter cranking up: "You know, General, those World War II troopers were undeniably 'The Greatest Generation,' but surely these soldiers are America's 'New Greatest Generation.'"

17. I had been selected for promotion to brigadier general and served briefly as the commanding general of Combined Joint Task Force 7-Forward, a position that rotated each month.

Prologue

1. I rode in the column and personally witnessed the events. For General Petraeus's view of the significance of this patrol, see Joe Klein, "David Petraeus," *Time,* December 19, 2007, http://www.time.com/time/specials/2007/article/0,28804,1690753_1695388_1695379,00.html.

2. Burning human refuse is a common field sanitation practice when proper sewage facilities are unavailable.

3. Kimberly Kagan, *The Surge: A Military History* (New York: Encounter, 2009), 19.

4. For other views of the devastation, see Linda Robinson, *Tell Me How This Ends: General David Petraeus and the Search for a Way Out of Iraq* (New York: PublicAffairs, 2008), 88, and Tom Ricks, *The Gamble* (New York, Penguin, 2009), 129.

1. A War Almost Lost

1. Multi-National Force–Iraq, Charts to accompany the testimony of GEN David H. Petraeus, 10–11 September 2007, Chart 3 (Iraq Civilian Deaths), http://www.defense.gov/pubs/pdfs/Petraeus -Testimony-Slides20070910.pdf. To provide context to this figure, if the same proportionate level of politically motivated violence were to occur in the United States, nearly thirty thousand people would die each month.

2. UN High Commissioner for Refugees, UNHCR Return Advisory and Position on International Protection Needs of Iraqis Outside Iraq, December 18, 2006, Corr. (April 2007), 2, note 5, http://www.unhcr.org/refworld/docid/46371aa72.html; and International Organization for Migration, Iraq Displacement 2006 Year in Review, http://www.google.com/url?sa=t&rct=j&q=iraq%20 displacement%202006%20year%20in%20review&source=web&cd=1&cad=rja&ved=0CC8QFjA A&url=http%3A%2F%2Fwww.iom.int%2Fjahia%2Fwebdav%2Fsite%2Fmyjahiasite%2Fshared%2F shared%2Fmainsite%2Fmedia%2Fdocs%2Fnews%2F2006_iraq_idp.pdf&ei=YERiUeOrHKfl4AP2 rYCgBA&usg=AFQjCNEkAlCXU5ai2Q6snLQvF3jH9F4mCA&bvm=bv.44770516,d.dmg.

3. For a superb treatment of the operational planning for the invasion of Iraq, see Michael R. Gordon and Bernard E. Trainor, *Cobra II: The Inside Story of the Invasion and Occupation of Iraq* (New York: Pantheon, 2006).

4. I am indebted to Dina Khoury of George Washington University for this thought, which she discussed in a paper at a panel, "The Iraq War Is History?," at the American Historical Association meeting in New Orleans on January 5, 2013.

5. Earl F. Ziemke, *The U.S. Army in the Occupation of Germany, 1944–1946* (Washington, D.C.: U.S. Army Center of Military History, 1975), 6.

6. Ibid., 31.

7. In the fall of 2002 the U.S. Army War College Strategic Studies Institute was tasked by the U.S. Army G-3 to prepare an assessment of the requirements that would follow a successful invasion. On February 1, 2003, Conrad Crane and Andrew Terrill published an assessment of the difficulty involved in occupying Iraq, *Reconstructing Iraq: Insights, Challenges, and Missions for Military Forces in a Post-Conflict Scenario* (Carlisle Barracks, Pa.: Strategic Studies Institute, 2003). The Department of Defense ignored their work in the belief that U.S. forces would not become engaged in a long-term occupation.

8. For the Bush administration's fixation on alleviating humanitarian suffering in postconflict Iraq, see George W. Bush, *Decision Points* (New York: Crown, 2010), 248.

9. For the dysfunction of postwar planning, see Rajiv Chandrasekaran, *Imperial Life in the Emerald City: Inside Iraq's Green Zone* (New York: Knopf, 2006), 28–37.

10. Gordon Rudd, *Reconstructing Iraq: Regime Change, Jay Garner, and the ORHA Story* (Lawrence: University Press of Kansas, 2011), chapter 2. For another view on the prerequisites for successful occupation of a foreign land, see David M. Edelstein, "Occupational Hazards: Why Military Occupations Succeed or Fail," *International Security* 29, no. 1 (2004), 49–91.

11. Rudd, *Reconstructing Iraq*, chapter 8.

12. Chandrasekaran, *Imperial Life in the Emerald City*, 70; L. Paul Bremer III, with Malcolm McConnell, *My Year in Iraq: The Struggle to Build a Future of Hope* (New York: Simon and Schuster, 2006), 39–40. Feith in turn had been influenced by the hard-line extremist views of Ahmed Chalabi and his compatriots in the Iraqi National Congress. Since Bremer was President Bush's envoy, he could have overridden the order provided to him by the Office of the Secretary of Defense, but chose not to.

13. Special Inspector General for Iraq Reconstruction (SIGIR), *Hard Lessons: The Iraq Reconstruction Experience* (Washington, D.C.: Government Printing Office, 2009), 71.

14. For the complete text of CPA Order 1, see http://www.iraqcoalition.org/regulations /20030516_CPAORD_1_De-Ba_athification_of_Iraqi_Society_.pdf.

15. Najim Abed al-Jabouri and Sterling Jensen, "The Iraqi and AQI Roles in the Sunni Awakening," *Prism* 2, no. 1 (2010), 8, http://www.ndu.edu/press/lib/images/prism2-1/Prism_3-18_Al-Jabouri_Jensen.pdf.

16. George Packer, *The Assassin's Gate: America in Iraq* (New York: Farrar, Straus and Giroux, 2005), 191.

17. For an excellent analysis of the impact of CPA Order 1, see W. Andrew Terrill, *Lessons of the Iraqi De-Ba'athification Program for Iraq's Future and the Arab Revolutions* (Carlisle Barracks, Pa.: Strategic Studies Institute, 2012).

18. For the complete text of CPA Order 2, see http://www.iraqcoalition.org/regulations/ 20030823_CPAORD_2_Dissolution_of_Entities_with_Annex_A.pdf. For the influence of Wolfowitz and Feith on the promulgation of the order, see Terrill, *Lessons of the Iraqi De-Ba'athification Program,* 15.

19. Gordon and Trainor, *COBRA II,* 479–480.

20. Ali A. Allawi, *The Occupation of Iraq: Winning the War, Losing the Peace* (New Haven: Yale University Press, 2007), 157.

21. Bremer and McConnell, *My Year in Iraq,* 53–58.

22. For the impact of the dissolution of the Iraqi Army on its officers and soldiers, see Allawi, *The Occupation of Iraq,* 158.

23. For the willingness of Iraqi military officers to work with the U.S. military and the adverse impact of CPA Order Number 2, see Packer, *The Assassin's Gate,* 194–195, and Chandrasekaran, *Imperial Life in the Emerald City,* 76–77.

24. President George W. Bush wrote later that in retrospect, he should have demanded more debate on Bremer's orders to de-Ba'athify Iraqi society and to disband the Iraqi Army. Bush, *Decision Points,* 259.

25. Bremer and McConnell, *My Year in Iraq,* 149.

26. Packer, *The Assassin's Gate,* 212–216; Allawi, *The Occupation of Iraq,* 166.

27. Terrill, *Lessons of the Iraqi De-Ba'athification Program,* xi.

28. Mark Moyar, *A Question of Command: Counterinsurgency from the Civil War to Iraq* (New Haven: Yale University Press, 2009), 254–255.

29. Ibid., 255.

30. Mark Grimsley, "Wars for the American South: The First and Second Reconstructions Considered as Insurgencies," *Civil War History* 58, no. 1 (2012), 6–36.

31. David H. Petraeus, "Learning Counterinsurgency: Observations from Soldiering in Iraq," *Military Review,* January –February 2006, http://www.army.mil/professionalWriting/volumes/vol ume4/april_2006/4_06_2.html.

32. Michael R. Gordon, "The Struggle for Iraq: Reconstruction; 101st Airborne Scores Success in Northern Iraq," *New York Times,* September 4, 2003, http://www.nytimes.com/2003/09/04/ international/worldspecial/04NORT.html.

33. Chandrasekaran, *Imperial Life in the Emerald City,* 63. Given Kissinger's penchant for centralization of power, this statement is quite an admission.

34. SIGIR, *Hard Lessons,* 100.

35. Ibid., 323.

36. Ibid., viii.

37. Peter R. Mansoor, *Baghdad at Sunrise: A Brigade Commander's War in Iraq* (New Haven: Yale University Press, 2008), 80–82; Bing West, *The Strongest Tribe: War, Politics, and the Endgame in Iraq* (New York: Random House, 2008), 24.

38. SIGIR, *Hard Lessons,* 83.

39. Ibid, 159.

40. For a discussion of this decision, see Gordon and Trainor, *COBRA II*, 460–461.

41. For an examination of the insurgent Ramadan offensive of 2003, see Mansoor, *Baghdad at Sunrise*, chapter 5.

42. Bob Woodward, *State of Denial: Bush at War, Part III* (New York: Simon and Schuster, 2006), 266.

43. Donald Rumsfeld, *Known and Unknown* (New York: Sentinel, 2011), 522.

44. H. R. McMaster, "Learning from Contemporary Conflicts to Prepare for Future War," *Orbis*, Fall 2008, 565.

45. For an indictment of U.S. military operations in the first three years of the Iraq War, see Thomas E. Ricks, *Fiasco: The American Military Adventure in Iraq, 2003–2005* (New York: Penguin, 2006).

46. Donald P. Wright and Timothy R. Reese, *On Point II: Transition to the New Campaign: The United States Army in Operation IRAQI FREEDOM, May 2003–January 2005* (Fort Leavenworth, Kan.: Combat Studies Institute Press, 2008), 116.

47. The administration had justified the war based on national security considerations and the need to find and destroy Saddam Hussein's weapons of mass destruction. After the collapse of the Ba'athist regime, researchers with access to Iraqi records determined that in fact Saddam had destroyed the weapons after the Gulf War, but he wanted to retain ambiguity as to whether or not Iraq possessed such weapons in order to deter Iran. See Kevin M. Woods et al., *Iraqi Perspectives Project: A View of Operation Iraqi Freedom from Saddam's Senior Leadership* (Norfolk, Va.: Joint Center for Operational Analysis, 2006).

48. Ricardo S. Sanchez, *Wiser in Battle: A Soldier's Story* (New York: HarperCollins, 2008), 321.

49. General David H. Petraeus, CENTCOM Update, Center for New American Security, June 11, 2009, Slide 8, "Security Incidents in Iraq," http://www.cnas.org/files/multimedia/documents/Petraeus%20Slides.pdf.

50. West, *The Strongest Tribe*, 7.

51. Lieutenant General Ricardo Sanchez, commander of CJTF-7, and General John Abizaid, head of U.S. Central Command, discussed a "window of opportunity" during this time, but could get no cooperation from Bremer to alter his chosen political course. See Sanchez, *Wiser in Battle*, 310–311.

52. International Crisis Group, "In Their Own Words: Reading the Iraqi Insurgency," *Middle East Report*, February 15, 2006; West, *The Strongest Tribe*, 28–29.

53. General John Abizaid, head of U.S. Central Command, thought that U.S. forces in Iraq were "antibodies," but the virus analogy is more correct.

54. Bing West, *No True Glory: A Frontline Account of the Battle for Fallujah* (New York: Bantam, 2005), 59; Sanchez, *Wiser in Battle*, 371.

55. West, *No True Glory*, 90–93; Vincent L. Foulk, *The Battle for Fallujah: Occupation, Resistance and Stalemate in the War in Iraq* (Jefferson, N.C.: McFarland, 2007), 28.

56. West, *No True Glory*, 119–120; Chandrasekaran, *Imperial Life in the Emerald City*, 276; Michael R. Gordon and General Bernard E. Trainor, *The Endgame: The Inside Story of the Struggle for Iraq, from George W. Bush to Barack Obama* (New York: Pantheon, 2012), 61–62. In his memoirs, Sanchez states his belief that President Bush and the National Security Council ordered Bremer to halt the offensive; otherwise, he would not have interfered so blatantly in a military operation. Sanchez, *Wiser in Battle*, 354. But Rumsfeld states in his memoirs that the decision to halt the operation was Bremer's, and that the president backed the judgment of his envoy on the ground in Iraq. Rumsfeld, *Known and Unknown*, 533–534.

57. Technically, U.S. Marines turned the city over to a sham entity called the Fallujah Brigade, but in reality it had no power and the city remained under control of Sunni militants.

58. Patrick Cockburn, *Muqtada: Muqtada Al-Sadr, the Shi'a Revival, and the Struggle for Iraq* (New York: Scribner, 2008), 135–136; Chandrasekaran, *Imperial Life in the Emerald City*, 264.

59. Mansoor, *Baghdad at Sunrise*, 280–281.

60. Bremer and McConnell, *My Year in Iraq*, 319.

61. West, *The Strongest Tribe*, 39–40.

62. Rumsfeld, *Known and Unknown,* 547, 550–551.

63. Ibid., 38.

64. The examples included (among others) the Second Anglo-Boer War, the Philippine Insurrection, the Arab Revolt, Iraq in 1920, French Indochina, the Huk Rebellion in the Philippines, the Vietnam War, the Soviet-Afghan War, and other insurgencies in Malaya, Kenya, Algeria, Aden, Cuba, Columbia, Northern Ireland, Oman, Sri Lanka, Palestine, Rhodesia, El Salvador, Nicaragua, Kashmir, Somalia, Chechnya, Afghanistan, and Iraq.

65. Kalev Sepp, "Best Practices in Counterinsurgency," *Military Review,* May–June 2005, 8.

66. Ibid.

67. Ibid., 8–12. For the importance of good leadership in counterinsurgency warfare, see Mark Moyer, *A Question of Command: Counterinsurgency from the Civil War to Iraq* (New Haven: Yale University Press, 2009).

68. Sepp, "Best Practices in Counterinsurgency," 12.

69. The Counterinsurgency Center for Excellence opened at Taji in November 2005, nearly eighteen months into Casey's tenure as MNF-I commander. See George W. Casey, *Strategic Reflections: Operation Iraqi Freedom, July 2004–February 2007* (Washington, D.C.: National Defense University Press, 2012), 73.

70. MNF-I, "Campaign Plan: Operation Iraqi Freedom, Partnership: From Occupation to Constitutional Elections," August 5, 2004, 14; declassified September 29, 2009, copy located in the General George Casey Papers, National Defense University Archives.

71. The Special Forces community has many parts, including, among others, special mission units, U.S. Army Special Forces (the "Green Berets"), the 75th Ranger Regiment, U.S. Navy SEALs, and U.S. Air Force Pararescue teams. The U.S. Army Special Forces traditionally are used to train and advise foreign militaries with a secondary role as direct action units. In Iraq, these roles were reversed as direct action took precedence over training the new Iraqi Army.

72. MNF-I Red Team, "Building Legitimacy and Confronting Insurgency in Iraq," July 15, 2004, 3; declassified September 29, 2009, copy located in the General George Casey Papers, National Defense University Archives.

73. Ibid., 6.

74. MNF-I, "Campaign Plan," August 5, 2004, 14.

75. Ibid., 15.

76. Ibid., 6.

77. Ibid., 16.

78. West, *The Strongest Tribe,* 48–49.

79. Ibid., 55–60; West, *No True Glory,* chapters 24–28, describes the battle in detail. For a description of the fighting at the small-unit level, see David Bellavia, *House to House* (New York: Pocket Books, 2008).

80. MNF-I, "Campaign Progress Review," December 12, 2004, 12; declassified September 29, 2009, copy located in the General George Casey Papers, National Defense University Archives.

81. West, *The Strongest Tribe,* 70.

82. See, for instance, MNF-I, "MNF-I Campaign Action Plan for 2005—Transition to Self-Reliance," April 22, 2005, 2–3; declassified September 29, 2009, copy located in the General George Casey Papers, National Defense University Archives.

83. An August 2005 MNF-I survey found that unit operations in Iraq reflected "an understanding of COIN theory, doctrine, and 'best practices' and that generally our COIN strategy was understood and in operation." MNF-I, "The September Assessment," September 23, 2005, 17; declassified September 29, 2009, copy located in the General George Casey Papers, National Defense University Archives.

84. "MNF-I Campaign Action Plan for 2005," 4 and 6.

85. MNF-I, "CONPLAN—Transition to Iraqi Security Self-Reliance and Coalition Transformation," April 25, 2005, 11; declassified September 29, 2009, copy located in the General George Casey Papers, National Defense University Archives.

86. Ibid., 12–13.

87. President's Radio Address, August 27, 2005, http://georgewbush-whitehouse.archives.gov/news/releases/2005/08/20050827.html.

88. Casey, *Strategic Reflections,* 80.

89. "The September Assessment," 1–3.

90. Ambassador Zalmay Khalilzad and General George Casey, "Joint Mission Statement: Building Success—Completing the Transition," December 6, 2005, 6; declassified September 29, 2009, copy located in the General George Casey Papers, National Defense University Archives.

91. Timothy S. McWilliams and Kurtis P. Wheeler, eds., *Al-Anbar Awakening,* vol. 1, *American Perspectives: U.S. Marines and Counterinsurgency in Iraq, 2004–2009* (Quantico, Va.: Marine Corps University Press, 2009), 9–10; West, *The Strongest Tribe,* 101–102.

92. George Packer, "The Lesson of Tal Afar," *New Yorker,* April 10, 2006, http://www.new yorker.com/archive/2006/04/10/060410fa_fact2; Ricardo A. Herrera, "Brave Rifles at Tall 'Afar, September 2005," in *Case Studies from the Long War,* ed. William G. Robertson (Fort Leavenworth, Kan.: Combat Studies Institute Press, 2006), 1: 125–152.

93. White House, "National Strategy for Victory in Iraq," November 30, 2005, http://www .globalsecurity.org/military/library/policy/national/ns-victory-iraq_051130.htm.

94. Elise Labott, "Rice: U.S. Will Defeat Insurgency, Rebuild Iraq," CNN Politics, October 19, 2005, http://articles.cnn.com/2005-10-19/politics/iraq.rice_1_provincial-reconstruction-teams -number-of-american-forces-insurgency?_s=PM:POLITICS.

95. Bob Woodward, *State of Denial: Bush at War, Part III* (New York: Simon and Schuster, 2006), 418.

96. Ricks, *Fiasco,* 424.

97. Dick Cheney, *In My Time: A Personal and Political Memoir* (New York: Threshold, 2011), 433; Woodward, *State of Denial,* 382.

98. Chandrasekaran, *Imperial Life in the Emerald City,* 297.

99. For the impact of Iranian funding on Shi'a political parties, see Gordon and Trainor, *The Endgame,* 183.

100. For an analysis of the initial election of 2005 and its adverse impact on the situation in Iraq, see Pauline H. Baker, "Lessons from the January Elections: Iraq as a Failed State," Fund for Peace, August 15, 2005, http://www.isn.ethz.ch/isn/Digital-Library/Publications/Detail/?ots591 =0c54e3b3-1e9c-be1e-2c24-a6a8c7060233&lng=en&ord866=grp2&id=44454. The drafter of this report states, "Policy options facing the United States at this point are not simple and they contain many contradictions. The U.S. strategy is to press for parliamentary democracy, train local forces, and try to establish a governance infrastructure so American and coalition forces can go home. The indicators suggest, however, that this strategy is having a boomerang effect: democratization is un- wittingly fueling the conflict, the presence of foreign forces is enflaming the insurgency, and state- building without political inclusiveness is deepening sectarian divisions within the society"; ibid., 11.

101. David Galula, *Counterinsurgency Warfare: Theory and Practice* (Westport, Conn.: Prae- ger, 1964).

102. David Kilcullen, "Counter-insurgency *Redux,*" *Survival* 48, no. 4 (2006–2007), 111–130.

103. Edward Wong, "U.S. Splits With Iraqi Official Over Prisoner Abuse," *New York Times,* November 17, 2005.

104. "Deadly Attacks Rock Baghdad, Karbala," CNN World, March 2, 2004, http://articles.cnn .com/2004-03-02/world/sprj.nirq.main_1_suicide-bombers-karbala-zarqawi?_s=PM:WORLD.

105. Cockburn, *Muqtada,* 179–180.

106. Text from a letter written by Abu Musab al-Zarqawi captured in a safe house in Baghdad on January 23, 2004, available at http://newamericancentury.org/middleeast-20040212.htm.

107. Allawi, *The Occupation of Iraq,* 447–448.

108. MNF-I, "Campaign Progress Review, December 2005–June 2005," June 27, 2005, 9; de- classified September 29, 2009, copy located in the General George Casey Papers, National Defense University Archives.

109. Robert F. Worth, "Blast Destroys Shrine in Iraq, Setting Off Sectarian Fury," *New York Times,* February 22, 2006, http://www.nytimes.com/2006/02/22/international/middleeast/22cnd-iraq.html?_r=1&hp&ex=1140670800&en=1077baccd068bf6b&ei=5094&partner=homepage.

110. Ellen Knickmeyer and K. I. Ibrahim, "Bombing Shatters Mosque in Iraq," *Washington Post,* February 23, 2006, http://www.washingtonpost.com/wp-dyn/content/article/2006/02/22/AR 2006022200454.html.

111. Worth, "Blast Destroys Shrine in Iraq."

112. MNF-I, "Strategic Directive—Golden Mosque Bombing," February 24, 2006; declassified September 29, 2009, copy located in the General George Casey Papers, National Defense University Archives.

113. Ellen Knickmeyer and Bassam Sebti, "Toll in Iraq's Deadly Surge: 1,300," *Washington Post,* February 28, 2006, http://www.washingtonpost.com/wp-dyn/content/article/2006/02/27/AR2006 022701128.html.

114. Cockburn, *Muqtada,* 175–186.

115. Allawi, *The Occupation of Iraq,* 442–443.

116. Ibid., 445.

117. Ibid., 449–450.

118. David Cloud and Greg Jaffe, *The Fourth Star: Four Generals and the Epic Struggle for the Future of the United States Army* (New York: Crown, 2009), 230.

119. U.S. Mission Iraq and MNF-I, "Joint Campaign Plan, Operation Iraqi Freedom: Transition to Iraqi Self-Reliance," April 28, 2006, 11; declassified September 29, 2009, copy located in the General George Casey Papers, National Defense University Archives.

120. Ibid., 17.

121. Ibid., 22–23.

122. Casey, *Strategic Reflections,* 107–108; Linda Robinson, *Tell Me How This Ends: General David Petraeus and the Search for a Way Out of Iraq* (New York: PublicAffairs, 2008), 16.

123. U.S. Mission Iraq and MNF-I, "2006 Joint Campaign Action Plan: Unity, Security, Prosperity," June 9, 2006, 7 and 11; declassified September 29, 2009, copy located in the General George Casey Papers, National Defense University Archives.

124. U.S. Mission Iraq and MNF-I, "Campaign Progress Review," June 14, 2006, 4 and 7; declassified September 29, 2009, copy located in the General George Casey Papers, National Defense University Archives.

125. Casey, *Strategic Reflections,* 113–116.

126. Cloud and Jaffe, *The Fourth Star,* 232.

127. Gordon and Trainor, *The Endgame,* 223–228.

128. Joint Campaign Plan, April 28, 2006, 28.

129. Rumsfeld, *Known and Unknown,* 698.

130. James A. Baker, III, and Lee H. Hamilton, "The Iraq Study Group Report," December 6, 2006, 15, available at http://media.usip.org/reports/iraq_study_group_report.pdf.

131. Petraeus, CENTCOM Update, slide 9.

132. That is, every line of operation was failing exception "Transition," which was MNF-I's main priority in 2006.

133. U.S. Mission Iraq and MNF-I, "Campaign Progress Review, June 2006–December 2006," 2; declassified September 29, 2009, copy located in the General George Casey Papers, National Defense University Archives.

134. Ibid., 6.

135. Baker and Hamilton, "The Iraq Study Group Report," 15.

2. Designing the Surge

1. Ralph Peters, "Progress and Peril: New Counterinsurgency Manual Cheats on the History Exam," *Armed Forces Journal,* (February 2007, http://armedforcesjournal.com/2007/02/2456854.

2. These were the words used by a native chieftain to decry Rome's wanton killing and destruction to suppress revolts, as recorded by Tacitus in *Agricola,* chapter 30, http://www.gutenberg.org/dirs/etext05/8aggr10.txt.

3. Field Manual 3-24, *Counterinsurgency* (Washington, D.C.: Department of the Army, 2006), chapter 1.

4. Ibid., 1–13.

5. For the historical basis of the troop ratio, see James T. Quinlivan, "Force Requirements in Stability Operations," *Parameters* 23 (1995–1996), 59–69. For an example of the reporting on the troop ratio see Dan Murphy, "New Commander, New Plan in Iraq," *Christian Science Monitor,* February 9, 2007, http://www.csmonitor.com/2007/0209/p01s03-woiq.html. The manual was contentious even within the military. John McGrath at the Combat Studies Institute at Fort Leavenworth conducted a study that determined that a ratio of 13.26 troops per 1,000 people was more appropriate, roughly one-third of whom should be employed as police. John J. McGrath, *Boots on the Ground: Troop Density in Contingency Operations* (Fort Leavenworth, Kan.: Combat Studies Institute, 2006). McGrath's study, however, included relatively benign occupation zones such as postwar Germany and Japan, as well as peacekeeping operations in Bosnia. These examples of constabulary and peacekeeping operations were vastly different in degree of violence from operations in a country such as Iraq, gripped by a full-blown, robust insurgency. For an even more recent examination of this issue, see Steven M. Goode, "A Historical Basis for Force Requirements in Counterinsurgency," *Parameters* 39 (2009–2010), 45–57.

6. The Future Combat System and similar weapons systems were predicated on a "revolution in military affairs" ushered in by the marriage of precision guided munitions with advanced intelligence, surveillance, and reconnaissance systems. Its proponents pointed to the decisive U.S. victory in the 1991 Gulf War as proof of this revolution, but they ignored the historical antecedents that would have painted a different conclusion. Historian Williamson Murray writes, "American victory in the Second Gulf War indeed represented—as advertised—a revolution in military affairs. But it was less a triumph of American technology than a triumph of concepts and doctrine that rested firmly on an understanding of the fundamental nature of war. . . . But that 'revolution in military affairs' is over. Present and future opponents and allies of the United States know what U.S. forces can do. . . . The watchword during the post–Cold War drawdown has been that a generic technological superiority—rather than any searching ongoing reassessment of strategic, operational, and conceptual possibilities—is the key to the future. And the services, with the exception of the U.S. Marine Corps, have predictably once again focused solely upon the procurement of sophisticated high-cost weapons systems while slighting intellectual and conceptual preparation for war"; Williamson Murray, "The Future Behind Us," in *The Dynamics of Military Revolution, 1300–2050,* ed. MacGregor Knox and Williamson Murray (Cambridge: Cambridge University Press, 2001), 189–192.

7. E-mail, Colonel Peter Mansoor to Lieutenant General David Petraeus, September 17, 2006.

8. Thomas E. Ricks, *The Gamble: General David Petraeus and the American Military Adventure in Iraq, 2006–2008* (New York: Penguin, 2009), 89–90.

9. Michael R. Gordon, "Military Team Undertakes a Broad Review of the Iraq War and the Campaign against Terror," *New York Times,* November 11, 2006; Elaine M. Grossman, "Pace Group to Put Forth Iraq Strategy Alternatives by Mid-December," *Inside the Pentagon,* November 9, 2006.

10. In discussing the role of the United States in the world today, at one point one of the chiefs quipped, "Others see the U.S. as the last vestige of imperialism—but we're shitty at it."

11. A full discussion of the thesis that the major conflicts in the post–Cold War era would be between and among competing civilizations is found in Samuel P. Huntington, *The Clash of Civilizations and the Remaking of World Order* (New York: Simon and Schuster, 1996).

12. A version of this meeting is recorded in Ricks, *The Gamble,* 103–104.

13. A version of this episode is recorded in Thomas E. Ricks, "Pentagon May Suggest Short-Term Buildup Leading to Iraq Exit," *Washington Post,* November 20, 2006.

14. Dick Cheney, *In My Time: A Personal and Political Memoir* (New York: Threshold, 2011), 439.

15. George W. Bush, *Decision Points* (New York: Crown, 2010), 363.

16. Bob Woodward, *The War Within: A Secret White House History, 2006–2008* (New York: Simon and Schuster, 2008), 102.

17. Bush, *Decision Points*, 364.

18. The details of this meeting are covered in Woodward, *The War Within*, 88–99.

19. Bush, *Decision Points*, 371.

20. Woodward, *The War Within*, 179.

21. Bush, *Decision Points*, 372. The options are also detailed in Woodward, *The War Within*, 190–192.

22. General Petraeus's comment on author's draft manuscript, August 9, 2011.

23. Cheney, *In My Time*, 442–443; Donald Rumsfeld, *Known and Unknown* (New York: Sentinel, 2011), 705–706. The president's thoughts on replacing Rumsfeld are detailed in Woodward, *The War Within*, 196–197.

24. Woodward, *The War Within*, 207–208.

25. Peter D. Feaver, "The Right to Be Right: Civil-Military Relations and the Iraq Surge Decision," *International Security* 35, no. 4 (2011), 106.

26. The memo was promptly leaked to the *New York Times*, which published it in full on November 29.

27. Memo, National Security Adviser Stephen J. Hadley to President George W. Bush, November 8, 2006, http://www.nytimes.com/2006/11/29/world/middleeast/29mtext.html?_r=1&page wanted=all.

28. Ibid.

29. "Bush, Maliki News Conference Transcript," NPR, November 30, 2006, http://www.npr .org/templates/story/story.php?storyId=6559560.

30. Bush, *Decision Points*, 374; Woodward, *The War Within*, 256–257.

31. General Casey wanted a reinforcement of two brigades to help secure Baghdad and two Marine battalions to assist in ongoing counterinsurgency efforts in Anbar province, but he was increasingly out of step with the administration on this issue. George W. Casey, *Strategic Reflections: Operation Iraqi Freedom, July 2004–February 2007* (Washington, D.C.: National Defense University Press, 2012), 145.

32. James A. Baker, III, and Lee H. Hamilton, "The Iraq Study Group Report," December 6, 2006, available at http://media.usip.org/reports/iraq_study_group_report.pdf.

33. Ibid., 6.

34. Ibid., 30.

35. Ibid., 50.

36. Frederick W. Kagan, "Choosing Victory: A Plan for Success in Iraq," American Enterprise Institute, January 5, 2007, http://www.aei.org/paper/foreign-and-defense-policy/regional/middle -east-and-north-africa/choosing-victory-a-plan-for-success-in-iraq-paper/.

37. Woodward, *The War Within*, 279–281; Linda Robinson, *Tell Me How This Ends: General David Petraeus and the Search for a Way Out of Iraq* (New York: PublicAffairs, 2008), 32–34.

38. Cheney, *In My Time*, 449–451; Woodward, *The War Within*, 279–282; Robinson, *Tell Me How This Ends*, 35; Ricks, *The Gamble*, 98–101. It is interesting that President Bush does not mention the meeting in his memoirs, but the record for its importance is fairly clear.

39. Bush, *Decision Points*, 376; Cheney, *In My Time*, 451–453. See also the discussion of this meeting in Feaver, "The Right to Be Right," 107–108.

40. A few members stayed on to re-form the organization with new members in order to examine the war in Afghanistan, but the group never again had the impact on the national stage of the original council.

41. Casey, *Strategic Reflections*, 143.

42. David Cloud and Greg Jaffe, *The Fourth Star: Four Generals and the Epic Struggle for the Future of the United States Army* (New York: Crown, 2009), 241–242.

43. Casey, *Strategic Reflections*, 142; see also General Casey's testimony to the Senate Armed

Services Committee, February 1, 2007, in which he confirmed his support for just two surge brigades.

44. Casey, *Strategic* Reflections, 138.

45. Cloud and Jaffe, *The Fourth Star,* 247.

46. Bush, *Decision Points,* 377.

47. Michael R. Gordon and General Bernard E. Trainor, *The Endgame: The Inside Story of the Struggle for Iraq, from George W. Bush to Barack Obama* (New York: Pantheon, 2012), 307; Woodward, *The War Within,* 296–299.

48. President Bush would later authorize "enablers" like aviation and engineer units to support the surge, which would grow closer to forty thousand additional troops at its height.

49. "President's Address to the Nation," January 10, 2007, http://georgewbush-whitehouse. archives.gov/news/releases/2007/01/20070110-7.html.

50. Bush, *Decision Points,* 375.

51. Feaver, "The Right to Be Right," 114.

52. H. R. McMaster had published one of the groundbreaking books on the Vietnam War, *Dereliction of Duty: Johnson, McNamara, the Joint Chiefs of Staff, and the Lies That Led to Vietnam* (New York: HarperCollins, 1997), in which he analyzed the pernicious role of the Joint Chiefs of Staff in allowing President Lyndon B. Johnson and Secretary of Defense Robert S. McNamara to commit U.S. combat forces to Vietnam in 1965 without a clear strategy or enough resources to achieve victory.

53. Ricks, *The Gamble,* 143–145.

54. Thomas E. Ricks, "Officers With PhDs Advising War Effort," *Washington Post,* February 5, 2007.

55. Babak Dehghanpisheh and John Barry, "Brainiac Brigade," *Newsweek,* September 15, 2007, http://www.thedailybeast.com/newsweek/2007/09/15/brainiac-brigade.html.

56. Transcript, "General Petraeus's Opening Statement," January 23, 2007, http://www.ny times.com/2007/01/23/world/middleeast/24petraeustextcnd.html.

57. Ibid.

58. Private security contractors lack the accountability of soldiers who wear the uniform of a nation-state. Due to a Coalition Provisional Authority decree signed by Ambassador L. Paul Bremer III and still in force, contractors were immune to prosecution by Iraqi courts. Lack of accountability led to a number of problems that adversely affected our counterinsurgency mission in Iraq.

59. Paula Broadwell, *All In: The Education of General David Petraeus* (New York: Penguin, 2012), 237.

60. General David Petraeus, "Change-of-command remarks," February 10, 2007, http://www .militaryconnection.com/columns/david-petraeus/change-of-command.html.

61. Ibid.

62. General Petraeus's comment on author's draft manuscript, August 9, 2011.

3. Fardh al-Qanoon

1. The Iraqi government came up with the name Fardh al-Qanoon for the operation. In an attempt to translate the phrase into one understandable to a Western audience, for a short time MNF-I called the plan Operation Law and Order. Sadi and Heather quickly complained that "law and order," translated back into Arabic, lost the meaning of the original phrase. General Petraeus then decided to call the operation by its Iraqi name. The phrase was more difficult for Americans to understand, but it was more important from an informational standpoint that the Iraqi people understand what the operation was all about.

2. Author interview with Colonel (Ret.) James Hickey, February 2, 2011.

3. Dale Kuehl, "Inside the Surge: 1-5 Cavalry in Ameriyah," *Small Wars Journal,* October 26, 2008, http://smallwarsjournal.com/mag/docs-temp/118-kuehl.pdf.

4. Hickey interview. Of course, the MNC-I focus in late 2006 made sense in the context of a strategy focused on targeting terrorist and insurgent operatives and transferring security responsibilities to Iraqi control.

5. Ibid.

6. Hickey had served as a brigade commander under Odierno in the 4th Infantry Division (Mechanized) from 2003 to 2005.

7. General Raymond Odierno, unpublished and undated article on the surge, copy provided by General Odierno to the author, 19; Kimberly Kagan, *The Surge: A Military History* (New York: Encounter, 2009), 17–18.

8. Colonel James B. Hickey, "The Art of Operational Battle Command: The Surge of 2007," unpublished manuscript, 3.

9. General Raymond Odierno, unpublished and undated article on the surge, 19.

10. Hickey interview.

11. Ibid.

12. General David H. Petraeus, Open Letter to the Troops of MNF-I, February 10, 2007, http://smallwarsjournal.com/blog/general-petraeus-letter-to-mnf-i.

13. This incident is recounted in the Prologue.

14. Kagan, *The Surge*, 37.

15. Michelle Tan, "Security Stations Support Constant Presence," *Army Times*, March 4, 2007, http://www.armytimes.com/news/2007/03/ATbaghdadsecurity070304/.

16. Kagan, *The Surge*, 33. This was the location of General Petraeus's first patrol into Baghdad after assuming command of Multi-National Force–Iraq, as recounted in the Prologue.

17. Commander, MNF-I, "SECDEF WEEKLY UPDATE, 3–9 MAR 07," 3, originally classified SECRET-NOFORN, redacted and declassified May 2012, Petraeus Papers, National Defense University. The length of the surge was the focus of a bitter political debate in Washington at the time. General Petraeus wanted to ensure that his superiors understood that to succeed, the surge had to last longer than just a few months.

18. Lieutenant General Raymond Odierno, Opening Remarks to the Union League, February 19, 2008.

19. LTC Jim Crider, "Inside the Surge: One Commander's Lessons in Counterinsurgency," CNAS Working Paper, June 2009, 11, http://www.cnas.org/files/documents/publications/CNAS_Working%20Paper_Surge_CriderRicks_June2009_ONLINE.pdf.

20. Ibid., 12.

21. Commander, MNF-I, "SECDEF WEEKLY UPDATE, 10–16 MAR 07," 1, originally classified SECRET-NOFORN, redacted and declassified May 2012, Petraeus Papers, National Defense University.

22. Marc Santora, "2 Car Bombs Kill Scores at Packed Market in Baghdad," *New York Times*, January 23, 2007, http://www.nytimes.com/2007/01/23/world/middleeast/22cnd-iraq.html.

23. Scott Conroy, "Baghdad Bomb Kills 121, Wounds Hundreds," CBS News, February 3, 2007, http://www.cbsnews.com/stories/2007/02/03/iraq/main2428779.shtml.

24. "Baghdad Bombing Death Toll Rises," CBS News, February 4, 2007, http://www.cbsnews.com/stories/2007/02/04/iraq/main2430116.shtml.

25. Damien Cave, "Two Markets Bombed in Central Baghdad, Killing at Least 67 and Wounding 155," *New York Times*, February 12, 2007, http://www.nytimes.com/2007/02/13/world/middleeast/13iraq.html.

26. Kimberly Kagan, "Transcript of Interview with COL J. B. Burton," November 14, 2007, http://www.understandingwar.org/press-media/webcast/isw-interview-col-jb-burton-commander-dagger-brigade-baghdad-iraq, 6.

27. See, for instance, Julian Borger, "Security Fences or Barriers to Peace?" *The Guardian*, April 23, 2007, http://www.guardian.co.uk/world/2007/apr/24/iraq.julianborger.

28. David Galula, *Counterinsurgency Warfare: Theory and Practice* (Westport, Conn.: Praeger, 1964, rpt. 2006), 82.

29. Thomas E. Ricks, *The Gamble: General David Petraeus and the American Military Adventure in Iraq, 2006–2008* (New York: Penguin, 2009), 167.

30. James R. Crider, "A View from Inside the Surge," *Military Review,* March–April 2009, 83.

31. Ibid., 84.

32. Ibid., 85.

33. Jody Kieffer and Kevin Trissell, "DOD Biometrics—Lifting the Veil of Insurgent Identity," ARMY AL&T, April–June 2010, 17, http://asc.army.mil/docs/pubs/alt/2010/2_AprMayJun/articles/14_DOD_Biometrics—Lifting_the_Veil_of_Insurgent_Identity_201002.pdf.

34. General Petraeus comment on draft manuscript, August 11, 2011.

35. Kagan, *The Surge,* 110–111.

36. Ibid., 34.

37. David Cloud and Greg Jaffe, *The Fourth Star: Four Generals and the Epic Struggle for the Future of the United States Army* (New York: Crown, 2009), 230–231.

38. Commander, MNF-I, "SECDEF WEEKLY UPDATE, 30 September–6 October 07," 3, originally classified SECRET-NOFORN, redacted and declassified May 2012, Petraeus Papers, National Defense University.

39. Linda Robinson, *Tell Me How This Ends: General David Petraeus and the Search for a Way Out of Iraq* (New York: PublicAffairs, 2008), 87. General Petraeus personally recounted this episode to me shortly after it happened.

40. Commander, MNF-I, "SECDEF WEEKLY UPDATE, 24 FEB–2 MAR 07," 1, originally classified SECRET-NOFORN, redacted and declassified May 2012, Petraeus Papers, National Defense University.

41. For a synopsis of these earlier operations, see Peter R. Mansoor, *Baghdad at Sunrise: A Brigade Commander's War in Iraq* (New Haven: Yale University Press, 2008), chapter 3 "Bad Karmah."

42. "Insurgent Bomb Factory Found in Baghdad," *USA Today,* February 23, 2007, http://www.usatoday.com/news/world/iraq/2007-02-23-bomb-factory_x.htm.

43. For a more complete account of General McChrystal's accomplishments in Iraq, see his memoir, *My Share of the Task* (New York: Portfolio Penguin, 2013).

44. Stanley A. McChrystal, "It Takes a Network: The New Frontline of Modern Warfare," Foreign Policy, February 22, 2011, http://www.foreignpolicy.com/articles/2011/02/22/it_takes_a_network.

45. Ibid.

46. Ibid.

47. See, for instance, Bob Woodward, *The War Within: A Secret White House History, 2006–2008* (New York: Simon and Schuster, 2008), 380.

48. For a synopsis of the uprisings of 2004 and their aftermath, see Mansoor, *Baghdad at Sunrise,* chapters 9 and 10.

49. Patrick Cockburn, *Muqtada: Muqtada al-Sadr, the Shia Revival, and the Struggle for Iraq* (New York: Scribner, 2008), 190.

50. Kagan, *The Surge,* 54–55.

51. Bill Roggio, "Three Iranian Qods Force Agents Captured in Iraq," *Long War Journal,* March 13, 2009, http://www.longwarjournal.org/archives/2009/03/three_iranian_qods_f.php; see also General Petraeus's testimony to Congress on April 8, 2008 at http://www.washingtonpost.com/wp-srv/politics/documents/iraq_hearing_040808.html.

52. Martin Chulov, "Qassem Suleimani: The Iranian General 'Secretly Running' Iraq," *Guardian,* July 28, 2011, http://www.guardian.co.uk/world/2011/jul/28/qassem-suleimani-iran-iraq-influence.

53. Kagan, *The Surge,* 166.

54. On February 11, 2007, coalition spokesman Major General Bill Caldwell laid out evidence of Iranian smuggling networks bringing arms and explosives into Iraq; Bill Roggio, "Evidence of Iran Supplying Weapons, Expertise to Iraqi Insurgents," *Long War Journal,* February 11, 2007, http://www.longwarjournal.org/archives/2007/02/evidence_of_iran_sup.php; see also Dick Cheney, *In My Time: A Personal and Political Memoir* (New York: Threshold, 2011), 437.

55. Sudarsan Raghavan and Robin Wright, "Iraq Expels 2 Iranians Detained by U.S.," *Washington Post,* December 30, 2006, http://www.washingtonpost.com/wp-dyn/content/article/2006 /12/29/AR2006122901510.html. The Iraqi government honored Iran's claim that the two Qods force operatives held diplomatic immunity and released them.

56. Bill Roggio, "Iranian Qods Force Agents Detained in Irbil Raid," *Long War Journal,* January 14, 2007, http://www.longwarjournal.org/archives/2007/01/iranian_quds_force_a.php.

57. Roggio, "Three Iranian Qods Force Agents Captured in Iraq."

58. Bill Roggio, "The Karbala Attack and the IRGC," *Long War Journal,* January 26, 2007, http://www.longwarjournal.org/archives/2007/01/the_karbala_attack_a.php.

59. Commander, MNF-I, "SECDEF WEEKLY UPDATE, 17–23 MAR 07," 1, originally classified SECRET-NOFORN, redacted and declassified May 2012, Petraeus Papers, National Defense University. The Qazali network and the Sheibani network were the two most important special groups receiving support from Iran.

60. Michael R. Gordon and General Bernard E. Trainor, *The Endgame: The Inside Story of the Struggle for Iraq, from George W. Bush to Barack Obama* (New York: Pantheon, 2012), 327.

61. This information was made public in an MNF-I press conference held by Brigadier General Kevin Bergner in Baghdad on July 2, 2007. Bill Roggio, "Iran, Hezbollah Train Iraqi Shia 'Secret Cells,'" *Long War Journal,* July 2, 2007, http://www.longwarjournal.org/archives/2007/07/ iran_hezbollah_train.php; Kagan, *The Surge,* 177–178.

62. General Petraeus discussed the capture of the Qazali brothers and the seizure of the documents in a press conference in Washington, D.C., on April 26, 2007, http://www.defense.gov/tran scripts/transcript.aspx?transcriptid=3951.

63. Bill Roggio, "U.S. Finds Karbala PJCC Mockup Inside Iran," *Long War Journal,* June 9, 2007, http://www.longwarjournal.org/archives/2007/06/us_finds_karbala_pjc.php.

64. Roggio, "Iran, Hezbollah Train Iraqi Shia 'Secret Cells.'" U.S. authorities handed Daqduq over to Iraqi custody when U.S. forces departed Iraq at the end of 2011. The Iraqi government freed him on November 16, 2012, after which the U.S. government sanctioned Daqduq as a foreign terrorist, a largely symbolic gesture, given the inability of the U.S. government to apprehend him as he traveled back to his native Lebanon; Institute for the Study of War, Iraq Update #47, November 21, 2012, https://app.e2ma.net/app/view:CampaignPublic/id:1409103.12955393034/rid:f5f6d4af5c29 f42de6be805b69d9c516. Qais Qazali was turned over to Iraqi custody and released in 2010. Asaib Ahl al-Haq remains in operation today.

65. "UK Sailors Captured at Gunpoint," BBC News, March 23, 2007, http://news.bbc.co.uk/2/ hi/uk_news/6484279.stm.

66. Gordon and Trainor state that the Iranians asked for the release of Qais Khazali in exchange for the detained British seamen; *The Endgame,* 353. Iran later released the hostages unharmed on April 4, 2007.

67. Commander, MNF-I, "SECDEF WEEKLY UPDATE, 13–19 May 07," 2, originally classified SECRET-NOFORN, redacted and declassified May 2012, Petraeus Papers, National Defense University; Bill Roggio, "Azhar al-Dulaimi, the Tactical Commander of the Karbala PJCC Attack, Killed," *Long War Journal,* May 21, 2007, http://www.longwarjournal.org/archives/2007/05/azhar_ aldulaimi_the.php. Azhar al-Dulaimi's fingerprints had been lifted from one of the SUVs used in the Karbala operation.

68. George W. Bush, *Decision Points* (New York: Crown, 2010), 374.

69. News Transcript, U.S. Department of Defense, January 19, 2007, http://www.defense.gov/ Transcripts/Transcript.aspx?TranscriptID=3870.

70. Jeanne F. Hull, "Iraq: Strategic Reconciliation, Targeting, and Key Leader Engagement," Strategic Studies Institute, September 2009, http://www.strategicstudiesinstitute.army.mil/pubs/ display.cfm?PubID=938.

71. See Chapter 5 for an in-depth discussion of the Sunni Awakening and its impact on the Iraq War.

72. The largest of these gas attacks occurred on March 16, 2007, when more than 350 Sunnis in al-Anbar province were injured by chlorine gas.

73. "Suicide Bomber Strikes at Heart of Iraqi Parliament Building," *The Times,* April 12, 2007, http://www.thetimes.co.uk/tto/news/world/middleeast/iraq/article1991155.ece.

74. On February 22, 2009, investigators accused Sunni lawmaker Mohammed al-Daini of aiding and abetting the terrorist attack. The Council of Representatives lifted his immunity. Al-Daini attempted to flee to Jordan, but his aircraft was forced to return to Baghdad, where he faced criminal charges. "Iraqi Lawmaker's Immunity Lifted," BBC, February 25, 2009, http://news.bbc .co.uk/2/hi/middle_east/7910807.stm.

75. "Suicide Bomber Kills 41 at Baghdad College," AP, February 25, 2007, http://www.msnbc .msn.com/id/17326397/ns/world_news-mideastn_africa/.

76. Edward Wong, "Baghdad Car Bomb Kills 20 on Booksellers' Row," *New York Times,* March 5, 2007, http://www.nytimes.com/2007/03/06/world/middleeast/06iraq.html.

77. Saddam Hussein banned Shi'a religious observances of Ashura and Arba'een for precisely this reason.

78. "TIMELINE: Major Bombings in Iraq Since 2003," Reuters, August 22, 2007, http://www .reuters.com/article/2007/08/22/us-iraq-blasts-timeline-idUSL2280890120070822.

79. Alissa J. Rubin, "Iraq Says Truck Bomb in North Killed 152," *New York Times,* April 1, 2007, http://www.nytimes.com/2007/04/01/world/middleeast/01iraq.html.

80. Joshua Partlow, "More Than 100 Killed in Baghdad, Nearby Town," *Washington Post,* March 30, 2007, http://www.washingtonpost.com/wp-dyn/content/article/2007/03/29/AR2007032 900385.html.

81. Qassim Abdul-Zahra, "Al-Qaida Targets Iraqi Infrastructure," *Washington Post,* June 12, 2007, http://www.washingtonpost.com/wp-dyn/content/article/2007/06/11/AR2007061101099.html.

82. "At Least 45 die in Baghdad Sectarian Bombings," Associated Press, April 15, 2007, http://www .msnbc.msn.com/id/18116217/ns/world_news-mideast_n_africa/t/least-die-baghdad-sectarian -bombings/. This article contains the updated casualty statistics for the attack in Karbala a day earlier.

83. "At Least 190 Dead in Baghdad Bombings," Voice of America, April 18, 2007, http://www .voanews.com/english/news/a-13-2007-04-18-voa9-66549262.html.

84. "Car Bomb Kills 58 at Shiite Shrine in Karbala," Associated Press, April 28, 2007, http:// www.msnbc.msn.com/id/18367419/.

85. Ross Colvin and Yara Bayoumy, "Sadr Ministers Quit Iraq Government over U.S. Troops," Reuters, April 16, 2007, http://www.reuters.com/article/2007/04/16/us-iraq-idUSPAR3407302007 0416.

86. Commander, MNF-I, "SECDEF WEEKLY UPDATE, 13–19 May 07," 2, originally classified SECRET-NOFORN, redacted and declassified May 2012, Petraeus Papers, National Defense University.

87. These events are recounted in Chapter 9.

88. "Senator Reid on Iraq: 'This War Is Lost,'" CBS News, April 20, 2007, http://www.cbsnews .com/stories/2007/04/20/politics/main2709229.shtml.

89. Bush, *Decision Points,* 382.

90. General Petraeus's wife, Holly, moved the household to Fort Myer, Virginia, after he left for Iraq. The families of the other officers and noncommissioned officers on the team remained in Kansas for the duration of their stay in Iraq.

4. Tower 57

1. Linda Robinson, *Tell Me How This Ends: General David Petraeus and the Search for a Way Out of Iraq* (New York: PublicAffairs, 2008), 173.

2. For the view of this bureaucratic struggle from Admiral Fallon's viewpoint, see Bob Wood-

ward, *The War Within: A Secret White House History, 2006–2008* (New York: Simon and Schuster, 2008), 342–343.

3. David Cloud and Greg Jaffe, *The Fourth Star: Four Generals and the Epic Struggle for the Future of the United States Army* (New York: Crown, 2009), 258–259.

4. I received my Ph.D. from Ohio State in 1995, while my daughter Kyle would enter the University of Kansas as a freshman in the summer of 2007.

5. William Westmoreland, *A Soldier Reports* (New York: DaCapo, 1989), 364.

6. Richard A. Oppel, Jr., "U.S. Seizes Son of a Top Shiite, Stirring Uproar," *New York Times,* February 24, 2007, http://www.nytimes.com/2007/02/24/world/middleeast/24iraq.html.

7. A staff officer later told me that General Casey did not attend all the meetings on the battle rhythm, but rather used it as a menu of activities that he could go to as time and inclination permitted. I have no idea whether this was the case, but if General Casey and his team actually followed the battle rhythm we inherited for the two and a half years they were in Iraq, I can only imagine the fatigue they must have endured.

8. General David H. Petraeus, "Ambassador Ryan C. Crocker: Diplomat and Partner Extraordinaire," *Army,* April 2011, 17.

9. Commander, MNF-I, "SECDEF WEEKLY UPDATE, 24–30 MAR 07," 2, originally classified SECRET-NOFORN, redacted and declassified May 2012, Petraeus Papers, National Defense University.

10. Robinson, *Tell Me How This Ends,* 115–117.

11. Peter Mansoor, *Baghdad at Sunrise: A Brigade Commander's War in Iraq* (New Haven: Yale University Press, 2008), 287–288.

12. Donna Miles, "Army Focuses on Families' Needs in Light of Unit Extension in Iraq," American Forces Press Service, June 28, 2006, http://www.defense.gov/news/NewsArticle.aspx?ID=292.

13. Ann Scott Tyson and Josh White, "Strained Army Extends Tours to 15 Months," *Washington Post,* April 12, 2007, http://www.washingtonpost.com/wp-dyn/content/article/2007/04/11/AR2007041100615.html.

14. General David H. Petraeus, Open Letter to the Troops of MNF-I, March 15, 2007, http://council.smallwarsjournal.com/archive/index.php/t-2227.html.

15. MNF-I Counterinsurgency Guidance, June 2007, http://council.smallwarsjournal.com/showthread.php?t=3177.

16. Carl von Clausewitz, *On War,* ed. and trans. Michael Howard and Peter Paret (Princeton: Princeton University Press, 1976), 87.

17. General David Petraeus e-mail to author, September 5, 2011.

18. On May 1, 2003, President Bush flew on a U.S. Navy aircraft and landed on the deck of the U.S.S. *Abraham Lincoln,* where he gave a speech announcing the end of major combat operations in Iraq beneath a banner that proclaimed, "Mission Accomplished." Regardless of the message intended, the banner became a symbol of the president's overreaching goals for and insufficient understanding of the war in Iraq.

19. These reports are housed in the Petraeus Papers in the archives at the National Defense University. They have been redacted to remove still-classified information and are now available for use by researchers.

20. Eliot A. Cohen, *Supreme Command: Soldiers, Statesmen, and Leadership in Wartime* (New York: Free Press, 2002), 212.

21. George W. Bush, *Decision Points* (New York: Crown, 2010), 385.

22. Ibid., 362.

23. "McCain lauds security during Baghdad visit," CNN, April 1, 2007, http://articles.cnn.com/2007-04-01/world/iraq.main_1_shorja-mccain-baghdad?_s=PM:WORLD.

24. John McCain, "The War You're Not Reading About," *Washington Post,* April 8, 2007, http://www.washingtonpost.com/wp-dyn/content/article/2007/04/06/AR2007040601781.html.

25. For an example of this invective, see Joe Conason, "McCain's Magic Carpet Ride," Truthdig.com, April 5, 2007, http://www.truthdig.com/report/item/mccains_magic_carpet_ride/.

26. Regrettably, General Petraeus later violated his own rules in Afghanistan, which eventually led to an affair after his retirement with his biographer, Paula Broadwell.

27. I am indebted to Colonel (Ret.) Steve Boylan for his thoughts and assistance with the preceding paragraphs on public affairs and strategic communications.

28. Anne Garrels, "Iraq Power Restoration Hampered by Security Risk," NPR, September 20, 2007, http://www.npr.org/templates/story/story.php?storyId=14556337; Cloud and Jaffe, *The Fourth Star*, 261.

5. The Awakening

1. Colonel Peter Devlin, "State of the Insurgency in al-Anbar," August 17, 2006, reprinted in Thomas E. Ricks, *The Gamble: General David Petraeus and the American Military Adventure in Iraq, 2006–2008* (New York: Penguin, 2009), appendix A.

2. MNF-I, "Strategic Planning Directive—Defeat Al Qa'ida in Iraq and Associated Terrorists and Foreign Fighters by the End of 2006," May 4, 2006, 3, declassified September 29, 2009, copy located in the Army Historical Office in the Pentagon.

3. Alan Beyerchen, "Clausewitz, Nonlinearity and the Unpredictability of War," *International Security* 17, no. 3 (1992), 59–90.

4. Ibid.

5. Ibid.

6. Major General James N. Mattis, "Preparing for Counterinsurgency," interview by Dr. Charles P. Neimeyer, June 17, 2009, in *Al-Anbar Awakening*, vol. 1, *American Perspectives: U.S. Marines and Counterinsurgency in Iraq, 2004–2009*, ed. Timothy S. McWilliams and Kurtis P. Wheeler (Quantico, Va.: Marine Corps University Press, 2009), 33.

7. Lieutenant General John R. Allen, Commanding General, II Marine Expeditionary Force (Forward), Multi-National Force–West, January 2007 to February 2008, "Turning the Tide, Part II," in McWilliams and Wheeler, *Al-Anbar Awakening*, 1: 228.

8. Interview with Major Alfred B. Connable, Senior Intelligence Analyst/Fusion Officer, I & II Marine Expeditionary Forces, 2005–2006, in McWilliams and Wheeler, *Al-Anbar Awakening*, 1: 124.

9. Gary W. Montgomery, Introduction to *Al-Anbar Awakening*, vol. 2, *Iraqi Perspectives: From Insurgency to Counterinsurgency in Iraq, 2004–2009*, ed. Timothy S. McWilliams and Kurtis P. Wheeler (Quantico, Va.: Marine Corps University Press, 2009), 11–12.

10. Connable interview, 1: 133.

11. Niel Smith and Sean MacFarland, "Anbar Awakens: The Tipping Point," *Military Review*, March–April 2008, 41–52.

12. Jim Michaels, *A Chance in Hell* (New York: St. Martin's, 2010), 22–23.

13. Smith and MacFarland, "Anbar Awakens," 49.

14. Interview with Colonel Michael M. Walker, Commanding Officer, 3d Civil Affairs Group, I Marine Expeditionary Force, October 2003 to September 2005, in McWilliams and Wheeler, *Al-Anbar Awakening*, 1: 71–72.

15. Austin Long, "War Comes to Al Anbar: Political Conflict in an Iraqi Province," paper presented at the 2009 International Studies Association conference, 12; Smith and MacFarland, "Anbar Awakens," 42.

16. Michaels, *A Chance in Hell*, 102.

17. Interview with Dr. Thamer Ibrahim Tahir al-Assafi and Sheikh Abdullah Jallal Mukhif al-Faraji in McWilliams and Wheeler, *Al-Anbar Awakening*, 2: 40.

18. Ibid., 2: 35.

19. William Doyle, *A Soldier's Dream: Captain Travis Patriquin and the Awakening of Iraq* (New York: NAL Caliber, 2011), 5.

20. "Interview with COL Tony Deane," *Operational Leadership Experiences in the Global War on Terrorism* (Fort Leavenworth, Kan.: Combat Studies Institute, 2008), 4.

21. Interview with Sheikh Ahmad Bezia Fteikhan al-Rishawi, in McWilliams and Wheeler, *Al-Anbar Awakening*, 2: 46–47. The Anbar provincial council, composed mostly of members of the Iraqi Islamic Party that had participated in the January 2005 provincial elections, had fled to Baghdad and therefore held little sway in the province.

22. Najim Abed al-Jabouri and Sterling Jensen, "The Iraqi and AQI Roles in the Sunni Awakening," *Prism* 2, no. 1 (2010), 11, http://www.ndu.edu/press/lib/images/prism2-1/Prism_3-18_Al-Ja bouri_Jensen.pdf.

23. Lieutenant General John R. Allen, "Turning the Tide, Part II," in McWilliams and Wheeler, *Al-Anbar Awakening*, 1: 235–237.

24. Smith and MacFarland, "Anbar Awakens," 52.

25. Doyle, *A Soldier's Dream*, 99, 191–193.

26. For the history of the brigade during its time in Iraq in 2003–2004, see Peter R. Mansoor, *Baghdad at Sunrise: A Brigade Commander's War in Iraq* (New Haven: Yale University Press, 2008).

27. Smith and MacFarland, "Anbar Awakens," 45.

28. Michaels, *A Chance in Hell*, 37.

29. "Interview with Colonel Sean MacFarland," Contemporary Operations Study Team, On Point III, Combat Studies Institute, Fort Leavenworth, Kansas, January 17, 2008, 24.

30. Smith and MacFarland, "Anbar Awakens," 46.

31. Ibid., 44.

32. "Interview with COL Tony Deane," 12.

33. Doyle, *A Soldier's Dream*, 184–187.

34. Smith and MacFarland, "Anbar Awakens," 43.

35. For a thorough accounting of Captain Travis Patriquin's role in fostering the Awakening, see Doyle, *A Soldier's Dream*.

36. Ibid., 126.

37. Michaels, *A Chance in Hell*, 138.

38. Doyle, *A Soldier's Dream*, 143–144.

39. Ibid., 158–159.

40. Smith and MacFarland, "Anbar Awakens," 43–44, 51.

41. Ibid., 44.

42. Doyle, *A Soldier's Dream*, 205–206.

43. Smith and MacFarland, "Anbar Awakens," 47.

44. MacFarland interview, 33.

45. Mohammed M. Hafez, "Al-Qaeda Losing Ground in Iraq," *CTC Sentinel* 1, no. 1 (20007), 6–8.

46. Doyle, *A Soldier's Dream*, 222–227.

47. Smith and MacFarland, "Anbar Awakens," 49–50.

48. Lieutenant General John R. Allen, Commanding General, II Marine Expeditionary Force (Forward), Multi-National Force–West, January 2007 to February 2008, "Turning the Tide, Part II," interview by Timothy S. McWilliams, Central Command, Tampa, Florida, April 23, 2009, in McWilliams and Wheeler, *Al-Anbar Awakening*, 1: 230.

49. Ibid., 1: 231.

50. For a description of the "COP in a Box," see Michaels, *A Chance in Hell*, 61.

51. General Petraeus telephone interview with author, November 9, 2011.

52. Ibid.

53. General Petraeus was the president of the promotion board that advanced Colonel MacFarland to brigadier general, the first time a serving combat commander had been brought back to fulfill this duty. Colonel H. R. McMaster was also selected for one-star rank at the same time.

54. Sudarsan Raghavan, "Maliki, Petraeus Visit Insurgent Hotbed in Iraq," *Washington Post*, March 14, 2007, http://www.washingtonpost.com/wp-dyn/content/article/2007/03/13/AR200703 1301724.html.

55. Long, "War Comes to Al Anbar," 13.

56. Greg Jaffe, "Tribal Connections: How Courting Sheiks Slowed Violence in Iraq," *Wall Street Journal,* August 8, 2007, http://online.wsj.com/article/SB118653546614491198.html.

57. Interview with Brigadier General Martin Post, Deputy Commanding General, I Marine Expeditionary Force (Forward), Multi-National Force–West, February 2008 to February 2009, in McWilliams and Wheeler, *Al-Anbar Awakening,* 1: 254.

58. Kimberly Kagan, "The Anbar Awakening: Displacing al Qaeda from Its Stronghold in Western Iraq," *Iraq Report,* August 1, 2006, to March 30, 2007, 12, http://www.understandingwar.org/report/anbar-awakening-displacing-al-qaeda-its-stronghold-western-iraq.

59. Commander, MNF-I, "SECDEF WEEKLY UPDATE, 1–7 July 07," 2, originally classified SECRET-NOFORN, redacted and declassified May 2012, Petraeus Papers, National Defense University; Ann Scott Tyson, "A Deadly Clash at Donkey Island," *Washington Post,* August 19, 2007, http://www.washingtonpost.com/wp-dyn/content/article/2007/08/18/AR2007081801270.html.

60. Allen interview, *Al-Anbar Awakening,* 1: 233.

61. General Petraeus telephone interview with author, November 9, 2011.

62. Thomas R. Searle, "Tribal Engagement in Anbar Province: The Critical Role of Special Operations Forces," *Joint Forces Quarterly,* issue 50 (2008), 66.

63. Michael Gordon, "The Former-Insurgent Counterinsurgency," *New York Times Magazine,* September 2, 2007, http://www.nytimes.com/2007/09/02/magazine/02iraq-t.html?_r=1&oref=slogin.

64. Rod Nordland, "Baghdad Comes Alive," *Newsweek,* November 17, 2007, http://www.thedailybeast.com/newsweek/2007/11/17/baghdad-comes-alive.html.

65. Ghaith Abdul-Ahad, "Meet Abu Abed: The US's new ally against al-Qaida," *Guardian,* November 9, 2007, http://www.guardian.co.uk/world/2007/nov/10/usa-al-qaida. The story of the roadside bomb was told by Abu Abed directly to General Petraeus in a meeting in Amiriyah in late May 2007.

66. Linda Robinson, *Tell Me How This Ends: General David Petraeus and the Search for a Way Out of Iraq* (New York: PublicAffairs, 2008), 237.

67. Nordland, "Baghdad Comes Alive."

68. Ibid.

69. Lieutenant Colonel Dale Kuehl, "Ameriyah Update," *Michael Yon Online Magazine,* November 2007, http://www.michaelyon-online.com/ameriyah-update.htm.

70. Dale Kuehl, "Inside the Surge: 1-5 Cavalry in Ameriyah," *Small Wars Journal,* October 26, 2008, http://smallwarsjournal.com/mag/docs-temp/118-kuehl.pdf.

71. Robinson, *Tell Me How This Ends,* 238–239; General Petraeus's aide, then-Major Everett Spain, with whom I shared a room at the commanding general's quarters, related this event to me shortly after it occurred.

72. For an examination of the origins of the insurgency in Adhamiya, see Mansoor, *Baghdad at Sunrise,* chapters 5 and 6.

73. In fact, in 2004 my brigade targeted Wathiq for his involvement in the insurgency, but he eluded our attempts to apprehend him.

74. Robinson, *Tell Me How This Ends,* 208.

75. Kuehl, "Inside the Surge."

76. Ibid.

77. Ricks, *The Gamble,* 202 and 215.

78. See, for instance, the discussion of Concerned Local Citizen (CLC) groups in Commander, MNF-I, "SECDEF WEEKLY UPDATE, 23–29 September 07," 3, originally classified SECRET-NOFORN, redacted and declassified May 2012, Petraeus Papers, National Defense University.

79. Another way of looking at the SOI program is that it gave the coalition an additional 166 battalions of light infantry for security duties in Iraq.

80. For an analysis of the impact of formal and informal organizations on the war in al-Anbar province, see Long, "War Comes to Al Anbar," 21–27.

81. Gordon, "The Former-Insurgent Counterinsurgency."

82. Ibid.

83. Colonel Martin Stanton, Chief of Reconciliation and Engagement, MNC-I, Department of Defense Bloggers Roundtable, November 2, 2007, 3, http://www.defenselink.mil/dodcmsshare/BloggerAssets/2007-11/1102071717471102_stanton_Transcript.pdf.

84. Richard A. Oppel, Jr. and Ali Adeeb, "Iraq Bombing Kills Sunni Sheiks Allied with U.S.," *New York Times,* June 25, 2007, http://www.nytimes.com/2007/06/25/world/middleeast/25cnd-Iraq.html.

85. Michaels, *A Chance in Hell,* 231. Sean MacFarland gave this same assessment to me when we met in Baghdad in October 2007.

86. Al-Jabouri and Jensen, "The Iraqi and AQI Roles in the Sunni Awakening," 14.

87. Commander, MNF-I, "SECDEF WEEKLY UPDATE, 27 May–2 June 07," 4–5, originally classified SECRET-NOFORN, redacted and declassified May 2012, Petraeus Papers, National Defense University.

88. Michal Harari, "Uncertain Future for the Sons of Iraq," Institute for the Study of War Backgrounder, August 3, 2010. Jeanne F. Hull writes, "Although the outreach between U.S. military forces and Anbari shayks in Iraq was initially successful in combating al-Qaida's support in Iraq, dissention surfaced when the Iraqi government refused to acknowledge or assume control for the initiative and its requirement to integrate members of Anbari tribes into the Iraqi Security Forces or other salaried positions. Because the Iraqi government had no buy-in to the original initiative, they were suspicious of the concept and were unhappy with Coalition implementation. They were also skeptical about the political party formed by the Anbari shaykhs involved in the initiative, and implemented legislation that could have prevented that party and its affiliates from participating in the political process. Although the Iraqi government eventually found an Iraqi way to assume responsibility for the effort, the transition to Iraqi control was tenuous for months, and the initiative very nearly fell apart. The relations between the Iraqi government and the Sunni shaykhs who disavowed their allegiance to al-Qaida remains tenuous to this day"; Jeanne F. Hull, "Iraq: Strategic Reconciliation, Targeting, and Key Leader Engagement," Strategic Studies Institute, September 2009, http://www.strategicstudiesinstitute.army.mil/pubs/display.cfm?PubID=938, 11.

89. General Raymond Odierno, unpublished and undated article on the surge, copy provided by Gen. Odierno to the author, 15–16.

90. Kuehl, "Ameriyah Update."

91. Kuehl, "Inside the Surge."

92. Interview with Mr. James V. Soriano, Provincial Reconstruction Team Leader, U.S. Department of State, September 2006 to 2009, in McWilliams and Wheeler, *Al-Anbar Awakening,* 1: 280.

93. Ibid., 1: 281.

94. MacFarland interview, 33–34.

95. Bing West, "Groundhog War: The Limits of Counterinsurgency in Afghanistan," *Foreign Affairs,* September–October 2011, 171.

6. Turning the Tide

1. The coalition suffered 523 dead during the period from February to June 2007; Iraqi Coalition Casualty Count, http://www.icasualties.org/Iraq/index.aspx.

2. Damien Cave, "Search for 3 G.I.'s Abducted in Iraq Continues," *New York Times,* May 14, 2007, http://www.nytimes.com/2007/05/14/world/middleeast/14cnd-iraq.html.

3. Iraqi Coalition Casualty Count. The number of coalition soldiers killed in May 2007 was eclipsed only by the number of dead during the second battle of Fallujah in November 2004 (141 killed in action) and the number killed during the first battle of Fallujah and the uprising by Jaish al-Mahdi militants across south-central Iraq in April 2004 (140 KIA).

4. Mark Bowden, "The Professor of War," *Vanity Fair,* May 2010, http://www.vanityfair.com/politics/features/2010/05/petraeus-201005.

5. Commander, MNF-I, "SECDEF WEEKLY UPDATE, 6–12 May 07," 3, originally classified SECRET-NOFORN, redacted and declassified May 2012, Petraeus Papers, National Defense University.

6. Michael R. Gordon and Scott Shane, "U.S. Long Worried That Iran Supplied Arms in Iraq," *New York Times*, March 27, 2007, http://www.nytimes.com/2007/03/27/world/middleeast/27weapons.html; see also General Petraeus's testimony to Congress on April 8, 2008 at http://www.washingtonpost.com/wp-srv/politics/documents/iraq_hearing_040808.html.

7. Bill Roggio, "Al Qaeda in Iraq's Diyala Campaign," *Long War Journal*, April 26, 2007, http://www.longwarjournal.org/archives/2007/04/al_qaeda_in_iraqs_di.php.

8. Kimberly Kagan, *The Surge: A Military History* (New York: Encounter, 2009), 47.

9. Thomas E. Ricks, *The Gamble: General David Petraeus and the American Military Adventure in Iraq, 2006–2008* (New York: Penguin, 2009), 195.

10. E-mail, Colonel James Brown to author, November 5, 2011.

11. For Yingling's critique of American generalship in Iraq, see Lt. Col. Paul Yingling, "A Failure in Generalship," *Armed Forces Journal*, May 2007, http://www.armedforcesjournal.com/2007/05/2635198.

12. Commander, MNF-I, "SECDEF WEEKLY UPDATE, 13–19 May 07," 4, originally classified SECRET-NOFORN, redacted and declassified May 2012, Petraeus Papers, National Defense University.

13. E-mail, Colonel James Brown to author, November 5, 2011.

14. Colonel James B. Brown, Lieutenant Colonel Erik W. Goepner, and Captain James M. Clark, "Detention Operations, Behavior Modification, and Counterinsurgency," *Military Review*, May–June 2009, 40–47.

15. Ibid. Studies at Camp Bucca showed that the vast majority of insurgents were motivated primarily by monetary rewards.

16. Ibid.

17. Ibid. The release rate for these boards until November 2007 was roughly 40 percent.

18. Ibid. By way of contrast, the average recidivism rate for prisoners released from U.S. domestic jails is more than 50 percent.

19. "Blast Hits Key Iraq Shia Shrine," BBC, June 13, 2007, http://news.bbc.co.uk/2/hi/middle_east/6747419.stm.

20. General Raymond Odierno, unpublished and undated article on the surge, copy provided by General Odierno to the author, 25.

21. Bill Roggio, "Iraq Report: Attacking Mahdi, al Qaeda Prison Camp in Diyala," *Long War Journal*, May 27, 2007, http://www.longwarjournal.org/dailyiraqreport/2007/05/iraq_report_attacking_mahdi_al.php.

22. Kimberly Kagan, *The Surge: A Military History* (New York: Encounter, 2009), 119.

23. Institute for the Study of War, "Operation Arrowhead Ripper, June 2007 to August 2007," http://www.understandingwar.org/operation/operation-arrowhead-ripper.

24. Bill Roggio, "1920s Revolution Brigades turns on al Qaeda in Diyala," *Long War Journal*, June 12, 2007, http://www.longwarjournal.org/archives/2007/06/1920s_revolution_bri.php.

25. Kagan, *The Surge*, 112.

26. Odierno, unpublished and undated article on the surge, 26.

27. "US, Iraqi Raid on Sadr City Kills 26 Suspected Militants," Voice of America, June 30, 2007, http://www.voanews.com/english/news/a-13-2007-06-30-voa23-66779387.html.

28. Alissa J. Rubin and Stephen Farrell, "Insurgents Fire Shells into Baghdad's Green Zone, Killing 3," *New York Times*, July 11, 2011, http://www.nytimes.com/2007/07/11/world/middleeast/11iraq.html.

29. Kagan, *The Surge*, 120.

30. Ibid., 130–131.

31. Ibid., 152.

32. Comment made in a meeting on July 17, 2007.

33. In March 2009 Senator Lieberman invited me to testify before the land power subcommittee (which he chaired) of the Senate Armed Services Committee to discuss the future of the U.S. Army in the twenty-first century.

34. Thomas E. Ricks, *The Gamble: General David Petraeus and the American Military Adventure in Iraq, 2006–2008* (New York: Penguin, 2009), 123.

35. Comment made in a meeting on June 13, 2007.

36. Guidance given in a meeting on July 17, 2007.

37. Odierno, unpublished and undated article on the surge, 24.

38. Daniel Kimmage and Kathleen Ridolfo, *The War of Images and Ideas: How Sunni Insurgents in Iraq and Their Supporters Worldwide Are Using the Media* (Washington, D.C.: Radio Free Europe/Radio Liberty, 2007).

39. Jeff Zeleny, "G.O.P. Senators Press to Change Strategy in Iraq," *New York Times*, July 14, 2007, http://www.nytimes.com/2007/07/14/washington/14capital.html.

40. Ibid.

41. Comment made in a meeting with Ambassador Crocker and General Petraeus on July 9, 2007. For another view of the inside political view of the situation in Washington during the spring and summer of 2007, see Dick Cheney, *In My Time: A Personal and Political Memoir* (New York: Threshold, 2011), 460–462.

42. Michael E. O'Hanlon and Kenneth M. Pollack, "A War We Might Just Win," *New York Times*, July 30, 2007, http://www.nytimes.com/2007/07/30/opinion/30pollack.html.

43. Ibid.

44. Ibid.

45. Ibid.

46. Ibid.

47. Ibid.

48. Ibid. Michael O'Hanlon had been a Clinton supporter and Ken Pollack had served in the National Security Council during the Clinton administration, which added to the significance of their piece. Regrettably, both men received considerable criticism from fellow Democrat policy advisers for the publication of the op-ed, which may have cost them positions within the Obama administration when it came into office in 2009.

49. Damien Cave and Richard A. Oppel Jr., "Iraqi Parliament Speaker Ousted over Alleged Assault," *New York Times*, June 11, 2007, http://www.nytimes.com/2007/06/11/world/africa/11iht-baghdad.1.6091135.html.

50. Bill Ardolino, "Inside Iraqi Politics—Part 3. Examining the Legislative Branch," *Long War Journal*, February 13, 2008, http://www.longwarjournal.org/archives/2008/02/inside_iraqi_politic_2.php.

51. Comments made in a meeting on July 9, 2007.

52. Molly Hennessy-Fiske, "Asian Cup Victory Showers Iraq with Joy," *Los Angeles Times*, July 30, 2007, http://www.boston.com/sports/soccer/articles/2007/07/30/asian_cup_victory_showers_iraq_with_joy/.

53. Comments made in a meeting on August 1, 2007.

54. Ibid.

55. Greg Bruno, "What Are Iraq's Benchmarks?" Council on Foreign Relations, March 11, 2008, http://www.cfr.org/iraq/iraqs-benchmarks/p13333.

56. The White House, "Initial Benchmark Assessment Report," July 12, 2007, http://www.globalsecurity.org/military/library/report/2007/iraq-benchmark-assessment070712.htm.

57. Ibid.

58. Ibid.

59. Ibid.

60. Stephen Farrell, "Despite Appeals, Iraqi Legislators Take Break," *New York Times*, July 31, 2007, http://www.nytimes.com/2007/07/31/world/middleeast/31iraq.html.

61. The White House, "Initial Benchmark Assessment Report."

62. Ibid.

63. Brian Fishman and Joseph Felter, "Al-Qa'ida's Foreign Fighters in Iraq," Combating Terrorism Center at West Point, January 2, 2008, http://www.ctc.usma.edu/posts/al-qaidas-foreign-fighters-in-iraq-a-first-look-at-the-sinjar-records.

64. "Ambassador Ryan Crocker Interview with Katayoun Beglari-Scarlet," Voice of America, March 3, 2008, http://iraq.usembassy.gov/remarks_03032008y.html.

65. Linda Robinson, *Tell Me How This Ends: General David Petraeus and the Search for a Way Out of Iraq* (New York: PublicAffairs, 2008), 289.

66. Kimberly Kagan, "Interview and Moderated Q&A with General Petraeus," Institute for the Study of War, January 22, 2010, http://www.understandingwar.org/press-media/webcast/cent com-2010-views-general-david-h-petraeus-video.

67. Commander, MNF-I, "SECDEF WEEKLY UPDATE, 27 May–2 June 07," 4, originally classified SECRET-NOFORN, redacted and declassified May 2012, Petraeus Papers, National Defense University.

68. U.S. Department of Defense, "Measuring Stability and Security in Iraq: Report to Congress in accordance with the Department of Defense Appropriations Act 2007 (Section 9010, Public Law 109–289)," September 2007, www.defense.gov/pubs/pdfs/Signed-Version-070912.pdf.

69. Jim Crider, "A View from Inside the Surge," *Military Review,* March–April 2009, 83.

70. The White House, "Initial Benchmark Assessment Report."

71. "The Report of the Independent Commission on the Security Forces of Iraq," September 6, 2007, 112, http://csis.org/files/media/csis/pubs/isf.pdf.

72. Ibid, 10.

73. Ibid.

74. Ibid., 126.

75. BBC News, "Iraq Stampede Deaths Near 1,000," August 31, 2005, http://news.bbc.co.uk/2/hi/middle_east/4199618.stm.

76. Odierno, unpublished and undated article on the surge, 21–22.

77. Author interview with Colonel (Ret.) James Hickey, February 2, 2011.

78. Ramadi, for instance, was the scene of multiple special operations raids each night in 2006, but the city remained out of control until operations to clear it with conventional forces were mounted.

79. Damien Cave and James Glanz, "Toll in Iraq Bombings Is Raised to More Than 500," *New York Times,* August 22, 2007, http://www.nytimes.com/2007/08/22/world/middleeast/22iraq-top .html?_r=1&hp&oref=login.

80. Roger Hardy, "Minority Targeted in Iraq Bombings," BBC News, August 15, 2007, http://news.bbc.co.uk/2/hi/middle_east/6947716.stm.

81. For the difficulties on one battalion in securing its area in the Shi'a community of southeastern Baghdad, see David Finkel, *The Good Soldiers* (New York: Picador, 2009), which chronicles the travails of 2-16 Infantry during its deployment to Iraq in 2007–2008.

82. "Roadside Bomb Kills Iraqi Governor," BBC News, August 20, 2007, http://news.bbc .co.uk/2/hi/middle_east/6954467.stm.

83. Stephen F. Farrell, "50 Die in Fight Between Shiite Groups in Karbala," *New York Times,* August 28, 2007, http://www.nytimes.com/2007/08/29/world/middleeast/29iraq.html?th.

84. For an account of this incident, see Robinson, *Tell Me How This Ends,* 285–286.

85. "Anti-U.S. Cleric Suspends His Militia in Iraq," CNN World, August 29, 2007, http://ar ticles.cnn.com/2007-08-29/world/iraq.main_1_sadr-karbala-thousands-of-shiite-pilgrims?_s= PM:WORLD.

86. Commander, MNF-I, "SECDEF WEEKLY UPDATE, 15–21 July 07," 5, originally classified SECRET-NOFORN, redacted and declassified May 2012, Petraeus Papers, National Defense University.

87. HQ, Multi-National Force–Iraq, Open Letter to the Troops, September 7, 2007, http://small warsjournal.com/blog/7-september-general-petraeus-letter-to-troops-of-mnf-i.

7. Testimony

1. Thomas E. Ricks, *The Gamble: General David Petraeus and the American Military Adventure in Iraq, 2006–2008* (New York: Penguin, 2009), 232.

2. Ibid., 233.

3. E-mail, General Petraeus to author, May 28, 2012.

4. Ibid.

5. National Intelligence Council Press Release, "Prospects for Iraq's Stability: Some Security Progress but Political Reconciliation Elusive," August 2007, http://http://www.dni.gov/files/documents/Newsroom/Press%20Releases/2007%20Press%20Releases/20070823_release.pdf.

6. Ibid., 4.

7. Ibid.

8. Ibid., 1.

9. Ibid., 2.

10. Mary Louise Kelly, "Good, Bad News in Iraq Intelligence Estimate," NPR, August 24, 2007, http://www.npr.org/templates/story/story.php?storyId=13920438.

11. I attended all the meetings in question. As usual, Bill Rapp took excellent notes that he distributed to a select group afterward.

12. Text available at "MoveOn's Hateful 'General Betray Us' Ad," Sweetness and Light, http://sweetness-light.com/archive/moveon-general-petraeus-or-general-betray-us.

13. The Fact Checker, "General Betray Us?" *Washington Post,* September 20, 2007, http://voices.washingtonpost.com/fact-checker/2007/09/general_betray_us.html.

14. As it turns out, MoveOn.org received a preferential advertising rate for its ad and only later paid the full price after public indignation at the decision by the *New York Times* to publish an attack of a personal nature, which ran counter to its own acceptability standards; Clark Hoyt, "Betraying Its Own Best Interests," *New York Times,* September 23, 2007, http://www.nytimes.com/2007/09/23/opinion/23pubed.html?n=Top/Opinion/The%20Public%20Editor.

15. Michael Hirsh, "The General as Salesman," Daily Beast, September 9, 2007, http://www.thedailybeast.com/newsweek/2007/09/09/the-general-as-salesman.html. The Daily Beast's date is incorrect; General Petraeus testified on September 10.

16. "Ranking House Committee Members Grill Crocker and Petraeus on U.S. Progress in Iraq," CQ Transcripts, September 10, 2007, http://media.washingtonpost.com/wp-srv/politics/documents/ranking_committee_members_grill_petraeus_crocker_10.html. All references in this and the following paragraphs to the testimony of General Petraeus and Ambassador Crocker before the joint meeting of the House Armed Services and Foreign Relations Committees are from the hearing transcript.

17. Of course, their request did not include all of the surge forces that eventually deployed to Iraq in 2007.

18. The firestorm over the validity of Multi-National Force–Iraq metrics influenced General Petraeus to convene a media conference later that fall in Baghdad, chaired by Colonel Bill Rapp, to discuss the coalition approach to gathering data.

19. "Ranking House Committee Members Grill Crocker and Petraeus on U.S. Progress in Iraq." All references in this and the following paragraphs to the testimony of Ambassador Crocker are from the hearing transcript.

20. Common Dreams News Center, "General Petraeus: Tosses a 4th Quarter Hail Mary Pass," September 10, 2007, http://www.commondreams.org/news2007/0910-13.htm.

21. Ibid.

22. John Bresnahan, "Wexler Compares Petraeus to William Westmoreland, U.S. Commander in Vietnam," The Politico, September 10, 2007, http://www.politico.com/blogs/thecrypt/0907/Wexler_compares_Petraeus_to_William_Westmoreland_US_commander_in_Vietnam.html.

23. "Crocker and Petraeus Testify Before the Senate Foreign Relations Committee on Iraq," CQ Transcripts, September 11, 2007, http://media.washingtonpost.com/wp-srv/politics/documents/

transcript_senate_hearing_on_iraq_091107.html. All references in this and the following paragraphs to the testimony of General Petraeus and Ambassador Crocker before the Senate Foreign Relations Committee are from this hearing transcript.

24. Babak Dehghanpisheh and John Barry, "Brainiac Brigade," *Newsweek,* September 15, 2007.

25. "Crocker, Petraeus Testify Before the Senate Armed Services Committee on Iraq," CQ Transcripts, September 11, 2007, http://media.washingtonpost.com/wp-srv/politics/documents/armed_services_cmte_hearing_091107.html. All references in this and the following paragraphs to the testimony of General Petraeus and Ambassador Crocker before the Senate Armed Services Committee are from this hearing transcript.

26. Tom Ricks also reports that General Petraeus expressed his disappointment over Senator Clinton's comments to his mentor, retired General Jack Keane; Ricks, *The Gamble,* 250.

27. Mark Bowden, "The Professor of War," *Vanity Fair,* May 2010, http://www.vanityfair.com/politics/features/2010/05/petraeus-201005.

28. Transcript, "Press Conference with Petraeus and Crocker," National Press Club, September 12, 2007, http://www.cfr.org/iraq/press-conference-petraeus-crocker-national-press-club/p14199?breadcrumb=%2Fpublication%2Fby_type%2Fessential_document.

8. Power Politics

1. General David Petraeus, "CENTCOM Update," June 11, 2009, slide 8, "Security Incidents in Iraq," http://www.cnas.org/files/multimedia/documents/Petraeus%20Slides.pdf.

2. Ibid., slide 9, "Violent Civilian Deaths."

3. Ibid., slide 10, "High Profile Attacks (Explosions)."

4. Some members of the media remained skeptical of the source of the statistics generated by Multi-National Force–Iraq. To allay their concerns, General Petraeus had Colonel Bill Rapp convene a three-day conference in Baghdad in November 2007, during which the statisticians in the Commander's Initiatives Group laid out the methodology they used to generate various statistics, such as killings due to ethnosectarian violence. The conference went a long way to easing anxieties over the reliability of data used to compile various reports. E-mail, Major General Bill Rapp to author, August 19, 2011.

5. Icasualties.org, Operation Iraqi Freedom, "Coalition Military Fatalities by Year and Month," http://icasualties.org/Iraq/index.aspx.

6. Ibid., "Iraqi Fatalities."

7. On December 8, 2004, Secretary of Defense Donald Rumsfeld, when asked by a soldier in Kuwait why his unit had to scrounge through scrap heaps to find armor plating for its vehicles before heading into Iraq, replied, "As you know, you go to war with the army you have, not the army you might want or wish to have at a later time"; Ray Suarez, "Troops Question Secretary of Defense Donald Rumsfeld about Armor," PBS NewsHour, December 9, 2004, http://www.pbs.org/newshour/bb/military/july-dec04/armor_12-9.html. Three years passed before the Department of Defense was energized enough to procure and ship MRAPs to Iraq.

8. Commander, MNF-I, "SECDEF WEEKLY UPDATE, 3–9 December 2007," 6, originally classified SECRET-NOFORN, redacted and declassified May 2012, Petraeus Papers, National Defense University.

9. Commander, MNF-I, "SECDEF WEEKLY UPDATE, 21–27 January 2008," 2, originally classified SECRET-NOFORN, redacted and declassified May 2012, Petraeus Papers, National Defense University.

10. David Johnston and John M. Broder, "F.B.I. Says Guards Killed 14 Iraqis Without Cause," *New York Times,* November 13, 2007, http://www.nytimes.com/2007/11/14/world/middleeast/14blackwater.html?ex=1352696400&en=4d3e7a7a4fbc5721&ei=5088&partner=rssnyt&emc=rss.

11. Sudarsan Raghavan, Joshua Partlow, and Karen DeYoung, "Blackwater Faulted in Military Reports from Shooting Scene," *Washington Post,* October 5, 2007, http://www.washingtonpost.com/wp-dyn/content/article/2007/10/04/AR2007100402654.html?nav=hcmodule.

12. Charlie Savage, "Judge Drops Charges from Blackwater Deaths in Iraq," *New York Times*, December 31, 2009, http://www.nytimes.com/2010/01/01/us/01blackwater.html.

13. Linda Robinson, *Tell Me How This Ends: General David Petraeus and the Search for a Way Out of Iraq* (New York: PublicAffairs, 2008), 114.

14. Commander, MNF-I, "SECDEF WEEKLY UPDATE, 11–17 February 2008," 7, originally classified SECRET-NOFORN, redacted and declassified May 2012, Petraeus Papers, National Defense University. Prime Minister Maliki expressed his disappointment at the verdict, lamenting to General Petraeus and Ambassador Crocker "that the trial meant the entire Iraqi judicial system was in danger." Commander, MNF-I, "SECDEF WEEKLY UPDATE, 3–9 March 2008," 5, originally classified SECRET-NOFORN, redacted and declassified May 2012, Petraeus Papers, National Defense University.

15. Michael R. Gordon, "In Baghdad, Justice Behind the Barricades," *New York Times*, July 30, 2007, http://www.nytimes.com/2007/07/30/world/middleeast/30military.html?pagewanted=1.

16. Commander, MNF-I, "SECDEF WEEKLY UPDATE, 31 December 2007–6 January 2008," 6, originally classified SECRET-NOFORN, redacted and declassified May 2012, Petraeus Papers, National Defense University.

17. General Raymond Odierno, unpublished and undated article on the surge, copy provided by Gen. Odierno to the author, 16–17.

18. Commander, MNF-I, "SECDEF WEEKLY UPDATE, 10–16 December 2007," 4, originally classified SECRET-NOFORN, redacted and declassified May 2012, Petraeus Papers, National Defense University.

19. Special Inspector General for Iraqi Reconstruction, Quarterly Report to Congress, January 30, 2008, Section 2, 122, http://www.sigir.mil/files/quarterlyreports/January2008/Section2_-_January_2008.pdf#view=fit.

20. "Stabilizing Iraq's Economy: An Interview with the DOD's Paul Brinkley," *McKinsey Quarterly*, April 10, 2010, reprinted at http://seekerblog.com/2010/04/10/stabilizing-iraqs-economy-an-interview-with-the-dods-paul-brinkley/.

21. Odierno, unpublished and undated article on the surge, 18.

22. Ibid.

23. Ibid.

24. Meeting on November 14, 2007.

25. The White House, "Initial Benchmark Assessment Report," July 12, 2007, http://www.globalsecurity.org/military/library/report/2007/iraq-benchmark-assessment070712.htm.

26. For an example of the relationship in action, see Robinson, *Tell Me How This Ends*, 260.

27. The exchange occurred during a meeting on October 10, 2007.

28. Commander, MNF-I, "SECDEF WEEKLY UPDATE, 14–20 October 2007," 1, originally classified SECRET-NOFORN, redacted and declassified May 2012, Petraeus Papers, National Defense University; "Iraqi PM Outraged over Alleged Civilian Casualties," CNN, October 21, 2007, http://articles.cnn.com/2007-10-21/world/iraq.fighting_1_civilian-casualties-al-maliki-sadr-city?_s=PM:WORLD.

29. "SECDEF WEEKLY UPDATE, 3–9 December 2007," 1.

30. Commander, MNF-I, "SECDEF WEEKLY UPDATE, 26 November–2 December 2007," 5, originally classified SECRET-NOFORN, redacted and declassified May 2012, Petraeus Papers, National Defense University.

31. "SECDEF WEEKLY UPDATE, 3–9 December 2007," 1.

32. "House Committee Approves Armenian Genocide Resolution," CNN Politics, October 10, 2007, http://articles.cnn.com/2007-10-10/politics/us.turkey.armenians_1_armenian-genocide-resolution-nabi-sensoy-historic-mass-killings?_s=PM:POLITICS.

33. Ivan Watson and Melissa Block, "Turkish Troops Bolster Mountainous Iraq Border," NPR, October 23, 2007, http://www.npr.org/templates/story/story.php?storyId=15567219.

34. I did not accompany General Petraeus on this mission, but he furnished the details of this incident in an e-mail to me on August 5, 2012. The mission is covered more generally in Com-

mander, MNF-I, "SECDEF WEEKLY UPDATE, 28 Oct–3 November 2007," 1, originally classified SECRET-NOFORN, redacted and declassified May 2012, Petraeus Papers, National Defense University.

35. Ibid.

36. Commander, MNF-I, "SECDEF WEEKLY UPDATE, 18–24 February 2008," 1, originally classified SECRET-NOFORN, redacted and declassified May 2012, Petraeus Papers, National Defense University.

37. Commander, MNF-I, "SECDEF WEEKLY UPDATE, 28 January–3 February 2008," 6, originally classified SECRET-NOFORN, redacted and declassified May 2012, Petraeus Papers, National Defense University; Commander, MNF-I, "SECDEF WEEKLY UPDATE, 10 March–16 March 2008," 4–5, originally classified SECRET-NOFORN, redacted and declassified May 2012, Petraeus Papers, National Defense University.

38. Commander, MNF-I, "SECDEF WEEKLY UPDATE, 21–27 October 2007," 5 and Commander, MNF-I, "SECDEF WEEKLY UPDATE, 31 December 2007–6 January 2008," 5, originally classified SECRET-NOFORN, redacted and declassified May 2012, Petraeus Papers, National Defense University.

39. Meeting with President Bush and General Petraeus on December 10, 2007.

40. "SECDEF WEEKLY UPDATE, 10–16 December 2007," 1.

41. Robinson, *Tell Me How This Ends*, 328.

42. Commander, MNF-I, "SECDEF WEEKLY UPDATE, 17–23 December 2007," 1, originally classified SECRET-NOFORN, redacted and declassified May 2012, Petraeus Papers, National Defense University.

43. Meeting with General Petraeus on December 18, 2007.

44. Author interview with Colonel (Ret.) James Hickey, February 2, 2011. Security in Mosul had deteriorated significantly since General Petraeus and the 101st Airborne Division had departed northern Iraq in the winter of 2004. U.S. military leaders had replaced the division with a force one-third its size. The lack of forces, combined with the gnawing impact of de-Ba'athification and other policies, led to the growth of the insurgency and al-Qaeda in northern Iraq.

45. "SECDEF WEEKLY UPDATE, 10 March–16 March 2008," 1.

46. Commander, MNF-I, "SECDEF WEEKLY UPDATE, 7–13 January 2008," 1, originally classified SECRET-NOFORN, redacted and declassified May 2012, Petraeus Papers, National Defense University.

47. Michael Howard, "New Iraqi Flag Hailed as Symbolic Break with Past," *Guardian*, February 5, 2008, http://www.guardian.co.uk/world/2008/feb/06/iraq.international.

48. "SECDEF WEEKLY UPDATE, 11–17 February 2008," 1.

49. Ibid., 6.

50. E-mail, General Petraeus to author, August 5, 2012.

51. Thomas P. M. Barnett, "The Man Between War and Peace," *Esquire*, April 2008, http://www.esquire.com/features/fox-fallon.

9. Charge of the Knights

1. For the history of the fighting in Karbala in the spring of 2004, see Peter R. Mansoor, *Baghdad at Sunrise: A Brigade Commander's War in Iraq* (New Haven: Yale University Press, 2008), chapter 10.

2. Patrick Cockburn, *Muqtada: Muqtada al-Sadr, the Shia Revival, and the Struggle for Iraq* (New York: Scribner, 2008), 196.

3. This discussion of British operations in Iraq is adapted from Peter R. Mansoor, "The British Army and the Lessons of the Iraq War," *British Army Review* 147 (Summer 2009), 11–15.

4. Brigadier Nigel Aylwin-Foster, "Changing the Army for Counterinsurgency Operations," *Military Review*, November–December 2005, http://www.army.mil/professionalWriting/volumes/volume4/february_2006/2_06_1.html.

5. E-mail, Richard Iron to author, September 5, 2012.

6. E-mail, General (Ret.) Petraeus to author, September 16, 2012.

7. Richard Iron, "Basra 2008: Operation Charge of the Knights," *British Generals in Blair's Wars,* ed. J. Bailey, R. Iron, and H. Strachan (Farnham, U.K.: Ashgate, 2013, in press).

8. Cockburn, *Muqtada,* 196.

9. Iron, "Basra 2008." Iron estimates that the Jaish al-Mahdi garnered at least $30,000 every day just from taxing truck drivers at the port of Um Qasr.

10. Ibid.; Commander, MNF-I, "SECDEF WEEKLY UPDATE, 3–9 March 2008," 3, originally classified SECRET-NOFORN, redacted and declassified May 2012, Petraeus Papers, National Defense University.

11. Commander, MNF-I, "SECDEF WEEKLY UPDATE, 17 March–23 March 2008," 2, originally classified SECRET-NOFORN, redacted and declassified May 2012, Petraeus Papers, National Defense University.

12. Iron, "Basra 2008."

13. Ibid.

14. Ibid.

15. Commander, MNF-I, "SECDEF WEEKLY UPDATE, 24 March–30 March 2008," 2, originally classified SECRET-NOFORN, redacted and declassified May 2012, Petraeus Papers, National Defense University.

16. E-mail, General (Ret.) Petraeus to author, September 16, 2012.

17. Iron, "Basra 2008."

18. Ibid.

19. Mohammed Tawfeeq and Jonathan Wald, "Sources: Iran Helped Prod al-Sadr Cease-Fire," CNN World, March 31, 2008, http://articles.cnn.com/2008-03-31/world/iraq.main_1_al-sadr-sadrist-dawa-party?_s=PM:WORLD; Linda Robinson, *Tell Me How This Ends: General David Petraeus and the Search for a Way Out of Iraq* (New York: PublicAffairs, 2008), 341; Institute for the Study of War, "Operation Knight's Charge (Saulat al-Fursan)," http://www.understandingwar.org/operation/operation-knights-charge-saulat-al-fursan.

20. Robinson, *Tell Me How This Ends,* 341–342.

21. "SECDEF WEEKLY UPDATE, 24 March–30 March 2008," 3.

22. David E. Johnson, M. Wade Markel, and Brian Shannon, "The 2008 Battle of Sadr City" (Santa Monica, CA: RAND Corporation, 2011), 4, http://www.rand.org/pubs/occasional_papers/OP335.

23. Ibid., 8.

24. Ibid., 8.

25. Ibid., 10.

26. "How Technology Won Sadr City Battle," CBSNews.com, February 11, 2009, http://www.cbsnews.com/2100-18560_162-4511800.html.

27. Ibid.

28. For an analysis of how U.S. forces waged the battle for Route Gold, see Johnson, Markel, and Shannon, "The 2008 Battle of Sadr City."

29. Mansoor, "The British Army and the Lessons of the Iraq War," 11–15.

30. Iron, "Basra 2008."

31. Ibid.

32. Ibid.

33. Ibid.

34. Ibid.

35. Ibid.

36. "SECDEF WEEKLY UPDATE, 24 March–30 March 2008," 2.

37. Commander, MNF-I, "SECDEF WEEKLY UPDATE, 14–20 April 2008," 3, originally classified SECRET-NOFORN, redacted and declassified May 2012, Petraeus Papers, National Defense University.

38. Commander, MNF-I, "SECDEF WEEKLY UPDATE, 7–13 April 2008," 3, originally clas-

sified SECRET-NOFORN, redacted and declassified May 2012, Petraeus Papers, National Defense University.

39. Transcript, "Petraeus, Crocker Testify at Senate Committee on Armed Services Hearing on Iraq," CQ Transcripts Wire, April, 8 2008, http://www.washingtonpost.com/wp-srv/politics/documents/iraq_hearing_040808.html. All references in this and the following paragraphs to the testimony of General Petraeus and Ambassador Crocker before the Senate Armed Services Committee are from this hearing transcript.

40. See also Multi-National Force–Iraq, "Charts to accompany the testimony of GEN David H. Petraeus, 8–9 April 2008," http://www.afa.org/PresidentsCorner/Other/Petraeus.pdf.

41. Slide 8 in the charts.

42. Commander, MNF-I, "SECDEF WEEKLY UPDATE, 5–11 May 2008," 1–2, originally classified SECRET-NOFORN, redacted and declassified May 2012, Petraeus Papers, National Defense University.

43. Commander, MNF-I, "SECDEF WEEKLY UPDATE, 12–18 May 2008," 1, originally classified SECRET-NOFORN, redacted and declassified May 2012, Petraeus Papers, National Defense University.

44. Commander, MNF-I, "SECDEF WEEKLY UPDATE, 2–8 June 2008," 2, originally classified SECRET-NOFORN, redacted and declassified May 2012, Petraeus Papers, National Defense University.

45. Commander, MNF-I, "SECDEF WEEKLY UPDATE, 16–22 June 2008," 2, originally classified SECRET-NOFORN, redacted and declassified May 2012, Petraeus Papers, National Defense University.

46. Reproduced in Appendix 2.

47. General David H. Petraeus, CENTCOM Update, Center for New American Security, June 11, 2009, slide 8, "Security Incidents in Iraq," http://www.cnas.org/files/multimedia/documents/Petraeus%20Slides.pdf.

48. Commander, MNF-I, "SECDEF WEEKLY UPDATE, 7–13 July 2008," 1, originally classified SECRET-NOFORN, redacted and declassified May 2012, Petraeus Papers, National Defense University.

49. Commander, MNF-I, "SECDEF WEEKLY UPDATE, 2–8 June 2008," 3.

50. Commander, MNF-I, "SECDEF WEEKLY UPDATE, 14–20 July 2008," 3, originally classified SECRET-NOFORN, redacted and declassified May 2012, Petraeus Papers, National Defense University.

51. Commander, MNF-I, "SECDEF WEEKLY UPDATE, 18–24 August 2008," 3, originally classified SECRET-NOFORN, redacted and declassified May 2012, Petraeus Papers, National Defense University.

52. R. Chuck Mason, "U.S.-Iraq Withdrawal/Status of Forces Agreement: Issues for Congressional Oversight," Congressional Research Service, July 13, 2009, www.fas.org/sgp/crs/natsec/R40011.pdf.

53. CBS, *60 Minutes*, February 22, 2009, http://www.cbsnews.com/video/watch/?id=4819435n.

10. The Surge in Retrospect

1. For an incisive analysis of the final years in Iraq and the missteps of the Obama administration in cementing the gains of the surge, see Michael R. Gordon and General Bernard E. Trainor, *The Endgame: The Inside Story of the Struggle for Iraq, from George W. Bush to Barack Obama* (New York: Pantheon, 2012), part 3, "New Dawn." Emma Sky, General Odierno's political adviser from 2007 to 2010, also agrees with this assessment; see Emma Sky, "Iraq in Hindsight," Center for New American Security, December 14, 2012, http://www.cnas.org/iraqinhindsight.

2. See for instance Gian Gentile, "COIN Is Dead: U.S. Army Must Put Strategy over Tactics," *World Politics Review*, November 22, 2011, http://www.worldpoliticsreview.com/articles/10731/coin-is-dead-u-s-army-must-put-strategy-over-tactics.

3. Iraq Body Count, "Iraqi Deaths from Violence, 2003–2011," October 23, 2012, http://www
.iraqbodycount.org/analysis/numbers/2011/.

4. Thomas E. Ricks, *The Gamble: General David Petraeus and the American Military Adventure in Iraq, 2006–2008* (New York: Penguin, 2009), 292.

5. Ryan Crocker, "Dreams of Babylon," *National Interest,* June 22, 2010, http://nationalinterest
.org/article/dreams-of-babylon-3541.

6. Bing West, "War Fighting Factors in Iraq and Afghanistan," address to the Marine
Corps Heritage Foundation Museum, March 5, 2009, smallwarsjournal.com/blog/journal/docs
-temp/197-west.pdf.

7. See, for instance, Gian Gentile, "A Strategy of Tactics: Population-Centric COIN and the
Army," *Parameters* 39, no. 3 (2009), 5–17.

8. The first Anaconda Strategy was the North's original strategy in the U.S. Civil War. Among
other elements, it featured a blockade of the southern seacoast to strangle the Confederacy economically.

9. Fusion centers collected intelligence from all available sources and provided it as quickly as
possible to the operators who could act on it. The initiative to form fusion centers at division level
began under General Casey. See George W. Casey, *Strategic Reflections: Operation Iraqi Freedom,
July 2004–February 2007* (Washington, D.C.: National Defense University Press, 2012), 71.

10. A conclusion reached as well by Gordon and Trainor, *The Endgame,* 385, and Fred Kaplan,
"The End of the Age of Petraeus: The Rise and Fall of Counterinsurgency," *Foreign Affairs,* January–
February 2013, 85.

11. T. E. Lawrence, "Twenty Seven Articles," *Arab Bulletin,* August 20, 1917, http://wwi.lib.byu
.edu/index.php/The_27_Articles_of_T.E._Lawrence.

12. Ibid.

13. "Interview with Colonel Sean MacFarland," Contemporary Operations Study Team, On
Point III, Combat Studies Institute, Fort Leavenworth, Kansas, January 17, 2008, 46.

14. Ibid., 47.

15. Crocker, "Dreams of Babylon."

16. See, for instance, Peter D. Feaver, "The Right to Be Right: Civil-Military Relations and the
Iraq Surge Decision," *International Security* 35, no. 4 (2011), 92–92.

17. Stephen Biddle, Jeffrey A. Friedman, and Jacob N. Shapiro, "Testing the Surge: Why Did
Violence Decline in Iraq in 2007?" *International Security* 37, no. 1 (2007), 1–34.

18. Ibid., 3.

19. One of General Petraeus's first actions upon taking command of Multi-National Force–
Iraq was to stop transitions for a period, as well as to halt temporarily the release of detainees from
coalition facilities.

20. Kimberly Kagan, *The Surge: A Military History* (New York: Encounter, 2009), 146.

21. For a summation of this argument, see Biddle, Friedman, and Shapiro, "Testing the Surge,"
6–9.

22. Linda Robinson, *Tell Me How This Ends: General David Petraeus and the Search for a Way
Out of Iraq* (New York: PublicAffairs, 2008), 268.

23. Nine hundred four U.S. soldiers were killed in 2007; Iraq Coalition Casualty Count, http://
icasualties.org/.

24. Commander, MNF-I, "SECDEF WEEKLY UPDATE, 31 December 2007–6 January 2008,"
3, originally classified SECRET-NOFORN, redacted and declassified May 2012, Petraeus Papers,
National Defense University.

25. Jim Michaels, *A Chance in Hell* (New York: St. Martin's, 2010), 5.

26. Commander, MNF-I, "SECDEF WEEKLY UPDATE, 24–30 December 2007," 5, originally classified SECRET-NOFORN, redacted and declassified May 2012, Petraeus Papers, National
Defense University. General Stanley McChrystal, who commanded the Joint Special Operations
Command during the Iraq War, agrees with General Petraeus's assessment. McChyrstal writes,
"The tactics that we developed do work, but they don't produce decisive effects absent other, complementary activities. We did an awful lot of capturing and killing in Iraq for several years before it

started to have a real effect, and that came only when we were partnered with an effective counter-insurgency approach"; "Generation Kill: A Conversation with Stanley McChrystal," *Foreign Affairs*, March–April 2013, 7.

27. George W. Bush, *Decision Points* (New York: Crown, 2010), 389.

28. Ricks, *The Gamble*, 150–153.

29. Alan Beyerchen, "Clausewitz, Nonlinearity, and the Unpredictability of War," *International Security* 17, no. 3 (, 1992), 59–90.

30. Ibid.

31. Sky, "Iraq in Hindsight," 7.

32. Brett H. McGurk, Testimony before the Senate Armed Services Committee, November 15, 2011.

33. The importance of Iraq to the Obama administration is evident in the president's reduced involvement in the negotiations that failed to create a new status-of-forces agreement that would have allowed U.S. troops to remain in the country. Certainly President Obama was not as involved in moving the negotiations forward as President Bush had been during his tenure in office.

34. Ironically, then–CIA Director Petraeus arrived in Baghdad in mid-December 2011 shortly after the departure of U.S. forces and the day after the political crisis precipitated by the charges announced for Hashemi. With the U.S. ambassador having just departed on leave, Director Petraeus found himself shuttling around Baghdad and then to the Kurdish region to appeal to Iraqi leaders of all sects, parties, and ethnic groups to engage in dialogue and resolve the new dispute in that manner rather than in resorting to violence; e-mail, General (Ret.) Petraeus to author, December 23, 2012.

35. Crocker, "Dreams of Babylon."

36. Sky, "Iraq in Hindsight," 8.

37. I was able to travel to Afghanistan in December 2010, along with Max Boot, at the invitation of General Petraeus. We observed the outstanding counterinsurgency practices being put into place by U.S. Army and Marine forces, but it was clear that tactical success alone would not lead to victory without the cooperation of a viable Afghan government and the reduction of insurgent sanctuaries in Pakistan.

38. For the failure of the U.S. military to retain the lessons learned from the Vietnam War, see Conrad Crane, *Avoiding Vietnam: The U.S. Army's Response to Defeat in Southeast Asia* (Carlisle Barracks, Pa.: Strategic Studies Institute, 2002), http://www.strategicstudiesinstitute.army.mil/pubs/download.cfm?q=58.

39. LTC Jim Crider, "Inside the Surge: One Commander's Lessons in Counterinsurgency," CNAS Working Paper, June 2009, 19, http://www.cnas.org/files/documents/publications/CNAS_Working%20Paper_Surge_CriderRicks_June2009_ONLINE.pdf.

40. See, for instance, Lieutenant General James M. Dubik, "Operational Art in Counterinsurgency: A View from the Inside," Institute for the Study of War Best Practices in Counterinsurgency Report no. 5, 2012, http://www.understandingwar.org/sites/default/files/Operational Art_in_COIN.pdf.

41. Donald Stoker, "Six Reasons Insurgencies Lose: A Contrarian View," *Small Wars Journal*, July 4, 2009, http://www.smallwarsjournal.com/blog/journal/docs-temp/268-stoker.pdf.

42. Thucydides, *The Peloponnesian War*, trans. Rex Warner (New York: Penguin Classics, 1954), 1.22.

43. Marcus Jones, "Bismarckian Strategic Policy, 1871–1890," conference paper, In Pursuit of Successful Strategy, Arlington, Virginia, April 2012.

44. David Kilcullen, *The Accidental Guerrilla: Fighting Small Wars in the Midst of a Big One* (New York: Oxford University Press, 2009), 185.

Appendix 1. Report to Congress on the Situation in Iraq

1. All slides from General Petraeus's testimony can be viewed at http://www.lib.utexas.edu/maps/middle_east_and_asia/petraeus-testimony-slides20070910.pdf.

Index